CHANGING
PATTERNS of
SOCIAL
PROTECTION

International Social Security Series

In cooperation with the
International Social Security Association (ISSA)
Neil Gilbert, Series Editor

Targeting Social Benefits:
International Perspectives and Trends
Neil Gilbert, editor

Social Security at the Dawn of the
21st Century: Topical Issues and New Approaches
Dalmer D. Hoskins, Donate Dobbernack, and
Christiane Kuptsch, editors

Activating the Unemployed: A Comparative
Appraisal of Work-Oriented Policies
Neil Gilbert and Rebecca A. Van Voorhis, editors

Recent Health Policy Innovations
in Social Security
Aviva Ron and Xenia Scheil-Adlung, editors

Who Returns to Work and Why: A Six-Country
Study on Work Incapacity and Reintegration
Frank S. Bloch and Rienk Prins, editors

Building Social Security:
The Challenge of Privatization
Xenia Scheil-Adlung, editor

Employability: From Theory to Practice
Patricia Weinert, Michèle Baukens, Patrick Bollérot,
Marina Pineschi-Gapènne, and Ulrich Walwei, editors

Social Security in the Global Village
Roland Sigg and Christina Behrendt, editors

Changing Patterns of Social Protection
Neil Gilbert and Rebecca A. Van Voorhis, editors

CHANGING PATTERNS of SOCIAL PROTECTION

Neil Gilbert
Rebecca A. Van Voorhis
editors

International Social Security Series
Volume 9

Transaction Publishers
New Brunswick (U.S.A.) and London (U.K.)

Fourth printing 2009

Copyright © 2003 by Transaction Publishers, New Brunswick, New Jersey.

The International Social Security Association (ISSA) was founded in 1927. It is a nonprofit international organization bringing together institutions and administrative bodies from countries all over the world dealing with all forms of compulsory social protection. The objective of the ISSA is to cooperate at the international level, in the promotion and development of social security throughout the world, primarily by improving techniques and administration in order to advance people's social and economic conditions on the basis of social justice.

The responsibility for opinions expressed in signed articles, studies, and other contributions rests solely with their authors, and publication does not constitute an endorsement by the International Social Security Association of the opinions expressed by them.

Library of Congress Catalog Number: 2002043001
ISBN: 978-0-7658-0989-6
Printed in the United States of America

Library of Congress Cataloging-in-Publication Data

Changing patterns of social protection / Neil Gilbert and Rebecca A. Van
    Voorhis, editors.
        p. cm.—(International social security series; v. 9)
    Includes bibliographical references and index.
    ISBN 0-7658-0989-3 (pbk.: alk. paper)
    1. Public welfare — Cross-cultural studies. 2. Social policy — Cross-cultural studies. 3. Social security — Cross-cultural studies. I. Gilbert, Neil. II. Van Voorhis, Rebecca A. III. Series.

HV70.C53 2003
361.6—dc21   2002043001

Contents

Acknowledgments

This volume concludes a cross-national study of continuities and change in modern welfare states, which was initiated in 1997 under the co-sponsorship of the International Social Security Association (ISSA) and the Center for the Comparative Study of Family Welfare and Poverty at the School of Social Welfare, University of California, Berkeley, and with the support of a foundation grant.[1] The research group conducting this study met on several occasions at various stages of the project to refine the study framework, report on current policy developments in their countries and review their preliminary findings.

In 2000, a final meeting was held at the Rockefeller Foundation Conference Center in Bellagio, Italy. We are indebted to the Rockefeller Foundation and its staff at the Bellagio Center for the gracious setting they provided in support of what turned out to be in many ways a highly productive meeting. In addition to members of the research team who contributed to this volume, the participants at that meeting included a number of outside experts who joined our conversation on the preliminary chapter drafts, which were presented by the authors. We should like to thank the members of this expert group whose views and insights stimulated a lively exchange of ideas: Lucy ApRoberts, Cathy Drummond, Keith Fontenot, Chris Foster, Richard Hauser, Dalmer Hoskins, Inger Marklund, Francois Merrien, Warren McGillivray, Stein Ringen, Roland Sigg and Hans Svensson.

A special gratitude is owed to Dalmer Hoskins, Secretary General of ISSA for his continuing encouragement of this project. Although we benefited from the friendly support and good counsel of the Secretary General and the ISSA staff, it should be noted that responsibility for results and interpretations reported in this volume rests entirely with the contributors.

Note

1. Two volumes have come out of the earlier stages of this project: Neil Gilbert (ed.), *Targeting Social Benefits: International Perspectives and Trends* (New Brunswick, NJ: Transaction Publishers, 2001) and Neil Gilbert and Rebecca A. Van Voorhis (eds.), *Activating the Unemployed: A Comparative Appraisal of Work-Oriented Policies* (New Brunswick, NJ: Transaction Publishers, 2001).

Introduction: New Configurations

Neil Gilbert and Rebecca A. Van Voorhis

Today we know that rumors about the impending divestiture of the welfare state circulating in the mid-1980s were greatly exaggerated. Although there was much concern about the fiscal capacity of the welfare state and its moral legitimacy, the frequently cited "crisis" never erupted into a full-blown emergency (Mishra, 1984; O'Connor, 1983; OECD, 1981). Indeed, by the 1990s prominent authorities such as Paul Pierson (1996) and Gosta Esping-Andersen (1990) had reached the verdict reached that, perhaps, some fat had to be trimmed from the margins of social welfare arrangements, but the welfare state as it was known certainly was not being dismantled.

While the growth of social welfare expenditures had leveled off and even taken a slight dip by the early 1990s, there was no acute decline in social spending, which was taken as a sign of the welfare state's viability.[1] However, the slight decline in social spending as a proportion of the GDP in the fifteen countries of the European Union may be more telling than it appears because it occurred at a time when there was no apparent abatement of demand for social benefits—unemployment rates were still relatively high and the population was aging. Of course, it is hard to imagine that *dismantling* of the welfare state was ever a serious political option. Citizens of the advanced industrialized countries have long grown accustomed to social security pensions, varying levels of health, unemployment and disability insurance, family assistance benefits, and the plethora of social services available to protect them against the risks of modern life. Political leaders with an explicit agenda to dismantle these arrangements would soon be looking for a new job.

To recognize that institutional arrangements for social protection are still with us at the dawn of the twenty-first century, however, is not to say that things have remained basically the same. Over the last two decades there have been many reforms in social policy dealing with the mainline programs of protection: old age pensions, disability, unemployment, family assistance, health, and social services. There is general agreement that the directions of

1

reform are toward narrower criteria for the allocation of social provisions, more involvement of the private sector in the delivery of benefits, and a great emphasis on work-related measures than in the two decades preceding the 1980s. Succinctly characterized as *targeting, privatization, and workfare*, movements in these directions are evident in almost all of the advanced industrialized welfare states, though the speed and distance covered vary. There are examples of policies that run counter to these trends, such as the reversal of the Accident Insurance reform in New Zealand, which shifted the insurance coverage from private back to public provision. But these cases constitute isolated pockets of resistance—not enough to reverse the main currents of reform.

Why have these reforms occurred during the last two decades? How are they manifest in the basic design and implementation of social policies? And to what extent would one say that the sum total of these reforms amount to a change in the essential character of social welfare? Addressing these questions, this volume analyzes the changing patterns of social protection in eight advanced welfare states: France, Britain, Germany, United States, Italy, Sweden, New Zealand, and the Netherlands.

These countries represent three distinct welfare state models—liberal, corporatist, and social democratic regimes—formulated by Esping-Andersen (1990) using empirical indicators based on data that went up to the early 1980s. One of the key indicators in this analysis involved a decommodification index that sought to represent the degree to which a country's social policies provided unemployed people easy accessible and generous benefits that dispensed a certain immunity from market forces—protecting their labor from being treated purely as a commodity.[2] Applying the scores on this index, the countries in his sample were clustered into three groups: high scoring social democratic regimes, which included the Netherlands and Sweden; moderate scoring corporatist regimes, which included Italy, France, and Germany; and low scoring liberal regimes, which included New Zealand, Britain, and the United States.[3] In response to the questions noted above, researchers from each of the countries studied in this volume were asked to analyze the economic and social context that had shaped social welfare reforms in recent years, to present the facts about policy trends and emerging patterns in their countries, and to offer their interpretations of the directions and significance of these changes.

Among the influences emanating from the socioeconomic context over the last two decades, the demands of aging populations, constraints dictated by the globalization of the economy, needs of changing family structures, growing labor-force participation of women, and the strains of immigration have generated, perhaps, the greatest impetus for the reformulation of social welfare policies. These developments may be seen as some of the basic features of advanced capitalism (discussed in chapter 5). On the international plane, the context was framed by economic misfortunes stemming from the oil shocks in the early and late 1970s. While locally, pressures for change flowed from an increasing recognition of the disincentives bred by generous and easily accessible social benefits and the corrosive effects of long-term dependency on these benefits. In addition to these general influences, there were also particular forces for change in different countries such as the costs of reunification in Germany, the political havoc of the clientelistic approach to social welfare practiced in Italy, the unprecedented level of claims for disability benefits in the Netherlands, and the 1991 "earthquake" election in Sweden, which removed the Social Democrats from power for the first time since the 1920s.

Analyses of the socioeconomic context in the following chapters reveal a broad range of similarities as well as country-specific influences that precipitated policy reforms. Likewise, examinations of the substantive nature of these reforms demonstrate a general pattern of corresponding principles that advance policies along the same tracks, with variations in their design and implementation more a matter of alternative approaches and gradation than direction. The direction is toward market-oriented social welfare policies that promote privatization, work, and narrower targeting of existing social benefits to those most in need.

The movement toward privatization includes a number of dimensions that involve finance, provision, and the locus of decision (examined in chapter 4). In Britain, the "pure" public provision (publicly provided, financed, and decided) of the personal social services declined by 30 percent between 1980 and 1996. The shift toward private financing in Germany is reflected in increasing use of private co-payments for several services in the sickness insurance scheme, at the same time that increasing private provision is manifest in opening up the delivery of long-term care to private for-profit providers. In the United States, privatization through purchase of service arrangements with for-profit agencies for the delivery of services—including child welfare, daycare, homemakers, and nursing home care—expanded in the 1980s as the number of paid employees in these service agencies increased by 38 percent (proportionately twice the increase of employees in voluntary nonprofit social service agencies). The subtle promotion of privatization occurs when levels of public provision are allowed to decline to a point at which people feel the need to seek private compensatory arrangements. Thus, in 1991 cuts in basic benefit rates in New Zealand resulted in a tremendous increase in demand for assistance from voluntary social service agencies. In Sweden, a part of the contributions to the public pension system is now invested in private individual accounts dependent on market returns. In Italy, a policy reform in 2000 formulated a comprehensive framework for the management of social care services, which emphasized the utilization of voluntary agencies in the public-private mix. The movement toward privatization appears to have advanced most slowly in France, where plans to promote private pension funds are still being debated.

In addition to privatization, all of the countries in this volume report on new social welfare measures designed to promote work. In Britain, for example, the Blair government set forth several key principles to guide future developments of the British welfare state, the first of which was, "The new welfare state should help and encourage people of working age to work where they are capable of doing so" (cited in chapter 4). Similarly, (as noted in chapter 1) Chancellor Schroder's government promised to transform the German social security system "from a potential inactivity trap to an enabling springboard."

Referred to variously as "activation," "insertion," and "workfare," these new work-oriented measures are reshaping the character of programs related to disability, unemployment, and social assistance. Benefits in these program areas are increasingly being tied to the applicants' compliance with activation plans—quasi-contractual agreements between applicants and program officials, which stipulate the various efforts that both parties will make to return the applicant back to work and the consequences (or sanctions) that might be applied if applicants fail to live up to their part of the contract. Desmond King's (1999) trenchant analysis suggests that "...the movement to a contractual workfare system of welfare assistance in Britain is of fundamental importance." As he sees it, "...the sharpness of the new initiatives is striking as is its break with the 1945-75 universalist welfare state" (p. 256).

The countries vary in the rigor with which activation plans are implemented and to the extent in which they focus on work, training opportunities, subsidized jobs, and other activities. Thus, in France within three months of claiming benefits under the *revenu minimum d'insertion (RMI)* program, participants and program officials are supposed to sign a *contract d'insertion*, which delineates a range of activities that are to be undertaken to assist the participant to become integrated within society. Some of these activities are employment-oriented, while others involve housing, health, and counseling. Although the RMI policy requires the development of these quasi-contractual agreements, since 1988 about half of the program's participants have not signed a *contract d'insertion* and only a small fraction of participants (5-6 percent) have been sanctioned for failure to comply with the policy. Here, street-level bureaucrats and local traditions cut a great deal of slack in the implementation of national policy.

Most of the work-oriented reforms employ a mix of incentives and sanctions. Under the 1996 reform of social assistance in Germany, authorities are obliged to reduce benefits by at least 25 percent for claimants who refuse an offer of suitable employment. In practice, sanctions tend to be imposed less frequently than incentives. The incentives include efforts to increase the rewards of low-paying jobs through the provision of tax credits such as the independent family tax credit in New Zealand, the Earned Income Tax Credit in the United States, and the Working Families Tax Credit in Britain, as well as measures that allow for the exemption of a certain amount of earned income in the calculation of assistance benefits.

The third major track of policy reform—the increased targeting of social benefits—involves the narrowing of eligibility criteria, which sharply focuses benefits on those most in need, and the tightening of benefit levels directly through lowering replacement rates, lengthening the waiting time, and shortening the duration of benefits. Benefits have also been lowered indirectly through the use of claw-back taxes, which reduce the value of cash assistance at the point of consumption. In New Zealand the system of family assistance moved from a universal benefit in 1984 to an income tested benefit in 1991. The trend in Germany has been away from general entitlements toward contingent, categorically differentiated provisions, particularly in relation to allocations for foreigners and families. In Sweden, home care services for the elderly were reduced and concentrated on the most infirm and incapacitated elderly. Many countries have introduced stricter rules that intensify initial medical assessments for disability benefits and require periodic reexaminations. Access to old age pensions has been tightened by lifting the standard age of retirement or increasing the period of contribution required to qualify for benefits. In the United States, targeting of pubic assistance benefits has gone beyond basic criteria of need to include behavioral requirements—such as having one's children immunized and completing high school degree programs—that imbue the allocation of social benefits with moral overtones.

How significant are the changing patterns of social protection and what do they augur for future developments? In assessing the larger meaning of recent shifts in social welfare policy the authors offer varying interpretations. Viewing Swedish policy reforms as an adaptation of the existing system, Seven Hort sees no end to the Swedish welfare state model. He concludes, "Maybe the model is wounded, even severely wounded. However, it has survived the deadly threats of the 1990s and as the century turns the future of the durable or resilient welfare state has seen the light of day." Valeria Fargion is undecided about the future of the Italian system of social protection. Although the reforms of the 1990s have advanced the Italian welfare state, much remains to be done. "As things now stand," she finds, "Italy is half way through the ford in reforming its welfare state, and the future appears uncertain." Piet Keizer observes that policy changes over the last few decades have made the Dutch social welfare system more sober and efficient. But he contemplates a continuing need for reforms that will shrink benefits to the lowest level acceptable in society and reinforce the obligation to work. Keizer emphasizes that the effective functioning of social protection involves not only the design of rules that are fair and efficient, but the exercise of individual discipline and personal responsibility in following these rules.

Analyzing the numerous innovative policy reforms since the 1990s, Jean-Claude Barbier and Bruno Théret detect a general trend toward further incorporation of Beveridgean principles into the traditionally Bismarckian-oriented approach to social protection in France. This shift moves the French system from a Bismarckian model characterized, in part, by an emphasis on delivering earnings-related benefits to occupational groups via the mechanism of social insurance financed by employee and employer contributions, and administered by the social partners (unions and employer associations) toward greater reliance on a system of uniform tax-financed non-contributory benefits provided to everyone by the state, often on a sliding scale related to income. As for the future, however, Barbier and Théret are not entirely confident that this new welfare mix will be able to resist pressures from globalization, which they see as clearly favoring the development of liberal systems of social protection based on minimalists standards (as suggested by Keizer). Surveying the British experience, Linda Bauld, Ken Judge, and Iain Paterson observe that the current round of policy reforms is shifting the boundaries of the welfare state as the Blair government has sought to chart a centrist approach—popularly referred to as the "Third way." They suggest that at its core the third way is "an attempt to reconcile the promotion of growth in the market system with social democratic goals." Among its objectives, the third way seeks to prevent discrimination and prejudice, to promote equality of opportunity—which enables individuals to take advantage of opportunities, to balance social rights with individual responsibilities, and to support the structures and institutions of civil society. Bauld, Judge, and Paterson see the British welfare state pointing in a new direction, but caution that how far it will travel down this path remains to be seen. In the United States, taken as a whole policy reforms in recent times are seen to represent a significant break from the welfare state of several decades ago. For the immediate future the course of social welfare policy developments is expected to continue to embrace "market-oriented solutions that involve increasing commodification of labor, greater reliance on private initiative, greater demands on personal responsibility of social welfare recipients and a decreasing consideration for social rights."

Examining the life course of New Zealand's welfare state, Ross Mackay likens the policy reforms in the 1980s and 1990s to a sort of mid-life crisis—a reassessment and change of direction spurred by lack of progress and expectations that exceed results. Mackay suggests that the social policies measures implemented over the last two decades have restructured the borders of the welfare state in quite significant ways: benefits are more parsimonious and directed toward those in greatest need; private arrangements for social provisions have expanded; and greater emphasis has come to be placed on the responsibility of individuals to provide for themselves. But he questions whether these changes have greatly affected the main edifice of the welfare state and informs us that plans to reverse these changes are already on the agenda of the incoming Labor-led government. Appraising the impact of changes in the German welfare state Jens Alber submits that "it now looks as if we have arrived at a new liberal break in the welfare state"—comparable to the liberal break in early nineteenth-century Britain. The current liberal orientation includes an emphasis on individual responsibilities, the design of categorical allocations that distinguish between deserving and less deserving claimants, and concerns about how nation states can maintain their competitive edge. As for the future, Alber suggests that the task before us is to integrate the American regard for individual responsibility with the European structure of social protection. He concludes that "the concept of an enabling state which helps citizens to help themselves may become the basis of a synthesis of American freedom and European security"—a harmonious thought to carry in mind as we explore the changing patterns of social protection in the following chapters.

Notes

1. For two widely used measures that reveal similar trends in social expenditure, see Eurostat (2000) and OECD (2000).
2. For a critical assessment of the methods and measures used to construct this index, see Van Voorhis (forthcoming).
3. We might note that a number of scholars have found the three-regime model in need of refinement. Castles and Mitchell (1990) proposed four types of regimes: conservative, social democratic, liberal, and radical welfare state. Ferrera (1996), Leibfried (1992), and others have suggested that the "Southern Model," which includes Italy, Spain, Greece, and Portugal, constitutes a fourth regime. Finally, in a more recent assessment, Esping-Andersen (1999) concludes that the Netherlands no longer fits the criteria of a social democratic regime.

References

Castles, F. G., and Mitchell, D. (1990). Three Worlds of Welfare Capitalism of Four, *The Australian National University Discussion Paper, No. 21*, Canberra.

Esping-Andersen, G. (1990). *Three Worlds of Welfare Capitalism*. Princeton, NJ: Princeton University Press.

Esping-Anderson, G. (ed.). (1996). *Welfare States in Transition: National Adaptations in Global Economies*. London: Sage Publications.

Esping-Andersen, G. (1999). *Social Foundations of Postindustrial Society*. New York: Oxford University Press.

Eurostat. (2000). *Social Protection Expenditure and Receipts: Data 1980-1997*. Luxembourg: European Communities.

Ferrera, M. (1996). The 'Southern Model' of Welfare in Social Europe. *Journal of European Social Policy* 6:1, 17-37.

King, D. (1999). *In the Name of Liberalism: Illiberal Social Policy in the United States and Britain*. New York: Oxford University Press.

Leibfried, S. (1992). Towards a European Welfare State? On Integrating Poverty Regimes into the European Community in Zsuzsa. In Ferge and Jon Kolberg (eds.), *Social Policy in a Changing Europe*. Boulder, CO: Westview Press.

Mishra, R. (1984). *The Welfare State in Crisis*. Brighton: Wheatsheaf Books.

O'Connor, J. (1983). *The Fiscal Crisis of the State*. New York: St. Martin's Press.

OECD. (1981). *The Welfare State in Crisis*. Paris: OECD.

OECD. (2000). *Social Expenditure Database 1980-1997*. Paris: OECD.

Pierson, P. (1996). "The New Politics of the Welfare State." *World Politics*, 48:2.

Van Voorhis, R. (forthcoming). "Different Types of Welfare States? A Methodological Deconstruction of Comparative Research," *Journal of Sociology and Social Welfare*.

1

Recent Developments in the German Welfare State: Basic Continuity or a Paradigm Shift?

Jens Alber

Institutional Structure and Past Development of the German Welfare State: An Introductory Overview[1]

The German welfare state is dominated by work-related social insurance programs that cover the vast majority of persons in dependent employment, but exclude most of the self-employed and civil servants.[2] There is still some institutional fragmentation with specific programs for various occupational categories (such as farmers or miners), but the major schemes for workers and employees have become virtually integrated, even though they are still kept apart technically. Laws *regulating* the schemes are made on the federal level, with a federal Ministry of Labor and Social Affairs bearing the responsibility for social insurance matters. In the case of the social assistance or poor relief scheme, the federal framework legislation is specified by state legislation, and the administration of the scheme rests with state and local government.

The federal government has only a limited share in the financing of welfare state programs. It participates in the *financing* of the pension insurance, and the unemployment insurance scheme, but it does not (or only marginally) contribute to the other insurance programs. The assistance scheme is exclusively financed from state and municipal general revenues. Both the employers and the trade unions are strongly involved in the functioning of social insurance programs. Employees and employers each pay identical shares of earmarked contributions, and they also share equally in the administration of the self-governing insurance funds which are managed by elected representatives who are nominated basically by the associations of business and labor.[3]

The German constitution declares the Federal Republic to be a *federal and social state* under the rule of law. Hence, social policy is subjected to *judicial review* by independent courts which include not only the general Constitutional Court (*Bundesverfassungsgericht*), but also a special Federal Social Court (*Bundessozialgericht*). These courts have recurrently established general principles that public policies have to respect, for example by regulating that pension entitlements are equivalents of personal property, which can only be curtailed by the law-maker within certain limits, or by obliging the government to exempt incomes below a certain minimum from taxation.

On the side of the clients, there are several rather weak and fragmented associations, but the unions continue to be considered the major spokesmen of social insurance beneficiaries. The churches are rather strongly involved in the German welfare state, because they are linked closely to the voluntary welfare associations which play a major role as providers of services in the social assistance scheme. In addition, the churches maintain strong links to the workers' wing of the Christian Democratic Party, from whose ranks the Minister of Labor is usually selected when the conservatives are in power. Outside the assistance scheme, providers' associations only play a prominent role in the sickness insurance scheme, where they function jointly with the sick funds as state recognized regulators who issue guidelines for medical practice. Unions, churches, and welfare associations frequently act together as advocates of people who depend on social transfers and public services.

The five social insurance schemes which represent the institutional core of the German welfare state now represent roughly two-thirds of the social outlays that are reported in the government's social budget. The social budget is the most comprehensive official statement of social spending in Germany. It is published in two versions, in an *institutional* and in a *functional* classification. The former classifies receipts and expenditure by the legislative programs or schemes for which they arise, the latter lumps together those expenditure items from various programs that serve a common function. Regrouping the official classification by institutions somewhat, we may distinguish *eight broad institutional expenditure categories* (see table 1.1).

First, there are the five social insurance schemes with fairly extended coverage. The two big schemes among them—pension and sickness insurance—represent roughly one-half of the social budget. *Family allowances* also have wide coverage. If the universal child allowance scheme is added together with the child rearing allowance for parents who opt out of employment in favor of child rearing for two years, the two forms of family support represent almost 5 percent of the social budget. Various social security schemes for specific occupations—such as civil servants, farmers, or various professions—claim about 8 percent of the social budget. Among them, the various benefits

Table 1.1
The composition of the German Social Budget in 1998

SCHEME AND 1998 EXPENDITURE	IN % OF TOTAL SOCIAL BUDGET	COVERAGE/ENTITLEMENT BASIS
SOCIAL INSURANCE SCHEMES	65.1 % (21.8 % of GDP)	
- Pension insurance (3 branches)	31.3 %	All persons in dependent employment
- Sickness insurance	19.3 %	Persons in dependent employment below rather high income-limit including middle mass
- Unemployment insurance/ Employm.Promotion	10.5 %	All persons in dependent employment
- Accident insurance	1.6 %	All persons in dependent employment plus pupils and students
- Long-term care insurance	2.4 %	Practically universal
FAMILY ALLOWANCES	4.5 % (0.2 % of GDP)	
- Child allowance	3.9%[1]	All parents of minors
- Child rearing allowance	0.6%	Parents below a fairly high income limit, including middle mass
SOCIAL SECURITY FOR SPECIAL GROUPS	8.1 % (2.7 % of GDP)	
- Farmers' pensions	0.5	All self-employed farmers
- Professions' pensions	0.3	Compulsory for members of specific professional chambers
- Civil service scheme		Tenured civil servants
- pensions	5.0 %	
- family increments	1.1 %	
- sickness cost	1.2 %	
MEANS-TESTED OR INCOME-TESTED SCHEMES	5.4 % (1.8 % of GDP)	
- Social assistance	3.9 %	All persons below means-tested subsistence level; excl. middle mass
- Housing allowance	0.6 %	Income-tested rent support with low income limit excl. middle mass
- Education allowance	0.1 %	Means-tested/categorical for pupils/students. incl. middle mass
- Support of property formation	0.8 %	Subsidization of savings for formation persons below fairly high income limit, including middle mass
PUBLIC SERVICES[2]	2.7 % (0.9 % of GDP)	
- Youth support services	2.4 %	General service/control functions
- Public health service	0.3 %	General service/control functions
CATEGORICAL COMPENSATION	1.2 % (0.4 % of GDP)	Special benefits for specific groups, e.g.
- Social compensation		war victims/military service
- Equalisation of war burdens		civilian war victims
- Compensation of Nazi victims		Holocaust survivors and others
- Other compensation		Immigrants of German origin
EMPLOYERS' BENEFITS	7.1% (2.4 % of GDP)	
- Wage continuation	3.4 %	All dependently employed persons during first 6 weeks of sickness
- Occupational pensions/public sector	1.2 %	Compulsory for workers/employees in public sector
- Occupational pensions/private sector	2.2 %	Voluntary/collective agreements
- Other employer benefits	0.3 %	Voluntary
INDIRECT TAX SUBSIDIES	5.8%[3] (2.0 % of GDP)	Categorical entitlements for special groups, e.g. housing constructors
TOTAL SOCIAL BUDGET in 1998: 1,272 bio. DM = 33.5 % of GDP		

[1] Since 1996 the child allowance is administratively ranked as a tax credit and hence appears under indirect payments in the social budget.

[2] The social budget ranks these items together with the means-tested items above.

[3] The government social budget now includes the child allowance reported above under this item so that 9.8% of the social budget is now ranked as indirect expenditure.

Source: Bundesministerium für Arbeit- und Sozialordnung, 1999: Sozialbudget 1998.

for civil servants are by far the most important, as they alone add up to some 7 percent of social expenditure.

Targeted schemes with means-tests or income-tests for low-income groups excluding (most of) the middle classes play only a minor role in the German welfare state. The four targeted schemes with limited coverage—social assistance, housing allowances, education allowances, and the somewhat more comprehensive subsidization of property formation—together represent only a little over 5 percent of the social budget. Various *categorical compensation schemes* deal with special contingencies that are related to war or war-like damages. Together, the different schemes grouped under this heading amount to about 1 percent of the social budget. Two types of *public services*—youth support services and the public health service—remain fairly limited in scope claiming together not even 3 percent of social expenditure.

In addition to benefits paid from the public purse, the social budget also includes various benefits paid by employers. This includes the *mandatory wage continuation* scheme under which earnings for workers and employees continue to be paid for up to six weeks in case of illness, *occupational pensions* and other benefits paid on a voluntary basis or on the basis of collective agreements, and the *mandatory occupational pensions* which augment the compulsory public pension schemes for employees *in the public sector*. Together, these employers' benefits amount to roughly 7 percent of the social budget, or 2.4 percent of GDP. Finally, the social budget also includes various types of tax expenditure as so-called *indirect benefits* which amount to almost 6 percent of the social budget.[4] Taken together, all schemes included in the social budget amount to 1.3 trillion DM or 33.5 percent of GDP in 1998. This figure, then, is the *official social expenditure ratio* according to German government statistics.

Including indirect tax subsidies as well as various fringe benefits paid by employers on a voluntary basis, the German social budget is more comprehensive than the social expenditure data reported by most international organizations, which are usually confined to direct payments and to mandatory benefits. It is noteworthy, however, that neither education nor housing are usually considered to form part of social policies as traditionally defined in Germany. As we will follow here the narrow German notion of social policy rather than a more general concept of welfare state policies, a few words about education and housing must be added.

The strong traditional differentiation between social policies and *educational policies* is related to contingencies of historical sequence. Whereas the adoption of social programs followed the mobilization of industrial workers in the last quarter of the nineteenth century, the universalization of primary compulsory education was achieved in Prussia about half a century earlier. As Germany had the highest educational enrollment ratios in Europe at the end of the nineteenth century (Schneider, 1982), widening the access to institutions of learning was not considered to be part of the so-called "social question" related to industrialization. In line with this tradition, the social budget today only encompasses two minor parts of educational expenditure, that is, current outlays for kindergartens within its item "youth assistance" and the outlays for educational allowances which we have grouped here with the targeted schemes. An embracive educational budget is published separately by the Ministry of Education and Research.[5] After having increased to a high of 5.5 percent in 1975, the education expenditure ratio declined considerably thereafter and is currently still below the 5 percent threshold (table 1.2).[6]

Just like education, housing policy is usually not considered to form part of social policy as traditionally defined, and the social budget covers only a minor part of all housing expenditure. *Public housing* has always been of limited importance in Germany. In the Federal Republic, the state combined *housing allowances* for low-income tenants under a fairly low-income ceiling with three other instruments: regulative tenant protection legislation, a subsidization of housing supply that meets certain regulative standards, and tax credits for private builders. The latter two forms of supply-side subsidies are usually referred to as "object-promotion." The so-called "social housing construction" program (*sozialer Wohnungsbau*) which coupled public subsidies with regulations concerning the maximum rent, the income of tenants,

Table 1.2
The Development of Public Educational Expenditure

Year	Total expenditure		Distribution (% of total expenditure)			
	Total of GDP	per cent sector	Pre-school	Schools	Post secondary sector	Other*
1965	15,676	3.4	3.9	65.1	22.6	8.4
1970	27,759	4.1	3.2	61.4	24.8	10.5
1975	56,835	5.5	4.3	57.7	23.9	14.2
1980	77,127	5.2	4.6	56.8	23.0	15.6
1985	85,264	4.7	5.0	54.9	25.1	15.0
1990	102,795	4.2	5.8	51.2	29.5	13.4
1995	168,610	4.9	9.5	50.8	28.1	11.7
1998	173,964	4.6	9.6	50.1	28.8	11.5

*Adult education, education allowances, research promotion.

Sources: Bundesministerium für Bildung und Forschung: Grund- und Strukturdaten eds. 1999/00: 304; 1987/88: 259, and own calculations.

and the size and quality of the dwelling was originally the predominant policy tool. During the 1980s, the government shifted the thrust of its subsidization from the social construction program to the free housing market, however. As tax credits for private builders became more important, the number of units built under the social housing program declined from more than 300,000 originally to below 50,000 in the late 1990s. In the late 1990s expenditure for the program even decreased in absolute terms (see table 1.3a).

Total public expenditure for housing purposes is difficult to estimate, because there are no comprehensive official statistics, as the responsibility for housing policies is divided among various levels of government. Information on the subsidies in the social housing program and estimates of the amount of the various tax credits vary widely by official source.[7] Concise figures are only available for the outlays on housing allowances, which also appear in the social budget. These allowances for low-income tenants are financed jointly by the federal government and by state governments. Expenditure declined during the 1980s, but rose again after unification. It currently corresponds to some 0.2 percent of GDP, and goes to some 8 percent of all households (see table 1.3b).[8]

Table 1.3a
The Development of Housing Construction Subsidies

Years	Expenditure mio DM	As % of BIP
1970	1,294	0.19
1975	2,640	0.26
1980	3,646	0.25
1985	3,001	0.16
1990	4,102	0.16
1995	6,947	0.20
1996	6,120	0.17
1997	5,988	0.16
1998	4,567	0.12

Sources: Statistisches Bundesamt: Statistisches Jahrbuch (various editions), Table: Bewilli-gungen im sozialen Wohnungs-bau; Bundes-/Landesmittel insgesamt. These figures reported by the Federal Statistical Office are only about 40 percent of the outlays for social housing which the Ministry of Labor and the Association of Tenants give concurrently in their publications (e.g. 16.1 bio DM in 1995 and 13.6 bio DM in 1997).

Table 1.3b
The Development of Housing Allowances

Years	Expenditure (Social Budget) mio DM	As % of BIP	Recipients (Households) 1,000	As % of all private households
1970	660	0.10	908	4.1
1975	1,797	0.18	1,666	7.0
1980	2,009	0.14	1,486	6.1
1985	2,714	0.15	1,357	5.3
1990	3,923	0.16	1,531	5.4
1995	6,209	0.17	2,595	7.0
1996	6,614	0.19	2,719	7.3
1998	7,556	0.20	2,947	7.9

Sources: Frerich/Frey 1993: 375; Statistisches Bundesamt: Statistisches Jahrbuch 1999: 473; 2000: 474; Bundesministerium für Arbeit und Sozialordnung: Übersicht über das Sozialrecht 1998: 642 (for 1970; figures on recipients in later years partly deviate from Frerich/Frey).

Returning to social policies as defined in the social budget, it is noteworthy that the government complements its institutional break-down of expenditure (by programs) with a functional classification (by purpose). The official statistics distinguish *five functions* of social spending, that is, for *old age and survivors*, for *health* (including invalidity and rehabilitation), for *unemployment compensation and employment promotion*, for *marriage and families*, and for *various other purposes* (including housing and specific contingencies such as poverty relief or war-related compensation programs). The relative importance of expenditure for old age and survivors declined in the most recent period, albeit this function is still predominant (see table 1.4). In contrast, health expenditure increased its share from about one-fourth in 1960 to roughly one-third in 1998, and employment-related spending grew in the context of rising unemployment from 3 percent in the 1960s to over 12 percent in the united Germany. Marriage and family-related expenditure more or less maintained its expenditure share despite declining birth rates, whereas the share of various other functions decreased to an insignificant magnitude The changing structure of social outlays was accompanied by a sizeable increase in the expenditure ratio. In the golden age of welfare state expansion up to the mid-1970s, the social expenditure share in GDP grew from originally 22 to 33 percent. It has since oscillated around this level.

Table 1.4

Changes in the Composition of the German Social Budget by Function
(% of total social expenditure)

	1960	1975	1990	1998
Old age and survivors	44.3	39.8	40.3	37.0
Health (incl. invalidity and rehabilitation)	27.6	29.9	34.2	32.8
Employment	2.7	6.9	8.5	12.5
Marriage and families	16.5	15.6	12.7	13.7
Other functions (incl. housing, war-related contingencies etc.)	8.9	7.8	4.3	3.9

Source: Bundesministerium für Arbeit und Sozialordnung: Hauptergebnisse der Arbeits- und Sozialstatistik 1999: 106

Bundesministerium für Arbeit und Sozialordnung: Statistisches Taschenbuch 1999: 7.2 (for 1975)

Figures for 1990 and 1998 are for the united Germany.

If we look at the financing structure of the social budget, the lion's share of almost two-thirds of all receipts comes from contributions from insured persons (including pensioners) and from employers (including the imputed contributions for employer benefits). Subsidies and grants from various levels of government represent only about one-third of all income. The federal government's share amounts to roughly one-fifth. Over time, the share of contributions from insured persons has shown a steep increase, while the employers' share remained stable, and the share contributed by public authorities declined (see table 1.5).

Deficits in social insurance schemes do not belong to the typical characteristics of the German welfare state, although they do occur occasionally. Where deficits were recorded in the most recent period after unification, they were exclusively the result of developments in East Germany and a consequence of the massive transfers that were shoveled from the western to the eastern parts of the country. Thus, one study (Meinhardt 1997) showed that the West German pension insurance scheme would have been in an uninterrupted surplus throughout the 1990s despite the massive increase in unemployment and in the number of pensioners, if the pension scheme had not been made responsible for paying redistributive measures in favor of Eastern pensioners.

Table 1.5
The Changing Financing Structure of Social Expenditure in Germany
(total receipts by sources in percent)

	1960	1970	1975	1980	1990	1998
Insured persons (incl. pensioners)	20.7	22.6	24.3	25.2	28.8	30.9
Employersincl. imputed contributions for employer benefits	34.4	35.8	34.5	37.4	38.6	33.4
Subsidies and grants	42.6	39.7	39.2	36.0	30.9	34.4
(Of which: Federal government)	(25.1)	(23.6)	(24.4)	(22.3)	(18.6)	(20.0)
Various other receipts	2.3	1.9	1.9	1.4	1.7	1.3

Source: Bundesministerium für Arbeit und Sozialordnung: Hauptergebnisse der Arbeits- und Sozialstatistik 1999: 111

Bundesministerium für Arbeit und Sozialordnung: Statistisches Taschenbuch 1999: 7.3; 7.4

As the major part of the social programs is financed from earmarked contributions, the avoidance of deficits had its price in a massive increase in contribution rates. Since 1975 the aggregate contribution rate for all social insurance schemes rose by more than ten percentage points. It peaked above 42 percent in 1998 and declined moderately afterwards (see table 1.6).[9] The present policy goal is to push the contribution rate under the 40 percent threshold. Of course, the contribution rate has to rise either when the wage sum shrinks, for example, due to mass unemployment, when the number of beneficiaries increases, or when new schemes—such as the long-term care insurance are introduced. However, the political scientist Frank Nullmeier (1992) has argued that increasing contribution rates are not only a function of growing unemployment or growing numbers of welfare state beneficiaries, but also the consequence of what he calls the "predatory politics of the state." This means that the federal government, which has the power of legislation, tends to shift the costs from itself to other contributors in schemes that are financed from multiple sources, especially if the other parties are not involved in the decision-making process and hence cannot successfully mobilize resistance.[10]

If we take a bird's eye look at the postwar development of the German welfare state, we can identify five phases. After a phase of heavy extension up to 1958, there was a phase of moderate growth until the mid-1960s (Alber,

Table 1.6
The Development of Contribution Rates in Social Insurance Schemes
(institutionally defined percentage of gross earnings)

	1975	1980	1985	1990	1995	1998	2000
Pension insurance	18.0	18.0	19.2	18.7	18.6	20.3	19.3
Sickness insurance	10.4	11.4	11.8	12.6	13.2	13.6	13.5
Unemployment insurance	2.0	3.0	4.1	4.3	6.5	6.5	6.5
Long-term care insurance	-	-	-	-	1.0	1.7	1.7
Total	**30.4**	**32.4**	**35.1**	**35.6**	**39.3**	**42.1**	**41.0**

Source: Bundesministerium für Arbeit und Sozialordnung: Statistisches Taschenbuch 2000: 7.7

1986). This was followed by a very steep and rapid expansion of welfare state schemes until the mid-1970s. Judging by the usual ILO, OECD, or EU data, this expansionary trend of social spending has clearly been broken afterwards (see figure 1.1). Even though the different statistical definitions of social outlays used in various sources lead to discrepant levels of the expenditure ratio, they all agree in the result that the phase of steep growth up to the mid-1970s was suddenly brought to halt in 1975. The major discontinuity thus occurred not under the bourgeois government headed by Chancellor Kohl, but under the social-liberal coalition, after Chancellor Brandt had been replaced by Chancellor Schmidt. Under the Kohl government, the social expenditure ratio remained more or less stable, until the German unification ushered in a phase of renewed expansion. Up to the unification, the developments looked much like the "growth to limits" which Peter Flora (1986) has described as typical for European welfare states, with consolidation rather than massive retrenchment as the outstanding characteristic. The very special circumstances of the German unification then made for a new upsurge in social spending. This is mostly due to the exorbitant social outlays in East Germany where the social expenditure ratio amounted to 65 percent in 1992 and still to 56 percent in 1998 (Bundesministerium für Arbeit und Sozial-ordnung, 2000a). In sum, the growth of social spending had been successfully checked in the old Federal Republic, but the most recent period brought some new problems and challenges to which we shall now turn.

Figure 1.1
The Development of the Social Expenditure Ratio in Germany According to Different Data Sources

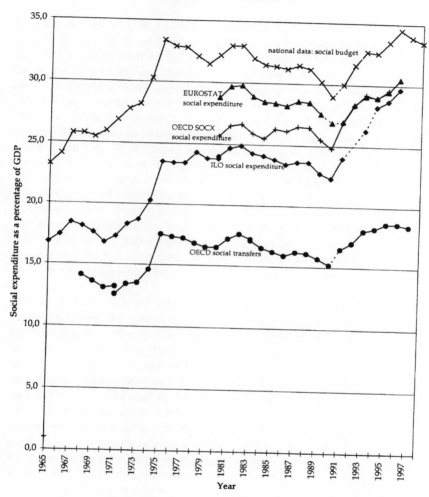

Data refer to Western Germany until mid 1990 (national data), 1991 (EUROSTAT,OECD), and 1993 (ILO). Major changes in the underlying data limit the comparability of the data between 1989 and 1990 (EUROSTAT) and between 1993 and 1994 (ILO).

Sources: Sozialbudget 1998; EUROSTAT Social protection: expenditure and receipts 1980 1994 and 1980-1996; ILO The Cost of Social Security, various volumes; OECD Historical Statistics, various volumes.

Adjustment Problems and Challenges

Adjustment Problems and Constraints

Ever since the two oil-price shocks of 1973 and 1979 brought the postwar prosperity in Germany to a halt, unemployment has been high, economic growth sluggish, and the public sector had to fight with incessant deficits (see table 1.7 on the context of social policies). Hence, the welfare state was faced with fiscal and political difficulties. When unemployment suddenly increased in the mid-1970s, even some social insurance schemes began to record deficits, and Chancellor Brandt was replaced by Chancellor Schmidt who subscribed to a policy of austerity. The new goal was to curb deficits and to stimulate growth and private investment by cutting taxes, and this led to a series of welfare state curtailments which began in 1975. When inflation increased and unemployment leaped to a new record of 9 percent in the early 1980s, the social democratic government was superseded by a conservative-liberal coalition under Chancellor Kohl which continued the policy of welfare state retrenchment with new vigor. The public deficit was curbed, unemployment could gradually be reduced, and inflation was successfully checked. When the wall between the two Germanies fell unexpectedly in October 1989, there were widely shared hopes for a new prosperity in a unified Germany.

The high-flying hopes that accompanied the German unification soon gave way to sobering encounters with a harsh reality. The monetary union, which had been implemented rapidly in July 1990 in order to forestall further increases in east-west migration, entailed an explosion of the labor costs of East German enterprises that suddenly had to pay their wages—as well as their other bills—in hard western currency. As the mushrooming costs outran their productivity by far, about 80 percent of all industrial firms in the East went bankrupt. The continuing union demand for "equal pay for equal work" made Eastern wages rise to about 80 to 90 percent of the West German levels, even though the Eastern productivity still is only at about 60 percent of the Western level. As a result, unemployment in the Eastern territories soared. In 1998, the jobless rate stood at 20 percent on average, with even higher levels in particular regions. In order to cope with the massive problems of transition, some 140 billion DM are transferred from the Western to the Eastern territories every year.

While unification brought about growing demands for public transfer payments, the ongoing process of standardization in the European Union put social and economic policies under heavy constraints. The *Maastricht treaty*, which went into effect in November 1993, defined five economic criteria that member countries of the European Union had to meet in order to qualify for the European Monetary Union that was to be implemented by 1999.[11] With

Table 1.7

The Changing Political-Economic Context of Welfare State Development in Germany

Years	Political-economic phase	GDP growth	Unemployment	Inflation	Public deficit (in % of public expenditure)	Election year(s) / Economic peak*) / Economic trough
1969-1973	Golden age of the social-liberal coalition	5.0	0.9	4.6	+0.9	Election years 1969 / 1972 / Economic peak 1969 7.4 / Economic trough 1970 3.1
1974-1975	Mid-seventies recession and change from Brandt to Schmidt as chancellor	1974: -0.0 / 1975: -0.1	3.7	6.5	-7.1	Economic peak 1974 -0.0 / Economic trough 1075 -1.1
1976-1979	Chancellor Schmidt's success years	3.9	4.3	3.7	-5.6	Election year 1976 / Economic peak 1976 5.5 / Economic trough 1977 2.6
1980-1982	Doom of the social-liberal government	-0.1	5.6	5.6	-6.6	Election year 1980 / Economic peak 1980 0.9 / Economic trough 1982 -1.1
1983-1987	Chancellor Kohl's muddling through in context of rising unemployment	2.2	9.1	1.6	-3.7	Election years 1983 / 1987 / Economic peak 1984 3.1 / Economic trough 1987 1.5
1988-1991	Short dream of unification with prosperity	4.6	7.5	2.6	-4.0	Election year 1990 / Economic peak 1990 5.5 / Economic trough 1988 3.7
1992-1998	Gradual decline of the Kohl government	1.2	10.8	2.6	-7.1	Election years 1994 / 1998 / Economic peak 1992 2.1 / Economic trough 1993 -1.2

*) Real economic growth rate

Sources: Bundesministerium für Arbeit und Sozialordnung: Statistisches Taschenbuch 1999: 1.1 (BIP); 2.10 (unemployment); 6.9 (inflation, cost of living index);

Deficit: (Sachverständigenrat zur Begutachtung der gesamtwirtschaftlichen Entwicklung: Bundestagsdrucksache 12/3774: 321; 1999/2000: 257) considerable difficulty, the Federal Republic managed to fulfill these criteria. The institutionalization of these economic criteria of rationality in the European Union and the neglect of other potential criteria of stability—such as a low level of unemployment or of strikes—put a high premium on fiscal consolidation policies and made active social policies much more difficult.

On the other hand, the social problems and policy tasks connected with the German unification continued to require vast resources. Under the dual pressure of the Maastricht constraints and the German unification problems, the Christian Democratic government retrenched welfare programs not only reluctantly in order to adapt to changing economic contexts—as its predecessor had done—but it also propagated an active restructuring of the welfare mix with a shift from welfare state to welfare society. Although the issue remained embattled among the various wings of the party, those affiliated with business interests warned of the growing cost of labor connected with high social insurance contributions, and of the shrinking attractiveness of the country for foreign capital given the high level of taxation and regulation. In order to break the spiral of rising expectations and of growing public deficits, a revival of self-help activities was now propagated. Some even advocated a retrenchment of social security schemes that would replace the status preservation enshrined in the traditional social insurance schemes by state-guaranteed minima (Miegel and Wahl, 1985).

In addition to the problems originating from German unification and the Maastricht criteria, some other challenges put traditional welfare policies under strain. After the collapse of the communist regimes in Eastern Europe, a massive emigration from Eastern countries set in. This was grounded in the fact that the German constitution guarantees not only asylum to the victims of political persecution, but also citizenship to all people of German descent who had been forced to remain in Eastern Europe after the second world war. From 1989 to 1995 roughly 9 million people immigrated into Germany, among them 1.6 million asylum seekers and more than 1.5 million German "expatriates" (*Aussiedler*) from Eastern Europe (see table 1.8). As the Federal Republic accepted more asylum seekers than all other EU member countries together, the proportion of foreigners grew rapidly. In the territories of the old Federal Republic, it more than doubled from 4 percent in 1970 to 10.5 percent by 1997 (Statistisches Bundesamt 2000). As most foreigners flocked to urban life, some of the big cities—such as Frankfurt, Munich, or Stuttgart—now count proportions of foreigners in the area of 25 to 30 percent. This massive influx put the social assistance scheme and also the pension scheme under heavy strain. In the pension scheme, the claims of German expatriates were honored basically as if they had been working and contributing in Germany, until a 1996 reform act curtailed the entitlement for all those who had come after 1990. In the social assistance scheme, the proportion of foreigners among those drawing the basic income support (outside

Table 1.8
Immigration and Asylum Seekers

	Total numer of immigrants thousands	Number of asylum seekers	Percentage of foreigners	
			Old Federal Republic	Germany
1970	1072		4.3	
1971	988			
1972	903	5289		
1973	968	5595		
1974	630	9424		
1975	456	9627		
1976	499	11123		
1977	540	16410		
1978	576	33136		
1979	667	51493		
1980	768	107818		
1981	625	49391		
1982	421	37423		
1983	372	19737		
1984	457	35278		
1985	512	73832		
1986	597	99650		
1987	645	57379	6.8	
1988	904	103076		
1989	1186	121318	7.7	6.4
1990	1652	193063	8.2	6.8
1991	1199	256112	8.8	7.3
1992	1502	438191	9.5	8.0
1993	1277	322599	9.9	8.5
1994	1083	127210	10.1	8.6
1995	1096	127937	10.2	8.8
1996	960	116367	10.4	8.9
1997	841	104353	10.5	9.0
1998	802	98644		

Sources: Statistisches Bundesamt: Statistisches Jahrbuch, various editions; Datenreport 1999: 45, 48

of institutions) had increased to over one-third in the early 1990s. In response, asylum seekers were shifted to a special new relief scheme,[12] and the proportion of foreigners in the social assistance scheme dropped to currently about one-quarter.

In the most recent period, the supranational social policy making in the European Union constitutes a major adjustment problem. The European Court of Justice quite frequently rules clauses in national social legislation to be incompatible with European law. Thus, when Germany credited years of child-raising with pension insurance contributions, it could not uphold the clause that the children had to be raised within the country, because this violated the non-discriminatory spirit of EU legislation. The German sickness insurance funds cannot effectively control the number of physicians admitted to practice under the sickness insurance regulations, because doctors from other EU countries are free to move in. A clause permitting the funds to limit their payments to services rendered within the country also violates EU law. Because of such tensions with supranational EU regulations, proposals to augment all pensions to a certain minimum level have become discredited in recent years, as the increments would also have to be paid to migrant foreign workers. Several verdicts of the European Court of Social Justice have strengthened the principle that social benefits—including the recently introduced long-term care allowance—must be freely exportable to other EU member countries.

In addition to constraints caused by external factors and events, some changes within German society also bring about new adjustment problems. The most serious of these changes is *population aging*. The population share of the elderly (65 +) has been fairly stagnant around 16 percent since 1980. The twenty-first century will be marked by a rapid greying of Germany, however. Following projections by the OECD, the proportion of elderly people will increase by scarcely 10 percentage points until 2030 on average, but by 13.2 percentage points in Germany, so that the country will have the highest elderly share among OECD countries by 2030 (OECD 1997: 101). Twenty-eight percent of the population will then be older than 65 years, and every elderly person will be faced by only two persons in the age group 15-64. This radical demographic transition will put the pension scheme under heavy strain, and it is now the consensus that it calls for further reforms. As the net reproduction rate among German women has fallen to below 0.60, there is little chance that the demographic situation will soon be redressed. In fact, having children seems to become less and less popular. Whereas only one out of ten women born in 1940 stayed childless for a lifetime, the proportion is estimated to be one-third among those born in 1970. Shrinking birth rates are not only a constraint for Germany's "Pay-As-You-Go" pension system, but they also give rise to a growing demand for services in old age that might substitute for the shrinking support potential within families.

Old and New Needs and Demands

If external pressures and internal transitions are the basis of serious new *constraints* on welfare state programs, there are also old and new social needs which constitute *demands* for continuous state action. The first and foremost social problem in any welfare state is the persistence of poverty. Judging from comparative data from the Luxembourg Income Study (LIS) or the European Union, Germany belongs to the countries with the lowest rates of relative income poverty in Europe (measured as below 50 percent of the mean income weighted by household size). However, the percentage of people living in "rigid" poverty (as defined by the 40 percent threshold) has increased in recent years from 3.9 percent in 1990 to 6.1 percent in 1995 (Statistisches Bundesamt 1997: 518). Particularly high poverty risks are reported for unemployed persons (34 percent), for families with children under 18 (21 percent), for families with three or more children (31 percent), and for single-parent households (42 percent).[13] The structure of poverty has changed considerably over time. Whereas up to the 1980s it was the elderly population who had overproportionate poverty risks and above average social assistance take-up, the poverty risk is now increasingly moving to younger age groups, especially to children (Hauser, 1995; Hauser, 1999).

Dynamic poverty research based on panel studies has shown that the risk to become poor is much more widespread than cross-sectional data suggest. Within a period of six years, about *one-quarter of the population* fall at least once under the 50 percent poverty threshold, and 10 percent remain under this poverty line for three years or more (Statistisches Bundesamt, 1997). Most poverty spells seem to be of fairly short duration, however, and there is a high proportion of people who would be entitled to public poor relief, yet choose not to claim it. The typical finding for the 1990s is that only about half of all potential claimants who would pass the means-test actually make a claim (Neumann, 1999). Over time, the proportion of the population claiming the basic income support tripled from about 1 percent in 1970 to 3.5 percent in 1997.[14] Whereas the average duration of welfare dependency is 26 months, in about one-half of all cases, benefits are drawn for less than a year.[15] In sum, the need for an effective anti-poverty policy persists, since the risk to become poor has become more widespread, and now affects especially children.

Another basic goal of the welfare state besides fighting poverty is to promote social integration by smoothing out social inequalities. In a comparative perspective, Germany belongs to the countries with a below average degree of income inequality in the European Union (Eurostat, 1998). Compared with the United States, the disposable household income is distributed much more equally among quintiles.[16] However, recent years witnessed a widening income gulf also in Germany. Whereas the originally vast East-

West disparities could be reduced, because incomes rose much more quickly in the East, the income inequality *within* the two territories has been growing. Compared to the situation twelve years earlier, West German incomes were distributed considerably more unequally in 1996, with the shares of the two bottom deciles falling, and the ratio of the top to the middle decile—the so-called 90/50 income threshold comparison—growing from 1.74 to 1.92 (Sachverständigenrat zur Begutachtung der gesamtwirtschaftlichen Entwicklung, 1999/2000). The size of the middle class—i.e., those having between 75 and 150 percent of the median disposable equivalent income—has been shrinking from 55 percent in 1983 to 50 percent in 1995 (Hauser, 1999). Even the Council of Economic Advisors, which usually sees its role as a prophet of the blessings of the free market economy, drew attention to the growing inequality and recognized that redistributive state programs have so far contributed to smooth out the disparities (Sachverständigenrat zur Begutachtung der gesamtwirtschaftlichen Entwicklung, 1999/2000). Obviously the existing redistributive measures have not been sufficient to neutralize the trend towards growing inequality, however.

One of the currently most pressing problems is the persistence of unemployment and the growth in *long-term unemployment*. Neglecting short-term fluctuations with the business cycle, unemployment has grown in three big leaps (1975, 1983, 1992) from originally 1 to 12 percent in 1999. The average duration of unemployment increased from four to nine months over the past two decades (Institut für Arbeitsmarkt-und Berufsforschung, 2000). In 1975, only 10 percent of the unemployed had been out of work for more than a year, but by 1998 this percentage had increased to 37 percent, and one out of five unemployed persons had been out of work for more than two years. The risk of unemployment and long-term unemployment is particularly high for unskilled workers and for older people above age 55. For both groups the jobless rate was above 20 percent in the 1990s. This shows the importance of vocational training and re-qualification measures that would help to avoid a segmentation of the labor market into insiders and permanent outsiders.

One particular problem in this respect results from the educational revolution with its inflationary upgrading of educational degrees. Among older age cohorts, more than 75 percent used to have no more than a regular high school diploma (*Hauptschulabschluss*) as the highest educational degree. Among the youngest age cohorts, however, most go on to institutions of higher learning so that only 15 percent now leave the educational system with a high school diploma (Statisches Bundesamt, 2000a). School leavers with nothing more than this degree are now in a radical minority position and will have increasing difficulties to find jobs in post-industrial labor markets that require high skills and have an abundant supply of better-educated groups. The de-qualification of those with merely basic education entails a serious risk of the growth of an underclass, and this will require new public efforts to ensure social cohesion and to integrate the marginal groups into the democratic order.[17]

A fourth problem consists of the changing household and family structures connected with the social mobilization of women. The labor force participation ratio of women aged 30 to 35 increased from 45 percent in 1970 to 71 percent in 1997, while that of married women grew from 36 to 49 percent (Bundesministerium für Arbeit und Sozialordnung, 1999a). More than half of all mothers with children under 18 are now economically active in West Germany, and in East Germany the figure is 71 percent. One-quarter of all mothers with children under three now hold a job, and 16 percent of all family households consist of single parents (Bäcker et al., 2000). This means that there is growing demand for more day care facilities, for extended youth services and for more social services in general which would increase the compatibility of vocational life and family life. Kindergartens and schools with day-long opening hours are still a rare exception in Germany. Whereas there is sufficient supply of kindergarten places for the age group 3 to 6, places for infants and toddlers below age three are in notoriously short supply (see table 1.9). Hence, public action to provide services for parents will be called for, especially since the right to a place in a kindergarten was enshrined in law following the unification. As the shrinking birth rates lead to a diminishing number of kin capable of providing long-term care in old age, there

Table 1.9
The Supply of Facilities in the Pre-School Sector

Years	0-3 years	3-6 years
1965		33
1975		66
1980		79
1985		80
1987	3	
1994		91
		3-8 years
1993	9.9	72
1995	7.7	70
1998	7.4	78

Sources: Bundesministerium für Bildung und Wissenschaft: Grund- und Strukturdaten 1991/92: 32; Statistisches Bundesamt: Statistisches Jahrbuch 1999: 471; Datenreport 1997: 50; Kom-mission der Europäischen Gemein-schaften 1990: 12.

will also be a continuing demand for social services for the elderly. The long-term care insurance scheme, which was introduced in 1994, may be seen as a response to this new challenge and will provide a platform for such demands in the future.

Current Issues and Debates

Changing Views of Solidarity

In the social policy discourse of the Federal Republic, it used to be a fairly uncontested idea that the combination of the market economy with a system of state redistribution served important integrative functions. It was widely accepted that the life chances of the population hinged upon two independent, but interlocking spheres of income distribution: (1) *The labor market* with collective bargaining arrangements at the industry level, which guaranteed that more general economic interests above the firm level would be taken into account and that firms of a given industry would not outbid each other in their competition for human capital; and (2) *A system of public transfer payments* with earnings-related public income maintenance schemes for the dependent labor force as its core. In the assessment of the sociologist Rainer Lepsius (1995), this dual system of income determination served to legitimize existing inequalities for two reasons. First, the existence of two separate arenas of decision-making helped to fragment conflicts over issues of social justice into technical details rather than ideologically charged matters of principle, because it directed the welfare claims of the population towards separate actors in differentiated systems of distribution; the mutual independence of the two spheres helped to isolate potential objects of conflict and to prevent distributional conflicts from developing into constitutional issues. Secondly, both arenas coupled decision-makers to the consent of the people, since political elites must be elected, and the results of collective bargaining require the approval of the members of the trade unions and of the employers' associations. Lepsius perceived the fragmentation of welfare issues and the dual feedback loop between decision makers and the public in two separate spheres of decision making as major stabilizers of the democratic order.

Today new concepts contest the conventional wisdom. In the *system of primary distribution*, unions collectively pressing for high wages and employment regulation are now seen as egotistically promoting the interests of those who possess a job at the expense of those who are unemployed. The new concept here is the segmentation of the labor force into privileged "insiders" and excluded "outsiders" whose interests are not represented at the bargaining table. High wages are no longer seen as a basis of purchasing power and mass consumption, but as an impediment to employment, especially in the context of growing competition from low-wage countries in a global economy. Many now recommend the creation of a low-wage sector which would provide jobs for unskilled workers who presently do not find jobs because their productivity is not high enough to warrant the level of pay enforced by the unions. Various employers and scholars now call for a "combination wage" following the logic of the American Earned Income Tax Credit (EITC), which would subsidize the low earnings that are paid at market clearing levels in the labor market (see Scharpf, 1995, 2000).

In the *system of public transfers,* basic income security for all citizens rather than status preservation in earnings-related social insurance schemes is now advocated by many. Though still representing only a minority view, it is now propagated by factions among the liberals, the Christian Democrats, and the Green Party alike (see e.g., Kaltenborn, 1995; Kommission für Zukunftsfragen der Freistaaten Bayern und Sachsen, 1997; Miegel, 1995; and Schmid, 1986). The existing system of basic income support in the social assistance scheme is no longer seen as an effective safety net for those who fall between the cracks of the affluent society, but perceived as a poverty trap that keeps people out of the labor market. It is claimed that the basic income support is too high and produces two unintended effects: (1) In the absence of a relevant difference between wages and benefits there is hardly any work incentive so that the recipients prefer to stay on welfare; and (2) Given the growing wedge which taxes and social insurance contributions drive between gross and net wages, employers find it increasingly difficult to pay the high gross wages that would be necessary to yield a net wage above the level of the basic income support (Scharpf, 1995). Even though dynamic poverty research has proven many of the assumptions underlying these arguments to be false showing that employment problems are less related to an insufficient search for (or supply of) labor among assistance recipients than to an insufficient demand for low-skill labor among employers,[18] the new views are becoming increasingly popular, and quickly disseminate into the political parties.[19]

There is also a new intellectual view of the cleavages that shape social policy developments. Traditionally, social policies used to be analyzed in terms of the *class cleavage* which was perceived to shape the interest in more or less vertical redistribution, and in terms of *religious cleavages* which shape the interest in more or less voluntary action in the welfare mix. Now special attention is given to specific life situations that give rise to different needs such as having children or being childless, having to cope with divorce, long-term illness, or with the loss of physical autonomy. It is claimed that needs tied to such contingencies arise independently of the position in the class structure and are not well voiced by the organizations built on the class cleavage. This has been termed "the new social question," and it gave rise to demands to shift the focus of welfare state action from the old and partially solved social question concerning the position of workers in capitalist society to new social questions concerning citizens with little bargaining power (Geissler, 1976; Miegel, 1983).

Secondly, there is concern that there will be a growing *generation cleavage*, as the twin demographic change of declining net reproduction rates and increasing life expectancy lead to a very unfavorable cost-benefit ratio for younger generations in the PAYG pension scheme. The ongoing debate about the profitability of various kinds of pension arrangements may lead to a new pension mentality which might be marked by a utilitarian calculus of the "individual rates of return" rather than by the moral sentiment that there ought to be "solidarity among the generations" (as advocated in the official slogan of the current Pay-As-You-Go pension scheme).

Finally, the mobilization of women brought about *gender conflicts* as a third form of new cleavages shaping social policy. Here, the adequacy of female pension entitlements and the availability of social services which would allow one to have children, and a job simultaneously, are core issues. Interestingly, the German feminists were deeply divided over the issue of whether the informal work of women in households should be credited with pension insurance contributions as an equivalent of contributions from formal work. While some welcomed the change as a recognition of women's contribution to society, others criticized it as perpetuating the traditional division of labor by introducing new incentives for women to stay content with family work. These debates suggest that conflicts in the sphere of reproduction may increasingly complement the old social policy cleavages which were rooted in the class conflict and in inequalities formed in the sphere of production (see Nullmeier and Rüb, 1993).

Opinion polls have so far failed to provide convincing evidence of the salience of new cleavages. Attitudes towards the welfare state seem to be (still) predominantly structured by the position in the class structure and by party affiliation (Roller, 2000; Svallfors, 1997). It may be, however, that new cleavage structures manifest themselves first and foremost on the level of organizations rather than on the level of mass attitudes. In this sense, it might be interpreted as a sign of a coming pension backlash among the younger generation that all youth organizations of the leading parties, with the exception of the young socialists, have recently come forth with independent pension reform proposals that advocate the introduction of funded elements (Richter, 1999; Fischer, 1999). Richter's account of the 1997 pension reform shows that the young representatives did not yet get together for joint meetings across party lines, but in the case of gender issues discussed in the 1989 pension reform, the female factions of various parties did actually get together to modify parts of the government's bill in favor of women (Richter, 1999).

Financing Issues

Financing issues have assumed the front stage of social policy debates in recent years. The most commonly voiced argument developed by the European Commission, the OECD, and scholars like Scharpf (1986, 2000) or Esping-Andersen (1996) alike, is that social insurance contributions drive a wedge between the net wages workers receive and the gross wages employers must pay, and that this drives unskilled work with low productivity out of the labor market. Hence, a change to new forms of financing is advocated which would shift from contributions to general or earmarked taxation, thus doing away with four weaknesses of the contribution system: (1) It only falls on income from dependent labor, thus exempting other sources of income as well as various social categories such as civil servants or the self-employed; (2) It extends only to income up to a contribution ceiling, thus exempting all income above the threshold; (3) It is not progressive, but proportional; and (4) In contrast to the income tax, it does not exempt income below the subsistence minimum from taxation. So far, even the new red-green coalition government shied away from a radical reform of the financing mode. In 1999, it did, however, introduce a new ecology or energy tax (especially on gas) which was used to raise the federal share in the financing of the pension insurance scheme so that the contribution rate could be lowered from 20.3 to 19.5 percent and to 19.1 percent by 2001.

The most heated debate concerning financing issues arose with respect to the viability of the PAYG pension scheme. Many fear that the present scheme cannot be kept solvent given the coming demographic burden. Paul Samuelson (1958) has shown that the real rate of return in a mature pay-as-you-go system is equal to the sum of the rate of growth in the labor force and the rate of growth in productivity. As fertility rates go down, labor force growth ends if the declining birth rates are not counteracted by immigration (which is usually costly in terms of social integration). This puts downward pressure on the rates of return in pay-as-you-go schemes and makes alternative forms of providing for old age more attractive. Since fertility rates have gone down dramatically over the past decades, and Germany is expected to have the most unfavorable elderly dependency ratio in OECD countries by 2030, many policy pundits advocate the transition to a funded scheme or at least the introduction of elements of such a scheme (Breyer, 1997, 2000; Börsch-Supan, 2000; Kommission für Zukunftsfragen der Freistaaten Bayern und Sachsen, 1997; see also Schmähl, 2000). As a profound system change to a funded scheme would involve a huge double payment problem for the transition generation, nobody seriously advocates a complete change, however. The emerging consensus, now also shared by the churches, is that the existing scheme should be curtailed so that the contribution rate can be stabilized, and that the demographic risk should be dispersed by a portfolio solution which would put public subsidies on private investments in funded schemes that would top the state program. This, at least, is what the most recent reform legislation by the new government provides for.[20]

Allocation Principles: Changing Priorities

The Pattern of Cutbacks

In a period of austerity, changing priorities and allocation principles should become visible in the different degrees to which various policy fields or different policy programs become vulnerable to retrenchment. Hence, we will take a look at the cutbacks in some core schemes. The pension insurance scheme has been at the center of curtailment efforts of both, the social-liberal coalition and the Christian-liberal coalition ever since 1977.[21] Following the long series of stepwise curtailments, the standard pension[22] is now roughly one-fifth lower than it would be, if the pre-1977 legislation were still in effect.[23] The most recent reform legislation foresees to further lower the level of the standard pension from (currently) 70 percent to 67 percent in order to cap the future contribution rate at 22 percent. Considering that pensioners were also obliged to pay individual sickness insurance contributions and higher consumption taxes from their pension, the real cutback is even higher. On the other hand, despite all curtailments, and due to the increase in wages to which pensions are indexed, the purchasing power of the standard pension is higher now than in 1975 before the cutbacks (for data see Alber, 2000). Access to invalidity, survivors' and premature pensions has been seriously reduced. The age-limit for pensions for women was raised from 60 to 65 years, but in exchange for this 18 percent cut of female entitlements, child-rearing and family work have been increasingly recognized as equivalents to contributions.

The *unemployment insurance scheme* was also subject to sizeable curtailments during the past two decades. The earnings replacement rate was lowered mildly from 68 percent to 67 percent for parents of dependent children, but more severely from 68 percent to 60 percent for childless people. Unemployment assistance—the means-tested component of the unemployment compensation program—was cut back a little less markedly, from 58 percent to 57 percent for parents, and from 58 percent to 53 percent for singles. In addition to the cutbacks, there were more stringent controls of benefit recipients in both branches as well as higher pressure to accept jobs even if they are below the applicants' level of qualification. On the other hand, the maximum duration of benefits for older people with long insurance records was almost tripled, and some new instruments, such as wage subsidies for employers willing to hire unemployed people were enacted (see section on social activation for more details).

Rather profound changes occurred in the sickness insurance scheme. The sickness insurance cash benefit was cut twice through legislation in 1983—which made the benefit subject to compulsory contributions for pension and unemployment insurance—and in 1996—which reduced the statutory wage continuation during the first six weeks of an illness from 100 percent to 80 percent and reduced the subsequent sickness benefit from 80 percent to 70 percent. The medical benefits were retrenched in a stepwise fashion by various acts that stretched over twenty years. Co-payments for pharmaceuticals, hospital stays, and various appliances were raised several times. On the other hand, risks which previously had to be borne privately came under public coverage. Thus, in 1988, the official plan for the health reform law was to save 14 bio DM, or some 10 percent of the sickness insurance expenditure, in order to use half of the savings to cover the cost of a new home-care benefit. A 1992 act then aimed at savings of roughly 11 bio DM or 6 percent of sickness insurance expenditure. Again, the savings were partly designed as a basis for getting the liberal party's consent to the introduction of the new long-term care insurance which the Christian union was then advocating, which was enacted after long political struggles in 1994.

The *social assistance or poor relief* scheme which provides for minimum income support was also subject to curtailments. The benefits of the scheme are designed to bridge the gap between the countable private means of a household and a standard of need which is considered a socially acceptable minimum (the so-called *Regelsatz*). If the means-test reveals no countable private income, the scheme carries the full cost of subsistence according to the standard, which varies with family size and to some extent also with the age of the family members.[24] The phase of retrenchment began in 1981, still under the social-liberal coalition government, when special increments for specific groups such as elderly persons were reduced from 30 percent to 20 percent, and the annual adjustment of benefits to inflation was suspended in favor of lower discretionary increases. The new conservative government continued this policy by postponing the adjustment for half a year and by capping its rate in 1982 and 1983. No further curtailments were legislated in the second half of the 1980s. Renewed attempts at cost control set in after the German unification and after the Constitutional Court had declared the minimum subsistence level to be tax exempt. A 1993 cur-tail-ment act suspended the regular adjustment mechanism of benefits and redefined the need standard as providing only the "indispensable" standard of living. Later acts also ruled that the assistance level of households with up to five members must remain under the level of net wages in the low wage sector (including child and housing allowances). A series of subsequent acts emphasized a shift from welfare-to-workfare to which we will return in the section on social activation.[25]

Summarizing the *pattern of cutbacks*, there is a fourfold conclusion: (1) No particular program has been spared; (2) There is no obvious difference in the vulnerability of long-term and short-term benefits; (3) The means-tested assistance scheme has not fared any worse than the more inclusive insurance programs; and (4) Cutbacks were frequently coupled with the introduction of new benefits. The retrenchment did not amount to an outright dismantling of welfare-state schemes but rather to a downscaling which brought the benefit levels roughly back to the standards reached in the late-1960s before the social-liberal reform government had come to office (see table 1.10 and Alber, 1980). The outstanding feature of German cutbacks is that the curtailments were administered remarkably symmetrically across the various social programs which we discussed here. This also implies that there has not been any conscious attempt to move the German welfare state into the direction of more residual type following the Anglo-Saxon model.[26]

If there was a conscious policy goal governing the retrenchment process, it was to arrive at a system stabilization by moving from *open-ended need-satisfaction to budgeting and contribution-defined spending*. This was reflected in the political slogan to subject social policies to the principle of "revenue-dependent expenditure policy" (*"einnahmen-orientierte Ausgabenpolitik"*). This new principle left a mark on several programs. In *pension policy*, it expressed itself most clearly in the recent capping of the future contribution rate and before in the new indexation method which tied pension adjustments to the development of net rather than gross wages so that rising taxes and social insurance contributions would translate into lower pension increments. In *sickness insurance*, fixed lump sum payments replaced open-ended entitlements, for example in the case of prescriptions for pharmaceuticals or medical appliances. In the new *long-term care insurance scheme*, benefits were graded by the severity of the impairment, but in each category they were capped with the goal to make the outlays of the scheme contribution-defined rather than need-defined (Rothgang, 1994). In *social assistance,* the departure from need-defined payments occurred when the regular annual adjustment procedure was dispensed and when the calculation of the standard rate was tied to earnings and consumption patterns in the low-wage sector.

The new emphasis on budgeting also meant that there was more effort to distinguish between necessary and merely desirable benefits. In Hugh Heclo's (1974) terms, there was now more collective "puzzling" about priorities, and this was accompanied by a trend to move from *undifferentiated general entitlements to more contingent, categorically defined provisions*. In the pension scheme, for example, the level of *widows'* pensions is now dependent upon *earnings*; the entitlements for *students* were lowered, whereas the pensions for *women doing family work* were upgraded. In the sickness insurance scheme a partial privatization of some risks in the form of co-payments for

Table 1.10

The Provisions of Social Insurance Laws in the Federal Republic of Germany at the Beginning and at the End of the Kohl Era

	Pension Insurance		Health Insurance		Unemployment Insurance		Accident Insurance	
	1981	1997	1981	1997	1981	1997	1981	1997
Scope of insurance No. insured (% of labour force)	22 Mio. (78%)	W: 24.3 Mio (75.8%) E: 6.9 Mio.(84.1%) tot: 31.2 Mio.(77.5%)	20.6 Mio. (74%) 25.1 Mio. (87%) 56.6 Mio. (92%)	29.7 Mio. (73.7%) 35.8 Mio. (88.8%) 71.6 Mio. (87.2%)	21.6 Mio. (77%)	27.2 Mio. (67.4%)	25 Mio. (1982) (89%)	38.4 Mio (95%)
Income limit for compulsory coverage	all workers and employees	all workers and employees	3,300 DM (1.27 times av. wages)	6,150 DM (1.40 times av. wages) (1.58 times av. wages) 5,325 DM (E)	all workers and employees	all workers and employees	all employed persons + students and school children (ca. 15 Mio.)	all employed persons + students and school children (ca. 16.8 Mio.)
Benefits absolute amounts in DM and percentage of net average wages	after 45 years: 1,282 DM (69.4%) (69.9%, BMAS); average pension: 821 DM (44.4%)	after 45 years: W: 1,975 DM (70.6%) E: 1,683 DM (W: 70.5%, BMAS) (E: 69.0%, BMAS) average pension: W: 1,280 DM (45.8%) E: 1,388 DM (58.4%)	first six weeks: full salary, payed by employer later: 80% of gross earnings (not exceeding net earnings)	first six weeks: 80% of full salary, payed by employer (alternative: 100% of gross earnings, but loss of one vacation day per 5 days illness) later: 70% of gross earnings (not exceeding 90% of net earnings)	1,256 DM for earners of average wages 68% (58% in unemployment assistance)	W: 1,873/1,678 DM E: 1,592/1,426 DM for earners of average wages 67% for unemployed with child(ren); 60% for single (57%/53% in unemployment assistance)	full salary for first 6 weeks; later: 80% of gross earnings, (not exceeding net earnings) care benefits (1980): 326-1.300 DM Pensions: 2/3 of prev. earnings	full salary for first 6 weeks; later: 80% of gross earnings, (not exceeding net earnings) care benefits: W: 537-2,147 DM E: 454-1.815 DM Pensions: 2/3 of prev. earnings
Duration of benefits	-	-	max. 78 weeks in a period of three years	max. 78 weeks in a period of three years	max. 52 weeks + unemployment assistance	max. 52 weeks under the age of 45; above this age increasing until age 57, when maximum of 32 months is reached + unemployment assistance	-	-
Contributions as % of gross wages	18.5	20.3	11.8	13.3 (West) 13.7 (East)	3.0	6.5	no data available	no data available
Source of funds: share paid by insured persons and employers (+ state share)	each 50%; State: 16.3% of cost (18.2%, own calc.)	each 50%; State: 21.7% of cost (21.4%, own calc.)	each 50% (employer pays full salary for first 6 weeks)	each 50% (employer pays 80% salary for first 6 weeks)	each 50% state pays assistance and deficit	each 50% state pays assistance and deficit	employers only	employers only
Income limit for contribution purposes	4,400 DM (1.70 times av. wages)	8,200 DM (W) (1.87 times av. wages) 7,100 DM (E) (2.10 times av. wages)	3,300 DM (1.27 times av. wages)	6,150 DM (W) (1.40 times av. wages) 5,325 DM (E) (1.60 times av. wages)	4,400 DM (1.70 times av. wages)	8,200 DM (W) (1.87 times av. wages) 7,100 DM (E) (2.10 times av. wages)	-	-
Controls: length of waiting period	-	-	0	0	0	0	0	0

Source: Alber (2000)

certain services went along with the collectivization of the risk of long-term care. In unemployment insurance and assistance, benefits were graded depending on the family situation of the recipient, and people successfully searching for work were allowed to receive wage subsidies or draw partly uncurbed benefits in addition to earnings from employment. Thus, an element of discretion was inserted into the schemes that took the life situation and the behavior of recipients into account.

The new trend towards more categorically differentiated entitlements made itself felt most visibly in two fields: the treatment of foreigners and of families. The massive influx of asylum seekers had coincided with a climate of economic nationalism in the context of globalization debates, and with the mobilization of cultural nationalism in the context of German unification (Alber, 1995). When the proportion of foreigners receiving the standard income support of the social assistance scheme surged from 8 percent to 35 percent within one decade, a public debate on the abuse of the asylum laws set in. In the end, asylum seekers lost their entitlement to social assistance payments and were shifted to a new special scheme with lower benefits in 1993. Asylum seekers thus became losers of the process to distinguish more consciously between various (more or less) deserving "risk categories."[27]

In contrast, parents and children were increasingly recognized as deserving public support. Whereas *child benefits* deteriorated in several other European countries, they were stable or even upgraded in Germany (Alber, 2000). In 1974, when the general child allowance scheme was introduced, the allowance stood at 50 DM for the first child and 120 DM for the third and further children. In 1998 the respective numbers were 220 and 300 DM in nominal terms.[28] In real terms, this corresponded to more than a doubling for the first child and a 26 percent increase for the third child.[29] The upgrading was mostly due to the 1992 Constitutional Court which strengthened the right to subsistence and exempted income up to the subsistence level from taxes. The government then integrated the child allowance scheme into the system of tax credits. This means that the fiscal authorities now pay either tax credits at the amounts stated above, or deduct the tax-exempted income from taxable income if the latter method is more advantageous (which only happens rarely in the case of high income earners who are subject to highly progressive tax rates).

The new emphasis on children and families is also reflected in the grading of social insurance curtailments by family status. This was most pronounced in pension insurance, where the policy of contribution credits shifted from credits for schooling to a bonus for child-rearing. The credit was extended from one year per child in 1981 to three years in 1989, and in addition, the computation base for credits was raised from 75 percent to 100 percent of average earnings in 1997. On the other hand, years of schooling were significantly devalued, from a credit of up to 13 years, counted as the equivalent of

200 percent of average earnings, to a credit of merely 3 years, counted at 75 percent. This meant a considerable redistribution from a credit favoring the middle classes to a more focused measure in favor of women with small entitlements due to short employment careers (see also section 6).

The new focus on family policies was spurred not only by family-friendly decisions of the Constitutional Court, but also by the findings from poverty research which had shown children rather than elderly people to be disproportionately hit by poverty (Hauser, 1995). In addition, the declining net reproduction ratio had begun to capture the attention of politicians, and concerns about the shrinking population size increasingly shaped the public discourse in which the precarious supply of social services became a central topic.

New Priorities and New Programs: The New Emphasis on Families and Services

The new emphasis on families, children, and social services led to an extension of welfare-state schemes into hitherto uncovered fields. Already in 1979, the old social-liberal coalition had adopted a *child alimony security law* (*Unterhaltsvorschussgesetz*). This introduced public advance payments for single parents (mostly mothers) who did not receive alimony from the liable parent (mostly fathers).[30] In 1986, this early initiative was followed by the introduction of a new *parental allowance* (*Erziehungsgeld*) and an entitlement to *parental leave* (*Erziehungsurlaub*). If the household income is below a (fairly high) income limit and the parent works less than 19 hours per week, he or she is entitled to a monthly parental allowance of 600 DM per month for a period of up to 24 months after the birth of a child. The benefit tops the general child allowance and is designed as an incentive to cater for small children. It has a high take-up with some 95 percent of all potential claimants—almost exclusively mothers—drawing the benefit. A reform act initiated by the new red-green government in 2000 extends the scope of the law, by giving both parents an entitlement to work part-time (up to 30 hours) for up to three years after birth. Other measures to facilitate the combination of work and family obligations included the introduction of a legal entitlement in 1996 to place children aged 3 to 6 in kindergarten.

In 1994, a new long-term care insurance scheme extended the scope of compulsory social insurance to a previously uncovered field. In an attempt to unburden families as well as local government, which was paying an ever-growing share of institutional care as part of the social assistance scheme, the task to care for frail elderly people was shifted from private households and local authorities to professional care workers and a compulsory public scheme. Based on compulsory contributions from practically the entire population, including pensioners and members of private health insurance, it introduced a legal entitlement to publicly financed long-term care. Three categories of need were distinguished, and in each category, benefits with a fixed ceiling were introduced which were designed to cover the (partial) cost of care. Claimants have the choice between a higher benefit in-kind designed to pay professionally provided services and a lower cash benefit which may be used to pay caretakers in the recipients' private household.

Limited as these innovations may have been, the restructuring that did take place left a clear mark on aggregate statistics showing the composition of social expenditure. One of the conventional wisdoms of comparative welfare-state research is that Germany belongs to the countries that put heavy emphasis on social transfers but have underdeveloped social services (Scharpf, 1986; Schmidt, 1988; Esping-Andersen, 1996). This has certainly been true in the past. Up until the 1980s, it also showed up—at least to some degree—in the OECD data on public and social expenditures. Thus, in 1980, the German social transfer ratio was clearly above average in a comparison of OECD countries, while the ratio of government civil consumption expenditure was below average, and social service outlays were slightly above the mean (see figures 1.2 and 1.3). By the mid-1990s, Germany could no longer

Figure 1.2a
The Structure of Social Expenditure in OECD Countries, 1980

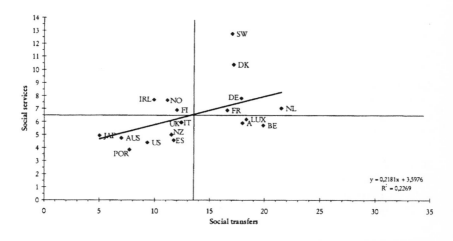

Social transfers are defined as social expenditure (public or mandatory private) on old age cash benefits, disability cash benefits, occupational injury and disease, sickness benefits, survivors' benefits, family cash benefits, unemployment (including active labour market programmes), housing benefits and other continegencies. Social service expenditure include services for the elderly, disabled people, families, and expenditure on health (without sickeness benefits). Data are missing from Canada, Greece, Iceland, and switzerland. Source: OECD Social Expenditure Database.

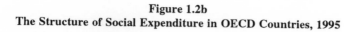

Figure 1.2b
The Structure of Social Expenditure in OECD Countries, 1995

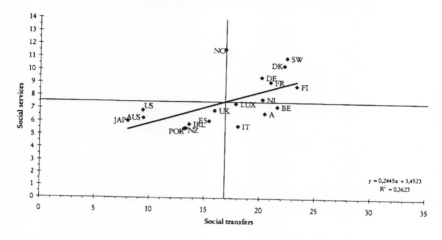

Social transfers are defined as social expenditure (public or mandatory private) on old age cash benefits, disability cash benefits, occupational injury and disease, sickness benefits, survivors' benefits, family cash benefits, unemployment (including active labour market programmes), housing benefits and other continegencies. Social service expenditure include services for the elderly, disabled people, families, and expenditure on health (without sickeness benefits). Data are missing from Canada, Greece, Iceland, and switzerland. Source: OECD Social Expenditure Database.

be ranked among countries that one might call transfer-intensive, however. In 1995, both the social services expenditure ratio and the government civil consumption expenditure ratio, had moved clearly above average, while the German social transfer ratio was now surpassed by several countries and moved slightly below the mean.[31] The German social budget also shows the German welfare state to have become much less transfer-intensive over time, as the share of transfers or cash benefits declined from 76 percent in 1970 to 60 percent in 1998 (Bundesministerium für Arbeit und Sozialordnung, 2000a; data for the old Federal Republic). While the importance of social services has thus been growing, there is one part of the service sector which has been conspicuously neglected by German policymakers. This is the field of education.

The Neglect of the Educational Sector

Educational policies had their heyday from the early 1960s to the mid-1970s when the postwar baby boomers began to pass through the institutions of higher learning. Compared to 1975, the educational expenditure ratio is

Figure 1.3a
The Structure of Public Expenditure in OECD Countries (1980)
(only civil government consumption; as a percentage of GNP)

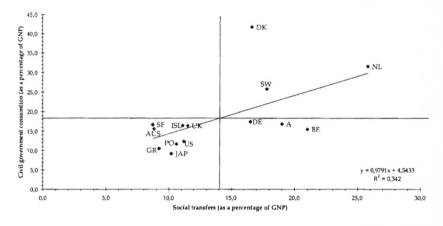

Source: OECD 1989: National Accounts (1975-1987), Vol. II: Tables 1,5,6; OECD 1985: Historical Statistcs (1960-1983), Tab. 6.5 and 6.3, Data for France, Canada, Ireland, Italy, Luzemburg, New Zealand, Norway, Switzerland and Spain are not avaiable.

Figure 1.3b
The Structure of Public Expenditure in OECD Countries (1995)
(only civil government consumption; as a percentage of GDP)

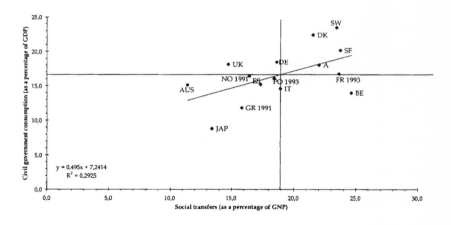

Source: OECD 1998: National Accounts (1984-1996), Vol. II: Tables 1,5,6; OECD 1995: Historical Statistics (1960-1995), Tab. 6.5 and 6.3. No date are available from Belgium, Canada, Ireland, Luxembourg, the Netherlands, New Zealand, Switzerland, and the USA.

now almost a full percentage point lower (see table 1.2). Of course, changes in educational expenditure reflect not only policy efforts, but also two other factors: demographic changes and educational mobilization. Demographic waves have been very intense in Germany. Whereas an annual number of about one million babies were born during the 1960s, the average number of births shrank to 600,000 in the period 1974 to 1989, and rose to some 700,000 in the 1990s (Statistisches Bundesamt, 1997).[32] Demographic waves of such magnitude must lead to a phase-specific shrinkage or expansion of the educational system. Between 1960 and 1975 the number of school children grew from scarcely 7 to over 10 million, while the number of students almost tripled (see table 1.11). In the next 15 years the number of students doubled, but the number of school children shrank almost back to its 1960 level. After unification, the ranks of school children swelled once more to above 10 million at the end of the decade, but it is now expected that the number will decline to some 8 million by 2015 (Statistisches Bundesamt, 2000a).

In addition to the demographic waves, there were two surges of educational mobilization. The first one occurred in the 1960s and early 1970s, the second one in the context of the unification. In the fifteen-year span from 1960 to 1975, the participation ratio of people at student age (19-26) in institutions of higher learning more than tripled, while the enrollment ratio for university entrants more than doubled from 8 percent to 20 percent among people aged 19 to 21 (see table 1.12). After a decade of stagnation, the enrollment ratio for entrants soared up once more by more than ten percentage points between 1985 and 1990.[33] Following unification, the 1990s saw another upsurge in student participation ratios.

Did educational policy keep pace with these leaps in educational participation? Up to the mid-1970s this was clearly the case. The huge increase in public expenditure was not merely the by-product of demographic changes or social mobilization processes, but was also the result of conscious policy efforts. This is most clearly reflected in student-teacher ratios (see table 1.12). While the number of university students barely tripled from 1960 to 1975, the number of professors more than quadrupled, thus considerably lowering the student-teacher ratio from 53 to 28. Similar changes occurred in the school system where the number of school children per teacher shrank by one-third between 1965 and 1980. In contrast, the 1980s and 1990s were marked by relative stagnation.[34] Whereas enrollment ratios continued to grow, the staffing of post-secondary institutions declined relative to the number of students. While student numbers doubled, and the number of university diplomas even tripled between 1975 and 1995, the number of professors just increased by the factor 1.2 (see table 1.11). By the end of the 1990s, the student-teacher ratios in German universities had roughly returned to the levels of the early 1960s, with some of the indicators even pointing to a heavier teaching burden for professors at the end of the twentieth century (see table 1.12).

Table 1.11
Teachers, Students, and Exams in Various Educational Sectors: Absolute Numbers in Thousands and Indices (1975 = 100)[1]

Years	All professors in post-secondary sector	University professors	Universities and colleges							Schools	
			Students		Entrants		Exams			School children in general schools (excluding vocational schools)	Teachers
			Total post-secondary sector	Universities	Total post-secondary sector	Universities	All exams	University diplomas	Doctoral exams		
1960	5.5	5.2	291.1	246.9	79.4	62.6	47.8	20.3	6.2	6,673	210
1965	9.4	8.8	384.4	308.4	85.7	63.8	66.5	25.5	7.0	7,325	243
1975	30.5 (100)	22.2 (100)	840.8 (100)	695.6 (100)	166.6 (100)	122.7 (100)	117.3 (100)	33.7 (100)	11.4 (100)	10,156 (100)	426 (100)
1980	32.9 (108)	24.2 (109)	1,044.2 (124)	842.2 (121)	195.0 (117)	139.7 (114)	123.7 (105)	46.3 (137)	12.2 (107)	9,186 (90)	498 (117)
1985	33.6 (110)	24.6 (111)	1,338.0 (159)	1,036.8 (149)	207.7 (125)	144.3 (118)	146.9 (125)	61.1 (181)	15.0 (132)	7,213 (71)	498 (117)
1990	33.0 (108)	22.8 (103)	1,585.2 (189)	1,212.5 (174)	278.2 (167)	198.0 (161)	166.1 (142)	81.5 (242)	18.5 (162)	6,882 (68)	493 (116)
Fed. Republic Germany 1990	34.6 (113)*	24.3 (109)*	1,717.4 (204)	1,344.9 (193)	317.7 (191)	237.5 (194)	.	.	.	8,649 (85)*	.
1995	41.8 (137)	27.3 (123)	1,858.4 (221)	1,409.4 (203)	264.3 (159)	181.0 (148)	229.9 (196)	105.7 (314)	22.4 (196)	9,932 (98)	670 (157)
1997	41.7 (137)	26.9 (121)	1,832.8 (218)	1,394.3 (200)	266.3 (160)	184.8 (151)	237.1 (202)	109.4 (325)	24.2 (212)	10,147 (100)	668 (157)
1998	41.5 (136)	26.7 (120)	.	.	.	.	.	.	.	.	.

[1]The index starts in 1975 as the end of the first phase of expansion.

*1991

Sources: Bundesministerium für Bildung und Wissenschaft: Grundund Strukturdaten, eds. 1998/99, 1987/88, 1981/82, and own calculations.

Table 1.12

The Development of Student Enrollment Ratios and Student-Teacher Ratios

| Year | Enrollment ratios — Post secondary sector | | Student-teacher ratios — Post secondary sector | | | | | | | Schools | | | | |
| | Students as % of age-group 19-26 | Entrants as % of age-group 19-21 | Universities | | Total post secondary sector | | Exams | | | Elementary ages 6-10 | Lower secondary ages 10-14 | Higher secondary | | All general schools |
			Entrants per professor	Students per professor	Entrants per professor	Students per professor	All post-secondary exams per professor	University diplomas per professor	Doctoral exams per professor			ages 10-16	ages 16-19	
1960	4.3	7.9	12.0	47.5	14.4	52.9	8.7	3.9	1.2			·	·	·
1965	6.6	13.3	7.3	35.0	9.1	40.1	7.1	2.9	0.8		33.1	·	·	28.3
1975	14.1	19.5	5.5	31.3	5.5	27.6	3.8	1.5	0.5		27.3	21.7	13.5	23.3
1980	15.9	19.1	5.8	34.8	5.9	31.7	3.8	1.9	0.5		21.6	20.4	12.9	18.5
1985	18.1	19.5	5.9	42.1	6.2	39.8	4.4	2.5	0.6	20.2	17.8 15.0	17.0	11.3	15.7
1990 Fed. Republic	22.0	32.2	8.7	53.2	8.4	48.0	5.0	3.6	0.8	20.5	14.3	15.3	10.6	
1990 Germany	19.6	29.6	9.8	55.3	9.2	49.6	·	·	·	·	·	·	·	·
1995	27.2	30.9	6.6	51.6	6.3	44.5	4.3	3.9	0.8	20.9	14.8	16.8	11.0	16.0
1997	29.0	30.4	6.9	51.8	6.4	44.0	5.7	4.1	0.9	21.6	15.0	17.4	11.7	·

Sources: Bundesministerium für Bildung und Forschung: Grund- und Strukturdaten, eds. 1998/99 and 1987/88; Statistisches Bundesamt: Datenreport 1997: 58 (for pupil-teacher ratio in all general schools in 1995).

Compared to colleges and universities, the schools fared much better. Here, the number of teachers kept growing after 1975 even though the number of pupils decreased so that pupil-teacher ratios continued to improve until 1990. When the number of pupils rapidly grew again during the 1990s, the expansion of staff did not keep pace. While pupil-teacher ratios went up again, the wheel was not turned all the way back to the early 1960s as in the university sector. The 1997 levels roughly corresponded to the situation in the mid-1980s (see table 1.12). The fact that schools fared better than universities in the phase of austerity is probably related to political factors. In the school sector, political responsibility is clearly concentrated on the state governments, and parents can be very angry voters. In the university sector, responsibility is divided between the federal government and the state governments, and the students are recruited from all over the country, so that they may not even have the right to vote at the site of their university. Besides, they know that their student status is only of a transitory nature.

The pre-school sector roughly tripled its share in educational spending since 1970. Germany has a fairly satisfactory, and compared to its neighboring countries in the EU, average supply of kindergarten centers for children aged 3 to 6, but it has remained conspicuous for its very limited supply of day- care for children aged 0 to 3.[35] After the introduction of a legal entitlement to a place in a kindergarten, the supply of day care facilities for the age group 3 to 6 expanded further, and the number of places now roughly corresponds to the number of children (see table 1.9). In the sector of infants and toddlers aged 0 to 3, however, there was no similar legislation, and the supply of facilities remained very limited particularly in the most recent period.

There is only one field in which educational policies proved to be a real success. Whereas class-specific discrepancies in educational participation persisted or became even more marked in recent years (Geissler, 1996; Bundesminister für Bildung und Forschung, 1998), gender-specific inequalities have diminished conspicuously. Representing only one of four students in 1960, women now account for one in two. Among doctoral dissertations, the proportion of women more than doubled to 32 percent. Among leading professions such as medical doctors, district attorneys or lawyers, women increased their representation from a miniscule share in the 1960s to one-fourth or even one-third at the end of the 1990s (see table 1.13). Thus, even in the absence of any affirmative action, gender-based inequalities are gradually vanishing.

The Shifting Axis of Benefit Delivery: Welfare Mix and Privatization

The production of social welfare has never been a state monopoly in Germany. As Wolfgang Zapf (1981) has shown, we must always conceive of social welfare as being produced jointly in various spheres of society, including the state, the market, associations, and private households. Even within

Table 1.13

The Percentage of Women in the Educational Sector and among the Professions

Year	Entrants		Students		Doctoral exams	Medical doctors	District attorneys	Judges
	Colleges and universities	(Universities)	Colleges and universities	(Universities)				
1960	27.0	(34.0)	23.9	(27.9)	14.5	15.2	2.0.	3.0.
1965	29.6	(39.8)	25.0	(30.9)	17.0	17.2	3.1	4.1
1970	28.8	(38.1)	25.6	(30.8)	15.1	19.2	4.3*	6.0*
1975	36.6	(41.0)	33.7	(35.8)	15.8	20.2	9.2	10.7
1980	40.1	(43.4)	36.7	(38.3)	19.6	21.6	10.1*	12.2*
1985	39.7	(43.3)	37.9	(40.3)	24.1	24.7	14.3	14.9
1990 Fed. Republic	39.3	(42.5)	38.3	(41.0)	27.8	.	17.6	17.6
1990 Germany	39.2	(41.9)	38.9	(41.4)	.	.	.	.
1995	47.5	(52.2)	41.6	(44.4)	31.5	35.9	28.9	26.3
1997	48.5	(52.4)	43.5	(46.3)	32.1	-	27.9	25.5
1998	.	.	.	.	.	36.4	.	.

*An upper star refers to one year before the given date, a lower star to the following year.

Sources: Bundesministerium für Bildung und Forschung: Grund- und Strukturdaten 1998/99: 144-145; for doctors, attorneys and judges: Statistisches Bundesamt: Statisti-sches Jahrbuch (absolute numbers in various editions, percentages own calculations).

the public schemes of the German welfare state, *corporate actors* have traditionally played an eminent role, as unions and employers participate in the financing as well as in the administration of social insurance. In addition, *occupational welfare* schemes have from the outset been complementing state provisions, first on a voluntary, later (partly) also on a mandatory basis (as in the wage continuation scheme in case of sickness). Finally, the *churches* have always been playing a very active role in the provision of social services. Their major welfare associations—*Diakonie* on the Protestant, and *Caritas* on the Catholic side—were already founded in the nineteenth century, and have always resisted state encroachments into their competences as suppliers of welfare services.[36] Today they employ more than 800,000 people, with the Catholic *Caritas* being Europe's biggest employer (Bauer, 1997). Hence, the question in recent debates never was whether to move from state to society in the provision of welfare, but how and to what extent the historically inherited composition of the welfare mix should and could be changed.

In this debate, welfare state schemes came under a dual attack. First, there were the traditional market-liberals who argued that an over-extended state action demanded too high a level of taxation, distorted the allocation of resources and impeded the competitiveness of German firms in international markets. In addition to this traditional liberal challenge, there was also growing concern that extended state responsibilities might weaken or even destroy solidarity networks in civil society, as individuals might increasingly turn to the state as the sole source of support. This criticism united parts of the Catholic proponents of subsidiarity with the new left in the student movement, in the Green party, and in the social democratic party. The latter argued that state bureaucracies will always tend to install a clientelistic system of rewards for those with the greatest bargaining power, thus neglecting the truly disadvantaged and impeding the liberation of civil society from the tutelage of the state (for a summary see Bauer, 1997).

The new intellectual mood combined with an expanding structural basis for voluntary action, as the reduction of work hours increased leisure time, and the growth in chronic illnesses fuelled a demand for self-help groups. Hence, voluntary activity became quite popular in recent years. Following German panel data, participation in voluntary action increased from 25 percent in 1985 to 35 percent in 1995 (Wagner et al., 1998; see table 1).[37] The growing basis for civic engagement led to political demands that the government support the proliferation of voluntary work with state subsidies (Kommission für Zukunftsfragen der Freistaaten Bayern und Sachsen, 1997). From the perspective of public policymakers seeking to avoid government overload in an era of diminishing resources, such demands are not unwelcome, since they open up a chance to reduce state responsibilities without losing legitimacy. To what extent, then, did the new spirit translate into visible changes in the welfare mix?

When we discuss changes in the production of social welfare, it is useful to distinguish between at least three dimensions: the *regulation* of welfare production, the *financing* of activities, and the *supply* of benefits and services. With respect to regulation, rather profound changes occurred only in the field of labor legislation and in the sickness insurance scheme. In the former field, the government asked an expert commission to draft plans for labor market deregulation in 1987, and it implemented some of its recommendations subsequently (Keller, 1997). In the sickness insurance scheme, several reform acts strengthened the capacity of corporatist bodies to negotiate agreements that would regulate the hospital sector and the pharmaceutical sector after the model of the ambulatory care sector, where the sickness funds and the physicians' assocations have a long tradition of determining the conditions of service in collective bargaining (Alber, 1992; Döhler and Manow-Borgwardt, 1992; and Manow, 1994). Reforms also strengthened the competition among the insurance funds by allowing free choice of a fund and by introducing a financial balancing mechanism that distributes the risks arising from different socio-demographic membership structures equally among all funds. The idea was that remaining differences in contribution rates should reflect differences in efficiency or service quality. Thus, an element of internal markets was introduced into the German sickness insurance scheme.

There was no new division of labor between various levels of government that could be described as a *decentralization* of regulation. Rather the opposite occurred, when local government associations pressured successfully for the introduction of the long-term care insurance scheme which shifted the burden of financing from state and local government to a new centrally regulated insurance institution.

With respect to financing, the most visible change occurred in the *sickness insurance scheme*, where private co-payments were introduced for several services which used to be provided free of charge. Thus, *prescription fees* were raised in several steps from 1 DM in 1977 to 3 DM in 1988. They were then graded by size in three classes and gradually augmented from 3/5/7 DM in 1992 to 9/11/13 DM in 1997, until the red-green government lowered them again to 8/9/10 DM. *Co-payments for hospitals* were introduced at 5 DM per day (up to two weeks) in 1982, and were raised stepwise to 17 DM by 1997; for the period 1997 to 1998 they were supplemented by a special annual hospital fee of 20 DM, payable by all insured persons, but the new red-green majority scrapped this charge again. *Co-payments for rehabilitation cures in spas* were set at 10 DM in 1982 and were doubled from 12 to 25 DM in 1996. *Co-payments for transportation costs* in case of illness were introduced at 3.50 DM in 1977, and successively raised to 20 DM in 1988. For *glasses,* a co-payment of 4 DM was introduced in 1981. Seven years later the funds' share was capped at 20 DM, and in 1996 it was abolished, so that glasses now have to be purchased privately. The private share in the cost of *dental prosthesis* was raised from 20 percent in 1977, to 40 percent in 1981, and to 100 percent for persons born after 1979 in 1996.[38] Estimates of the magnitude of these privatization measures are difficult to obtain. One attempt to quantify the co-payments in the pharmaceutical sector reckons with a sevenfold increase from 1.1. billion DM in 1987 to 7.3 billion in 1997 (Litsch and Schröder, 1997). Expressed in relation to the pharmaceutical expenditure of the sickness funds, this would correspond to an increase in the private share from 6 to 28 percent.[39]

In the footsteps of the introduction of co-payments in the health sector, there is now also a growing debate about introducing fees in the *educational sector.* The discussion is usually limited to the university level. One state, Baden-Wuerttemberg, recently pioneered with the introduction of a fee for students who study longer than a certain number of years.[40] In the context of the debate on globalization, a heavier reliance on fees and user charges is occasionally advocated also as an adequate response to the growing international tax competition (Scharpf, 1998; Scharpf and Schmidt, 2000).

The supply side of the welfare mix was changed, when the new long-term care insurance scheme not only collectivized the risk of long-term care, but also opened up the provision of care services to *private for-profit providers.* Breaking with the privileges which the social assistance scheme had traditionally granted to the voluntary welfare associations as a virtually exclusive welfare cartel, the new law explicitly put commercial providers on the same legal footing. This led to a rapid growth of private services which now represent about one-half of all services and one-third of all personnel in care services (Alber and Schölkopf, 1999).

Attempts to strengthen private providers are also being made in the *pension sector*, where the red-green government has just passed an act to subsidize private pension insurance contracts. Despite the existence of extended public pensions, private life insurance has always been flourishing in the Federal Republic. The total number of existing contracts exceeds the population size, more than seven million new contracts are added each year, and the total insurance sum corresponds to about 77 percent of GDP (Statistisches Bundesamt, 1999). Occupational pension schemes had been growing up to the 1980s, but are now back to the level of the late 1970s. Two-thirds of those employed in industry, and scarcely 30 percent of those employed in commerce are covered by an occupational scheme (Wirth and Paul, 1998). The average monthly benefit (DM 519 in 1993) corresponds to about a quarter of the standard pension in the public scheme. Given the proliferation of supplementary pensions and the considerable accumulation of private means after fifty years of peace and prosperity, some observers strongly recommend to limit the public scheme to the provision of effective minima (Miegel, 1983, 1995).

In the *educational sector*, private schools have always been around in a minority role. In recent decades, they increased their share in all pupils only moderately from 3 percent in 1970 to 5 percent in 1998 (Bundesministerium für Bildung und Forschung, 2000). Private universities are of more recent origin. The most recent statistical yearbook lists only eight with a miniscule share of all students below 1 percent. However, new initiatives are now popping up in several states and the numbers given in the statistical yearbook may soon be outdated. There now is a favorable climate for private provision, which makes continuous changes in the welfare mix rather likely. The present social democratic chancellor has frequently voiced the idea that the public sector should become a partner of private business, and he advocates a welfare state that is a springboard rather than a hammock.

Social Activation and Work-Oriented Policies

Concepts and Policy Goals

Comparative welfare state typologies usually rank Germany as the classical representative of the continental "Bismarck"-type (Esping-Andersen, 1996; and Manow and Seils, 2000). Under the influence of Catholic social doctrines and of the liberal party, social policies remain supposedly guided by the normative ideas of a male family breadwinner with lifetime employment and of women as housewives and mothers. Welfare state programs remain largely limited to the payment of social transfers, while the provision of services is left to private households. In such patriarchical welfare states, the trade unions have to press for high wages in order to enable their mostly male members to earn sufficient incomes for their families, but the resulting high cost of labor makes it increasingly difficult to find jobs, especially in the sector of unskilled workers with low productivity. In theory, conservative or Christian democratic welfare states typically react to such problems with labor shedding through early retirement. This strategy, however, requires higher taxes or contributions which widen the wedge between gross and net earnings and make labor even more expensive for employers. As a consequence, it leads to increasing unemployment especially among the unskilled. The labor market then becomes segmented into well-protected insiders on the one hand—usually younger, better-educated men—and outsiders who remain locked-out from employment on the other—usually older, less educated and female.

This interpretation has become widely disseminated by scholars, OECD reports, European Commission white papers, as well as various German expert commissions (Zukunftskom-mission der Friedrich-Ebert Stiftung, 1998; and Kommission für Zukunftsfragen der Freistaaten Bayern und Sachsen, 1997). It has also been shared by federal governments of different political leanings. The bourgeois coalition government which had superseded the social-liberal coalition in 1982 adopted the dominant problem diagnosis most vividly and in his policy statements opening the sessions of a new parliament, Chancellor Kohl repeatedly vowed to overcome the old policy legacy. After the red-green coalition government had come to power in 1998, Chancellor Schröder similarly highlighted the importance of lowering the cost of labor by reducing social insurance contributions. He also declared that his government of the "new center" would seek to transform the social security system from a potential inactivity trap to an enabling springboard, where education and training programs would be extended instead of channeling more funds into a mere compensation of unemployment (see Presse- und Informationsamt der Bundesregierung, 1998). Far from being merely lip service, these declarations translated into some marked policy changes.

Policy Changes

The policy change ushered in by the bourgeois government in the 1980s was first and foremost reflected in labor market policy (Keller, 1997). An employment promotion act, which went into effect in 1985, widened the possibility to offer short-term work contracts (up to 18 months). A 1986 act prohibited the payment of unemployment compensation to workers whose redundancy was indirectly caused by strikes in other collective bargaining areas, thus making the union tactic of focusing strikes on a particular region obsolete. A 1994 reform-act replaced the old work time regulations which traced back to 1938, and widened the possibilities to work at night or on holidays. The employment promotion act of the same year extended the 1985 deregulation measures and abolished the monopoly of public labor exchanges by allowing private placement services. In order to cope with the massive unemployment problems in the new eastern territories following the unification, the government also channelled sizeable sums into active labor market policies including retraining measures.[41] A shift towards more activating or enabling policies also occurred in several social policy programs.

From early retirement to activation policies in the pension schemes. There was a clear-cut policy reversal with respect to early retirement. Up until the early 1980s, the federal government had actively promoted early exit from the labor market in ways very much in line with the idea of labor shedding in Christian democratic welfare states. Until a 1957 pension reform, 65 years had been the regular and rigid age limit for retirement. The 1957 reform then introduced discrepant categorical entitlements for women, handicapped persons, and the unemployed. Women could go on old age pension at age 60 (provided they had an insurance record of a certain length). Unemployed persons could also draw an old age pension at age 60 if they had been unemployed for at least one year (the so-called 59er-clause for early exit). Handicapped persons could draw an either partial or a full disability pension independently of a specific age limit, provided that their earnings capacity was reduced by at least 50 percent. In the context of prosperity and pension fund surplus, the 1972 pension reform then introduced two new routes out of the labor market. The so-called flexible age limit allowed persons with a long employment and insurance record (35 years) to draw a full old age pension at age 63. In addition, severely handicapped workers were given the right to retire at age 62.

When unemployment struck in the mid-1970s, these categorical entitlements for specific groups began to be used actively as instruments of labor market policy. The way for massive early exit from work was paved in 1976, when the Federal Social Court ruled that the assessment of the degree of disability had to be based on concrete rather than abstract criteria. This meant that the entitlement to a disability pension depended no longer exclusively on medical criteria but also on the situation in the labor market. If the labor market did not provide a sufficient number of part-time jobs for handicapped persons, the pension insurance scheme now became obliged to pay a full disability pension even if the recipient was capable of part-time work.[42] A 1979 act then lowered the pensionable age for severely handicapped persons to 61 years, and to 60 years as from 1980. Within the unemployment insurance scheme, benefit duration was extended for older workers, with an extension of up to three years for those above age 57. This implied that people could now leave the labor market at age 57, draw an unemployment benefit for three years, and then convert it into a predated old age pension at age 60. Since older workers are hard to dismiss because they enjoy special employment protection, many employers used the new clause to reduce their work force or to exchange older workers for younger ones.[43]

When the massive cost of extended early retirement became gradually evident,[44] the Christian-liberal government initiated a major policy change. First the qualifying conditions for early pensions in case of unemployment were tightened, then access to disability pensions was narrowed. Eligibility for disability pensions was now made contingent upon a contribution record of at least three years within the five years preceding the claim.[45] As a consequence, the proportion of disability pensions among new pension claims decreased sharply. The general idea of the subsequent pension reform acts was to reinstate the pre-1957 threshold of 65 years as the regular age limit, and to introduce new forms of flexible retirement as an alternative. The raising of age limits took place in three steps. First, a 1989 pension reform act implemented in 1992 made 65 years the general age limit for all old age pensions and foresaw to gradually raise the lower age limits for particular categories from 2001. It also gave a general and unconditional possibility to retire at age 62, but this would now be coupled with actuarial reductions of 0.3 percent per pre-dated month. Secondly, acts passed in 1996 accelerated the raising of the age limits for specific categories so that the new general age-limit target of 65 years would already be implemented earlier. If future claimants wanted to draw a pension at the earlier categorically defined age limit, they could do so only at the price of an actuarial curtailment of 0.3 percent per month.[46]

Thirdly, the 1997 pension reform brought a major overhaul. By 2012 categorically defined age-limits for women or for unemployed people would completely cease to exist, and the age-limit for severely handicapped persons was to be raised in monthly steps from 60 to 63 years as from 2000. On the other hand, the age-limit for persons with long insurance records was lowered from 63 to 62 years. Age 62 was now to become the earliest possible age for a pension claim, and the actuarially reduced early pension would be 10.8 percent lower than the pension entitlement at age 65.[47] The new act also abolished the traditional separation into two forms of disability pensions (*Berufs-und Erwerbsunfähigkeits-rente*). The unified new disability pension varies only by the degree of incapacity. Persons capable of working more than six hours a day are no longer entitled to a pension. The assessment is to be made strictly on medical grounds again, and the availability of part-time jobs in the labor market will no longer be taken into account. In case a disability pension is claimed below age 63, it will now be reduced by 0.3 percent per month up to a maximum curtailment of 10.8 percent.

In addition to changing the traditional pension provisions, the government sought to create novel forms of a more flexible and gradual retirement. Thus, a 1984 Preretirement Act provided a legal framework for collective agreements between unions and employers. The idea of this temporary measure was to have workers go into retirement at age 58 and to bridge the remaining gap until the lowest possible pensionable age (e.g., 60 for women, and 63 for men with long insurance records).[48] When the Preretirement Act expired in 1988, it was superseded by various Old Age Part-Time Acts. The basic concept of these laws was to provide a frame for collective agreements. At age 58—later lowered to age 55—workers could reduce their weekly work time by one-half while receiving 70 percent of their net earnings. The employer would pay the 20 percent increment above half-time pay as well as pension insurance contributions based on 90 percent of the previous full-time earnings. If the newly created half-time position was filled by a formerly unemployed person, the federal Employment Office would reimburse the 20 percent increment as well as the higher pension insurance contributions to the employer. As unions and employers' organizations were hesitant to draft respective collective agreements, take-up of the 1989 scheme remained very low under the first act, and grew only slowly under the new provisions.

In order to provide for a more flexible transition from work to retirement the 1992 pension reform act (passed in 1989) also introduced the novel possibility of combining income from work (up to a ceiling) with a partial pension amounting to either one-third, one-half, or two-thirds of a full pension. This partial pension (*Teilrente*) can be drawn by anybody entitled to an old age pension, and if it is continued beyond age 65—thus postponing the payment of the full pension—the full pension will be increased by increments of 0.5 percent per month (or 6 percent per year).

Put in a nutshell, the recent reforms of early retirement and of the pension system pursued a triple goal. First, in order to safeguard the fiscal solvency of the pension scheme, the categorically defined age-limits for early retirement were to be raised so that age 65 would once again become the regular age of retirement. Secondly, rather than being categorically defined and being limited to specific groups, the possibility of early retirement should now be open to all, but it should only be available at the price of actuarial reductions that would ensure a stricter correspondence between benefits and contributions. Thirdly, the transition from work to retirement should be made more flexible by combining income from transfers with income from work.

Activating the unemployed. A new emphasis on workfare was also visible in the recent reforms of the unemployment compensation scheme. While active labor market policies were extended with an increase of people in retraining programs, the passive compensation payments were made less generous and became tied to much stricter controls. In addition to the curtailment of benefit levels (described under "Allocation Principles: Changing Priorities") various acts also changed the calculation of the earnings base to which the earnings replacement ratios apply. Hence, the full cutback of benefit levels is more severe than the 12 percent reduction in earnings replacement ratios for childless persons from 68 percent to 60 percent would suggest. The duration of unemployment assistance benefits drawn without any previous insurance benefits was limited to one year in 1994, and in 1996 the assistance benefits following insurance benefits were reduced by a redefinition of their calculation method. However, there were not only curtailments. The maximum duration of benefits became graded by age so that older people (beyond age 42) became entitled to longer spells. In 1986 the duration was extended to a maximum of two years for the oldest category of workers, and in 1987 it was extended to 32 months.[49] These changes help to explain why the proportion of unemployed people who receive benefits returned to some 75 percent in the mid-1990s, after it had been declining steeply during the 1980s.[50]

The *qualifying conditions* and the controls of benefit abuse were successively made more stringent. The criteria for suitable employment, which a beneficiary must accept, were made more restrictive in 1977, when the normal duration of assistance benefits was limited to one year, with subsequent re-examination. The controls were further tightened in 1981, when the definition of suitable employment was restricted again, and the disqualification period of voluntary unemployment or the refusal of suitable jobs was doubled (from 4 to 8 weeks). In 1985 the disqualification period was further extended to 12 weeks. Workers who are indirectly affected by strikes were barred from the receipt of benefits in 1986. A 1997 reform abolished the clause that a job offer must correspond to the recipient's level of training, and it extended the maximum commuting time which the recipient must accept as part of a suitable job offer to three hours per day.[51]

Two major reform acts of 1997 and 1998 combined retrenchment measures with new instruments for employment promotion. Wage subsidies for employers who hire long-term unemployed people were introduced in 1997 and extended in 1998. Take-up remained low, however, as only 2,782 "integration contracts" were concluded in 1998, even though the new contracts were not only subsidized, but also exempted from certain labor regulations (Sachverständigenrat zur Begutachtung der gesamtwirtschaftlichen Lage, 1999, 2000). In an attempt to avoid inactivity traps related to the receipt of means-tested unemployment assistance, the income limits for non-considered spouses' earnings had already been doubled in 1986 (to 150 DM per week). Following the Constitutional Court ruling that exempted income up to the subsistence level from taxation, a 1996-reform declared a further 25 percent of earned income compatible with eligibility for unemployment asssistance (which can now be combined with a spouse's income that amounts to some 29 percent of average gross earnings). Since 1999, the recipients are also entitled to add their own earnings of up to 315 DM—or some 7 percent of average gross earnings—to their benefits without any curtailment.

Welfare and workfare in the social assistance scheme. The social assistance scheme was originally designed to provide benefits for people in extraordinary circumstances who either were not fit to work or had exhausted their claims to unemployment benefits. From its beginnings in 1961, the scheme did have a so-called "assistance to work" component, but the purpose of this activating measure was mostly to give some opportunity to people with severe physical or psychological problems. When unemployment surged in the early 1980s, the social assistance clientele became much more heterogeneous, now including a growing number of jobless people who were fit for the labor market. In this situation, several municipalities began to implement the control elements of the "assistance to work" component which allowed to make the payment of public support contingent upon participation in training programs or active work (Lamping and Schridde, 1999).

Building on the early initiatives on the communal level, the 1990s also saw some new activities on the federal level. After considerable public debate about the principle of less eligibility and the supposedly "lavish" level of social assistance benefits which the employers' associations saw as a disincentive to work in the low-wage sector, a 1993 reform act provided that the sum of benefits for households with four or more persons must remain below the net wages of low wage earners (including child and housing allowances). In addition to more stringent controls of benefit abuse, the act also contained two innovative elements: Employers hiring welfare recipients could now receive training subsidies, and in order to increase the incentive for program clients to take up employment, an "appropriate" amount of earnings from work could be exempted in calculating the entitlement. In actual practice, this meant that up to 50 percent of the standard social assistance rate for a single adult could now be earned from work without curbing the assistance entitlement.

A further act passed in 1994 obliged all social assistance recipients who were fit for work to accept any kind of broadly defined suitable employment in the labor market. It also limited the principle of less eligibility to households with up to five persons thus exempting very large households from the restriction.[52] A 1996 social assistance reform act combined new sticks with new carrots. On the one hand it made the *principle of less eligibility* harsher by including one-time payments in the calculation of the benefit ceiling, and it also made it obligatory for municipal authorities to curtail the benefit in case of the refusal of suitable employment by at least 25 percent.[53] On the other hand, it introduced wage subsidies to employers hiring welfare recipients and it provided the possibility of augmenting the recipients' earnings from work for a period of up to six months.[54]

As a consequence of these new activating policies, the number of people on welfare who participate in assistance to work programs increased from some 20,000 in the early 1980s to an estimated 300,000 in 1998. The latter figure means that by now one out of ten recipients of regular social assistance outside of institutions participates in an activating measure (see table 1.14). The Council of Economic Advisors estimates 1 million welfare recipients to be actually fit for work, this would mean that about *one-third* of all able-bodied welfare recipients is now combining welfare with some kind of workfare.

Minor employment and the development of a low wage sector. As regularly paid jobs became scarce, an increasing number of people moved into so-called minor employment positions in the low-wage sector (*geringfügige Beschäftigung*). Minor employment—basically defined by income below the limit of 630 DM per month (some 12 percent of average gross monthly wages)—used to be exempted from social insurance contributions and from income taxes. Only the employer had to pay a tax of 23 percent. Estimates of the number of minor jobs in this sense varied around 5.5 million or 14 percent of the labor force.[55] A 1999 reform act passed under the new red-green coalition government made employers liable to report all people in minor jobs and to pay a 12 percent contribution to the pension insurance scheme, plus a 10 percent contribution to the sickness insurance scheme instead of the old proportional income tax. The major motive behind the reform was to alleviate the fiscal situation of the social insurance schemes, but the employers' contribution also leads to (reduced) individual pension entitlements for the employee (who can top the employer's contribution with a voluntary contribution in order to reach the full contribution rate giving rise to a regular entitlement).

Table 1.14
Welfare Recipients Participating in "Assistance to Work" in the Social
Assistance Scheme

Year	No. of people receiving assistance to work	As % of people receiving regular assistance outside of institutions (*Hilfe zum Lebensunterhalt ausserhalb von Einrichtungen*)
1982	20.000	2% (1,025)
1983	24.000	2% (1,141)
1993	110.000	5% (2.450)
1996	200.000	7% (1,689)
1998	300.000	10% (2.893/31.12.1997)

Sources: Estimates for 1980s: Hoppensack/Wenzel (1985: 156); for 1993/1996: Lamping/Schridde (1999: 95); for 1998: Deutscher Städtetag (1999; http://www.staedtetag.de/schlagz/s_19991021_ l.htm); percentages: own calculations, based on recipients data in Bundesministerium für Arbeit und Sozialordnung: Statistisches Taschenbuch (1997: 8.16, 1998: 8.16).

The Redefinition of What Constitutes Work

In addition to attempts to combat unemployment, recent years also saw a growing debate on the proper definition of work and on the relationship between formal and informal forms of activity. First steps towards an institutional redefinition of what constitutes work were taken in the pension scheme. In 1977, the pension entitlements accumulated during a marriage became split equally between husband and wife, so that after a divorce both spouses would have an equal claim on the jointly acquired pension rights. This was the first formal recognition of the work rendered in the family sphere. A second step was taken under the bourgeois government in 1986 when mothers were credited with one year of pension contributions for each child they had raised.[56] As the 1983 budget law had previously reduced the waiting period for old age pensions from 15 to 5 years, women could now build up pension entitlements even if they had been in formal employment for only brief periods. The 1989 pension insurance reform then raised the credit to three years for each child born in 1992 or later. The 1997 pension reform act strengthened *women's entitlements* further by raising the computation base for the contribution credits from 75 percent to 100 percent of average earnings and by allowing mothers to *add* the child-raising credit to entitlements based on *simultaneous* earnings from work. Raising one child is now formally recognized as equivalent to three years of employment with average earnings. In an indirect way, other family care work besides child-raising also became recognized as an equivalent of paid work when the 1989 reform act introduced so-called consideration periods (*Berücksichtigungszeiten*). These do not count as contribution equivalents but they are considered in calculating the waiting period for specific types of pensions.[57]

The fact that women's work in the family sphere is now recognized as an equivalent of wage labor that gives rise to (state-financed) pension entitlements must be considered a remarkable innovation. It signifies a clear departure from both the traditional *insurance* principle with its emphasis on an equivalence between entitlements and contributions based on earnings from employment, and from the traditional *patriarchical* model in conservative welfare states where entitlements were strictly based on formal work rendered by a male breadwinner.

To summarize, there have been some significant changes regarding the connection between welfare and workfare. Welfare state institutions have been used to change the social construction of what constitutes respectable work in society. Early withdrawal from the labor market in order to go on pension became heavily constrained, and the trend towards increasingly early retirement was stopped. Many welfare state benefits were made contingent upon credible efforts to find employment. Active labor market policies became more prominent, while passive compensation of unemployment became less generous and tied to stricter controls. Cheap jobs in the labor market that were previously exempted from social obligations were now at least partly incorporated into compulsory coverage of the social security scheme. As the last resort safety-net of the public welfare program, participation in work programs is no longer a rare exception, but has become a widespread practice.

Emerging Borders of the Welfare State?

Theoretical and Philosophical Debates on Normative Issues

The recent years saw a revival of fundamental debates about issues of social justice. A first questioning of the "social democratic consensus" sustaining the welfare state had already set in during the 1970s, when scholars and politicians of different political leanings had similarly attacked the welfare state as a new system of privilege which benefited mostly the well-organized sectors of society (Offe, 1972; Schelsky 1976; Geissler, 1976; and Lepsius, 1979). Claiming that the welfare state neglected the problems of groups with little political influence, attention was drawn to the so-called "new social question" which consisted of deprivation related to particular life-situations such as mental illness or dependence upon long-term care rather than to specific positions in the social structure. This debate waned somewhat in the 1980s, but in the 1990s philosophical debates about the normative principles underlying welfare-state action revived. A growing number of books and articles were now published on the subject, and in 1998, the social democrats used the slogan "innovation and justice" as the motto for their electoral campaign (Leisering, 1999; Nullmeier, 2000; Müller and Wegener, 1995; Döring et. al, 1995).

The recent revival of fundamental debates was ushered in by libertarian attacks which highlighted supposedly widespread benefit abuse and welfare scrounging, as well as perverse incentives in welfare programs and the declining competitiveness of German industry (Bruns, 1993; and Engels, 1986). The charges concerning abuse led to discourse on the proper balance between the rights and obligations of citizenship (Dahrendorf, 1985). Defenders of the welfare state usually counter the critics' arguments with reference to empirical analyses showing benefit abuse to be only of minor quantitative importance,[58] and claiming that tax evasion on the part of the rich is the much more relevant neglect of the obligations of citizenship. They also highlight that changes of the tax system were accompanied by growing shares of indirect taxes, and by a shrinking tax yield from the income tax levied on higher earning strata and from corporate taxes.[59]

In addition to the somewhat conventional clash of arguments between critics and defenders of the welfare state, there were some new social changes which fueled a novel debate on social justice. First, the massive transfers from West to East Germany after the German unification were partly financed from a special 7.5 percent "solidarity-surtax" on the wage and income tax. This surtax was introduced in 1991 and lowered to 5.5 percent in 1998. Even though introduced in the context of increasing concern about a growing tax wedge, the new tax did not give rise to much contention in the public. This suggests that redistribution in favor of national integration enjoys a higher legitimacy than redistribution designed to smooth out inequalities between social classes. However, in contrast to the situation after the second world war, when the government had levied a burdensome 50 percent tax on all property existing in 1948 in order to indemnify civilian war victims, this time the politicians shied away from a special tax on property owners.[60] Hence, a debate began on the concept of national solidarity and on the question of who should properly be held responsible for financing the unification. In addition, politicians in East Germany, such as prime minister Stolpe of Brandenburg, recurrently demanded that wages in the East should be raised to the same level as in the West, thus neglecting regional differences in productivity. This encouraged debates on whether *equality* and *need* rather than *equity* should be considered the proper criterion of social justice.

Secondly, as economic growth rates declined and real net earnings remained stagnant for protracted years, the relative position of groups in the income distribution began to attract increased attention. When income in-equalities widened during the 1990s, the old debate between those advocat-ing the stimulation of production and those calling for more redistribution was revived. The one side insists that economic growth will lift all boats with the rising tide and eventually "trickle down" to all income strata, the other holds that a mere promotion of growth would predominantly benefit the privileged few and contribute to polarizing tendencies which then require redistributive efforts by the state. There was also growing concern about the rise of an "underclass," and those fearing the social exclusion of sizeable minorities advocated to concentrate welfare state efforts on the provision of effective minima. Their argument is that earnings-related schemes provide effective social security only for the core sectors of society, and that they cement inequality because they focus on the preservation of status differen-tials. Thus, there is a renewed debate on criteria of justice: Should welfare state schemes primarily enhance the *equality* of citizenship by providing universal minima, or should they stress *equity* by providing earnings-related benefits (Dahrendorf, 1988; and Giddens, 1998)?

Thirdly, the changing structure of poverty gave rise to new concerns about social justice. As shown earlier, there was an *"infantilization"* of poverty in the sense that the risk of becoming poor shifted from elderly persons to chil-dren. In the 1990s, especially younger people and families with many chil-dren had high poverty risks (Hauser, 1995, 1999; and Palentien et al., 1999). This mobilized not only the Constitutional Court, but also the unions and churches. Prior to the most recent two federal elections, the Catholic and the Protestant churches had published a joint declaration in which they urged politicians to focus not only on issues of economic competitiveness, but also on the quality of life of children and other disadvantaged groups (Kirchenamt der Evangelischen Kirche in Deutschland/Sekretariat der Deutschen Bischofskonferenz, 1994; and Heimbach-Steims and Lienkamp, 1997). To-gether with concerned scholars, the activists formed a national poverty con-ference with the task to alarm the public. Based on such initiatives, the red-green coalition government has vowed to issue an official national report on poverty and deprivation (see also Hanesch et. al, 2000).

The shift of the poverty risk from the elderly to the young contributed to focusing the debate on social justice on two issues which, despite being intertwined, had previously not really been discussed in connection: the inequality between families with children and childless households, and the question of intergenerational justice. The former issue is not only a question of income poverty and taxation. It also concerns the degree of tolerance for children in modern neighborhoods, where two-thirds of all households are childless. With respect to income, Franz Xaver Kaufmann (1997) has argued that Germany has almost completely collectivized the task of maintaining the elderly, but predominantly privatized the task of bringing up children.

Since declining birth rates threaten the fiscal solvency of the pension scheme, and since childless persons do not contribute to a future stabilization of the ratio between beneficiaries and contributors, he advocates to move from the concept of a two-generation solidarity to a three-generation contract by grading pension insurance contributions according to the number of children. Another issue with respect to intergenerational equity is to what extent the curtailment of pensions can be seen as a just punishment for generations who failed to produce a sufficient number of children, and to what extent the increasing longevity of pensioners should be considered in the calculation of claims. By now there is widespread consensus that the equivalence principle tying benefits to contributions should be related to the accumulated total pension claim rather than to a particular monthly payment, so that a growing duration of the payment should translate into a lower benefit level (Breyer, 1997).

The debate about childhood poverty and pensions also fuelled concerns about gender-specific issues of social justice. As single parent households face vastly overproportionate poverty risks, and as these are predominantly headed by women, the issue is to what extent lone mothers deserve special state support. This also combines with the debate on women's position in the pension insurance scheme, where the question is how to ensure individual entitlements independently from husbands, without having periods of child rearing lower the pension entitlement to unacceptably low levels. Here, the women's quest for a solution that provides effective individual minima within the existing pension scheme has recently gained some momentum (Rolf and Wagner, 1996). On the other hand, minimum pensions which do not link benefits to contributions have also become subject to growing criticism, because they provide few work incentives and are seen to attract migration, especially from other EU countries, to which cash benefits must be exported under EU law.

Finally, there is the question of taxation and participation. Following the principle of the American Revolution—"no taxation without representation"—the steep increase in social insurance contribution rates should have been accompanied by growing participation rights of the insured population. This, however, has not been the case, as the insurance boards continue to be elected on the basis of "peaceful elections" (*Friedenswahlen*) which ensure that representatives chosen by the unions and the employers' associations run the boards. As legal regulations passed by Parliament leave very little leeway for autonomous action of the funds, turnout at these elections is usually below 40 percent. Hence, discussions occasionally come up as how to revitalize the tradition of self-administration in ways that might also strengthen social control functions. A novel idea concerning taxation and participation is to supplement the taxes on income by a *tax on time* that would recruit citizens including women who are still exempted from universal conscription for a period of social service (Dahrendorf, 1988). It is very likely, however, that the predominant discussions of social justice will soon move beyond the national arena, and turn to the topic of redistribution on a global scale.

The Scope and Legitimacy of National and Transnational Government

Income inequalities within Western countries are certainly not negligible, and they may also be growing. However, they are nothing compared to the stunning inequalities on a worldwide scale. Even if expressed in purchasing power parities rather than U.S. dollars, the differences in gross national income per capita range from below 700 PPP in some African and Asian countries to above 20,000 PPP in several OECD countries (Baratta, 2000). As television and other media make these differences painfully visible every day, and as many of the poorer countries are marked by civil strife, the already massive migration from poorer to richer countries is bound to increase. The rising tide of immigration leaves the rich-world countries only with the choice of erecting new iron curtains to stem the tide, or to bring some of their wealth and opportunities to the poor countries. To cope with this challenge will not be easy, and it will certainly be expensive, but the debate on how to achieve the task should become more intense.

Considering the growing international burden, there may be pressure to cut back domestic welfare programs even more. However, one should not overestimate the potential for further retrenchment. The open world economy and the new international division of labor also leave losers in Western countries, especially among unskilled workers. If these neither find a place in the labor market nor social security in public welfare programs, they may well turn against the modern order and support populist movements propagating economic nationalism. If Ralf Dahrendorf's pessimistic vision that the twenty-first century may become the century of authoritarianism is to be avoided, further efforts at a social integration of the disadvantaged are probably imperative (Dahrendorf, 1998; see also Rieger and Leibfried, 1997).

Within Europe, supranational developments on the EU level play an increasingly important role, as the European Commission seems to be determined to extend its regulative competence also to more welfare issues and to play a more active role in the development of social policies. There are many advocates of a further shift of responsibilities to the European level, because it is felt that the loss of control which national governments have suffered over economic affairs can only be redressed to a certain extent if regulatory competences are shifted to the supranational level (Streeck, 1995). Presently, one of the major impediments to a more active role of the EU is the requirement to decide social policy matters unanimously. Hence, many pundits recommend to shift to the simple majority principle. However, it must not be forgotten that redistribution requires legitimation (Majone, 1996). Presently, supranational European decisions are legitimized only indirectly by coupling the national governments who make the decisions in the Council to their voters in national elections. Decisions made by simple majority imply, however, that regulations become law also in countries whose governments objected to their introduction, but were overruled in the Council. Who does then legitimize the introduction of the norm in this country? As long as the legitimation of decision-making on the European level remains indirect and incomplete, extended responsibilities of the EU in social policies may entail a shrinking legitimacy of redistributive policies. Legitimation of such policies is easier in contexts where the voters have a sense of national identity and are ethnically and culturally homogeneous. Guaranteeing equal social rights of citizenship across ethnic or cultural divisions is politically much harder to achieve. Hence, redistributive policies would probably encounter stronger impediments on the supranational European level even if the decision-making process were made more immediately responsive to voters and to the European parliament.

Conclusion: Towards a New Combination of Freedom and Security in an Enabling State?

The past two decades have seen a reconsideration of the costs and benefits associated with welfare state growth. Curtailments, which first were made merely reluctantly as gradual adjustments to changing economic conditions, later became seen as necessary adaptations of historically inherited and partly outdated institutions to a new social environment. In the ongoing process of transformation, the old structures were modified, but not demolished. In some areas, such as the social transfer schemes, benefit levels of the German welfare state were driven back to roughly the levels of the late 1960s. This certainly meant retrenchment, but it also implied that we are still at levels of social security which had not been reached prior to the "golden age" of welfare state growth. In some fields, such as social services, the scope of public action was even extended, as new previously uncovered risks became part of state responsibilities. In this sense, there was some restructuring, but the basic institutional shape of the welfare state was preserved.

Gradual change and institutional continuity went together with an almost entirely new culture of interpretation, however. Historically, the transition from poor house to welfare state in the nineteenth century had been associated with a re-interpretation of the relationship between the individual and the state. Whereas the old poor laws had emphasized an *individual responsibility* for poverty and aimed at stabilizing the *collective order*, the new social insurance institutions highlighted *individual welfare* as the goal of public action and *collective processes* as the causes of destitution. Following

Rimlinger's notion of a "liberal break" in early nineteenth-century Britain (1971), it now looks as if we have arrived at *a new liberal break* in the history of the welfare state. Now, individual responsibilities are highlighted again, the competitiveness of nation states as collectivities has become the focus of concern, and there are new attempts to introduce categorical entitlements that distinguish more closely between deserving and less deserving social categories. The task ahead may be to link the American culture of individual responsibility with the European structure of welfare state safety nets. If deregulation makes dynamic change possible; social security must make it acceptable. The concept of an enabling state that helps citizens to help themselves may become the basis of a synthesis of American freedom and European security.

Notes

1 .   This chapter was written at the Hanse Institue for Advanced Study in Delmenhorst for whose generous support I am most grateful. I also wish to thank my collaborators at the University of Konstanz, Christina Behrendt, Kristina Haaf, Angela Lippus, and Dirk Radlinger, for technical assistance.
2 .   Civil servants are covered by contribution-free special schemes. The self-employed usually take private insurance.
3 .   In the case of the unemployment insurance scheme, the administrative boards are tripartite, including state representation.
4.   As the official reckoning now includes the child allowances which we here grouped as a direct payment, tax expenditure in the new definition even represents about 10 percent.
5.   Just adding up the expenditure reported in the social budget, the health budget, the housing budget, and the education budget would lead to considerable double counts.
6.   Following comparative figures published by the OECD, German educational spending roughly corresponds to the OECD mean (OECD, 1996).
7.   Subsidies and credits are usually paid jointly by the federal government and by the governments of the single states.
8 .   On average, the housing allowance reduced the rent burden of low-income households by about one-third in the 1990s, but it is estimated that only about one-half of all entitled households actually make a claim (Ulbrich, 1993).
9 .   The figures refer to the total rate which employees and employers have to pay up to an income ceiling.
10 .   Even though the empirical evidence is far from consistent, there are many examples of such predatory politics in which the federal government acts more or less like a robber. The financing share borne by employees and employers grew from 55 percent in 1960 to 64 percent in 1998. However, the most recent years also saw some reversals of the long-term German practice described by Nullmeier. Thus, in an example of policy learning and under pressure from the employers' associations, both the old bourgeois government under chancellor Kohl, and the new red-green coalition government lowered the contribution rate by increasing the federal share in the pension insurance scheme.
11.   There had to be stable exchange rates of the national currency for two years, public debt should be below 60 percent of GDP, the annual deficit of the state below 3

percent of GDP, the inflation rate (then) below 2.2 percent, and the long-term interest rate (then) below 6.6 percent.

12. The new benefit, drawn by about half a million people, is about 80 percent of the regular assistance level.

13. All figures refer to West Germany and to the 50 percent threshold (Statistisches Bundesamt, 1997).

14. It must be borne in mind that only about one third (37 percent) of all outlays of the social assistance scheme is spent on basic income support for people living outside of institutions. The dominant part consists of payments for special contingencies and for people living in institutions.

15. Only 10 percent are on welfare for more than five years (Statistisches Bundesamt, 1999: 464; see also Leisering/Leibfried, 1999).

16. The bottom 40 percent of the population have 22 percent of all income in Germany, but only 14 percent in the U.S., and the richest 20 percent have one-half of all income in the U.S., but only about one-third in Germany (see Sachverständigenrat zur Begutachtung der gesamtwirtschaftlichen Entwicklung (1999, 2000); Shapiro and Greenstein (1999); also Hauser (1999) for similar, yet slightly disvergent German data from 1991 to 1995.

17. About 9 percent of all school leavers, and one-quarter of all non-German pupils even drop out of school without any formal degree (Allmendinger, 1999). Their employment problems are also related to a new international division of labor, with a cheap but literate labor force in the southern hemisphere allowing industrial mass production with unskilled labor to be advantageously located in third world countries, while European countries increasingly specialize in high-quality products requiring highly specialized labor (Martin, 1997; Wood, 1994).

18. For empirical data, see Andreß/Strengmann-Kuhn, 1997; Gangl, 1998; Leisering/ Leibfried, 1999. Social assistance benefits can only surpass wages in the low wage sector in the case of large families with many children, because the assistance rates for children are higher than the general child allowance. Dynamic poverty research carried out by Leisering and Leibfried (1999) in Bremen has shown that unemployment is not a predominant cause for claiming social assistance (p. 71), most spells of social assistance claims are only of short duration below one year (p. 66), only 29 percent of the claims because of unemployment last longer than three years (p. 78), and families with three or more children receiving benefits close to the level of low wages do not achieve fewer exits from welfare rolls than other claimants (p. 152). Following the results of Gangl (1998) and Andreß/Strengmann-Kuhn (1997) more than 70 percent of the assistance recipients are in active search of jobs.

19. Thus, the leader of the Green Party, Fritz Kuhn, declared an overhaul of the social assistance scheme to be necessary, because it produces poverty traps (Süddeutsche Zeitung, 159, 13 July 2000).

20. It should be noted that funded systems are not immune to demographic changes, because a shrinking population means that the accumulated assets of the pensioner generation must be capitalized by selling them to shrinking numbers of potential buyers. Even if this problem might be circumvented in an open world economy, stock returns embody substantial phase-specific variation, and funded systems with decentralized individual accounts are notorious for their high administrative costs. (Orszag and Stiglitz, 1999; Schmähl, 1999; Breyer, 2000).

21. Following a 1997 government report, each of the two coalition governments contributed about one-half of the total cutbacks (Handelsblatt, 11.12.1997: 4).

22. The standard or model pension gives the amount a person receives after having worked with average earnings for forty-five years.

23. Without the curtailments, the net earnings replacement ratio would have surpassed 90 percent in 1997 (Bundesministerium für Arbeit und Sozialordnung, 1998d: 310).

24. Even though the principles of the need standard calculation are defined by national law, the actual payment standard is determined by state authorities, but there is little regional variation. Including special payments and housing costs, the standard rate corresponds to the minimum income which the Constitutional Court had ruled to be tax-exempt in 1992. In 1997 the monthly tax exempt minimum subsistence amounted to 1,008 DM per month for singles, and 2,016 DM for married couples (Bundesministerium für Arbeit und Sozialordnung, 1998b). This compares to average net earnings of the dependent labor force of 2,796 DM. As the rates for children are between 50 percent (below age 7) and 90 percent (ages 15-18) of the full rate for an adult, the total social assistance benefits for a family of four roughly corresponded to the average net wage. Assistance child benefits are higher than the general child allowance.

25. The various curtailments led to phase-specific variations in the purchasing power of benefits, but not to a long-term decline. In the late 1990s the purchasing power of the standard assistance benefit was higher than in the mid-1970s, and over the long run the standard benefit developed at a similar rate as the net wages of the dependent labor force.

26. It is true that the social assistance scheme doubled its share in total social expenditure from about 2 percent in the early 1970s to around 4 percent in the late 1990s, but this reflects merely the fact that the social assistance benefit remained fairly constant in real terms, so that the economic downturn—with more widespread unemployment of longer duration—made more people fall below the standard.

27. This is Peter Baldwin's (1990) term for the concept of "transfer classes" (Versorgungsklassen) which was developed by the German sociologist Rainer Lepsius (1979).

28. 350 DM were paid for fourth and further children. In 2000 the payment for first and second children was further raised to 270 DM.

29. The benefit for the second child remained practically identical in constant figures.

30. Public benefits, financed jointly from general revenues of the federal government and the respective state government, were originally paid for up to 36, now 72 months, for children twelve years of age whose father failed to support them. Private claims against the parent not meeting his liability were taken over by the state.

31. Of course, the figures also show how sensitive the calculation of means and other statistics is to the number of countries for which data are available.

32. The data refer to West Germany. In the new eastern territories the number of newborn babies shrank after unification from almost 200,000 in 1989 to roughly 79,000 in 1994.

33. This dynamic increase preceded unification and was spread fairly evenly over the years 1985 to 1990.

34. This change coincided with the shift from the social-liberal to the Christian-liberal coalition. It must be noted, however, that educational policies are largely in the competence of the single states so that the federal government has only limited power in this field.

35. This is probably related to the influence of the Catholic church which is strongly interconnected with the Christian parties and controls part of the voluntary welfare associations that supply social services.

36. The principle of subsidiarity, enshrined in the papal encyclical Quadragesimo Anno of 1931, was legally sanctioned in a 1961 Constitutional Court ruling which deter-

mined that the state can only provide various services financed by social assistance if private and voluntary action fail to provide a sufficient supply.

37. As most of the increase was among those who volunteer only occasionally, however, the percentage of those contributing on a regular basis remained practically constant.

38. Low income groups are usually exempted from co-payments (except those for hospitals). A clause in the 1988 reform-law stated that private co-payments are not to exceed 2 percent of annual household earnings for people below the contribution ceiling, and 4 percent for those above the ceiling.

39. It must be remembered that on the other hand some previously privatized risks became collectivized as the scope of sickness insurance scheme was extended to care services.

40. In the German university tradition, it is seen as part of academic freedom that students can extend their studies in public sector universities for as long as they want.

41. Whereas expenditure for active labor market policies represented only 0.8 percent of GDP in 1982, it rose to 1.7 percent by 1992, and was still at a level of 1.3 percent in 1995 (Schmid, 1997; Schmid and Reissert, 1988).

42. As a consequence, the proportion of male entrants to the pension scheme drawing the regular old age pension (age 65) dropped from 49 percent in 1970 to 15 percent in 1980, while the percentage of (various) disability pensions increased to 65 percent (see Alber and Schölkopf, 1999).

43. If the older employee agreed to give up the job, the employer would pay a sizeable lump sum and/or bridge the gap between the former net salary and the unemployment benefit until the premature pension payment for older unemployed people would set in at age 60.

44. A government report estimated the total cost of lowering the pension entrance age by one year as 27 bio. DM; this compares to total pension expenditure in the workers' and employees' scheme of 239 bio. DM in 1996 (Bundesministerium für Arbeit und Sozialordnung, 1998d).

45. This barred especially housewives without recent work experience from access. As a compensation, the waiting period for a regular old age pension was lowered from 15 to 5 contribution years, a reform which mostly benefited women. In addition, a 1986 act credited child rearing with one year of pension insurance contributions.

46. Thus, female retirees could still claim an old age pension at age 60, but if they did so, their pension would now be reduced by 18 percent.

47. In addition to the actuarial reduction, pensions drawn early are lower, because the length of the contribution record enters into the pension formula. Severely handicapped persons remained the only group with a categorically defined entitlement to retire at age 60, but this would also be subject to the usual actuarial reduction of 0.3 percent per month.

48. Employers were obliged to pay a pre-retirement benefit of at least 65 percent of previous gross earnings which could be increased on the basis of collective agreements. In case the employer hired a previously unemployed person to replace the preretiree, the Federal Employment Office would add a subsidy. As employers preferred the traditional route of early exit via the 59er regulation in the pension insurance scheme, take-up of the novel scheme remained very limited, however. When it expired in 1988, only some 107,000 persons were registered as preretirees (Jacobs et al., 1991).

49. There were also minor changes concerning the age limits for age-graded extensions of the benefit duration. In 1996, for example, the age limit for the lowest extension was raised from 42 to 45 years, for the highest extension from 54 to 57 years.

50. However, the proportion of the registered unemployed receiving the more generous insurance benefit is now only about half compared to two-thirds in the early 1970s.

51. In an act of symbolic politics, the new red-green majority lowered the limit to 2.5 hours.

52. The idea of the 1993 act had probably been to limit the payment for households with up to four persons, but the actual text had referred to households with four or more members.

53. In actual practice, about one-quarter of those who are offered a job refuse to take it. In this case, the social assistance rate is either curbed by the authorities, or the claimants withdraw the application.

54. The increment corresponds to the full social assistance rate in the first month and then decreases over time.

55. Most people in minor employment are married women, and in about one-fourth of all cases, minor jobs are combined with other jobs (Bogai and Classen, 1998; Schupp et al., 1997).

56. At first, this was still tied to the condition that there were no earnings from work in the period of credited child-raising.

57. Thus the special pension increment for low-income earners in the German pension scheme is only granted to people with long contribution records of at least 35 years, but years of child-raising or family care work are now credited as part of the qualifying period.

58. Empirical analyses usually show benefit abuse to be much less widespread than frequently assumed, i.e., well below 5 percent of all cases. Moreover, cases where potential claimants abstain from making a claim are much more frequent than cases of benefit abuse (Fehringer, 1998).

59. The share of wage taxes (Lohnsteuer) grew from 22 percent to 31 percent between 1970 and 1998, whereas the share of corporate and income taxes shrank from 16 percent to scarcely 6 percent (Bäcker et al., 2000).

60. This tax under the so-called equalization of war burdens scheme (Lastenausgleich) had to be paid in quarterly installments over a period of thirty years, thus amounting to annual payments of 1.66 percent of the property held in 1948.

References

Alber, Jens. (1980). Der Wohlfahrtsstaat in der Krise? Eine Bilanz nach drei Jahrzehnten Sozialpolitik in der Bundesrepublik, in *Zeitschrift für Soziologie* 9 (4): 313-342.

Alber, Jens. (1986). "Germany." In Peter Flora (ed.), *Growth to Limits. The Western European Welfare States Since World War II.* Band 2. Berlin/New York: de Gruyter.

Alber, Jens. (1992). *Das Gesundheitswesen der Bundesrepublik Deutschland. Entwicklung, Struktur und Funktionsweise.* Frankfurt: Campus.

Alber, Jens. (1995). Towards Explaining Anti-Foreign Violence in Germany. Cambridge: Harvard University Center for European Studies Working Paper Series No 53.

Alber, Jens. (2000). Der deutsche Sozialstaat in der Ära Kohl: Diagnosen und Daten. In Stephan Leibfried, Uwe Waagschal (eds.), *Der deutsche Sozialstaat—Bilanzen— Reformen—Perspektiven.* Frankfurt: Campus.

Alber, Jens, Martin Schölkopf. (1999). *Seniorenpolitik. Die soziale Lage älterer Menschen in Deutschland und Europa.* Amsterdam: G+B Fakultas.

Allmendinger, Jutta. (1999). Bildungsarmut: Zur Verschränkung von Bildungs- und Sozialpolitik. In *Soziale Welt* 50: 35-50.

Andreß, Hans-Jürgen, Wolfgang Strengmann-Kuhn. (1997). Warum arbeiten, wenn der Staat zahlt? Über das Arbeitsangebot unterer Einkommensschichten. In *Zeitschrift für Sozialreform* 43: 505-525.

Angestelltenkammer Bremen/Arbeiterkammer Bremen. (2000). Sozialpolitische Chronik. Die wesentlichen Änderungen im Bereich der Arbeitslosenversicherung, Rentenversicherung, Krankenversicherung, Pflegeversicherung und Sozialhilfe (HLU) in den vergangenen Jahren. Bremen.

Bäcker, Gerhard, Reinhard Bispinck, Klaus Hofemann, Gerhard Naegele. (2000). *Sozialpolitik und soziale Lage in Deutschland.* (2 vols.). Opladen: Westdeutscher Verlag.

Baldwin, Peter. (1990). *The Politics of Social Solidarity: Class Bases of the European Welfare State 1875-1975.* Cambridge: Cambridge University Press.

Baratta, Mario von (ed.). (2000). *Der Fischer-Weltalmanach 2000—Zahlen—Daten—Fakten.* Frankfurt: Fischer Taschenbuch Verlag.

Bauer, Rudolph, Klaus Grenzdörffer. (1997). Jenseits der egoistischen Ökonomie und des methodologischen Individualismus: Die Potentiale des intermediären Bereichs, in Leviathan 25: 338-361.

Beitragsexplosion verhindert (1997, December 11). *Handelsblatt,* p. 4

Bogai, D., M. Classen. (1998). Abschaffung der Sozialversicherungsfreiheit für geringfügige Beschäftigung? In *Sozialer Fortschritt* 47: 112-117.

Börsch-Supan, Axel. (2000). Zur Diskussion eines Übergangs vom Umlage—zum Kapitaldeckungsverfahren in der Gesetzlichen Rentenversicherung. In *Perspektiven der Wirtschaftspolitik* 1: 400-428.

Breyer, Friedrich. (1997). Sind "äquivalente" Renten fair? In Richard Hauser (ed.), *Reform des Sozialstaats I.* Berlin: Duncker & Humblot.

Breyer, Friedrich. (2000). Kapitaldeckungs—versus Umlageverfahren. In *Perspektiven der Wirtschaftspolitik* 1: 383-405.

Bruns, Werner. (1993). *Sozialkriminalität in Deutschland.* Frankfurt: Ullstein.

Bundesministerium für Arbeit und Sozialordnung. (1997). Statistisches Taschenbuch 1997. Bonn.

Bundesministerium für Arbeit und Sozialordnung. (1998a). Arbeits- und Sozialstatistik. Hauptergebnisse 1998. Bonn.

Bundesministerium für Arbeit und Sozialordnung. (1998b). Sozialbericht 1997. Bonn

Bundesministerium für Arbeit und Sozialordnung. (1998c). Statistisches Taschenbuch 1998. Bonn.

Bundesministerium für Arbeit und Sozialordnung. (1998d). Übersicht über das Sozialrecht. Bonn.

Bundesministerium für Arbeit und Sozialordnung. (1999a). Arbeits- und Sozialstatistik. Hauptergebnisse 1999. Bonn.

Bundesministerium für Arbeit und Sozialordnung. (1999b). Statistisches Taschenbuch 1999. Bonn.

Bundesministerium für Arbeit und Sozialordnung. (2000a). Sozialbudget 1999. Bonn (http://www.bma.bund.de).

Bundesministerium für Arbeit und Sozialordnung. (2000b). Statistisches Taschenbuch 2000. Bonn.

Bundesminister für Bildung und Forschung (ed.). (1998). Das soziale Bild der Studenten-schaft in der Bundesrepublik Deutschland. 15. Sozialerhebung des Deutschen Studentenwerkes. Bonn.

Bundesminister für Bildung und Forschung. (2000). Grund-und Strukturdaten 1999/ 2000. Bonn.

Dahrendorf , Ralf. (1985). *Law and Order*. Boulder, CO: Westview Press.

Dahrendorf, Ralf. (1988). *The Modern Social Conflict. An Essay on the Politics of the Liberty*. London: Weidenfeld and Nicolson.

Dahrendorf, Ralf. (1998). Anmerkungen zur Globalisierung. In Ulrich Beck (ed.), *Perspektiven der Weltgesellschaft*. Frankfurt: Suhrkamp.

Döhler, Marian, Philip Manow-Borgwardt. (1992). Korporatisierung als gesundheitspolitische Strategie. In *Staatswissenschaften und Staatspraxis* 3: 64-106.

Döring, Diether, Frank Nullmeier, Roswitha Pioch, Georg Vobruba. (1995). *Gerechtigkeit im Wohlfahrtsstaat*. Marburg: Schüren Presseverlag.

Engels, Wolfram. (1986). *Über Freiheit, Gleichheit und Brüderlichkeit*. Bad Homburg: Frankfurter Institut für Wirtschaftspolitische Forschung.

Esping-Andersen, Gøsta. (1996). Welfare States without Work: The Impasse of Labour Shedding and Familialism in Continental European Social Policy. In Gøsta Esping-Andersen (ed.), *Welfare States in Transition. National Adaptations in Global Economies*. London: Sage.

Eurostat. (1998). Analysis of Income Distribution in 13 EU Member States. Statistics in Focus, Population and Social Conditions no11/1998. Luxembourg.

Fehringer, Jochen. (1998). Die Mißbrauchsdebatte im deutschen Sozialstaat: Fakten und Analysen. University of Konstanz: Diploma Thesis (mimeo).

Fischer, Christian. (1999). Kapitaldeckungsverfahren in der Alterssicherung–ein Weg aus der Krise? University of Konstanz: Diploma Thesis (mimeo).

Flora, Peter (ed.). (1986). Growth to Limits. *The Western European Welfare States Since World War II*. (3 vols.). Berlin: DeGruyter.

Frerich, Johannes, Martin Frey. (1993). Handbuch der Geschichte der Sozialpolitik in Deutsch-land, Band 3: Bundesrepublik Deutschland bis zur Herstellung der Deutschen Einheit. Mün-chen-Wien: Oldenbourg.

Gangl, Markus. (1998). Sozialhilfebezug und Arbeitsmarktverhalten–Eine Längsschnittanalyse der Übergänge aus der Sozialhilfe in den Arbeitsmarkt. In *Zeitschrift für Soziologie* 27: 212-232.

Geissler, Heiner. (1976). *Die Neue Soziale Frage*. Freiburg: Herder.

Geissler, Rainer. (1996). Kein Abschied von Klasse und Schicht. In *Köl-ner Zeitschrift für Soziologie und Sozialpsychologie* 48: 319-338.

Giddens, Anthony. (1998). *The Third Way. The Renewal of Social Democracy*. London: Polity.

Hanesch, Walter, Peter Krause, Gerhard Bäcker. (2000). *Armut und Ungleichheit in Deutschland*. Reinbek: Rowohlt.

Hauser, Richard. (1995). Die Entwicklung der Einkommenslage von Familien über zwei Dekaden-einige empirische Grundlagen zur Würdigung der deutschen Familienpolitik. In Gerhard Kleinhenz (ed.), *Soziale Ausgestaltung der Marktwirtschaft. Festschrift zum 65. Geburtstag von Prof. Dr. Heinz Lampert*. Berlin: Duncker & Humblot.

Hauser, Richard. (1999). Die Entwicklung der Einkommensverteilung und der Einkommensarmut in den alten und neuen Bundesländern. In *Aus Politik und Zeitgeschichte* B18/99: 3-9.

Heclo, Hugh. (1974). *Modern Social Politics in Britain and Sweden. From Relief to Income Maintenance*. New Haven/London: Yale University Press.

Heimbach-Steins, Marianne, Andreas Lienkamp (eds.). (1997). *Für eine Zukunft in Solidarität und Gerechtigkeit: Wort des Rates der Evangelischen Kirche in*

Deutschland und der Deutschen Bischofskonferenz zur wirtschaftlichen und sozialen Lage in Deutschland. München: Bernward bei Don Bosco.

Hoppensack, Hans-Christoph, Gerd Wenzel. (1985). Hilfe zur Arbeit und Arbeitszwang. Sozialhilfe und administrative "Normalisierung" von Lohnarbeit. In Stephan Leibfried, Florian Tennstedt (eds.), *Politik der Armut und Die Spaltung des Sozialstaats*. Frankfurt: Suhrkamp.

Institut für Arbeitsmarkt-und Berufsforschung der Bundesanstalt für Arbeit (ed.). (2000). Zahlen-Fibel. Ergebnisse der Arbeitsmarkt- und Berufsforschung in Tabellen. Nürnberg.

Jacobs, Klaus, Martin Kohli, Martin Rein. (1991). Germany: The Diversity of Pathways. In Martin Kohli, Martin Rein, Anne-Marie Guillemard, Herman van Gunsteren (eds.), *Time for Retirement. Comparative Studies of Early Exit from the Labor Force*. Cambridge: Cambridge University Press.

Kaltenborn, Bruno (ed.). (1995). *Modelle der Grundsicherung: Ein systematischer Vergleich*. Baden-Baden: Nomos.

Kaufmann, Franz-Xaver. (1997). *Herausforderungen des Sozialstaates*. Frankfurt: Suhrkamp.

Keller, Berndt. (1997). *Einführung in die Arbeitspolitik*. München/Wien: Oldenbourg.

Kirchenamt der Evangelischen Kirche in Deutschland/Sekretariat der Deutschen Bischofs-konferenz (eds.). (1994). Zur wirtschaftlichen und sozialen Lage in Deutschland. Diskus-sions-grundlage über ein gemeinsames Wort der Kirchen. Hannover/Bonn (mimeo).

Kommission der Europäischen Gemeinschaften 1990: Kinderbetreuung in der Europäischen Gemeinschaft 1985-1990. Brüssel.

Kommission für Zukunftsfragen der Freistaaten Bayern und Sachsen. (1997). Erwerbstätigkeit und Arbeitslosigkeit in Deutschland. Entwicklung, Ursachen und Maßnahmen. Bonn. (3 vols.).

Lamping, Wolfgang, Henning Schridde. (1999). Konturen neuer Sozialstaatlichkeit: Sozialhilfepolitik zwischen Kontinuität und Wandel. In *Zeitschrift für das Fürsorgewesen* 51 (4): 74-100.

Leisering, Lutz. (1999). Eine Frage der Gerechtigkeit. Armut und Reichtum in Deutschland. In *Aus Politik und Zeitgeschichte* B 18/99: 10-17.

Leisering, Lutz, Stephan Leibfried. (1999). *Time and Poverty in Western Welfare States— United Germany in Perspective*. Cambridge: Cambridge University Press.

Lepsius, M. Rainer. (1979). Soziale Ungleichheit und Klassenstrukturen in der Bundesrepublik Deutschland. In Hans-Ulrich Wehler (ed.), *Klassen in der europäischen Sozialgeschichte*. Göttingen: Vandenhoeck & Ruprecht.

Lepsius, M. Rainer. (1995). Soziale Symmetrie, Tarifautonomie und staatliche Sozialpolitik. In Werner Fricke (ed.), *1995 Jahrbuch Arbeit und Technik*. Bonn: Dietz.

Litsch, Martin, Helmut Schröder. (1997). Zuzahlungserhöhung um weitere 5 DM: Auswir-kun-gen im Arzneimittelbereich. In *Sozialer Fortschritt* 46: 122-125.

Majone, Giandomenico. (1996). Redistributive und sozialregulative Politik. In Markus Jachtenfuchs, Beate Kohler-Koch (eds.), *Europäische Integration*. Opladen: Leske + Budrich.

Manow, Philip. (1994). *Gesundheitspolitik im Einigungsprozeß*. Frankfurt: Campus.

Manow, Philip, Eric Seils. (2000). Adjusting Badly: The German Welfare State, Structural Change and the Open Economy. In Fritz W. Scharpf; Vivien A. Schmidt (eds.), *Welfare and Work in the Open Economy, Volume II. Diverse Responses to Common Challenges*. Oxford: University Press.

Martin, Andrew. (1997). What does globalization have to do with the erosion of welfare states? Sorting out the issues (ZeS-Arbeitspapier 1/1997). Bremen: Zentrum für Sozialpolitik (mimeo).

Meinhardt, Volker. (1997). Vereinigungsfolgen belasten Sozialversicherung. In *DIW-Wochen-bericht* 40: 725-729.

Miegel, Meinhard. (1983). *Die verkannte Revolution.* Stuttgart: Bonn Aktuell.

Miegel, Meinhard. (1995). Perspektiven des Sozialstaats in Deutschland-ein Entwurf für die Jahre 2000 folgende. In Werner Fricke (ed.), *1995 Jahrbuch Arbeit und Technik.* Bonn: Dietz.

Miegel, Meinhard, Stefanie Wahl. (1985). *Gesetzliche Grundsicherung Private Vorsorge—Der Weg aus der Rentenkrise.* Stuttgart: Bonn Aktuell.

Müller, Hans-Peter, Bernd Wegener (eds.). (1995). *Soziale Ungleichheit und soziale Gerechtigkeit.* Opladen: Leske + Budrich.

Neumann, Udo. (1999). Verdeckte Armut in der Bundesrepublik Deutschland. Begriff und empirische Ergebnisse für die Jahre 1983 bis 1995. In *Aus Politik und Zeitgeschichte* B18/99: 27-32.

Nullmeier, Frank. (1992). Der Zugriff des Bundes auf die Haushalte und Gemeinden und Parafisci. In Hans-Hermann Hartwich, Göttrik Wewer (eds.), *Regieren in der Bundesrepublik IV.* Opladen: Leske+Budrich.

Nullmeier, Frank. (2000). *Politische Theorie des Sozialstaats.* Frankfurt: Campus.

Nullmeier, Frank; Friedbert W. Rüb. (1993). *Die Transformation der Sozialpolitik. Vom Sozialstaat zum Sicherungsstaat.* Frankfurt/New York: Campus.

OECD. (1996). Bildung auf einen Blick OECD-Indikatoren. Paris.

OECD. (1997). Ageing in OECD Countries. A Critical Policy Challenge. Paris.

Offe, Claus. (1972). Politische Herrschaft und Klassenstrukturen. Zur Analyse spätkapitalistischer Gesellschaftssysteme. In Gisela Kress, Dieter Senghaas (eds.), *Politikwissenschaft.* Frankfurt: Fischer.

Orszag, Peter R., Joseph E. Stiglitz. (1999). Rethinking Pension Reform: Ten Myths about Social Security Systems. Paper presented at the conference on "New Ideas about Old Age Security." The World Bank, Washington, D.C. (mimeo).

Palentien, Christian, Andreas Klocke, Klaus Hurrelmann. (1999). Armut im Kindes— und Jugendalter. In *Aus Politik und Zeitgeschichte* B 18/99: 33-38.

Presse und Informationsamt der Bundesregierung 1998: Die Regierungserklärung von Bundeskanzler Gerhard Schröder. Berlin.

Richter, Saskia. (1999). Ideen, Interessen, Institutionen–was be-stimmt den rentenpolitischen Entscheidungs-prozeß in Deutschland? Literaturkritik und empirische Überprüfung anhand des Renten-reformgesetzes 1999. University of Konstanz: Diploma Thesis (mimeo).

Rieger, Elmar, Stephan Leibfried. (1997). Die sozialpolitischen Grenzen der Globalisierung. In *Politische Vierteljahresschrift* 38 (4): 771-796.

Rimlinger, Gaston V. (1971). *Welfare Policy and Industrialization in Europe, America, and Russia.* New York: John Wiley.

Rolf, Gabriele, Gert Wagner. (1996). Alterssicherung in der Bundesrepublik Deutschkland. Stand und Perspektiven. In *Aus Politik und Zeitgeschichte* B35/96: 23-32.

Roller, Edeltraud. (2000). Ende des sozialstaatlichen Konsenses? Zum Aufbrechen traditioneller und zur Entstehung neuer Konfliktstrukturen. In Oskar Niedermayer, Bettina Westle (eds.), *Demokratie und Partizipation. Festschrift für Max Kaase.* Opladen: Westdeutscher Verlag.

Rothgang, Heinz. (1994). Die Einführung der Pflegeversicherung - Ist das Sozialversiche-rungsprinzip am Ende? In Barbara Riedmüller, Thomas Olk (eds.), *Grenzen des Sozialversicherungsstaates. Leviathan, Sonderheft 14.* Opladen: Westdeutscher Verlag.

Sachverständigenrat zur Begutachtung der gesamtwirtschaftlichen Entwicklung. (1999). Wirtschaftspolitik unter Reformdruck. Jahresgutachten 1999/2000 des

Sachverständigenrats zur Begutachtung der gesamtwirtschaftlichen Entwicklung. Stuttgart: Metzler-Poeschel.

Samuelson, Paul. (1958). An Exact Consumption-Loan Model of Interest with or without the Social Contrivance of Money. In *Journal of Political Economy* 66: 467-482.

Scharpf, Fritz. (1986). Strukturen der post-industriellen Gesellschaft oder: Verschwindet die Massenarbeitslosigkeit in der Dienstleistungs- und Informations-Ökonomie? In *Soziale Welt* 37: 1-24.

Scharpf, Fritz. (1995). Subventionierte Niedriglohn-Beschäftigung statt bezahlter Arbeitslosigkeit? In *Zeitschrift für Sozialreform* 41 (2): 65-82.

Scharpf, Fritz. (1998). The Adjustment of National Employment and Social Policy to Economic Internationalization. Köln: Max- Planck-Institut für Gesellschaftsforschung (mimeo).

Scharpf, Fritz. (2000). The Viability of Advanced Welfare States in the International Economy: Vulnerabilities and Options. In *Journal of European Public Policy* 7: 190-228.

Scharpf, Fritz, Vivien A. Schmidt (eds.). (2000). *Welfare and Work in the Open Economy.* (2 vols.). Oxford: University Press.

Schelsky, Hemut. (1976). *Der selbständige und der betreute Mensch.* Stuttgart: Seewald.

Schmähl, Winfried. (1999). Arbeit—Basis für die soziale Sicherung der Zukunft. In Winfried Schmähl/Herbert Rische (eds.), *Wandel der Arbeitswelt-Folgerungen für die Sozialpolitik.* Baden-Baden: Nomos.

Schmähl, Winfried. (2000). Perspektiven der Alterssicherungspolitik in Deutschland— über Konzeptionen, Vorschläge und einen angestrebten Paradigmenwechsel. In *Perspektiven der Wirtschaftspolitik* 1: 407-430.

Schmid, Günter. (1997). Beschäftigungswunder Niederlande? In *Leviathan* 25 (3): 302-337.

Schmid, Günter, Bernd Reissert. (1988). Machen Institutionen einen Unterschied? Finanzie-rungs-systeme der Arbeitsmarktpolitik im internationalen Vergleich. In Manfred G. Schmidt (ed.), *Staatstätigkeit. International und historisch vergleichende Analysen. PVS Sonderheft 19.* Opladen: Westdeutscher Verlag.

Schmid, Thomas (ed.). (1986). *Befreiung von falscher Arbeit: Thesen zum garantierten Mindesteinkommen.* (2nd. ed.) Berlin: Wagenbach.

Schmidt, Manfred G. (1988). West Germany: The Policy of the Middle Way. In *Journal of Public Policy* 7: 135-177.

Schneider, Reinhart. (1982). Die Bildungsentwicklung in den westeuropäischen Staaten 1870-1975. In *Zeitschrift für Soziologie* 11: 207-226.

Schupp, Jürgen, Johannes Schwarze, Gert Wagner. (1997). Erwerbsstatistik unterschätzt Beschäftigung um 2 Millionen Personen. In *DIW-Wochenbericht* 64 (38): 689-694.

Shapiro, Isaac, Robert Greenstein. (1999). *The Widening Income Gulf.* Washington, D.C.: Center on Budget and Policy Priorities (http://www.cbpp.org/9-4-99tax-rep.htm)

Statistisches Bundesamt (ed.). (1997). Datenreport 1997. Bonn: Bundeszentrale für politische Bildung.

Statistisches Bundesamt. (1999). Statistisches Jahrbuch 1999 für die Bundesrepublik Deutschland. Stuttgart: Metzler-Poeschel.

Statistisches Bundesamt (ed.). (2000a). Datenreport 1999. Bonn: Bundeszentrale für politische Bildung.

Statistisches Bundesamt. (2000b). Statistisches Jahrbuch 2000 für die Bundesrepublik Deutschland. Stuttgart: Metzler-Poeschel.

Streeck, Wolfgang. (1995). From Market Making to State Building? Reflections on the Political Economy of European Social Policy. In Stephan Leibfried, Paul Pierson (eds.), *European Social Policy. Between Fragmentation and Integration.* Washington, D.C.: Brookings.

Svallfors, Stefan. (1997). Worlds of Welfare and Attitudes to Redistribution: A Comparison of Eight Western Nations In *European Sociological Review* 13 (3): 283-304.

Ulbrich, Rudi. (1993). Wohnungsversorgung in der Bundesrepublik Deutschland. In *Aus Politik und Zeitgeschichte* B8-9/93: 16-31.

Wagner, Gert, Johannes Schwarze, Karin Rinne, Marcel Erlinghagen. (1998). "Bürgerarbeit"—Kein sinnvoller Weg zur Reduzierung der Arbeitslosigkeit. In *DIW-Wochenbericht* 65 (4): 82-85.

Wirth, Christian, Susanne Paul. (1998). Anreiz für Betriebsrenten. In *Bundesarbeitsblatt* 2/98: 43- 47.

Wood, Adrian. (1994). *North-South Trade, Employment and Inequality. Changing Fortunes in a Skill-Driven World.* Oxford: Clarendon Press.

Zapf, Wolfgang. (1981). Wohlfahrtsstaat und Wohlfahrtsproduktion. In Lothar Albertin, Werner Link (ed.), *Politische Parteien auf dem Weg zur parlamentarischen Demokratie in Deutschland.* Düsseldorf: Droste.

Zukunftskommission der Friedrich-Ebert-Stiftung. (1998). *Wirtschaftliche Leistungsfähigkeit, sozialer Zusammenhalt, ökologische Nachhaltigkeit. Drei Ziele— ein Weg.* Bonn: Dietz.

2

Remaking the Welfare State in New Zealand

Ross Mackay

Introduction

Over the past two decades, New Zealand has undergone a profound and comprehensive transformation of almost every aspect of its public and economic life. The economy has been restructured from top to bottom, through the deregulation of financial markets and dismantling of tariffs and import barriers. Public sector management has been totally rebuilt, with an emphasis on efficiency, managerial accountability and quality of services (Boston et al., 1999). New governance arrangements have been implemented in the education and health sectors, with policy separated from the delivery of services, with devolution of decisions about delivery of services closer to local communities. The industrial relations system has been radically overhauled, infusing a considerable dose of flexibility into the labor market. There have also been constitutional changes, the most important being an electoral reform that replaced from a first-past-the-post to a fully proportional system of electoral representation. These changes have also been associated with significant transformations of social attitudes. Taking them altogether, it is no exaggeration to say that the whole political economy of the country has been reshaped by these reforms.

The welfare system has not been immune to this reform. Indeed, much of government's reforming zeal became focused on the welfare system during the 1990s after most of the other reforms had been put in place. This has resulted in major changes that have reshaped the welfare system in quite profound ways, just as the wider reforms have reshaped the context in which it operates. There is now a sense in which a chapter of the story has ended, however, following a recent change of government. A new Labor-led government, elected in November 1999, has signalled a change of direction for future welfare policy. This makes it an opportune time to take stock and attempt an assessment of the extent to which the reforms have altered the fundamental shape of the welfare state in New Zealand.

The chapter maps out three broad shifts in social security policy. First, changes in the allocation of social benefits are described. Prominent among these have been a shift from universal to targeted benefits and a downward adjustment in the level of provision afforded by benefits. Secondly, changes in the welfare mix are discussed. The most publicly noted instances have been two failed privatization initiatives, in the area of accident compensation and the public pension. However, there have also been some significant, if less noticable, shifts, involving the retreat of the state from certain areas of provision and the consequent rise of private arrangements. One of these—a retreat of the state from any involvement in wage-fixing procedures, leaving wages to be determined purely by the market—occurred more gradually over a longer time frame than the other changes. Thirdly, changes in social activation and work-oriented policies are outlined. These include a range of welfare-to-work approaches that were introduced by the former center-right Nation-led government, some of which are now being unwound by the new center-left Labor-led government.

Before examining these changes in detail, it will be useful to provide a brief overview of the development of the welfare state in New Zealand and background of the welfare reforms.

Context and Adjustment Problems

If it is possible to talk about the evolution of the welfare state, the most apt explanatory framework, in New Zealand at least, is a theory of punctuated equilibrium. The history of the welfare state in New Zealand does not follow a gradual path of development, but rather shows an oscillation between bouts of rapid activity and long intermitting periods of relative stasis. In particular, we can discern three periods of rapid development: the last years of the nineteenth century when the foundations of the welfare state were laid down by an activist-Liberal government; the late 1930s when the structures of the modern welfare state were erected by the first Labor government; and the past decade and a half when these structures have been renovated by reformist right-oriented governments.

The present chapter is not concerned with the early origins of the welfare state, but focuses instead on how the structures created in the late 1930s have been modified by the recent reforms. The discussion opens with an account of the characteristics of the welfare state as created by the first Labor government. It is useful to devote some space to this, as New Zealand stands apart from the rest of the developed world in its welfare arrangements. In particular, little use is made in New Zealand of social insurance-based programs. Instead, the vast majority of programs can be characterized as social assistance, being funded from general taxation, income-tested and paid on a flat-rate basis, with no relation to prior earnings. These characteristics date from the very early years of the welfare state (Mackay, 2000).

Context: The Social Security Act of 1938

The modern welfare state in New Zealand dates from the Social Security Act of 1938. This systematized the coverage of provisions that had grown in a piecemeal way since the 1898 Old Age Pensions Act. The objectives of the 1938 Act, set out in its preamble, outlined the various social risks. The Act was to provide protection against, including "disabilities arising from age, sickness, widowhood, orphanhood, unemployment, or other exceptional circumstances." Accordingly, the Act established a range of statutory benefits to cover these (and other) contingencies, the principal of these being a sickness benefit, a widows' benefit, an invalids' benefit, an unemployment benefit, an age benefit, and a family benefit.

These benefits were all flat rate payments, with no connection to prior earnings, and were in the main subject to an income test, although there were a number of exceptions to this. A miners' benefit was exempt from the income test, largely for political reasons. The family benefit, initially subject to an income test, was converted into a universal payment in 1946, for reasons associated with the transition back to civil society after the disruption of world war—in particular to promote a resurgence in the birth rate and to ease women back into the home after taking up the call to work to support the war effort. A superannuation benefit, which provided a small universal payment to everyone from age 65, stood alongside the age benefit that was paid to everyone from age 60 at a higher rate but on an income-tested basis.[1] Apart from these three exceptions, all other benefits were subject to an income test.

The initial funding arrangements involved a mix of methods including a special social security levy on incomes (of 1 shilling in the pound or 5 percent of earnings, subsequently raised to 7.5 percent), and a contribution from general taxation revenues—and the funds were managed in a separate Social Security Fund on a pay-as-you-go basis. These arrangements were subsequently unwound, however. By 1958 the social security contribution had been integrated into the income tax system and by 1964, the Social Security Fund had been disestablished. Since then, social security has been financed purely out of consolidated revenues.

The Social Security Act of 1938 also established a new national health service. The government's aim was to provide comprehensive free health services, including hospital treatment, maternity care, prescription pharmaceuticals, and general practitioner care. The first three goals were achieved, but the government ran into fierce opposition from the medical profession over a free general practitioner service. The initial proposal for an annual capitation scheme was implacably opposed by the New Zealand branch of the British Medical Association (and described by the chairman of the doctors' health insurance committee as "state helotry[2]"). Doctors insisted instead on their right to set their own fees. A counter-proposal from the government, comprising a fixed fee of 5s. per consultation, was also resisted. In the end, the doctors were bought off with an increased offer of 7s. 6d. per consultation. As Sinclair (1976:162) noted, "...what was intolerable at five bob became quickly acceptable at seven and six."

Despite this one signal failure, the national health service was a significant and impressive achievement. Where the social security benefits had abolished the fear of destitution, the health service "abolished the economic corollary of illness—the fear of not being able to afford a doctor. Men stood now as equal before disease as before death" (Sinclair, 1991: 271).

In addition to these groundbreaking arrangements in health and social security, the first Labor government also placed a strong emphasis on education. New Zealand had had a system of universal, compulsory and secular primary education since 1877 and continued to develop its secondary education system during the early years of the twentieth century. In 1939, the Minister of Education affirmed the commitment of the Labor government to this tradition in a resounding speech to the House of Representatives:

> The Government's objective, broadly expressed, is that every person, whatever the level of his academic ability, whether he be rich or poor, whether he live in town or country, has a right as a citizen to a free education of a kind for which he is best fitted and to the fullest extent of his powers. (Peters and Olssen, 1999: 179)

Accordingly, the government extended the provision of free education up to the age of 19, thus providing all children with an entitlement to five-years' free secondary education. At the same time, the years of compulsory education were raised to the age of 15.

These new provisions for social security, health and education constitute the three principal pillars of New Zealand's modern welfare state. It is notable that they pre-date moves by most other Western states to introduce a comprehensive modern welfare state. Just as New Zealand had been one of the first nations to implement old age pensions in the late nineteenth century, so once again it was in the vanguard of reform in the next wave of welfare-state development.

These initiatives were attended by considerable rhetoric about the scope and function of the welfare state, in which a central recurrent phrase was the notion of the welfare state as a provider of security "from cradle to grave." The repetition of this formulation during the postwar years like some sort of incantatory mantra had a duly soporific effect. Once the changes were bedded down and the nation resumed the job of rebuilding home and family life after the trauma of world war, the appetite for reformist changes ebbed away. A long period of lull in the evolutionary process now succeeded.

It is not possible in the scope of this chapter to account for changes across the whole span of the welfare state. The remaining discussion will be restricted to changes in the social security system and how these have modified the original vision of the 1938 Social Security Act.

Adjustment Problems: Escalating Demands Amid a Climate of Fiscal Constraint

The initial motivation for the recent round of welfare reforms can be found in the deteriorating condition of the New Zealand economy, which led to increasing demands on the social security system at the same time as it restricted the country's ability to fund them.

Table 2.1 lays out some summary statistics that document the emerging development of economic problems from the 1960s. These include figures on expenditure on social security over the last four decades, together with some selected macroeconomic statistics—GDP growth, price inflation, and the rate of unemployment—all averaged over five yearly intervals.

By the 1960s social security expenditure was in decline. Between 1960 and 1970, expenditure on social security benefits fell from 20.7 percent to 17.9 percent of the government budget and from 6.5 percent to 5.1 percent of

Table 2.1
Five-Yearly Average Expenditure on Social Security Benefits and Selected Macroeconomic Statistics, 1961-2000

Year	Average % of government budget on social security benefits	Average % of GDP spent on social security benefits	Average rate of growth of GDP	Average rate of inflation	Average rate of unemployment
1961-65	19.5	5.9	4.9	2.6	0.1
1966-70	17.8	5.2	3.2	4.4	0.3
1971-75	18.9	5.5	4.4	9.6	0.2
1976-80	22.3	8.3	0.0	14.8	1.3
1981-85	26.3	10.5	2.9	12.1	4.6
1986-90	29.4	10.8	1.0	10.3	5.1
1991-95	32.3	12.4	2.5	2.3	9.2

GDP. A large part of this decline was due to the falling real value of the family benefit, which was not indexed to inflation and whose rate was only very infrequently reviewed, but it also reflects the general stasis into which the social security system had lapsed. It was soon to begin growing again, partly as a result of further elaboration of the system (in particular, the introduction in 1972 of a new benefit for single parents, known as the domestic purposes benefit), but also as a result of a rising tide of economic misfortune.

Economic clouds had been gathering over the economy since the late 1960s, caused by a long slow deterioration in the terms of trade, but it was not until the first oil shock of 1973 that the government was forced to recognize the real difficulties the economy was facing. The oil shock kick-started an inflationary cycle whose malign effects were soon felt throughout the whole of the economy. Average GDP growth rate averaged precisely zero in the second half of the 1970s and unemployment began an inexorable climb, fuelling an increase in outlays on social security. Between 1972 and 1979, public expenditure on social security benefits doubled as a percentage of GDP from 4.8 percent to 9.6 percent. The growth continued through the next decade and beyond, as unemployment surged to a peak of 10.9 percent in 1992, hoisting with it expenditure on social security to a peak of 13.2 percent of GDP.

The rise of spending on social security benefits—during the 1970s when it grew from 18 percent to 25 percent of the government budget, and the 1980s when it grew even faster to 33 percent of the budget—provides the background to the recent reforms. Governments became increasingly concerned with containing the demands that the welfare system made on the economy. Although the economy improved after 1992 and the unemployment rate dropped to 6.2 percent by 1996, the reduction in the number of people receiving unemployment benefits was offset by growth in the numbers of people receiving other benefits, particularly sickness, invalids, and domestic purposes benefits. This meant that there was no net reduction in expenditure to show for the economic upturn.

However, a concern with cost containment was not the sole motivation for the reforms. Government was also concerned about the corrosive effects of being dependent on benefits for long periods and the way in which this led to an atrophy of skills, erosion of work confidence, and loss of self-esteem, with second order impacts on children's well being. As unemployment had risen, a significant and rising proportion of people remained on benefits for longer periods, including invalids and single parents as well as the unemployed. Furthermore, dependence on welfare was disproportionately experienced by particular subgroups (especially young people, Maori and Pacific Islands people), and concentrated in particular geographic communities, with negative effects on social cohesion.

These were the facts that confronted decision-makers as they contemplated the welfare state in the late 1980s. The remainder of the chapter describes the responses made to these challenges. These were of three main types: shifts in the allocation of benefits, changes in the welfare mix, and expanded use of social activation approaches. The discussion is in the form of a descriptive narrative supported by illustrative statistics and interpretative commentary.

Allocation Principles: Changing Priorities

Some of the most important recent changes in New Zealand's social security policy have involved the reallocation of social benefits. Two broad shifts can be identified: a move from universal to targeted programs (although a significant counter-example is evident in the area of pension policy); and a downward shift in the real value of most benefits.

A Move from Universal to Targeted Assistance

A significant theme in the reforms has been an increasing emphasis on targeted assistance. This has taken a number of forms, three of which will be discussed here. The first change was a rapid and dramatic shift from a fully universal to a fully targeted system of family assistance. The second change has involved an increasing emphasis on second-tier supplementary assistance programs, which provide additional support, more tightly targeted on the basis of need, on top of the basic benefit. The third change has been the adoption of targeting in a wider range of social policy areas—in particular health and education. These three changes have predominantly affected the working age population. By contrast, there has been a move in the opposite direction—away from targeting and towards more universality—for people of pensionable age.

Family assistance. The area in which there has been the most significant movement from universal to targeted provisions has been family assistance. In the seven years from 1984 to 1991, New Zealand moved from a fully universal to a fully targeted system of family assistance. In 1984, family assistance was delivered through the family benefit program. This was a flat-rate demogrant, payable through the benefit system in respect of all dependent children at the weekly rate of $6 per child without any form of means test. By 1991, family assistance was delivered through the family support program. This was a tax credit, payable at the rate of $42 per week for the first dependent child and $22 per week for subsequent children, to families on an income-tested basis, with an annual income disregard of $17,500 and a withdrawal rate of 18 cents in the dollar up to $27,000 and 30 cents in the dollar thereafter.

The family benefit was instituted by the 1938 Social Security Act. The payment was initially subject to an income test, but this was removed in 1946, largely to assist the country to cope with the transition back to a peacetime economy. To this end, it was intended to signal a return to the "normal" family life that had existed before the war, where married women were expected not to work, but rather to be full-time caretakers for their children. Thus, the removal of the means test was aimed at stimulating the birth-rate and easing women out of the jobs they had taken up to support the war effort, in order to supply vacancies for returned servicemen.

Once these goals were achieved, the program was subject to somewhat benign neglect by the government—although the ability to capitalize it after 1958 afforded an important source of funding for first-time home buyers— and its value declined over the years. It was never indexed and the rate of payment was only very irregularly reviewed. In 1945, it had been payable at a rate equivalent to 25 percent of the single rate of unemployment benefit. However, by 1985, its value had atrophied to around 7 percent of the single rate of unemployment benefit.

By this time, a new targeted family assistance benefit had been instituted, which delivered higher levels of support to low-income families in employment. This program, known as family care, was short-lived, being replaced in 1986 by the family support program, which was available to all low-income families, including those reliant on income support. In contrast to family care, family support was paid by way of a tax credit and the level of payment—$36 for the first child and $16 for subsequent children—now totally dwarfed the family benefit, which was still worth only $6 per week per child. The writing was now on the wall for the old universal payment, although it was another five years before it was abolished, at which time the rate of payment of family support was increased to make up for its loss.

Thus, in the span of only seven years—from 1984 to 1991—New Zealand's system of family assistance had been moved from a fully universal basis to a fully income-tested basis.

Expansion of second-tier programs. Another significant shift has been the emergence of second-tier supplementary assistance programs that provide additional provision on top of the basic benefit, targeted on the basis of specific designated need. These second-tier programs grew from rather modest beginnings. The supplementary assistance program was initially established in 1952 to provide additional assistance to people in need, in the form of a weekly payment or a lump sum to purchase particular items, such as dentures or wheelchairs. It remained a quiet backwater off the mainstream social security system for the next twenty-five years. From the late 1970s, however, the system began to be elaborated into a number of separate programs, each aimed at meeting a different type of need.

By the mid-1990s, the range of programs included an accommodation supplement (for those with high housing costs), disability allowance (for those with regular ongoing costs associated with a disability or personal health need), handicapped child allowance (for those with a seriously disabled child who needed constant care and attention), child-care subsidy (for parents who needed, but could not afford, child day care), special benefit (for those with regular ongoing expenses, related to special circumstances, which exceeded their regular income), and special needs grant (for those with a special need which was not able to be met from other social security programs). In addition, a range of tax credit programs was available to supplement the incomes of low-income families, including family support and various in-work tax credits for low-income working families with children.

The successive addition of each of these programs meant that an increasing proportion of the total welfare spend was being paid by way of top-ups to the basic benefit. Table 2.2 gives details of the proportion of welfare expenditure allocated to supplementary assistance and tax credits.

As late as 1985, only around 1 percent of the total welfare spend was allocated to targeted second-tier assistance. This had grown to nearly 8 percent by 1990. The bulk of the growth during this period was due to the establishment of the targeted family support tax credit. By 1995, the amount of spending on targeted supplementary assistance and tax credit programs had grown at an even more rapid rate to 14.5 percent. This was due to a number of factors, including the abolition of the universal family benefit and the creation of a range of new supplementary assistance programs. It also reflects the cuts in benefit rates effected in 1991 (discussed subsequently), which not only reduced the amount of money paid by way of the basic benefit, but also led to increased demand for supplementary assistance—because of the more straitened circumstances of beneficiary households—which was accordingly expanded. By 1998, the amount of spending allocated to targeted programs had grown further to 18 percent.

Table 2.2
Expenditure on Supplementary Assistance and Tax Credits as a Percentage of Total Welfare Spending

Year	Total expenditure on welfare benefits	Total expenditure on supplementary assistance	Total expenditure on tax credits	Supplementary assistance and tax credits as a % of all welfare expenditure
1980	1922.9	22.9	-	1.2%
1985	4121.5	58.8	-	1.4%
1990	9195.4	246.3	465.0	7.7%
1995	10530.8	804.7	722.8	14.5%
1998	11945.0	1159.7	995.0	18.0%

Broader application of targeting in social policy. It is not only within the social security system that targeted assistance has expanded. Targeting has also been adopted in the health and education sectors as a means of allocating assistance to people at lower income levels.

In 1991, a new regime for targeting of health expenditure was introduced, involving the imposition of user charges for health services on middle- and high-income earners and increased subsidies to low-income earners. Public hospital services (which had previously been provided free of charge) now became subject to part-charges for middle- and high-income earners (although these were subsequently abolished). Nominal charges for pharmaceuticals were increased for middle- and high-income earners. Subsidies for general practitioner charges were increased for low-income earners and reduced for middle- and high-income earners. Access to the subsidies for low-income earners was obtainable by means of a community services card, entitlement to which was based on eligibility for social security benefits.

Assistance for tertiary education students has also, since 1991, been subject to an income-testing regime based on total family earnings, including those of the student's parents. Tertiary students between the ages of 18 and 25 have access to student living allowances, subject to the earnings test. Prior to this, all students enrolled full-time in recognized tertiary programs were eligible for non-income-tested tertiary study grants.

The pool of people who are targeted for assistance under these other policies overlaps considerably with those who are targeted in the social security system. While these policies serve to meet the goal of allocating scarce resources in the health and education fields, they further exacerbate the problem of high effective marginal tax rates that are produced by social security targeting mechanisms. Given that these rates approach 100 percent for a significant proportion of social security claimants over a relatively broad reach of the earnings distribution, these other targeting mechanisms are likely to boost effective marginal tax rates well above 100 percent for some people in some circumstances. Anyone facing such a high rate would be in the unfortunate position of being financially worse off after an earnings increase, due to the combined effects of tax on earnings and loss of entitlements to social security and other forms of assistance.

This difficulty was recognized by the government when it introduced these wider targeting policies. To alleviate the problem, a project was initiated to integrate the various disparate targeting mechanisms into a unitary targeting regime. The project did not proceed, however, and the problem of overlapping targeting regimes remains largely unresolved.

Pension policy: A counter-example. There has been one salient exception to the general trend for increased targeting—in the public pension, where the most recent change has been in the direction of less targeting. The background to this can be discerned in changes to the public pension in the 1970s.

In 1974, the third Labour government introduced a new compulsory contributions-based public pension scheme that was intended eventually to replace the existing age and superannuation benefits. The new scheme was scarcely bedded down when the government faced an election in 1975, in which much of the debate centered on pension arrangements. The new pension was opposed by the National Party, which proposed instead to introduce a flat-rate tax-funded pension, payable from age 60 without any means test. The rate at which it was to be paid (for couples) was 80 percent of average ordinary time earnings, with the single rate set at 60 percent of the couple rate. The relatively high replacement rate, the low age of eligibility, the universal coverage, and the absence of a means test meant that the proposal was very generous by any standards, at any time anywhere in the world. These features also provided an electoral advantage, in that there were few losers among new entrants to the scheme that had just been introduced by the Labor government.

The National Party duly won the election and introduced the new pension, which was known as National Superannuation. The generosity of the scheme contained the seeds of its own undoing, however, and it was not long before commentators began to point to the projected rising costs which were an inevitable consequence of population aging. The pressures for change began to build and reforms to the pension became irresistible. Three types of changes were introduced to contain the costs: increases in the age of eligibility; reductions in the replacement rate; and imposition of an income test in the form of a tax claw-back.

The first change involved a graduated increase in the age of entitlement to the pension, from 60 to 65, which it is scheduled to reach in 2001. The second change—a reduction in the replacement rate—was also gradually effected, through indexation of the payment to prices rather than wages. The indexation mechanism has not been a simple price link, but has retained a connection with wage levels, by requiring the rate to be maintained within a wage band, set at between 65 percent and 72.5 percent of average wages. As prices have grown more slowly than wages over the past two decades, the replacement rate has moved inexorably downwards to the floor of the band.[3]

The first change—the increase in age of eligibility—was largely accepted and the second change—the reduction in replacement rate—was little noticed (at least until the previous government's decision to reduce the floor of the wage band to 60 percent). However, the third change—involving the imposition of an additional tax surcharge on other income of superannuitants— proved to be politically contentious. The surcharge was initially introduced in 1985 by a Labor government and then intensified in 1993 by the succeeding National government (which had campaigned to remove it). Opposition to the surcharge crystallized around a new political party, New Zealand First, formed by a group that had splintered from the National government over the broken promise to repeal the surcharge. Abolition of the surcharge now became a defining political issue for the new party.

Following the 1996 election, which was held under changed electoral rules to produce a proportionally representative Parliament, New Zealand First entered government in coalition with the National Party. One non-negotiable item in the coalition deal was the tax surcharge, which was accordingly abolished in 1998. The public pension is now the only program in the New Zealand social security system that is not subject to an income test.

This means that the movement from universal to targeted provision has not been entirely consistent. Indeed, given that the pension is the biggest ticket item in the social security budget, accounting for 15 percent of total government expenditure, this is not a small exception. Nor can it be seen as an aberration, since the result was brought about by electoral politics that reflect the growing voting power of older people. This power is likely to grow as the population ages, with the proportion of over 65-year-olds projected to escalate significantly after 2011.

Downward Adjustments in the Real Rate of Payment of Benefits

In a flat-rate payment system like New Zealand's, where payments are not configured in relation to prior earnings, a key question is how to set the level at which benefits should be paid. In the absence of links to prior living standards at the individual level, another means must be found of linking benefits to prevailing living standards at an aggregated level. This is another area in which there has been a significant shift within the past decade.

The 1972 Royal Commission on Social Security Criterion: "Participation and Belonging." In the early 1970s, a Royal Commission on Social Security deliberated on this matter and propounded the view in its 1972 report that the system should aim "to ensure, within the limitations which may be imposed by physical or other disabilities, that everyone is able to enjoy a standard of living much like that of the rest of the community, and is thus able to feel a sense of *participation in and belonging to* the community." This italicized phrase[4] was subsequently much quoted and came eventually to be seen as describing a benchmark for the level at which benefits should be paid. "Participation and belonging" became part of the language used to describe the New Zealand social security system for the next two decades.

The challenge for the Royal Commission was how to operationalize this concept. Ideally, it would have liked to have had at its disposal some empirical evidence about living standards in the community. Such information was lacking, however, and the Commission was not in a position to commission such work. After rummaging through a range of alternatives, it fixed on two separate measures which it considered appropriate for the purpose of setting a benchmark for the benefit levels: the quartile earnings level calculated from the distribution of income statistics, and the ruling rate of wages for building and engineering laborers. In relation to the latter measure, the Royal Commission noted that

> Its primary advantage lies in the fact that it is an actual rate of pay for 40 hours of work. While it is by no means the highest rate in the work force, it is not the lowest. It represents, moreover, an amount of money on which (after payment of tax) a significant number of families depend for their standard of living and, as such, is an indicator of the "belonging" aim we have set for beneficiaries. (p. 189)

Conveniently, these two rates were found to be approximately equivalent, since it was considered important not to rely on a single benchmark. This rate was not simply to be translated into benefit levels; instead it was to be regarded as a reference point in the process of determining what that level should be. The Royal Commission considered that the actual rate must be set at a somewhat lower level than this benchmark, for four main reasons:

> First, to give an incentive margin, so that people are positively encouraged to work if they can; second, because it costs some part of a wage to travel to and equip oneself for work; third, to ensure that the number of beneficiaries who, with other allowable income, will have larger total incomes than many full-time wage-earners, does not become too great; and fourth, to take account of the fact that in many cases beneficiaries will have accumulated substantial assets. (p.190)

After further rumination, the Royal Commission concluded that the married rate of benefit should be set close to 80 percent of the designated earnings levels after payment of income tax, and that the unmarried rate should be set at 60 percent of the married rate. The married rate turned out to be close to the current couple rate, and the single rate was adjusted in 1973 to bring it into line with the recommended rate.

The indexation question: Attenuation of the wage relativity. Having set what it regarded as an appropriate benchmark for benefit levels, the Royal Commission considered the issue of adequacy of benefits to be largely settled. It gave little attention to the matter of how the rates should be reviewed from year to year. Indeed, it noted that, having considered the factors to be taken into account in fixing standard benefit levels, "little needs to be added about reviewing benefits and keeping them at appropriate levels." What seems to have escaped the Commission is that, if a link with wage levels was required to secure the "participation and belonging" goal, then setting benefit levels in relation to a designated level of wages was only half the task: To maintain the linkage, it would be necessary to have an adjustment mechanism which preserved the relationship with wages. In the event, government adopted an adjustment mechanism that relied purely on movements in prices.

Prices and wages followed different growth trajectories over the ensuing ten years, which had a significant impact on the relativities between benefit rates and wage levels. It is not possible to track changes in the ruling rate of wages for building and engineering laborers, since this rate was subsequently discontinued. Instead, we can compare the trajectory in average wage rates with price inflation. Between March 1973 and March 1982, gross average ordinary time weekly earnings grew by 272 percent, while prices grew by 233 percent. During the 1980s, wages ceased to outstrip prices as inflation spiralled upward. Indeed, during the period March 1982 to March 1991, prices increased by 124 percent compared with wage growth of 110 percent. This meant that benefit levels recouped some of the ground they had lost in comparison with wages in the earlier period. Nevertheless, by March 1991, benefit rates were significantly lower than they would have been if the rates had been indexed to wages after 1973.

Thus, by 1991, the link between benefit rates and wage levels had become relatively attenuated. By now, however, another change was in the offing that would have the effect of completely severing whatever remained (or was believed to remain) of the linkage with wages. This was the decision taken in December 1990, to cut benefit rates, effective 1 April 1991.

The 1991 benefit cuts. The background to the benefit cuts was a projected increase in the budget deficit. The fiscal position had been deteriorating during the course of 1990 as the economy slid into recession and the deficit was projected to rise possibly as high as 6.3 percent of GDP. However, the reasons for the cuts were more complex than this. Government also had a desire to create a wider differential between the benefit level and low wage rates. This had become imperative with the passing of the Employment Contracts Act, which had reformed the industrial relations and wage-fixing structures with the goal of infusing more flexibility into the labor market. This was likely to create downward pressure on wage levels for low-skilled jobs, thus reducing the incentives for people on benefits to move into employment.

Although benefit replacement rates have been reduced in many jurisdictions around the world as decisionmakers have attempted to curb the cost of welfare, in the vast majority of cases such cuts have been implemented in indirect ways—for example by altering the indexation regime, or by freezing rates at fixed values for a period, thus allowing their real value to fall. The New Zealand decisionmakers were more forthright. Eschewing such approaches by stealth, they decreed that benefit rates would be cut directly, by varying amounts dependent on the type of benefit, which would go into effect on 1 April 1991. Whatever else may be said about the decision—and it certainly met with much public criticism—at least it had the merit of transparency as it laid out the extent of the cuts quite publicly and explicitly.

The reductions in benefit rates were not uniform, but varied across different benefits. Indeed, not all rates were reduced, some were preserved, and a small number were increased. This had the effect of changing the allocation

Table 2.3
The 1991 Benefit Cuts: Examples of Rate Changes

Beneficiary type	Old rate	New rate	% Change
Invalid beneficiary, married, one child	$255.08	$270.44	+6.0%
Sickness beneficiary, unmarried, 18-24, no children	$162.26	$129.81	-20.0%
Unemployment beneficiary, unmarried, 18-24, no children	$143.57	$108.17	-24.7%
Lone parent beneficiary, one child	$213.14	$185.93	-12.8%

of assistance to people in different circumstances. Table 2.3 gives examples of rate changes for selected categories of beneficiaries.

Hardest hit were single unemployment beneficiaries aged 20 to 24 without children, whose rate was cut by a quarter. The steepness of the reduction for this group derived from the fact that they were, in effect, being subjected to two changes at once. In addition to the rate cut, the age band for the youth rate was increased from 18 to 24. Single young people aged 20 to 24 were moved to the youth rate (payable at 20 percent less than the adult rate), while the youth rate was itself cut by 5.8 percent. A new youth rate for sickness benefit was also created, involving a 20 percent reduction for single young people without children aged 20 to 24.

Recipients of the domestic purposes benefit fared differently depending on their status. The largest group (single parents) faced cuts of 12.7 percent. Women alone faced a higher cut of 16.7 percent, while those providing domiciliary care for dependent relatives had their rate preserved at the existing level. Invalids beneficiaries fared best under the changes. Those without dependants had their rates preserved at existing levels, as did single persons with dependants. Couples with dependent children received rate increases of 5 percent to 6 percent.

The benefit cuts placed most beneficiaries under additional financial pressure. Almost overnight, a new industry of food banks was created, as voluntary and community agencies sought to provide a new tier of last-resort provision for households that ran out of money between welfare checks. In the first quarter of 1991, just prior to the cuts, the Salvation Army had provided food assistance to 2,124 people nationally. By the first quarter of the following year, the number had exploded to 10,261. In 1989, there had been 16 food banks in the Auckland area. By 1994, the number had mushroomed to more than 130 (Mackay, 1995).

A new benchmark: "A modest standard." Until the benefit cuts, and despite the atrophy of the linkage with wages and thus with community living standards, the phrase "participation and belonging" had continued to be invoked as the aim (or, more latterly at least, the aspiration) of the social security system. However, the benefit cuts forced a re-evaluation of the way the system was described. If the principle of participation and belonging was dying a death of a thousand cuts as price inflation fell behind wage growth, the benefit cuts of 1991 killed it outright in one fell swoop.

In a supplement to the 1991 budget (promoted by the Minister of Finance as the "Mother of All Budgets"), the Minister of Social Welfare made the case for the change, which she characterized as a "major shift in perspective of social welfare."

> The state will continue to provide a safety net—a modest standard below which people will not be allowed to fall provided they demonstrate they are prepared to help themselves.... The Government reaffirms its commitment to protect those who are unable to protect themselves.... Assistance will be closely targeted on genuine need and people will be expected to support themselves when they have the ability to do so. (Shipley, 1991: 13)

The vision of social security articulated here is a more restricted one than the "participation and belonging" formulation of the Royal Commission. In place of the Commission's more embracing and inclusive view, this envisions a more residual role for the state—to provide a safety-net only for those unable to protect themselves, to deliver targeted assistance to those in genuine need, and to furnish those who meet these tests with a modest level of support.

Shifting Axis of Benefit Delivery: Welfare Mix and Privatization

The process of privatization can happen in different ways. The most obvious forms—conversion of a public agency into a private one, or opening up of a public monopoly to competition from the private sector—necessarily occur quite overtly, and thus attract the attention of opposed interests. However, there are also more subtle ways in which the process of privatization can occur, through changes in levels of public provision that encourage people to make their own private arrangements for coverage. In addition, the withdrawal of the state from certain areas of public provision can stimulate the provision of assistance by third-sector organizations. Some of the most important shifts in the welfare mix in New Zealand have had this more subtle character, without attracting significant public notice.

Meanwhile, public attention has largely focused on two failed privatization initiatives of the former type. In the area of accident compensation, a privatizing reform similar to the Dutch disability insurance reforms was introduced by the former National-led government and subsequently reversed by the new Labor-led government. Secondly, a proposed privatizing reform of the public pension, involving compulsory individual retirement accounts on the Chilean model, was resoundingly rejected in a public referendum.

The following discussion will consider these two failed overt privatization moves, together with an account of other more subtle moves that have shifted the welfare mix in the direction of increased private responsibility. One of these changes has been the retreat of the state, over an extended time period, from any involvement in wage-fixing arrangements. Where these were for many years required by statute to deliver a "living wage" sufficient to enable a working man to support a family, they are now conducted purely as a market transaction.

Accident Compensation: To Market and Back Again

New Zealand's social security arrangements have involved very limited use of social insurance-based systems and are almost entirely funded from general taxation, rather than contributions of workers and employers. This has restricted the scope for the types of privatization initiatives that have been undertaken in other countries, such as the Netherlands. One part of New Zealand's social security system which is founded on social insurance principles—and which stands apart from other social security arrangements for this reason—is the accident compensation system. This is a compulsory public system providing no-fault compensation for personal injury (originally to earners only, but soon extended to include non-earners). Funding is drawn from levies on employers, workers and motor vehicle owners, supplemented by a contribution from general revenues. The scheme is administered by the publicly owned Accident Compensation Corporation (ACC).

In a recent reform of the scheme, the Accident Insurance Act 1998 provided for the entry of private providers into the market for insurance cover of personal injury. Under this change, employers were still required to purchase certain levels of cover for their employees, but were able to choose the provider from which they purchased cover. For their part, insurance providers were able to vary the price of the cover offered to employers, thus furnishing an incentive for employers to manage the risk of accidents so as to attract lower premiums.

Prior to their implementation, the changes were subject to some criticism, on a number of grounds. First, it was contended by some commentators that administrative costs would rise, because of the need for marketing by competing providers and because of the loss of economies of scale in collection of levies, as each insurer would need to establish a separate system for this. Secondly, it was argued that, while the new regime would provide choice for employers, there was no element of choice for the people for whom the cover was provided, that is workers and non-earners. This would mean that any advantage delivered to employers by way of lower costs would only be achieved at the expense of the covered population, through tighter controls over entitlement to compensation and rehabilitation (Stritch, 1998).

The new scheme was implemented in July 1999 by the former National-led government. Private providers were free to enter the market and a number of new enterprises were spun off from ACC to face the challenge from the private sector. Anecdotal evidence suggested that, initially at least, the new arrangements led to reductions in employer levies, especially for large-scale enterprises. The changes were opposed by the Labour-led Opposition, however, which pledged to unwind them in a campaign pledge in the 1999 election. The government was duly defeated in the election and the reform has now been reversed. New contracts entered into with private providers were allowed to run their course until 30 June 2000. The spun-off businesses were then reintegrated back into ACC, which has again resumed responsibility for all insurance cover for personal injury.

Pension Reform Rejected: Overwhelming Preference for Retention of Public System

In 1998, another privatization opportunity arose, this time in the public pension, now known as New Zealand Superannuation. This arose out of the changed political landscape brought about by a reform of the electoral representation system. The 1996 election was the first to be held under the new proportional representation rules and the deal-making that followed brought the New Zealand First Party into coalition with the National Party, which had formerly governed in its own right. As noted above, a considerable part of New Zealand First's electoral appeal derived from its policies on the public pension. Two changes were high on the party's bargaining priorities in the coalition negotiations. The first was the abolition of the controversial tax surcharge. The second was a national referendum on the introduction of a new compulsory private superannuation scheme.

The proposed scheme had the following features, which bore a resemblance to the reformed Chilean pension: it was to be funded entirely from worker's contributions; the contributions were to be paid into privately managed funds; contributors were to be free to choose the fund to which they contributed; the funds were to be free to compete for clients; and contributors were to be free to switch between funds, subject to specified notice periods.

It differed from the Chilean scheme by incorporating a stronger mechanism for reducing the degree to which retirees would be exposed to the risk of low income in old age. Once an individual reached age 65, the accumulated fund held in the individual's name was to be used to purchase a fixed-rate annuity. If the balance fell short of the amount needed to purchase the annuity, a top-up would be provided by the government. If it exceeded this requirement, the excess would revert to the contributor. Women would be provided with a special top-up to recognize the higher market price for female annuities because of their longer life expectancy.

In the event, however, these guarantees of a basic pension right were insufficient to persuade the public to vote for the scheme and it was decisively rejected by the electorate by a margin of 92 percent against and 8 percent for. The New Zealand public thus resoundingly restated their preference for a taxpayer-funded pay-as-you-go public pension scheme.

It is instructive to contrast the New Zealand decision to stick with its public pension with the Australian case, where a compulsory contributory private retirement scheme was implemented in 1993, which also bore a familial resemblance to the reformed Chilean pension. There were some design differences between the New Zealand proposal and the Superannuation Guarantee Charge (SGC), as the new Australian scheme is known, which may help to explain the different receptions they were accorded by their respective publics.

First, the SGC exists as a separate and complementary pillar alongside the public pension that continues to exist as a safety net provision, subject to income and asset tests. While the internal income guarantee in the proposed New Zealand scheme would have performed the same function of ensuring a minimum income in old age for all citizens, it is possible that there was a perception in New Zealand that the new private scheme was about to swallow the existing public pension, where in Australia there was a clearer appreciation of the distinct roles of the separate pillars. Secondly, the Australian scheme was to be funded initially by employers' contributions, with employees' contributions only to be phased in over time. By contrast, the proposed New Zealand scheme was to be funded entirely by employees' contributions, which were to be offset by tax cuts. This difference is also likely to have contributed to the difference in acceptability of the proposals to the two electorates.

Whatever the reason, the referendum result has set New Zealand on a different policy trajectory from its trans-Tasman neighbor for the foreseeable future. It will be of interest to observe how the two countries fare in managing the challenges posed by aging populations.

From Family Wage to Market Wage

In contrast to these failed privatization initiatives, there have been a number of other changes which have produced a shift in the welfare mix in the direction of increased private responsibility. In most cases, these have resulted from the withdrawal of the state from involvement in public provision of various sorts, which has stimulated the growth of private and community-level arrangements. One such shift, which worked itself out over a long timetable, has been the withdrawal of the state from wage-fixing arrangements.

For much of its history, New Zealand relied upon the wage-fixing system to ensure that families were provided with sufficient resources to raise children. A key institution in this system was the Arbitration Court. Like many other of New Zealand's early welfare arrangements, the Court was created by the socially activist Liberal government, in 1894. It was empowered to make determinations relating to wages and allowances that would apply to all members of unions in a designated class of labor. The Court based its determinations on the concept of a "fair wage," founded on observations about what employers were actually paying for a particular class of labor.

The family wage. Over time, the Court's notion of a "fair wage" came to be conceived in terms of a "living wage" that would allow the raising of a family. By 1925, the Court declared that a minimum basic wage should be sufficient to maintain a man, his wife, and two dependent children. Although this represented a significant achievement, which afforded a significant level of social protection for its members, the union movement considered this to be no time to rest on its laurels. The pronouncement was contested on a range of grounds, one of which was that a more appropriate standard would be a man, his wife and three dependent children. This became a point on which the unions kept up a sustained campaign. In 1936, when a Labor government had finally come to power, the goal was eventually achieved and, moreover, written into legislation. The Industrial Conciliation and Arbitration Amendment Act of 1936 contained the following provision in section 3(5):

> The basic rate of wages for adult male workers fixed under the authority of this section shall be such a rate as would, in the opinion of the Court, be sufficient to enable a man in receipt thereof to maintain a wife and three children in a fair and reasonable standard of comfort. (Woods, 1963: 138)

As Woods notes, the government had thus conceded a point that the Court itself had steadfastly refused to grant on the grounds that this was larger than the average family size.

> There was offered no material justification for such a basis other than a suggestion that it would enable and encourage workers to have larger families and thereby be to the advantage of the country. There was no refutation of the Court's own view in earlier years that in paying for the maintenance of three children per family industry would be paying out on non-existent children. (Woods, 1963: 138)

The landmark Social Security Act of 1938 thus set down the rule that male wages had to be fixed at a level which would allow a worker to support a wife and three children. The male wage—unlike female wages, which were set at lower levels—was to be considered as a family wage.

It is possible to overstate the importance of this provision. The Court made no inquiry into the actual level of income that might be required to support a man, his wife, and three dependent children. Rather it made some desultory inquiries into various related and unrelated statistics and then, without further analysis, settled on a minimum wage rate which resulted in no general wage increases, since the majority of awards current at the time already exceeded the amount laid down by the Court.

> Many workers had expected a substantial gain through the application of the man, wife, and three children formula, but the trade unions generally accepted the basic wage of 1936 as a reasonable satisfactory minimum of protection. The decision clearly indicated a recognition in the Court and outside that the Court must deal with realities and not theoretic propositions.... Families were already living on the remuneration their breadwinners were receiving. (Woods, 1963: 142)

The basic wage was never subsequently updated by the Court and eventually became, in Woods' term, a "dead letter." When the Industrial Conciliation and Arbitration Act was re-enacted in 1954, the clause was quietly omitted.

Nevertheless, while its effect on actual wage levels may have been slight, its symbolic value was significant. Its presence in the legislation stood as a powerful reminder of the role of the state in protecting the interests of workers and their families.

Over time, though, the weaknesses of such a basis of wage fixing became more apparent. As Easton (1980) noted, "whatever the good intentions of such a wage strategy, its weakness is that if a wage is basic for a family of five, it is luxurious for a single man, and penurious for a family of nine. Moreover, one could hardly ask employers to pay rates according to the worker's family circumstances, if only because it would provide an incentive to employ single men and women" (p. 105). By 1951—significantly, after the demise of the first Labour government and with a conservative National government now in power—the Court specifically repudiated the principle of clause 3(5) of the old 1936 Amendment. As Woods notes,

> The Court firmly rejected a contention that it should base its decision on the requirements of a man, wife, and three children.... The Court also referred to the existence of universal family allowances as a separate measure to relieve the burden on the worker with children to support; the Court implied that in its view any submissions as to the adequacy with which a worker could support a family of more than average size should be addressed to the legislature which controlled family allowances rather than to the Court. (Woods, 1963: 173)

As this indicates, other ways had now been found to meet the needs of workers with families. These included not only family allowances (first instituted, on a means-tested basis, in 1927 and then extended, after 1946, to all children on a universal basis), but also tax rebates for families with children and child supplements for people receiving social security benefits.

The market wage. The old arrangements for wage-fixing came under pressure in the late 1960s as inflation began to rise and broke down completely in the 1970s, as wages and prices both spiralled ever upwards in ways that seemed beyond the power of government to control. A succession of stabilization acts and regulations ensued as governments tried to limit the damage of a never-ending round of wage claims, which both fed off and further stimulated other claims. A passing parade of institutions for wage-fixing each took their turn on the stage in place of the Arbitration Court—a Remuneration Authority, a Wages Tribunal, an Industrial Commission, a Wage-Hearing Tribunal, and then a revivified Arbitration Court. Periodically government took more direct control of the process by simply freezing wages, in despair at the lack of other alternatives.

These various arrangements through the course of the 1970s and 1980s merely served to reshuffle the same old deck. In effect, the days of a moribund ancient régime were numbered. The old institutions were eventually swept away by a new round of reform, commencing with the Labor Relations Act of 1987, implemented by the Labor government. As Walsh and Brosnan (1999) note, this enactment led to some significant restructuring of bargaining structures, and "pointed to the possibilities for much more flexible approaches to bargaining" (p. 118). However, it left intact the statutory monopoly of unions over the bargaining process on the employee side at a time when most other market areas had been deregulated. There was now a significant business lobby arguing for more radical reform. In particular, the case was made for employment arrangements to be negotiated at the enterprise level, to allow employment contracts between workers and employers to reflect the specific financial position of individual firms.

The National government, which had come to power in 1990, shared this view. The result was the Employment Contracts Act of 1991. This Act brought radical change to industrial relations arrangements, principally by redefining the role played by trade unions in wage-fixing procedures. As Walsh and Brosnan (1999) note, the Act broke the historical link between unions and negotiating authority by stipulating that "any employee or employer, in negotiating for an employment contract, may conduct the negotiations on his or her own behalf or may choose to be represented by another person, group or organisation." This meant that unions no longer had any monopoly right to represent workers in negotiations with employers over industrial matters, including wage-fixing.

While the Act preserved the right of workers to strike, strikes were not permitted where the matter at issue was whether a collective employment contract should bind more than one employer. This proved to be a crucial provision, since—at a time when more and more employers were seeing a need to negotiate contracts which reflected their own circumstances in the reformed marketplace and when the government supported them in these aims—union power was the only thing holding things together at the center. Once this power was removed, the centrifugal forces inherent in disparate employers' needs was likely to lead inevitably to a fragmentation of the bargaining process across a multitude of workplaces.

This indeed has been one of the major outcomes of the Act. As Walsh and Brosnan (1999) note, the major change to the bargaining process

> ...has been the abandonment of the multi-employer bargaining that typified the arbitration system for almost a century. This is a direct consequence of the provision in the Employment Contracts Act that allows employers to choose between enterprise and multi-employer bargaining, and prohibits unions from undertaking any industrial action to achieve a multi-employer contract. Employers have exercised this option decisively in favour of enterprise bargaining. Just on one-third of the workforce are employed on single-employer collective contracts, and only 7 percent on multi-employer contracts. (p. 128)

The consequences of this fragmentation are likely to have been significant, although these are difficult to map in detail since, as Walsh and Brosnan (1999) note, employment contracts are private documents and are not published. They point to a deterioration in employment conditions since 1991, particularly in areas such as penal and overtime rates, and cite Harbridge's (1994) finding that traditional wage relativities have been broken and that there is a wider dispersion of wage settlements under the Act. There is also evidence that real wages have continued to fall during the 1990s, although it is not possible to attribute this entirely to the Employment Contract Act, since it continues a longer-run trend dating from the 1980s.

The story does not quite end there. In October 2000, the Employment Contracts Act of 1991 was repealed by the new Labor-led government and replaced by the Employment Relations Act. The new law makes some significant changes to the industrial relations framework. In particular, it restores unions to primacy of place at the bargaining table: only registered unions and employers are now able to negotiate and enter into collective agreements. However, this provision is mitigated by a further provision that allows a union to be formed by as few as two people, provided certain other requirements are met. The bill also permits unions to strike in pursuit of single or multi-party collective agreements. However, it is unlikely that this provision will be able to reverse the significant decentralization in bargaining that has already been brought about by the Employment Contracts Act. That horse has now bolted. What the bill makes no attempt to restore is any notion of the family wage in the wage-fixing process. That ideal perished many years prior to the passing of the Employment Contracts Act.

Retreat of the State and Expansion of Private Arrangements

A range of other changes to the welfare mix has also come about as a result of the retreat of the state from social provision in various areas. Some of this has resulted from changes discussed elsewhere in this chapter—reductions in benefit entitlements, imposition of user charges for healthcare services, changed ages of entitlements to benefits—which have all had flow-on implications for the welfare mix, by stimulating the adoption of private arrangements and community-level provision to cover lost entitlements to public benefits.

The following discussion will refer briefly to four particular shifts. First, an increasing share of healthcare expenditure is privately funded. Secondly, new markets are emerging for private insurance for loss of earnings by reason of sickness and injury. Thirdly, the years of dependence of young adults on their families have increased, as a result of reduced entitlements to social security benefits. Finally, the third sector has assumed an expanded role in meeting the basic needs of families.

Growing private share of expenditure on health care. Prior to the Social Security Act of 1938, most healthcare outlays were privately funded. In 1925, private funding accounted for around 57 percent of total health expenditure. By 1945, however, the public share had grown to 74 percent of total health expenditure. This share continued to increase and by the early 1980s, it peaked at 88 percent (Ministry of Health, 2000).

During the mid-1980s, however, growth in public expenditure on health stalled. Over the eleven-year period between 1982 and 1993, real per capita public expenditure on health fell in seven of the eleven years. While the losses were counterbalanced by significant increases in the four intervening years, the real per capita value of public expenditure on health over this period changed only by the minuscule amount of 0.1 percent. Demand for health services was not stagnant, however, and the resulting deficit in expenditure was made up from private purses. Over the eleven-year period, real per capita private expenditure on health increased by 128 percent. Over the two decades between 1980 and 1999, private sector health expenditure grew at an average nominal rate of 13.5 percent, equating to 6.2 percent in real terms.

As a result of the different growth trajectories of public and private expenditure on health, by the year ending 30 June 1999, the public share of health expenditure had slipped back to 77 percent and private expenditure now accounted for nearly a quarter of all expenditure on health.

The largest portion of private health expenditure is out-of-pocket expenditure by private individuals. By 30 June 1999, this accounted for 71 percent of private expenditure and 16 percent of total expenditure on health. The remainder (apart from a very small share by not-for-profit organizations) is expenditure by private health insurers. In 1999, this accounted for 28 percent of private expenditure and 6 percent of all expenditure on health. The market for private health insurance has been growing rapidly over the past decade and a half. In 1980 total expenditure on private health insurance had amounted to $16 million. By 1990 this had expanded nearly ten-fold to $142 million, and by 1999 it had grown further to $520 million. The most rapid period of growth was in the early 1990s. Between the years 1990 and 1994, expenditure by private health insurers more than doubled, while the share of total health expenditure grew from 2.8 percent to 6.1 percent. This rapid growth is likely to have been stimulated by the new public health user charge regime which came into effect in 1991, increasing the costs for middle and high income earners.

Growth of new private insurance markets for loss of earnings. The growth of private health insurance is paralleled by the emergence of new markets for private insurance cover for loss of earnings, by reason of sickness and injury. While the public social security system provides benefits for people who are unable to work by reason of sickness or disability, the payments are flat-rate and bear no relation to private earnings. This provides an incentive for higher income earners to take additional insurance cover to replace lost income. Such schemes typically replace up to 75 percent of prior earnings. Insurance products are also available to cover mortgage repayments or repayments of other advances, including credit card debt, in the event of sickness or injury.

These new markets are relatively recent developments and information is difficult to come by on their size or rate of growth. No doubt they are still very minor components of the total insurance picture and expenditure on such products would be dwarfed by the scale of the public social security system. They are likely to be of interest primarily to professional salaried classes. The significant increases in income inequality over the past decade and a half, fuelled largely by high rates of growth at the top end of the income distribution, however, indicate that there is likely to be an assured future market for such products.

Lengthening years of dependence of young adults on their families. The 1991 budget introduced a number of changes that restricted the entitlement of younger people to social security benefits. Young people aged 16 and 17 were no longer eligible for unemployment benefit (although new provisions were created for restricted groups of young people, such as those whose relationship with their parents had irretrievably broken down). The level of provision for young adults was also reduced. Single unemployment and sickness beneficiaries aged 18 to 24 with no dependent children were now paid at the youth rate (set at 80 percent of the adult rate).

Similar changes were also made to tertiary student allowances. Universal student allowances were abolished in 1992 and replaced by income-tested allowances. Under the new income-test, eligibility for a student allowance was assessed not only against the claimant's income, but also (for those aged less than 25) against the claimant's parents' income.

These policy changes were based on the principle that parents should continue to have responsibility for providing financial support for their children up to the age of 25. This has been characterized by some commentators as lengthening the years of dependency of young people, and delaying the achievement of full adulthood until the age of 25.

Expanding role of the third sector in meeting basic needs. The cuts to basic benefit rates in 1991 placed beneficiaries under additional financial pressure. One result of this was an explosion in demand for assistance from voluntary social service agencies, in particular food banks. Prior to the benefit cuts, food banks had occupied a minor place in New Zealand's array of welfare services. At the end of the 1980s, there were 16 food banks operating in the Auckland metropolitan area, with its population of close to 900,000 (MacKay, 1995). By 1994, there were 130 food banks. Statistics from the Salvation Army, a major operator of a national network of food banks, show that between 1990 and 1992, the volume of food parcels provided in the first quarter of the year leapt from 1,226 to 10,261. In 1994, it was estimated that around $25 million of assistance was being provided annually by food banks, mainly to families reliant on income support (Mackay, 1995).

An increase in second-tier supplementary assistance in 1994 produced a significant decline in demand for food parcels in the Auckland area, estimated at 30 percent, and a more moderate decline elsewhere in the country, estimated at 13 percent (Mackay, 1995). Since then, robust statistics on demand for food parcels have been somewhat hard to come by. Food banks are run by a range of unrelated organizations and there is no comprehensive national collation of statistics. It is likely, though, that demand has not reduced to any significant further degree since the mid-1990s. Food banks continue to provide significant volumes of assistance to New Zealand families.

During the course of the 1990s, an accommodation was made between the public social security system and the third sector to ensure that food banks were not using their resources to meet needs for which public provision was available. Staff of the Department of Work and Income began to issue beneficiaries with statements verifying that they were receiving all the assistance to which they were entitled. Food banks would provide claimants with food parcels on presentation of such a certificate. This process provided formal recognition of the expanded role of the third sector in meeting the basic needs of low-income New Zealanders.

Social Activation and Work-Oriented Policies

Another significant shift in recent welfare reforms has been an increased emphasis on welfare-to-work goals (Mackay, 2001). These changes have involved a range of different policy instruments—including incentives, sanctions and facilitative assistance, as well as some institutional reform—all aimed at the goal of encouraging people to move off benefit and into employment.

One way of characterizing these reforms is as a shift from a passive system of income support (where the state's role is restricted to verification of eligibility for assistance and administering payments once eligibility is established) to a more active system (where the state assumes more interest in helping people move off benefit and into employment). Another way of characterizing the reforms is as a shift in the status of benefits as relatively unattached entitlements (whose recipients incur no obligation other than demonstrating that they fulfil the eligibility criteria) to a more contingent form of assistance (where the recipients incur a set of obligations in return for the assistance they receive). This constitutes a fundamental change in the relationship between the recipient of benefits and the state that provides them.

There are indications, however, that a limit may have now been reached to reform in this area, following the recent change of government. While there has been no change in the goal of encouraging movement off benefit and into employment, there has been a change in the way this is to be brought about, involving a different mix of policy instruments. In brief, the new government aims to place less reliance on mandatory requirements and more emphasis on facilitative assistance aimed at assisting people to make the transition into employment.

This section will provide an overview of the welfare-to-work reforms undertaken by National-led governments throughout the 1990s, locating these in context, with some additional comment on how these have been amended by the recent change of government.

Background to the Welfare-to-Work Changes

Until the mid-1980s, the income support system in New Zealand operated very much as a passive system, in which primary emphasis was placed on establishing the entitlement of a claimant to a benefit. Where an entitlement was established, payment was duly arranged as prescribed by statute and regulation. Once they were on the welfare rolls, little further attention was paid to beneficiaries and few conditions were imposed on them. Single parents were required to provide notification of any change in their circumstances (in particular if they had re-partnered or taken employment). In the absence of such change, they were entitled to continue to receive benefits until their youngest child turned 16. Invalids beneficiaries were generally regarded as likely to continue for long periods, and many continued benefits until they qualified for the public pension. Sickness beneficiaries were required periodically to provide certificates from a medical practitioner attesting their continuing incapacity to work, although in practice this proved only a formality for many people. Unemployment beneficiaries had a number of conditions imposed upon them. They were required actively to search for,

and be available to take up employment. Even for this group, the requirement was hardly onerous and required little enforcement while jobs remained
plentiful.

This system had worked reasonably well for most of the postwar period,
when plenty of work was available. While unemployment remained low—
and for much of the postwar period it was astonishingly low—the numbers of
people receiving unemployment benefits naturally also remained low, with
most staying on for short periods only, while the numbers receiving other
benefits were also at relatively low and stable levels.

Difficulties arose when—as in most other developed countries—the
economy began to experience some turbulence in the mid-1970s. The first oil
shock in 1973 plunged the New Zealand economy into a crisis which had
been pending for some years as a result of a long period of slowly declining
terms of trade. The effect on the unemployment rate was seismic: from March
1974 when only 483 people were receiving unemployment benefit, the numbers jumped to 17,484 in March 1978 and continued to grow past 50,000 in
1983, 100,000 in 1989, and 150,000 in 1992. The number of people who
were registered as unemployed was even higher and passed 215,000 in 1992.
In this year the official unemployment rate peaked at 10.9 percent. The effects flowed on to other benefits. As job opportunities evaporated, many
single parents and people with health problems withdrew completely from
the labor market, causing significant growth in other benefits.

Although the economy improved after 1992, with a drop in the unemployment rate (down to 6.2 percent by 1996), it was clear that the old days of
virtual zero unemployment were gone for good and that policy would now
have to be predicated on the existence of a sizeable pool of people who were
out of work, many of whom were finding it difficult to compete in the transformed labor market where skills were at a premium. This meant, in turn, that
many of those without skills were increasingly likely to spend longer spells
receiving benefits.

In addition, while the recovering economy generated sufficient jobs to
make significant inroads into unemployment—with the result that the number of people receiving unemployment benefit had fallen by more than 20
percent from 170,367 in 1992 to 134,133 in 1996, the number of people on
other benefits—especially sickness, invalids and domestic purposes benefits—had continued to grow. Indeed the growth in these latter benefits was
sufficiently large in that, despite the drop in numbers in unemployment benefit, the total number of people receiving benefits in 1996 was slightly higher
than in 1992.

This suggested that a broader view had to be taken of the issue of increasing dependency on welfare, since a focus on the unemployed would not be
sufficient to reduce the numbers of people in receipt of welfare benefits. For
this reason, the focus of policy reforms through the 1990s shifted to the

Figure 2.1
**Levels of Receipt of Unemployment and Training Benefit; Sickness and
Invalids Benefit; Domestic Purposes and Widows Benefit, 1970-1998**

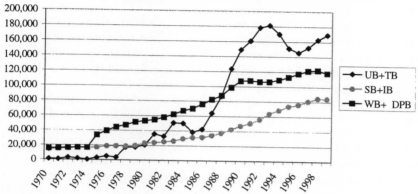

broader group of beneficiaries of working age—including single parents and
people with disabilities, sickness or injury—who were seen as at least potential participants in the labor force, and who were to be encouraged to take
steps towards more active participation in it. The new policy approach began
to cohere around the idea of welfare-to-work, applied to this broader group.

Under this new view, the primary goal in interactions with beneficiaries
was, wherever possible, to assist them to become self-supporting by taking up
work opportunities. To achieve the goal, income support policy was rede-
signed to provide a set of signals to encourage beneficiaries to take steps to
move into work. These included both negative measures—primarily in the
form of a strengthened work requirement, backed up by stiffer sanctions for
noncompliance with the requirement—and positive measures—primarily in
the form of facilitative assistance programs aimed at assisting people make
the transition to work, backed up by enhanced returns to work through establishment of in-work benefits and a relaxation in the rate of withdrawal of
benefit as earnings rise. These changes were accompanied by some restructuring of programs to emphasize the welfare-to-work message and changes in
service delivery aimed at supporting the new policy direction.

Strengthened Work Expectations

Historically, the only group of beneficiaries in New Zealand that had been
subject to a work test (that is, who were required to search actively for work
and to take up any employment opportunity that became available) were
people receiving unemployment benefit. In line with the new thinking, the
work test was extended to cover a broader range of income support claimants.

Three groups in particular were affected by the changes. From February 1999, single parents with children aged 14 or older became subject to a full-time work test, while those with children aged 6 to 13 became subject to a part-time work test.

The second group that was newly subject to a work test were spouses or partners of beneficiaries. Where there were children, the work test operated in the same way as for single parents. Prior to this change, the work test had covered only the individual recipient of the benefit, and spouses of beneficiaries had not been subject to any requirement.

The new work requirements were backed up with some additional assistance: a child care subsidy was made available to low-income working parents with children aged 5 to 13 to cover the costs of out-of-school care. Additional job search and training assistance was also made available to assist those who needed help to meet their new obligations.

The third group to be subject to a new work requirement were people with a disability, sickness or injury who were assessed as having a capacity for full-time work. This requirement was not to be introduced immediately, but trialed over a three-year period in a small selection of pilot sites, during which a newly developed procedure for testing work capacity would be fully evaluated.

The strengthened work requirements were backed up by a menu of sanctions that could be applied in cases of noncompliance with the requirement. Sanctions could be applied in a range of circumstances, including failure to accept an offer of suitable work, failure to participate in an organized activity (such as interviews, work assessment, training, work experience or medical or psychological assessments), unsatisfactory performance in an organized activity, and voluntary unemployment (including dismissal for misconduct).

The sanctions regime was a graduated one, with penalties becoming increasingly severe for repeated instances of noncompliance. For a first failure to accept a suitable job offer, for example, the benefit could be suspended for a minimum period of one week, and until such time as the person complied with the requirement. For a second failure, the benefit could be suspended for a period of thirteen weeks. In practice, however, these sanctions were applied only sparingly by the Department of Work and Income.

Many of these changes, however, are now being unwound by the new Labor-led government, and it appears that a limit has now been reached in welfare-to-work reforms based on mandatory sanction-based approaches. In particular, the new government has halted the trial of the work capacity assessment procedure and people with a sickness, injury or disability will not be brought within the work-testing framework. Secondly, the government has signalled an intention to review the work testing of single parents. Thirdly, the role of sanctions is also being re-examined by the new government and is likely to undergo some changes. In place of these mandatory sanction-based provisions, the new government has signalled that it intends to place more emphasis on facilitative assistance to help people make the transition into employment.

Enhanced Returns from Work

If the strengthened work requirements and sanctions that back them up represented a "stick," a "carrot" was also provided in the form of enhanced returns from work. A range of methods has been employed to improve the returns generated by work as people move off benefit and into employment. Recent reforms have focused on the use of in-work benefits and relaxation of the rate at which benefits are withdrawn as earnings increase.

Tax credit programs. In 1986, a tax credit program known as the guaranteed minimum family income had been introduced for full-time working families with children. This was intended to provide a minimum income guarantee to low-income earner families (now set at the level of $286 per week), and additionally to provide a margin between benefit levels and the minimum disposable income available to full-time earners. To qualify, a single parent had to be employed for at least 20 hours per week and a couple had to have a combined total of at least 30 hours' employment per week. It was not payable to anyone receiving benefits.

Another tax credit program, known as the independent family tax credit, was added in 1996 and again targeted at low-income families not receiving a benefit. This was a more highly developed program than the guaranteed minimum family income. The payment rate was graduated according to the number of children in the family and it delivered assistance to families higher up the income range. Government's specific goal in creating the new tax credit— rather than giving a flat increase in family assistance to all families with children—was to widen the margin between those in work and those on benefit. These two programs were subsequently repackaged as, respectively, the family tax credit and the child tax credit.

The incomes of low earners with children are likely to have been improved by these programs, although little is known about their effect in detail. No systematic research has been undertaken into their impact on labor supply behavior and so it is not possible to draw any firm conclusions about their effectiveness in contributing to welfare-to-work goals. However—although firm figures are hard to come by—it is known that take-up of both programs has been relatively low. There would appear to be a relatively low level of awareness and understanding of the nature and purpose of both programs among the general community, which is likely to be related to the lack of any significant effort to promote them. This raises a question as to the effectiveness of their contribution to welfare-to-work goals.

Relaxed abatement rates. One of the problems with income-tested benefits is the high effective marginal tax rates they produce, through the combined effects of tax on earnings and withdrawal of benefit payments as earned income rises. Typically, most beneficiaries in New Zealand face effective marginal tax rates of close to 100 percent for significant reaches of the potential earnings range, which means that for each dollar earned, little is retained after tax is paid and benefit income is withdrawn. As a result, people who take up work opportunities may not be much better off financially for their efforts. This results in a significant disincentive for people to move off benefit and into work.

In 1996, a policy change was made to improve the returns from employment for all beneficiaries, and to provide an additional advantage to invalids, widows and domestic purposes beneficiaries. The income disregard was increased from $50 (or $60 for those with children) to $80 per week for all beneficiaries. For the specified subgroup of beneficiaries, the rate of withdrawal (or, in New Zealand parlance, abatement) of the benefit was 30 cents for each dollar of earnings between $80 and $180 per week and 70 cents in the dollar above this level of earnings. Other beneficiaries faced an abatement rate of 70 cents for each dollar of earnings above $80 per week. (Prior to the change, the 30-cent rate had applied only up to $80 of earnings per week, for all beneficiaries, while the 70-cent rate had applied to all higher earnings.) The special regime that now applied to invalids, widows and domestic purposes beneficiaries recognized that single parents and people with disabling health conditions were often more easily able to take up part-time than full-time work.

Facilitative Assistance

These various incentives for beneficiaries to move into work were supported by a range of facilitative assistance programs aimed at assisting beneficiaries to make the transition to employment, including information and job search services, targeted training courses, work confidence seminars, work experience placements and wage subsidy programs.

In addition, specialized programs of facilitative assistance were targeted at particular subgroups of beneficiaries. One successful example was the Compass program for single parents. Compass was a voluntary program aimed at assisting single parent beneficiaries make the transition into education, training or employment through individualized case management, with referral to training opportunities and assistance with job search.

The program was piloted in selected sites in 1994-95. An evaluation demonstrated that participation in the program increased Compass volunteers' chances of going off benefit by 57 percent and increased their chances of starting new training or education by 207 percent (Rochford, 1995). On the basis of the successful pilot results, the program was rolled out nationally.

Such facilitative interventions were provided within the context of a case management model for managing interactions with income support beneficiaries. Under this model, each beneficiary was allocated to an individual case manager who took responsibility for all transactions with that beneficiary. The aim was not only to improve service levels to beneficiaries but also to increase their awareness of the need to plan for self-reliance. The beneficiary and the case manager were expected to prepare a plan to chart a route to self-reliance for the beneficiary, utilizing referrals to education, training and employment opportunities, as appropriate for each client.

Program Restructuring

In October 1998, the former unemployment and sickness benefits were disestablished, and were replaced by a new community wage program. The change in program title was significant, signalling a shift from a passive to a more active form of support: The payment was no longer to be regarded as a "benefit" for which no obligation is expected in return, while the word "wage" signalled the strengthened job search requirement. Under the new program, provision was also made for recipients to be required to undertake community work as an alternative to employment.

The disestablishment of a separate sickness benefit—instead people with temporary disabling health problems were able to apply for a temporary deferral of the work-test that applied to recipients of the community wage—was designed to prevent people with short-term health problems from becoming disconnected from the labor market and thus becoming exposed to the risk of long-term dependency on welfare. The rate differential that existed between the former sickness and unemployment benefits was eliminated, by freezing the rate at which former sickness beneficiaries were paid until the two rates attained equivalence. This rate differential, combined with the absence of a work-test for sickness beneficiaries, provided a double incentive for people to migrate from unemployment to sickness benefit. The conjoint attractions of a higher paying and comparatively hassle-free benefit—combined with the difficulty that people with low skills had in finding employment—was considered to have lain behind some of the growth in rates of receipt of sickness benefit in recent years.

These changes are also being unwound by the new Labor-led government. The community wage program is to be disestablished and beneficiaries will no longer be required to participate in community work, although they may continue to do so on a voluntary basis. Separate benefits will be re-established for the sick and the unemployed.

Institutional Changes in Delivery Mechanisms

These various changes were supported by service delivery reforms aimed at giving best effect to the welfare-to-work initiatives. In 1998, the former Income Support service (which was part of the Department of Social Welfare) and the New Zealand Employment Service (which was part of the Department of Labor) were merged into a new Department of Work and Income. The new department was responsible for provision of both income support and employment services. The bringing together of these two functions under a single roof was intended to allow a better integration of the two sets of services. In addition to assessing entitlements to benefits and making payments where these were met, the new department would apply the work-test and any other requirements placed on beneficiaries, and assist them to meet these obligations by providing job-search and other employment-related services.

The conjoint management of these functions was a crucial aspect of the change. This allowed an explicit connection to be made between benefit receipt and the work requirement. Interactions with claimants of income support were now premised on the basis that they would be expected to seek out and take up employment opportunities and helped to do so through the active assistance of their case management officer.

Implications: The Emerging Borders of the Welfare State

The changes outlined above have served to redefine the borders of the welfare state in quite significant ways. The restructured welfare state is now leaner and more parsimonious, directing more of its payments to those who are demonstrably in need. It has contracted its limits in certain areas, stimulating the emergence of other forms of private and community provision to make up the deficit. And it places more onerous requirements on recipients of benefits to ensure that they are receiving public support only while they are unable to provide for themselves. The implications of change in these three areas are discussed briefly below.

Changes in the Allocation of Social Benefits

In one sense, increased targeting involving more elaborate methods for assessing entitlement to benefits is simply a response to the increasing complexity of the world. A question may be raised, however, about the effectiveness of this response. A principal plank in the argument in favor of targeted assistance is that higher levels of assistance can be delivered to people in need by withholding assistance from those who are not in need. There is no doubt that the targeting changes have delivered a greater proportion of assistance to people in the lower reaches of the income distribution and a lesser proportion to those who are better off. On the face of it, it seems likely that this would have resulted in increased levels of social protection. However, such an outcome is by no means beyond doubt. There are a number of reasons why it may not come about in practice.

First, if programs become overly complex—making them difficult for claimants to understand, for delivery agency staff to explain and for governments to promote—then this is likely to result in lower rates of take-up, which, in turn, is likely to have a negative impact on overall levels of social protection. The New Zealand system has certainly become more complex and elaborate as a result of the targeting changes and there is some evidence that parts of the system are not well promoted and not well understood by potential claimants. It is difficult to be sure about the precise degree to which this may have compromised levels of social protection, since there is a dearth of evidence about levels of take-up of these programs.

Secondly, where increasing reliance on second-tier programs is accompanied by reductions in levels of assistance made available through the first tier—as has been the case in New Zealand, especially when benefit rates were cut in 1991—this is likely to exacerbate the problems of gaps in coverage, since second-tier programs generally have lower rates of take-up than first-tier provisions. In addition, the increased levels of supplementary assistance available to people in special need may not have left them any better off in real terms, since this may have only offset income lost in the cuts to the rate of basic benefit.

Thirdly, it might also be argued that excluding better-off citizens from significant dividends from the social security system carries a risk of undermining public support for the system, which may lead to progressive reductions in levels of provision. Under this scenario, once a state embarks on a course of targeted benefits, one possible outcome would be a degenerative spiral as levels of public support and levels of public provision wound down synchronously.

Levels of provision were reduced in New Zealand when most benefit rates were cut in 1991. However, this change did not seem to have been made primarily as a result of public pressure to reduce benefits. Indeed, at the time, it created considerable public debate and controversy. Even so (in contrast to the parallel controversy over means testing of the public pension), restoration of the previous level of provision has not been taken up by any political party as a defining "litmus-test" issue. The incoming Labor-led government has made no signal that it intends to restore the level of benefits to their pre-1991 levels, and policies to help the poor center rather on other concerns such as the move away from market rentals for state housing tenants.

Part of the reason for this may be that there is less scope to increase benefit levels in the light of changes in the labor market effected by industrial relations reform, which constrained wage levels for low-skilled jobs. Any upward adjustment of benefit rates would be likely to cause perverse incentives—both for those on benefits to cease active efforts to find work and for those in low-paying jobs to give up work and apply for benefits. But perhaps it also points to the lack of a broader public constituency for more generous levels of income support.

Overall, the 1991 benefit cuts were likely to have had a negative impact on levels of social protection. Even if it is true that benefit rates were relatively generous prior to the cuts, there is a range of evidence that some families are now experiencing difficulties in managing their incomes and are unable to feed themselves without recourse to food banks (Ministry of Health, 1999; Waldegrave et al., 1999), although there are few robust estimates of the proportion of the population experiencing such difficulties.

On the other hand, it is also possible that the benefit cuts may have stimulated some people receiving benefits to find work who otherwise might not have done so, and they may also have led others to make more strenuous efforts to avoid the need to rely on benefits, so that some individuals may be better off as a result. Overall, however, there can be no doubt that receiving benefits is likely to involve a higher risk of material hardship since the benefit cuts, even if there be fewer people on benefits who are exposed to that risk.

Changes in the Welfare Mix

The changes to the welfare mix have been more complex. While most of the public debate and discussion has focused on two failed privatization initiatives—in the public pension and accident compensation—other more subtle and subterranean shifts have occurred, involving a contracting of the limits of public provision and a corresponding growth of private and community provision to make up the deficit. These changes have involved a number of elements: flight of the middle class into alternative private insurance arrangements to cover health (and increasingly social security) risks; an expanded role for the third sector in meeting the basic needs of low-income New Zealanders; and lengthened years of dependency of young adults on their parents, when they become unemployed or sick. These changes have reinforced the shifts occurring elsewhere, by increasing the residualistic character of the welfare state and reducing the stake that the middle class has in it.

Over a much longer time frame, the state has also retreated from any involvement in wage-fixing procedures. Wage-fixing arrangements no longer make any reference to notions of a family wage and any connection with social protection goals has been quite severed (apart from the contribution to social protection which is made by the statutory minimum wage which underpins negotiation of all employment contracts). Social protection is now delivered through the social security system and, increasingly, the tax system, through the system of tax credits for low-income workers. Wage-fixing procedures now simply produce wages that reflect market realities—that is, the value of the skills that the worker has to sell and the capacity and willingness of the employer to pay.

This change itself may not have had a significant impact on levels of social protection. The idea of a family wage was never linked by empirical evidence to any real notion of living standards, and in practice, the wage often reflected market realities. There is also a more sophisticated income support system now in place to protect the living standards of families.

Moreover, the old system also resulted in some inequities. The presumption that men were breadwinners for a family led to a considerable inequity by gender, since women's wages were generally at a lower level than men's for the same work. For single people without dependants, the inequity was clear enough, since males were paid at a higher rate than females even though they had no dependants to support. For women without partners who were raising children alone, there was a double inequity, since they not only received lower wages than their male counterparts (which implied they were living on an income lower than a "living wage") but also received lower incomes than single men without dependants. These inequities show that the old system was not, in the long run, an efficient way to deliver support to families.

Changes in Social Activation and Work Orientation

Taken together, the welfare-to-work changes amount to a significant transformation in the relationship between benefit recipients and the providing state. Receipt of a benefit was now considered to imply that the recipient had incurred a reciprocal obligation, normally in the form of an expectation that he or she would actively search for work and accept any job opportunity that arose. This expectation was widened beyond the group of unemployed people that had traditionally been subject to it, and encompassed the spouses of unemployment beneficiaries, single parents, and (potentially at least) people with a disability, sickness or injury who were assessed as being capable of work. In effect, the work expectation was extended to the bulk of the working-age population, for whom receipt of a benefit was seen as a temporary and contingent form of assistance that was available only until the recipient was able to find employment.

The harder edge of some of these policies, however, was a step too far for the incoming Labor-led government, which has signalled its intent of reversing them. Rather than relying on mandatory participation in job search and other activities, backed by sanctions for noncompliance with these requirements, the new government has signalled that more emphasis is to be placed on helping beneficiaries to make the transition to work, through the provision of a range of programs they can access on a voluntary basis.

Again, it is possible to overestimate the significance of this change. Many of the changes were on the periphery of the system and in practice there was little active enforcement. Sanctions were only sparsely applied by the Department of Work and Income for noncompliance with program requirements. This means that the welfare-to-work reforms may have involved less change than they appeared to imply, so that the refocusing under the new government may also involve less immediate change.

The real significance of the change of government is that it has diverted the course of future development of the welfare system. The welfare-to-work changes of the former government represented not so much a set of fully realized policies as a potential future developmental path on which many of the details remained to be elaborated. The new government has steered the development of the welfare state onto a new path, although much of the detail, again, remains to be painted in.

Concluding Comments

New Zealand's welfare state was born in the late nineteenth century—one of the fruits of an activist Liberal government. Despite the prodigious fact of its birth—one of the first of its kind—in the far-flung outpost of empire that was New Zealand in the 1890s, it was in truth a rather puny infant and grew only slowly over the next four decades. It attained full maturity following a rapid developmental spurt in the late 1930s—much like the onset of a delayed adolescence—only after the election of the first Labour government. It entered upon its adult career with considerable confidence, although as time passed it failed to progress and develop. In the 1980s and 1990s, it began to be assailed by self-doubt. To press the metaphor perhaps beyond a serviceable point, the present travails of the welfare state in New Zealand might be likened to the type of mid-life reassessment or crisis not uncommonly seen in the human life cycle. This chapter has aimed to discern the outcome of such an assessment. What would it make of the figure peering out of the looking-glass, thinking back to its young adulthood?

On the face of it, the degree of change has been significant. Welfare payments are now much more tightly targeted to people on low incomes, and the middle-class taxpayers who largely fund them have lost their entitlement to the family benefit that was once payable in respect of all children. Levels of provision have been lowered significantly, so that the experience of living on a benefit is now more difficult, with considerable care needed to make ends meet from week-to-week and with little capacity to fund unexpected additional costs.

The demands made by the state on recipients of welfare checks have also escalated. Most beneficiaries are now expected to begin planning for their exit from benefit, by finding employment, from the moment they come onto the welfare roll. As a result, many beneficiaries are under increased pressure, both from financial constraints and from the hoops they are expected to jump through by the welfare bureaucracy to demonstrate their commitment to job search. For those who do find jobs, the labor market is much more relentlessly competitive and the wage-fixing system long ago shed any pretension to provide an adequate living wage to support families, instead paying only the going rate for the job. For those with few skills, it is more difficult to find work that will support a family. This is a picture which is vastly different from that envisioned by the legislators who framed the welfare state in the 1930s, although it must be conceded that the surrounding world has also changed in ways they would find difficult to comprehend.

And yet it is possible to overestimate the effect of the changes. The reality is that the welfare state goes on paying benefits to hundreds of thousands of New Zealanders who are unable, for a whole range of reasons, to provide for themselves through their own efforts in the labor market—indeed to more New Zealanders than ever before. Clearly, whatever changes have occurred have not prevented anyone in need of assistance from receiving a statutory benefit which provides a regular check for as long as they remain in need and are unable to find gainful employment. While it is true that increased emphasis has been placed on targeting, this is hardly a revolutionary change, since the New Zealand system has always been targeted through the use of income-tests. And in the case of one of the most significant targeting changes—the abolition of the universal family benefit—at the time of its disestablishment, it was payable at such a low level ($6 per week per child) that its loss meant little to the middle classes who forfeited it.

It should also be noted that many of the additional hoops through which beneficiaries were now expected to jump were either in peripheral areas (as in the work-testing of beneficiaries' spouses) or tentative (as in the pilot trial of a procedure to test the work capacity of sick, injured and disabled people) or not subject to much enforcement (as in the work-testing of single parents, few of whom were ever subject to a sanction for non-compliance with the work-test) or on too small a scale to make a significant difference to the great bulk of beneficiaries (as in the community work program, which only ever reached around 20 percent of work-tested beneficiaries). This suggests that the scope of the welfare-to-work changes may have been more apparent than real.

Furthermore, many of these changes are now in the process of being reversed by the incoming Labor-led government. In particular, three of the changes just mentioned—work capacity assessment of people with a disability, sickness or injury, work testing of single parents, and compulsory referral to the community work program—are areas which the new government has signalled it intends to change. Even in the absence of effective enforcement, the presence of these harder-edged provisions was, in the end, a step too far, at least in the present political environment.

Overall, we might conclude that the main edifice of welfare has been less affected by the coming and going of these changes than is commonly assumed. Notwithstanding the cuts to benefit rates, the increased reliance on targeted assistance and the increased emphasis on work expectations, expenditure on welfare has not been significantly reduced in the past decade. Rather these changes have only served to curb its ongoing growth. As Pierson (1994) found, the welfare state is remarkably durable and resistant to efforts to dismantle it. Pierson noted further that the politics of retrenchment often mean that reform efforts are more front than substance. This may also be true in New Zealand's case.

One thing that has undoubtedly changed out of recognition, though, is the tone of public debate about welfare. It has now been many years since the phrase "from cradle to grave" has been evoked as a serious portrait of the New Zealand welfare system. No longer is the state seen—and nor does it wish to portray itself—as the bearer of an open check to provide lifelong security for all New Zealand citizens. Rather it now sees itself as the provider of last resort, and a careful intermediary between the taxpayers who underwrite the provisions and the people who benefit from them, taking care while meeting the needs of the latter not to overburden the demands on the former.

Thus, recent governments have assumed a sterner face towards their less fortunate citizens, with constant trumpeting of the virtues of self-reliance and continual exhortation to make ever more strenuous efforts to move back into employment. Perhaps the rewritten social contract at the heart of the matter— more grudging on the part of taxpayers over the demands on their purses and more indignant on the part of recipients at the reduced deal they are getting— is the only way to secure the future of the welfare state. Further expansion of provision may risk loss of political support among middle-class taxpayers who, in a more tightly targeted regime, see less of the benefits, while further cutbacks may pose risks for social protection.

There is also another moral dimension to public discussions about welfare. Part of the debate about reciprocal obligations that are incurred by people when they accept state benefits has focused on the need to be "good citizens." The former National-led government took a further step along this path, by proposing the adoption of a code of social responsibility. This was not explicitly aimed at beneficiaries; rather it was an attempt to set down the types of obligations that all New Zealanders must shoulder, but it carried the implicit message that the requirements of good citizenship needed to be especially borne in mind by beneficiaries. These developments represent a considerable step away from the paternalistic vision of care from cradle to grave that was the blazonry of the first Labor government. By the 1990s, the nanny state had started to look more like a stern governess.

What may have changed most, then, is not so much the substantial content of the welfare state, but the edifice of public views and myths about it. With middle-class taxpayers increasingly excluded from its benefits, there is likely to be a less roseate view of the state as a beneficent provider. Viewed from this perspective, the welfare state may now rest on the foundation that is not so much like a social contract as a state of uneasy truce.

Coda: A Comment on Pension Politics

One area in which it is possible to discern some indication of the future trajectory of the welfare state is the widening divergence of pension policy from provisions for the working-age population. The decision to remove the tax surcharge, so that the pension is no longer subject to any form of income-test, goes against the grain of other reforms that have emphasized increased targeting of resources to people in particular need. This may indicate a difference in public perception about the role of the state in providing social protection for the old and for people of working age. The state's role with respect to the working-age population has increasingly taken on a residualistic character—largely providing temporary support while claimants are unable to support themselves through work—while its role with respect to the pensionable population has a more universal character—which might perhaps be regarded as a type of national dividend in recognition of pensioners' prior contribution to society.

The decision to remove the tax surcharge was not driven by policy elites, but rather derived directly from the electoral process, as part of the deal-making associated with the creation of New Zealand's first coalition government following a reform of the electoral system. This indicates that the votes of older people, and those approaching retirement age, are of considerable significance in the new political environment. This holds some lessons for the future, as the aging population is projected to swell to much greater numerical strength.

Much of the analysis surrounding demographic aging that has been published to date has focused on projected growth in the cost of supporting growing numbers of people in retirement. Another aspect of the issue, which has been less remarked, is how the changing demography will affect the political dynamic through the increasing strength of the grey vote. The divergence in policy directions for the aged and working-age populations might foreshadow a deeper division, with the pension becoming increasingly strongly protected through the growing electoral strength of its recipients, while the rest of the income support system for the working-age population becomes increasingly residual in character, as the electoral strength of its supporters becomes progressively diluted. This might lead to predictions that the pension will remain exempt from a means test, and that its real value will be protected through time, while access to other social security benefits will become increasingly restricted and their value will become progressively eroded through time.

The resounding defeat of the referendum over the proposed pension reform adds weight to the view that the pension is perceived differently by the New Zealand public at large. This provides evidence that the overwhelming bulk of the population considers that the pension should remain a charge on the public purse and should not be privatized by way of individualized contributions to private accounts. This lends strength to the above analysis, since it appears that the public pension is already capable of being defended through the electoral strength of those who consider themselves to have a vested interest in it. The lack of any equivalently strong electoral lobby to reverse the benefit cuts of 1991 might suggest that the remainder of the system will remain vulnerable to further winding back as the demographics continue to shift in favor of those of pensionable age.

This analysis in terms of electoral strength is, of course, a partial one, as is the analysis in terms of financing, and to descry the future of the pension with any real clarity would require an analysis from both perspectives. The two views lead to different predictions about future paths for pension policy: the analysis by costs suggests a winding back of pension entitlements and their associated costs, while the analysis by voting strength suggests that these entitlements are likely to be protected. Putting the two together might indicate that the future is likely to involve some degree of intergenerational conflict, as the older generation votes to protect its entitlements, while the younger generation lobbies to contain the costs to a reasonable loading on productive effort.

Such a future may not be an unrealistic prospect. The idea is not one that is completely foreign to New Zealand: Thompson (1996) has written extensively on the issue of intergenerational capture of the welfare state, in this case referring to an earlier generation. If Thompson's thesis holds, it is worth noting that the capture was not remarked particularly at the time it occurred and was left to be discovered only through later scholarly effort. In the scenario outlined above, however, the conflict would likely be much more overt and would likely dominate the political agenda for many decades to come—and indeed increase in salience after 2011 when the baby-boomers begin to pass into pensionable age. This suggests that the efforts of current generations of New Zealand politicians to forge multi-party accords on pension policy might be mere straws in the wind, since the real fight is not yet scheduled to begin in earnest, with the gloves off, for another decade or so.

Notes

1.   The age benefit was paid at the rate of £78 per annum, while the superannuation benefit was initially paid at the rate of £10 per annum and gradually increased over the years, until it finally reached parity with the age benefit in 1960. This hybrid

arrangement represented a compromise between the political desire of the new government to implement a universal pension and the fiscal difficulties of doing so.
2.   Dr. J. P. S. Jamieson, cited in Sutch, 1966.
3.   In 1999, the former National-led government lowered the floor of the wage band to 60 percent and the rate began to reduce to this lower level. However, this change was subsequently reversed by the new Labor-led government.
4.   The italics are not mine, but are in the original source document.

References

Boston, J. (1984). *Incomes Policy in New Zealand.* Wellington: Victoria University Press.

Boston, J., Dalziel, P., and St John, S. (eds.). (1999). *Redesigning the Welfare State in New Zealand: Problems, Policies, Prospects.* Auckland: Oxford University Press.

Boston, J., Martin, J., Pallot, J., and Walsh, P. (1996). *Public Management: The New Zealand Model.* Auckland: Oxford University Press.

Dalziel, P., and Lattimore, R. (1996). *The New Zealand Macroeconomy. A Briefing on the Reforms.* Melbourne: Oxford University Press.

Easton, B. (1980). *Social Policy and the Welfare State in New Zealand.* Auckland: George Allen and Unwin.

Harbridge R. (1994). *Labour Market Regulation and Employment: Trends in New Zealand.* Wellington: Industrial Relations Centre, Victoria University of Wellington.

Hawke, G. R. (ed.). (1991). *A Modest Safety Net? The Future of the Welfare State.* Wellington: Institute of Policy Studies.

Krishnan, V. (1995). Modest But Adequate: An Appraisal of Changing Household Income Circumstances in New Zealand. *Social Policy Journal of New Zealand 4,* 76-97.

Mackay, R. (1995). Foodbank Demand and Supplementary Assistance Programs: A Research and Policy Case Study. *Social Policy Journal of New Zealand 5,* 129-141.

Mackay, R. (2000). The New Zealand Model: Targeting in an Income-tested System. In N. Gilbert (ed.), *Targeting Social Benefits: International Perspectives and Trends.* New Brunswick, NJ: Transaction Publishers.

MacKay, R. (2001). Work-Oriented Reforms: New Directions in New Zealand. In N. Gilbert and R. A. Van Voorhis (eds.) *Activating the Unemployed: A Comparative Appraisal of Work-Oriented Policies.* New Brunswick, NJ: Transaction Publishers.

Mackay, R. (in press). Welfare-to-Work: New Directions in New Zealand. In N. Gilbert (ed.), *Welfare Benefits and Social Activation: A Comparative Analysis of Work-Related Policies.* New Brunswick, NJ: Transaction Publishers.

McClure, M. (1998). *A Civilised Community. A History of Social Security in New Zealand 1898-1998.* Auckland: Auckland University Press.

Mills, M. (1998). The Case for ACC Reform. *Social Policy Journal of New Zealand 11,* 83-94.

Ministry of Health. (1999). *The 1997 National Nutrition Survey.* Wellington: Author.

Ministry of Health. (2000). *Health Expenditure Trends in New Zealand 1980-99.*

Oliver, W. H., with Williams, B. R. (eds.). (1981). *The Oxford History of New Zealand.* Wellington: Oxford University Press.

Olssen, E. (1981). Towards a New Society. In W. H. Oliver (ed.), *The Oxford History of New Zealand.* Oxford University Press.

Palmer, G. (ed.). (1977). *The Welfare State Today.* Wellington: Fourth Estate Books.

Peters, M., and Olssen, M. (1999). Compulsory Education in a Competition State. In J. Boston, P. Dalziel, and S. St John (eds.), *Redesigning the Welfare State in New Zealand*. Auckland: Oxford University Press.

Pierson, P. (1994). *Dismantling the Welfare State? Reagan, Thatcher and the Politics of Retrenchment*. Cambridge: Cambridge University Press.

Rochford, M. (1995). Evaluating the Compass Pilot Program. *Social Policy Journal of New Zealand 5*, 163-172.

Royal Commission on Social Security. (1972). *Social Security in New Zealand: Report of the Royal Commission of Inquiry*. Wellington: Author.

Shipley, J. (1991). *Social Assistance: Welfare That Works*. Wellington: New Zealand Government.

Sinclair, K. (1976). *Walter Nash*. Auckland: Auckland University Press.

Sinclair, K. (1991). *A History of New Zealand*. Auckland: Penguin Books.

Stritch, A. (1998). Competition and Compensation: The Privatization of ACC. *Social Policy Journal of New Zealand 11*, 83-94.

Sutch, W. B. (1966). *The Quest for Security in New Zealand. 1840 to 1966*. Wellington: Oxford University Press.

Thompson, D. (1996). *Selfish Generations? How Welfare States Grow Old*. Cambridge: White Horse Press.

Trlin, A. D. (ed.). (1977). *Social Welfare and New Zealand Society*. Wellington: Methuen Publications.

Waldegrave, C., King, P., and Stuart, S. (1999). *The Monetary Constraints and Consumer Behaviour in New Zealand Low Income Households*. Wellington: The Family Centre Social Policy Research Unit.

Walsh, P., and Brosnan, P. (1999). *Redesigning Industrial Relations: The Employment Contracts Act and Its Consequences*. In J. Boston, P. Dalziel and S. St John (eds.), *Redesigning the Welfare State in New Zealand*. Auckland: Oxford University Press.

Woods, N. S. (1963). *Industrial Conciliation and Arbitration in New Zealand*. Wellington: Government Printer.

3

The French System of Social Protection: Path Dependencies and Societal Coherence

Jean-Claude Barbier and Bruno Théret

A Transformed Political and Economical Context

Trends explaining the main challenges the French *État social*, along with other welfare states, have been facing for the last twenty years, can be traced to the combined effects of (1) financial constraints, (2) labor markets under pressure to become more flexible, and (3) demography and family patterns. In any national system of social protection (NSSP) this combination of exogenous and endogenous changes is closely related to outcomes in terms of inequality, poverty, and unemployment. It has become conventional wisdom that even when they belong to different clusters, welfare states face "universal" challenges, such as fertility decline, unstable couples and families, single parenthood, child poverty, workless households, welfare traps, insufficient employment and activity rates for certain segments of the working-age population. For our part, we contend that NSSPs *diverge sufficiently* so as not to face the *same* challenges, although from a general perspective they obviously face *similar* challenges. The difference between sameness and similarity relates to different NSSPs' rationales. After exploring the global trends and the macroeconomic and political contexts, we will address these "universal challenges" in the specific terms in which they are constructed within the French System of Social Protection (FSSP).

Trends in Social Expenditure

In the second half of the 1990s, total social expenditure[1] amounted to around 37 percent of households' gross disposable income and nearly 30 percent of GDP[2] (Abramovici and Mathieu, 1999), that is, approximately the mean European ratio. At the beginning of the 1960s, the figure was 15 percent and it peaked at roughly 19 percent at the end of the "Fordist" era (1945 to 1975). From the mid-1970s on, the changes can be divided into three periods.

The first period (1974 to 1983) saw a sharp increase of the social expenditure ratio to GDP in the context of *stagflation*. It combined high inflation with a rapidly increasing unemployment rate and a steadily declining GDP growth rate (see figures 3.1 and 3.2). Sustained social expenditure growth during this period reflected expansion of the Fordist-Keynesian welfare state. A significant increase in unemployment insurance benefits took place in 1974, as well as an increase of family benefits in 1981 and a reduction of the legal retirement age from 65 years to 60 in 1982. Increasing social needs, growing unemployment and high inflation were addressed according to the previously established FSSP rules, and social benefits grew at a high nominal rate of 16 percent.

During the second period (1984 to 1993), the nominal growth rate of social expenditure decreased and stabilized at 6 percent, while measures were implemented to contain and reduce expenditure. Whereas the overall structure of the system remained unchanged, Beveridgean innovations surfaced during the late 1980s.[3] The social expenditure ratio to GDP in this period appears congruent with the growth cycle (first a decline and then a sharp climb until the 1993 recession as shown in table 3.1).

The third period begins in 1994, after which social expenditure has stabilized and even declined. Structural reforms have now been on the agenda for some time.

Pensions (12.7 percent of GDP and 43.5 percent of social transfers and services in 1998) and healthcare[4] (respectively 9.7 percent and 33.2 percent) account for the bulk of French social expenditure. The other areas are (1) family and housing benefits (4 percent of GDP and 13.7 percent of transfers), (2) unemployment and early retirement (2.4 percent and 8.2 percent), and (3) poverty and "social exclusion" (respectively 0.4 percent and 1.4 percent).

Table 3.1 shows social expenditure for the years 1981 to 1998. The pensions' share grew by 2 percent of GDP points between 1981 and 1998 and healthcare by 1 percent, while from 1983 on, family/ housing benefits and unemployment compensation (including early retirement) have been effectively contained. The doubling of resources allocated to poverty and social *exclusion* should also be stressed, despite their relatively small share in the total.

During the last twenty years, endogenous rather than exogenous factors chiefly explain this structural evolution: population aging for pensions and a growing demand (and supply) for healthcare services (most of which go to the elderly). The three other "risk areas" (unemployment, family and anti-poverty programs) experienced evolutions linked to labor market imbalances.

In terms of the overall rationale of the NSSP, they are significant with regard to their contribution to the social protection crisis, while limited in terms of financial impact. Thus, the main challenges have not been directly linked to the impact of globalization, and according to pension reform experts (Dupont and Sterdyniak, 2000), contrary to conventional wisdom, "objective" financial constraints do not exist. Choices are of a social and political nature, closely connected to national welfare regimes, which allow for degrees of freedom vis-à-vis economic challenges. Economic interests and neoliberal social forces (i.e., insurance companies, banks, international financial organizations, state financial élites) nevertheless tend to use these challenges as opportunities for radically changing the system. It is no wonder that they press for solutions such as privatization in the most potentially profitable sectors (i.e., retirement and healthcare). On the other hand, the areas of unemployment, family/housing, and poverty within the FSSP, face challenges related to transformations in gender relationships and family structures. But these areas are dialectically related to the labor market situation and depend on labor relations and wage policies. These are impacted by trade liberalization and neo-mercantilist strategies of corporate and governmental élites. All in all, two distinct "risk groups" within the FSSP tend to emerge. This clear difference will appear later in the chapter.

The Macroeconomic and Political Context

As social expenditure and GDP growth rates are linked, it is remarkable that the three periods referred to above are also business cycles.[5] Traditionally business cycles "stylize" economic facts. Reference to them had disappeared in continental Europe during the Fordist era. However, they returned with the mid-1970s crisis. As figure 3.1 shows, links between social expenditure and production are not only explained in terms of economic cycles but also in terms of their corresponding underlying economic policies.

1. From 1975 to 1983, a first cycle encompassed both a fast recovery with sustained growth around 3.5 percent of GDP (1976-1979) and a gradual contraction resulting in a new recession in 1983. Fordist-Keynesian fiscal and monetary policies were maintained during this cycle, although they proved unsuccessful. They did not fit in with an economy whose internationalization increased quickly. Growth was more export-led and wages emerged less as a factor of internal demand than as a cost to be reduced. Hence, the doubling of the unemployment rate from 4 percent in 1975 to 8.1 percent in 1983 was accompanied by persisting high inflation (a mean rate of 10.6 percent for 1976 to 1983) (see figure 3.2). Along with high inflation, came financing difficulties either through the state budget or payroll contributions. *Stagflationist* tensions revealed the contradiction existing between Keynesian policies and internationalization. In 1983,

Table 3.1
Social Transfers and Services

% GDP	1981	1982	1983	1984	1985	1986	1987	1988	1989	1990	1991	1992	1993	1994	1995	1996	1997	1998
Total Healthcare	8.8	9.0	9.1	9.3	9.2	9.3	9.1	9.1	9.1	9.2	9.2	9.6	10.0	9.9	9.8	10.0	9.8	9.7
Sickness	6.5	6.7	6.7	7.0	6.9	7.0	6.8	6.8	6.9	7.0	7.0	7.4	7.7	7.7	7.8	7.9	7.6	7.7
Disability	1.5	1.6	1.7	1.6	1.6	1.7	1.7	1.7	1.6	1.6	1.6	1.6	1.7	1.7	1.5	1.6	1.5	1.5
Industrial Accidents	0.8	0.7	0.7	0.7	0.7	0.6	0.6	0.6	0.6	0.6	0.6	0.6	0.6	0.5	0.5	0.5	0.5	0.5
Old Age Pensions	10.5	10.7	10.9	11.1	11.3	11.2	11.2	11.2	11.1	11.2	11.5	11.8	12.3	12.4	12.6	12.8	12.8	12.7
Family	3.1	3.2	3.2	3.1	3.0	2,9	2.8	2.8	2.7	2.6	2.6	2.6	2.8	2.8	3.0	3.0	3.1	3.0
Housing	0.5	0.6	0.7	0.7	0.7	0.7	0.7	0.7	0.7	0.8	0.8	0.8	0.9	0.9	0.9	0.9	1.0	1.0
Family – Housing	3.6	3.8	3.9	3.8	3.7	3,6	3.5	3.5	3.4	3.4	3.4	3.4	3.7	3.7	3.9	3.9	4.1	4.0
Early Retirement	0.5	0.7	1.1	1.1	1.2	1.0	0.9	0.7	0.6	0.5	0.4	0.3	0.3	0.3				
Unemployment	1.6	1.8	1.5	1.6	1.6	1.7	1.8	1.8	1.7	1.7	2	2.2	2.4	2.2				
Unemployment-Early Retirement	2.1	2.5	2.6	2.7	2.8	2.7	2.7	2.5	2.3	2.2	2.4	2.5	2.7	2.5	2.6	2.6	2.5	2.4
Poverty – "Social exclusion"	0.2	0.2	0.2	0.2	0.2	0.2	0.2	0.2	0.3	0.3	0.4	0.4	0.4	0.5	0.4	0.4	0.4	0.4
Total	25.2	26.2	26.7	27.1	27.2	27.0	26.7	26.5	26.2	26.3	26.9	27.7	29.1	29.0	29.3	29.7	29.6	29.2
															1995	New	base	
% TOTAL	1981	1982	1983	1984	1985	1986	1987	1988	1989	1990	1991	1992	1993	1994	1995	1996	1997	1998
Total Healthcare	34.9	34.4	34.1	34.3	33.8	34.4	34.1	34.3	34.7	35.0	34.2	34.7	34.4	34.1	33.6	33.6	33.2	33.4
Sickness	25.8	25.6	25.1	25.8	25.4	25.9	25.5	25.7	26.3	26.0	26.0	26.7	26.5	26.6	26.8	26.6	26.4	26.6
Disability	5.95	6.11	6.37	5.9	5.88	6.3	6.37	6.42	6.11	6.08	5.95	5.78	5.84	5.86	5.1	5.2	5.2	5.2
Industrial Accidents	3.17	2.67	2.62	2.58	2.57	2.59	2.25	2.26	2.29	2.28	2.23	2.17	2.06	1.72	1.8	1.7	1.7	1.6
Old Age Pensions	41.7	40.8	40.8	41.0	41.5	41.5	41.9	42.3	42.4	42.6	42.8	42.6	42.3	42.8	43.0	43.1	43.2	43.5
Family	12.3	12.2	12.0	11.4	11.0	10.7	10.5	10.6	10.3	9.89	9.67	9.39	9.62	9.66	10.2	10.1	10.5	10.3
Housing	1.98	2. 29	2. 62	2.58	2.57	2.59	2.62	2.64	2.67	3.04	2.97	2.89	3.09	3.1	3.07	3.03	3.38	3.42
Family – Housing	14.3	14 ,5	14.6	14.0	13.6	13.3	13.1	13.2	13.0	12.9	12.6	12.3	12.7	12.8	13.3	13.1	13.9	13.7
Early Retirement	1.98	2.67	4.2	4.06	4.41	3.7	3.37	2.64	2.29	1.9	1.49	1.08	1.03	1.03				
Employment	6.35	6.87	5.2	5.9	5.88	6.3	6.74	6.79	6.49	6.46	7.43	7.94	8.25	7.59				
Unemployment-Early Retirement	8.33	9.54	9.4	9.96	10.3	10.0	10.1	9.43	8.78	8.37	8.92	9.03	9.28	8.62	8.87	8.75	8.45	8.22
Poverty – "Social exclusion"	0.79	0.76	0.75	0.74	0.74	0.74	0.75	0.75	1.15	1.14	1.49	1.44	1.37	1.72	1.37	1.35	1.35	1.37
Total	100	100	100	100	100	100	100	100	100	100	100	100	100	100	100	100	100	100

Source: SESI=DREES

President Mitterrand eventually opted for the *"franc fort"* (strong franc) strategy and restrictive fiscal policies.

2. The French socialists' abrupt conversion to monetarism in 1983 and the subsequent change in economic policy explain the second cycle's new profile. *"Désinflation compétitive"* (competitive disinflation[6]) and a strong franc tightly connected to the Deutsche Mark, as well as a restrictive fiscal policy resulted in: (1) the economic recovery being impaired, in

Figure 3.1
GNP Growth Rate (1990 Prices)

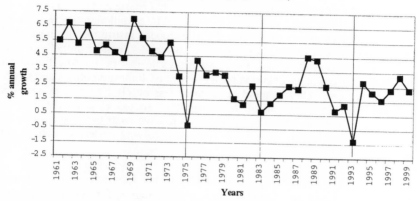

Source: National accounts

stark contrast with the fast 1975 to 1976 recovery. The upward trend of unemployment was thus not reduced (this rate however decreased from 10.4 percent in 1987 to 8.9 percent in 1990). Unemployment remained higher than in the contraction phase of the previous business cycle (see figure 3.2); (2) a steep continuous fall in GDP growth rates (from 4.3 percent to −1.3 percent) from 1989 to 1993. At that time France experienced its worst recession since World War II and its unemployment rate peaked at 11.7 percent (a 44 percent increase if compared to the 1983 recession). Simultaneously, the inflation rate dropped from 9.7 percent in 1983 to 2.5 percent in 1993. In spite of the currency's overvaluation and as a result of disinflation, the French economy was able to sustain the high degree of international opening-up established in the previous period. Allowing for persistent high unemployment and interest rates' growth, the monetarist economic policy forbade any rise in resources, while social needs kept increasing, because of long-term unemployment and poverty. Hence, successive retrenchment plans were implemented that lowered social protection coverage and contributed to the emergence of "social exclusion." In this period, welfare reforms responded to strict financial considerations. Major institutional changes may also be ascribed to European Union developments, that is, the single market and monetary union preparations. Indeed neoliberal policies of deflation, deregulation and privatization were directly dependent on the EMU political agenda (Jobert and Théret, 1994).

3. The third cycle is currently underway. Here we find a very low level of inflation along with a rather steady and relatively low rate of GDP growth (around 2.5 percent). Economic recovery is export-led and a positive trade balance helps interest rates decrease. Thus, real interest rates have fallen and eased fiscal deficits and public debt constraints. Unemploy-

ment has started to drop (see figure 3.2). In fact, 1994 initiates a new period marked by the completion of the European single market, with economic policies abiding by the Maastricht criteria and the first steps of the euro. From a political point of view, EMU completion has resulted in a new agenda where the legitimacy of European institutions is questioned (Quermonne, 1999). European citizenship and "Social Europe" are discussed as well (Maurice, 1999) and times seem ripe for true European politics. But time is also ripe for a renewal of domestic politics and structural reforms. These should be dictated less purely by financial reasons and take more account of the "forgotten" sociological dimensions of social protection. The Juppé plan seems to have contributed to a return of the political debate on welfare reform, involving collective actors and civil society.

Nevertheless a mooted point remains whether Economic and Monetary Union (EMU) will be able to open new perspectives for coordinated economic policies at the Union's level (Boyer, 1999). These policies could be more employment-friendly and the contribution of social protection to economic growth could be emancipated from strict financial constraints. It will depend on which of the following two opposite and currently competing agendas will be chosen: (1) a strict market-driven orientation aiming at convergence towards residual social protection in an Europe only conceived of as a free-trade zone; or (2) the promotion of the EU as a new political and

Figure 3.2
Macroeconomic Indicators

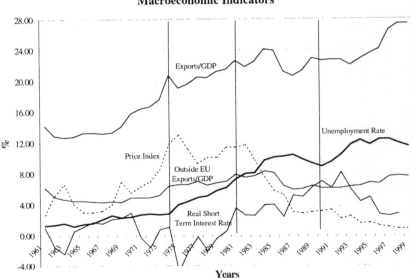

cultural entity with a specific social model—a mix of Bismarckian, social-democratic, and Beveridgean traditions. The extent to which the European level of government will influence the future architecture of national systems obviously will be the outcome of national options towards either the residualist or social-democratic regimes.

However, the challenges the French system is currently facing are obviously not only external—being related to the European Union building process or to globalization. Internal challenges concerning unemployment and inactivity, poverty and inequalities, family and demographic transformations during the last two decades should also be reviewed.

The Employment and Activity Regime

In France, the number of employed people was 21.25 million in 1972, 22.32 million in 1990 and reached 22.43 million in 1997. Adjustments of the French labor market for the last twenty years have been made through two channels: explicit unemployment (whether or not eligible for benefits), and participation in state subsidized employment and insertion programs (as illustrated in table 3.2).

These overall labor market developments for the last twenty-five years constitute a major factor in the transformation of the FSSP. Whereas the French "welfare state" has not been rolled back, it has certainly undergone a major transformation via the emergence of *"politiques d'insertion"* and employment policies.

Table 3.2
Unemployment, Employment, and Labor Market Programs (1972-1996)

(thousands)	1972	1996	Variation
1 Total employment	21,253	22,321	+ 1068
2 Subsidized	2	2065	+ 2063
3 Non-Subsidized	21,251	20,256	- 995
4 Unemployment (ILO)	669	3,248	+ 2,579
5 Early retirements (state funded)	93	850	+ 757
6 Active population (1+4)	21,922	25,569	+ 3,647
7 Potentially active population (6+5)	22,015	26,419	+ 4,404
8 Total of participants in government programs (2+5)	95	2,915	+ 2,820

Source: DARES, 1997 (PS 97.07, n° 27.1)

Table 3.3 illustrates the last decade's employment rates, breaking down the figures according to age and gender. France's labor market nowadays is marked by very low employment rates[7] at both ends of the age spectrum (the young mainly enrolled in education and training programs and older workers commonly retiring early). A second structural feature of the employment regime is the persistent gap between male and female activity rates, which is nevertheless decreasing. A higher unemployment rate for women, roughly 4 percent higher than the male rate, has also persisted for the last twenty years. The gap is about double for those under 25 years of age. Nevertheless, because of a large quantitative development of employment policies (see table 3.2) France has not experienced "welfare-to-work" or "dependency" problems for single parents.

Overall, immigration has not had a heavy impact on the labor market. Immigration for new workers was stopped in 1974 and this resulted in a radical restriction of flows. Since then, the proportion of foreigners in the French population (5.6 percent in 1999, or 7.4 percent including immigrants who have acquired French nationality) and labor force has remained roughly constant. However, during the first two periods under review (before 1993), the foreign labor force was at the forefront of the labor market

Table 3.3
Employment Rates (1985-1997)

	(age)	1985	1997
All	15-24	38.7	24.4
	25-54	77.3	77.1
	55-64	33.6	29.1
	Total	62.0	60.1
Men	15-24	43.3	27.1
	25-54	91.6	86.5
	55-64	42.1	33.2
	Total	73.9	67.7
Women	15-24	34.6	22.0
	25-54	63.1	67.9
	55-64	26.0	25.2
	Total	50.7	52.7

Source: EU, Employment report (1998)

adjustment. From 1975 to 1990, 40 percent of the industrial job positions employing foreigners were eliminated (roughly 500,000 jobs). As a result, foreigners only represented less than 7 percent of the labor force in firms with more than ten staff in 1995 down from 12 percent in 1973 (CERC, 1999).

Poverty and Inequality

The three periods under review are contrasted with respect to developments of inequality. From 1975 to 1984, the distribution of households' incomes concentrated around the median income—as the rich became relatively less rich and the poor less marginalized (Chauvel, 2000). Transfers contributed to this as flat-rate family benefits were raised in 1981 and tax policies fostered further reduction of income inequality. With the change in economic policy in 1983 to 1984, as "solidarity" was substituted for equality as a policy objective (Jobert and Théret, 1994), this process was brought to a halt. Several factors explain this situation: the wage hierarchy widened; the minimum wage (SMIC) played a lesser role in pushing up low wages; "precarious" jobs spread; capital income grew at labor income's expense; less redistributive tax and transfers policies were implemented (for instance, personal income tax's progressivity was reduced) (Théret, 1991). Moving into the third and present period, concerns about vertical redistribution have come back on the political agenda. Data, however, fail to establish whether income inequality has again started to decrease. Since the early 1990s, because it is capitalized and not distributed, capital income is likely to have had a neutral impact on income distribution (Lollivier, 2000). Moreover, given the scraping of ceilings for social contributions and the increasing role of CSG, "social security," [whose relative performances in terms of vertical redistribution have traditionally been regarded as very weak (Palier, 1999)], has turned out more neutral at the end of the periods under review.

Being steadily reduced (see table 3.4), income distribution among the old however has fared differently. Thus, inequality between the active population and pensioners has also been reduced to the point where both now enjoy the same mean income.

This situation may be ascribed to the gradual increase in the number of pensioners with full pension entitlements (see later). However, poverty still exists among the old. When it is defined as earning less than half the national mean income, 114 aged persons (over 65) were poor in 1993 for every 100 poor people in the rest of the population. Moreover, poverty has evolved between 1984 and 1993. The young (ages 16 to 24) now have a higher probability of being poor: 185 are in this category for every 100 poor people in

Table 3.4
Distribution of Income by Consumption Unit

Taxable Income	Inequality index	1970	1984	1990	1996
Employees	Interdecile ratio	4.8		4.4	4.9
	Gini Index	0.343		0.312	0.325
	Theil index	0.204		0.165	0.173
Pensioners	Interdecile ratio	8.7	5.3		4.2
	Gini Index	0.407	0.339		0.302
	Theil index	0.274	0.194		0.150
Disposable income					
Employees	Interdecile ratio	3.6		3.0	3.2
	Gini Index	0.287		0.247	0.255
	Theil index	0.142		0.104	0.110

Source: INSEE, *Revenus et Patrimoines des ménages*, collection "Synthèses," n° 28, 1999; Lollivier, 2000—capital income excluded, 1996 FF

the rest of the population. Although it is not high on the French social policy agenda,[8] the risk for single parents being poor is twice the risk for the whole of the population. This higher probability is correlated with the fact that one-third of single parents' households are composed of people who are not working (as against 8 percent for all households).

Because of the combined effect of labor market and family conditions, France also has seen the emergence of a "working poor" population. If poverty is measured as earning less than half the median net disposable income, 5.5 percent of workers employed for at least six months were poor in 1995 (as compared to 12.1 percent for the inactive or for those who had been employed or active for less than six months).[9]

Measured as a proportion of the population earning less than half the national mean income, the French poverty rate was 16 percent in 1993 and the proportion of the poor among the long-term unemployed was 30 percent (Paugam, 1999).[10] The proportion in low-income[11] categories is 16 percent in 1995, and the Gini Index is less than 0.30 (Eurostat, 1999).

Demographic Trends

France's *population increase* results mainly from internal growth, with immigration having had a relatively low impact on total increase for the last twenty-five years. With 4.3 per thousand in 1999 (3.2 in 1995 compared to 4.6 in 1985), France's population growth presently ranks among the highest rates in the EU (Beaumel et al., 1999). It is estimated that it will keep increasing until 2020 (between 1990 and 1999, the annual increase oscillated between 190 to 250 thousands for a population which grew from 56.7 to 58.6 million[12]). This annual change entails a substantial yearly flow of new entrants on the labor market.

Fertility rates have decreased for the last twenty-five years. The birth rate—13.4 per thousand in 1990—decreased to 12.3 in 1994 but has since recovered to 12.7 for the last four years. Relatively high fertility rates in France have traditionally been ascribed—partially at least—to a specific set of family policies (see later), including measures encouraging full-time employment for mothers (mainly childcare benefits and services). This means that a "double earner" pattern for couples has been established in France for a longer time than elsewhere in Europe.[13]

Matrimonial behaviors have also changed significantly over the last twenty-five years. Divorce is more frequent (38 percent of 1995 marriages are expected to end in divorce). The proportion of unmarried couples has also increased. The number of marriages has decreased by 32 percent since 1972, but marriage rates have recently increased again (4.9 per thousand in 1999 compared to 4.4 from 1993 to 1995, but 7.8 in 1970). Marriages are concluded later in life, and nearly 40 percent of children are now born out of wedlock (6.8 percent in 1970 and 19.6 percent in 1985). Around 14 percent of all families with children[14] are single parent families (84 percent of these are single women). Single parents have traditionally been economically active (more than 70 percent of single mothers were active in 1996. Of single parents with two children, 86 percent were active at the same time). Additionally, their activity pattern has been predominantly full-time (only one-third presently have a part-time job). For this reason the "single parent question" has not been so crucial in social policy which again may be ascribed to the traditional French family policies which encourage economic activity.[15]

As in all European countries, population aging trends appear inexorable in France. However, conclusions drawn from indicators give rise to controversy about the basic demographic tenets of pension reform. Population aging is the result of increasing life expectancy and stagnating births and immigration. Presently, the proportion of people over 65 in the total population is 15.9 percent; this will roughly keep steady until 2011 (16.8 percent and 20.6 percent are the present estimates for 2010 and 2020) (Levy, 2000). The proportion of those over 60 will increase substantially from 2006 when the 1946 baby-boomers are 60. This proportion was 20 percent in 1995 and it is supposed to reach 27 percent by 2020 and 33 percent by 2040 (Concialdi, 1999). A specific French feature is the high gap existing between life expectancies of men and women (82.4 for women and 74.9 for men in 1999[16]). The question of dependency ratios is more controversial and constitutes one of the factors explaining the wide discrepancies in current debates about pension reform.

Concialdi (1999a) discusses an "economic dependency ratio" from the Charpin report,[17] which takes into account the overall "burden" of the non-working population (including the unemployed). He emphasizes the considerable difference existing between the "old-age dependency ratio" and the "economic dependency" ratio. Whereas the former (see table 3.5) is expected to grow steadily from 100 (1995) to 182 (2040), the latter would decrease from 100 (1995) to 86 (2010) and then again increase to 106 (2040). The main explanation for such a situation is that the increased burden of pension funding (contributions) in the future will be at first outweighed, and then partly balanced, by the reduction of social expenditure for the young and the unemployed. Such calculations ought to be contrasted with the current alarming discourse concerning age dependency ratios that the European Union estimates will increase by 50 percent between now and 2020 in the member states.[18]

A New Funding Pattern

Paradoxically, France emerges as the country where "welfare stateness" (Flora, 1986) is the lowest in Europe. Until 1994, social contributions accounted for 80 percent of total social security resources. The changing ratio of social contributions to GDP may be analyzed according to the three periods previously identified. During the first period, social contribution increased steadily from 16.9 percent of the GDP in 1974 to 22.3 percent in 1983. It subsequently stabilized (at roughly 22.7 percent until 1992), and then started to decline.[19] However, these developments are connected to a

Table 3.5
Alternative Ratios of Dependency

	2005	2010	2020	2030	2040
Old-age dependency ratio	103	110	136	164	182
Demographic dependency ratio	99	105	115	129	137
Economic dependency ratio	90	86	93	101	106

Source: Concialdi (1999) (1995=100)

major innovation with respect to funding principles. From 1991, *Contribution sociale généralisée* (CSG) gradually and increasingly substituted for payroll contributions. Being neither a tax nor a social contribution proper, CSG combines features of both, and its taxing base extends to all incomes (i. e., wages, benefits and capital earnings).

Contribution Sociale Généralisée (CSG): An Innovative Mix of Tax and Social Contribution

This innovation is as important as the 1988 introduction of the *Revenu Minimum d'Insertion* (RMI). It was devised to placate political controversy in the 1980s and 1990s relating to what was seen as excessive reliance on social contributions. Critics argued in favor of enlarging social protection's tax base and adopting a more Beveridgean type of funding. Social contributions allegedly endangered international competitiveness because they impacted indirect labor costs. But international comparison of unitary labor costs showed that the latter were not significantly higher in France. Social contributions, it was further argued, especially impacted low wages and unskilled labor in industries competing with low-wage countries. Incentives to substitute capital for labor were assumed to be responsible for high unemployment and long-term unemployment, as well as for increasing poverty and creating a built-in social security deficit. Adopting a Beveridgean stance, critics exposed the inadequacy of social insurance principles to fund national solidarity, family and healthcare benefits. National solidarity, it was contended, ought not be linked to payroll contributions but to citizenship's rights. Supply-side economic policy resulted in the gradual extension of breaks on employers' contributions on wages (up to 1.3 and even 1.8 SMIC— the minimum wage—in some cases). Contributions breaks have also been massively implemented for unskilled workers, apprentices, young workers with no qualifications, as well as the long-term unemployed. Given that these breaks have been (partially) compensated by state subsidies to social security funds, it is no wonder that the share of social contributions dropped.

Table 3.6 displays the structure of contributions and other resources from 1981 and beyond. Until1994, at a mean of 78 percent, the share of social contributions remained roughly stable. However, this apparent stability hid a significant substitution for employers' by employees' contributions. From 1994 on, the employers' share was stabilized, but employees' contributions were subsequently substituted for by CSG.[20] Throughout the periods under review, the state budget's share remained around 15 percent.

While swapping employers' and employees' contributions did not alter the Bismarckian rationale, CSG emerged as the main effective Beveridgean innovation. In 1991 it was initially fixed at 1.1 percent of all incomes and attributed to CNAF (*Caisse Nationale des Allocations familiales*) (the Fam-

Table 3.6
Net Resources

	1981	1985	1989	1993	1994	1995	1996	1997	1998
Employers' Contributions	55.2	52.4	52.0	49.9	49.5	47.2	46.6	46.2	46.7
Current						37.9	37.3	37.2	37.9
Reconstituted						9.1	9.2	8.9	8.8
Employees' Contributions	18.4	19.4	22.4	22.5	22.3	22.4	22.6	21.3	16.1
Independent Workers' Contributions	5.1	4.8	5.2	4.9	4.7	4.0	4.2	3.9	3.4
Contributions on Benefits	0.1	0.7	0.7	0.7	0.7	0.7	0.9	0.9	0.1
Total social Contributions (1)	78.8	77.3	80.3	78.0	77.2	74.3	74.3	72.3	66.3
Special Taxes (2)	2.3	3.2	3.1	5.7	4.5	7.1	7.2	9.2	15.8
Total Ratio (1+2)	81.1	80.5	83.4	83.7	81.7	81.4	81.5	81.5	82.1
State Budget Contribution	15.7	16.4	14.2	14.1	16.1	15.1	15.3	15.3	14.8
Total Taxes	18.0	19.6	17.3	19.8	20.6	22.2	22.5	24.5	30.6
Other resources	3.2	3.1	2.4	2.2	2.2	3.5	3.2	3.2	3.1
TOTAL	100	100	100	100	100	100	100	100	100
French francs (Billions)	852.8	1,386	1,730	2,119	2,189	2,355	2,459	2,539	2,640

ily Benefits Fund) for financing family and "solidarity" benefits (it substituted for employers' contributions reintegrated in gross wages). CSG rates subsequently increased at a regular rate, first to 2.4 percent in 1993 (1.3 points going to a *Fonds de Solidarité Vieillesse*—FSV—for noncontributive pensions). In 1997 the CSG taxing base was enlarged and its rate fixed at 3.4 percent. Additional resources went to CNAM (*Caisse Nationale d'Assurance Maladie*) (the Healthcare Fund), compensating for a drop of 1.3 percent on employees' contributions. In 1998 the CSG rate more than doubled at 7.5

percent on wages and capital incomes, and at 6.4 percent on benefits. Additional resources again went to healthcare funds and balanced further drops in social contributions. Overall, CSG now accounts for over 78 percent of all taxes tied to social security expenditure.

Analytically, CSG should be regarded as a typical hybrid resource, mixing social insurance and tax. Inasmuch as it is generalized to all incomes, it undoubtedly bears the characteristics of a proportional tax, given that it is universal and that it was initially not deductible from taxable income. However, many of its characteristics make it distinct. It is strictly earmarked to finance benefits and it cannot be used for other destinations. Moreover, CSG is collected along with social contributions within the "social security" system and not through state central administration. CSG thus emerges as an endogenous institutional innovation that alters the previous internal balance in favor of national, instead of "professional"[21] solidarity.

The Social Budget Deficit

The "social security deficit" has been the subject of controversy for the last twenty-five years in France. Indeed it provided a prevailing cognitive basis for political arguments and acted as a crucial justification for welfare reform.[22] When the deficit is a priority, dominant actors tend to use it as an opportunity for reform in order to strengthen their position. Nevertheless, at a time when FSSP expansion was a matter of consensus, both the government and social partners were against state budget contributions, and this provided a built-in arbitration mechanism for disputes. The government kept opposing state budget subventions for obvious financial reasons, while social partners would stick to the Bismarckian rationale of the system and their power positions. Arbitration generally followed a two-stage pattern: first, trade unions and employers' associations fought each other over employers' and employees' contributions. Whenever this first negotiation failed, the government would then enforce new financing rules and trade one-off financing of the deficit with expenditure reduction.

This negotiation process, however, has been fragmented and differentiated into multiple schemes and funds (*régimes*)[23] (ApRoberts et al., 1997). Four different configurations of negotiation involve (1) state companies (*régimes spéciaux* for the railways, gas and electricity, the post, etc.); (2) the *régime général* (mainstream fund for private sector employees); (3) *régimes complémentaires* (supplementary pensions, AGIRC, ARCCO); and (4) the Unemployment Insurance Fund (UNEDIC). Moreover, under state supervision, structural imbalances between *régimes* may be compensated through special transfers,[24] based on national and "inter-professional" solidarity. Tackling the deficit varied significantly according to our three periods.

During the first business cycle (1975 to 1983), things remained unchanged: social contributions kept increasing in order to match growing expenditure. The government, nevertheless, gradually increased its intervention in order to reduce healthcare expenditure's growth. During the second economic cycle (1984 to 1993) adjusting contributions to expenditure proved very difficult, as the weakest actors, trade unions, had to accept a gradual substitution for employers' contributions by employees. To compensate for their weakness, they tried to abide strictly by Bismarckian social insurance and "professional" solidarity principles. Conversely, they called for the state to contribute for national solidarity risks. Accepting these transfers over to the state budget, the government staged a trade-off in 1993. In exchange for taking charge of non-contributive pensions (*minimum vieillesse*), trade unions tacitly approved the Balladur pension reform for the *régime général* (see later). A new configuration emerged from 1994, and especially with the 1995 "*Plan Juppé*" (Dehove and Théret, 1996). Prime Minister Juppé forced the passing of his secretly conceived plan through Parliament, while resisting all forms of negotiation with social partners. His plan encompassed wide ranging reforms: privatization of the national railway company (SNCF), an overall reform of social security financing, and reform of healthcare and public companies' pensions schemes. A powerful popular movement subsequently paralyzed the country for two months and defeated Juppé's plan—at least partially. Both SNCF's privatization and the pension reform had to be cancelled. Essential elements of the reform nevertheless were retained. Of particular interest with respect to the FSSP's power structure were: (1) the principle of an annual Parliament approval of a Social Security Bill; (2) the transfer of aggregated social security funds' debt to a state-run special fund, CADS (*Caisse d'amortissement de la dette sociale*). It was agreed that the debt would be financed via CRDS (*Contribution pour le remboursement de la dette sociale*), a new contribution akin to CSG. These moves have represented a significant shift of power over to the state, thus reinforcing the Beveridgean component of the French system.

*   *   *

Globally, the challenges to the FSSP have been addressed very differently according to the three periods reviewed above. The situation of pensions and healthcare, on one hand, and other welfare areas on the other, remains structurally very different. For pensions and healthcare which absorbed little over three-quarters of the social budget, important political decisions are still pending. For the other areas significant transformations have already been implemented.

Family and Unemployment Benefits: Areas for Targeting?

Targeting and Universalism

Conventional wisdom generally opposes *targeting* and universalism. However, this opposition is not clear-cut. In a certain sense, welfare schemes are intrinsically selective, because benefits are only available when beneficiaries face *actual* risks. The only universalistic scheme would be a universal minimum income, which exists nowhere.

If poverty and social exclusion, for instance, are considered social risks, the right to be protected from them becomes universal, but one has to prove effectively poor under an income-test to be eligible. Which suggests that universalism and selectivity (or targeting) are not contradictory. The universality criterion applies to entitlements to benefits, not to effective access to the benefits themselves.

On the other hand, targeting may be opposed to universalism when it is based on conditions that only apply to closed groups, or groups targeted for specific reasons (such as skin color, disability, residency, etc.).

Rather than opposing targeting and universalism, it would thus seem more adequate to contrast two different "universalisms": (1) Liberal universalism implies flat-rate benefits for all and coexists with targeting the poor; and (2) "Social-democratic" universalism allows for modulating benefits, for vertical redistribution purposes, and incorporates targeting in the perspective of equal outcomes.

There has been no significant transformation of targeting practice in health and old age pensions in France. "Targeting" health risk, strictly speaking, only applies to the disabled and has not changed significantly since 1975.[25] With respect to old age pensions, "targeting" has long been decreasing, because of the gradual extension of the social insurance system. However, "targeting" seems to have increased over the last twenty-five years in France in two main areas: "family policy" (in an extensive sense, it includes housing benefits) and unemployment benefits.

Within the complex array of benefits that constitute "family policies," an increasing proportion has tended to focus on vertical redistribution. But, at the same time, universalistic principles have not really been challenged, except for a short-lived reform of the Child Benefit in 1998. Yet, in a period of mass unemployment, a growing proportion of the unemployed has been shifted over to assistance benefits, without significant social unrest—with the notable exception of the winter movement in 1997-98 led by the unemployed associations. New minimum incomes (*minima sociaux*) have targeted "social exclusion." Since 1975, these have, in fact, been introduced in three stages:[26] (1) renewed benefits for the disabled (AAH, *allocation d'adulte handicapé*) in 1975, and single parents and widows' minimum incomes in 1976 and 1980; (2) new benefits that emerged in the mass unemployment period [allocation d'insertion (AI) and *allocation de solidarité spécifique* (ASS)] created in 1984; (3) RMI (*revenu minimum d'insertion*) created in 1988 (because of its link to the "welfare-to-work" rationale, it will be extensively reviewed later).

Family and Housing Benefits

France has had a long-lasting and wide-ranging system of family policies (Barbier, 1990). Family programs include: tax credits through *"quotient familial"*;[27] quasi-universal provision of early education (*écoles maternelles* for children from 3 to 6); the vast array of benefits managed by the Family funds (CAF, *Caisses d'allocations familiales*); the *départements*' general social assistance and families assistance; and the municipalities' childcare services and crèches.

Some family benefits in the French context would not be considered as such in other national contexts. Because of institutional settings and the pivotal role played by CAF, family policies in the French sense also encompass programs focused on social exclusion and housing. Traditionalists have made much use of the fact that family policy in France has become blurred because of its three concomitant objectives (the so-called "natalistic" one; horizontal redistribution, envisaged as "compensation" for larger families with a given income level; and vertical redistribution).

Initiating a shift from the 1970s, vertical redistribution objectives became more prominent within family policy. This development is obviously related to the declining, albeit not disappearing influence of "family lobbies." "Social" benefits rather than strict "family" benefits kept being introduced in this period (benefits for widows and for the young disabled, most of them being administered by CAFs). Most new benefits have been likened to income conditions, and some were differential, like the single parent benefit introduced in 1976 (*Allocation de parent isolé*, API). During the same period, income-tested housing benefits were gradually extended. Housing benefits have tended to play an increasing role in alleviating poverty and the number of beneficiaries (currently more than 5.7 million) has increased sharply during the 1990s (Barbier and Théret, 2000).

From 1984 to 1993, the focus was on childcare services, for which France occupies an intermediate position in Europe. Benefits linked to labor market situations were also modified or introduced during this period. For instance, from 1985, *Allocation parentale d'éducation* (APE), provided for a replacement income for parents (in fact, 90 percent women) who temporarily left employment to care for a third child at home. This benefit was attributed under strict work conditions (two years in employment during the 30 months before the birth of the third child). Worsening conditions of the labor market in that period undoubtedly account for work conditions being relaxed in 1986 (2 out of the 10 years before the birth).

In 1994 and with a new majority in Parliament, innovations were limited, except for the APE where the child's rank was transformed into a *second* child condition; moreover, women who kept a part-time job also became eligible for APE. On the other hand, various measures were taken to increase childcare support (tax credits, social contributions exemptions for caretakers employed at home, and services in-kind). Also linked to the developments of the labor market and the low activity rates among the young (see later) was the new stress put on the extension of the age limit for children's eligibility, which was supposed to gradually increase from 18 to 22. Families with children up to 20 years of age are now eligible for a child benefit,[28] irrespective of the dependent children's status (training, education) provided they are inactive. For a very short period in 1998, the Child Benefit was "income tested."[29] This resulted in benefit cuts for a small number of richer families (351,000 families targeted in that year lost their entitlement, a proportion of 8 percent of all Child Benefit claimants). However, this measure, taken by the new socialist administration, was considered very unpopular and after a symbolic *"Conférence de la famille"* in June 1998, the universal Child Benefit was restored.[30] Financially and politically, the government preferred to cap tax allowances available to richer families (capping the *"quotient familial"* credit for 400,000 more families among the richest).

Given the multiple objectives of family policies, *if "strict" family policies are considered,* the general picture has been one of stability for the last twenty years. But the growing importance of *minima sociaux* and housing benefits appears much more significant than minor inflexions during the period.[31] Indeed, the vertical redistribution element has become more and more prominent. The increased proportion of benefits based on income conditions (*sous conditions de ressources*) provides a good index for that development. Of all benefits currently delivered by CAF, 60 percent are income tested, whereas only 12 percent were in 1970. This is strictly linked to housing benefits and *minima sociaux* (Join-Lambert et al., 1997).[32]

A certain "natalistic" orientation has persisted, mostly during the 1970s and 1980s. Indeed, during a short period in the 1980s, family policy seemed to turn back to its historical natalistic objectives, providing more explicit supplements and advantages in the hope of encouraging families to have a third child. But that policy was short-lived. The specific French compromise between actors in family policy matters should, however, not be underestimated, proven by the failed attempt to tax family benefits in 1996. Indeed, although the natalistic element should now be regarded more as symbolic than substantive,[33] the resilience of distinctions among justifications for programs in terms of supporting families should not be discarded as rhetoric. The characteristics of the single parent's issue in France and the redistribution outcomes in terms of a relatively low rate of child poverty testify to the continuing interests in family support (Chambaz, 1997).

Less important trends are also to be observed in the childcare system, due to allowances and tax deductions available to richer families, who can afford hiring caretakers at home on a regular basis (these measures have been linked explicitly to their potential employment impact in services). These programs have de facto targeted the rich but their overall impact on expenditure has been limited.

Unemployment: Benefits Reduction and Transfer from Insurance to Assistance

Considering income replacement for the unemployed, the French system has clearly diversified over the last twenty-five years. Strictly determined by the emergence of mass unemployment, this process has also contributed to a transformation of the general structure of rights and obligations (which will be dealt with extensively later on).

On the assistance side, two benefits (*minima sociaux*) were introduced for the registered unemployed lacking adequate insurance coverage (although tax funded, these are delivered through the Unemployment Insurance Fund administration). Since 1984, ASS (*allocation de solidarité spécifique*) has been provided to the long-term unemployed with no insurance entitlements remaining. Its conditions of eligibility were restricted in 1992 and 1997. These now include not only income-tests, but also age limits, and recipients must have contributed at least five years out of their last ten years of employment.[34] The number of recipients has increased nearly six-fold since the beginning of the programme. AI (*allocation d'insertion*) was also introduced in 1984 for specific categories of job seekers with no entitlements (young people, single mothers, refugees, recently freed prisoners, etc.). Since 1992, this benefit was cut for two important categories of individuals initially eligible: under 25 young job seekers and single mothers.[35]

On the insurance[36] side, payments have been earnings-related from the start and subjected to a ceiling, but the main innovations were introduced after 1984. From 1992 to 1997, gradually decreasing insurance benefits were introduced after 6 months, and up to the end of the entitlement (15 to 30 months for those under 50, depending on their work record, those over 50 being entitled for longer periods under strict conditions).[37] At the same time eligibility employment periods of contributions were increased. It is remarkable that these retrenchments did not provoke any significant organized opposition. The co-steering coalition between the unions and employers' associations (it has run the insurance fund since 1958 on a *paritarisme* ba-sis[38]) was at that time transforming itself, CFDT emerging as business's privi-leged partner.

Over the two last periods, income replacement levels of assistance, as com-pared to standard insurance benefits, were greatly reduced. Whereas in 1984, ASS and insurance benefits were roughly equivalent, by 1997 ASS had de-clined by 27 percent relative to the standard insurance benefit (Daniel and Tuchszirer, 1999). That marks the first prominent feature of the present income replacement system: levels of incomes' replacement have widely diversified.

Moreover, the reform entailed adjustments allowing for a gradually in-creasing linkage between entitlements and participation in specific programs. The general purpose of increasing incentives for active behavior and for "activating" expenditure has, in fact, been present since 1988 and the intro-duction of *Allocation Formation Reclassement* (AFR) for those unemployed that engaged in vocational training. This trend at first encountered fierce opposition from the trade unions, especially FO, which was the leading union in the unemployment insurance. Consequently the diversification of catego-ries among the unemployed also entailed diversification among their obliga-tions. But it is only during the last period (from 1993) that a forceful "activation" rationale emerged, culminating in an open public debate in 2000, over a possible strengthening of the "actively seeking" work clause.

On the whole, these reforms have resulted both in an increase in the share of the unemployed being served by the assistance system and an overall decrease of the proportion of the registered unemployed eligible for insur-ance benefits, as shown in table 3.7.[40] An exceptional social movement was started at the end of 1997 by several organizations of the unemployed that were protesting against government's refusal to increase minimum incomes.

During the same period the number of RMI recipients rose to over 1 mil-lion in 1999 and the 1990s restrictions in unemployment benefits resulted in a transfer of ASS recipients over to the general assistance RMI.

Table 3.7
Insurance and Assistance (RMI excepted) for the Unemployed

Year	Insurance recipients	Assistance recipients	All recipients (excluding RMI)	% of recipients/ all unemployed registered[40]
1987	1 416 041	455 262	1 871 303	60.2
1992	1 929 830	371 787	2 301 021	62.4
1997	1 831 200	492 500	2 323 700	53.5

Source: Daniel and Tuchszirer, 1999.

These developments are however not equivalent to a "targeting" process in the terms of liberal welfare regimes. Rather they result from a mix of social insurance with a fragmentation of categories, and universal social democratic Beveridgean principles. Nevertheless, income replacement levels for a major part of the unemployed are presently significantly less generous than in the Nordic systems. This change, as in other countries, has been accompanied by an increasing—however contained—stress on "activation" policies. At the time of writing (winter 2000), this latter issue is high on the agenda of social partners negotiating a new contract for the unemployment fund. Trade unions have split again during the negotiation, a provisional contract with the employers' associations first being agreed on by only two unions (CFDT and CFTC). The government is currently in the process of approving the new regulation after a six-month conflict.

The Scope for Privatization and Individualization of Healthcare and Pensions

Pressures for more privatization and/or individualization of rights are at work in healthcare and pensions, but shifts in both policy areas have been limited so far. Opposite tendencies towards universalism and increased statism are clearly observable in health, while resistance to pension individualization (via funding schemes) appears very strong. State and nonstate social actors are looking for a new balance between "professional" solidarity (the Bismarckian tradition) and "national solidarity" (allowing for a Beveridgean adjustment to financial interests' pressure).

The Health System: From Limited de facto Privatization to Universal Coverage: From Demand to Supply Management

The French health system encompasses nineteen health insurance funds.[41] Services are delivered either by public or private hospitals (including private services within public hospitals), and by private providers for ambulatory care (medical and paramedical professions). The system therefore relies on contradictory principles. On the one hand, private liberal medical practice prevails: patients choose their practitioners freely in the private or public sectors and pay them on a fee-for-service basis. On the other hand, health costs (care and prescriptions) are reimbursed to patients as contributors to a fund. Fees for care as well as for prescriptions are flat fees approved after agreements negotiated between funds and professional associations.

Apart from public hospitals, government is thus unable to directly control the supply and it is inclined to exert indirect pressure on the demand side (via increasing social contributions and/or patient charges). Leaving aside objective factors (like for instance population ageing or AIDS) an "inflationist coalition" prevailed on the supply side until the early 1990s. As co-administrators of CNAM, trade unions and employers' associations accepted fast expenditure growth (Damamme and Jobert, 2000), under the influence of a powerful pharmaceutical industry and of physicians' organizations. Indeed this coalition was quite efficient during the Fordist era. But slowing economic growth and recurrent recessions no longer allowed for such management, resulting in the system being pictured as more expensive and less efficient than in other European countries.

Therefore, retrenchment and cost control have been on the government's agenda since 1975. Three successive strategies have been implemented, from the politically easiest to the hardest, which roughly coincide with the three periods noted earlier. During the first stagflationist cycle (1975-83), payroll contributions were increased to adjust resources to expenditure. This was achieved through the removal of ceilings at the employees' expense. Increases in patient charges' were supposed to foster incentive for patients to "self-adjust."[42] But these measures failed to contain spending, which continued to grow faster than GDP. During the "competitive disinflation" cycle (1984-93), three more radical institutional innovations concerning hospital and ambulatory care were implemented. A typical "demand-side" measure, a daily hospital patient charge (*forfait hospitalier*) was introduced. Moreover, public and nonprofit private hospitals received a cap on their annual funding (*dotation globale*). Dotation globale, effective in terms of capping staff costs, proved largely inefficient to contain medical expenditures especially the most costly types of care.

Pursued through *dotation globale*, this inadequate stabilization of hospital costs was accompanied by growing inefficiency in the regional allocation of resources because the funding cap entrenched existing inequalities between hospitals. Moreover, budget control was not extended to private hospitals where costs kept soaring.[43] At the end of the day, financial constraints and competition with the private sector proved detrimental for the less well-off patients and those on the margins of society, which appeared contrary to traditional French public hospital standards.

Thirdly, in a clear departure from the rules established in 1971, a second sector was created in 1980 for practitioners (*secteur II*). It allowed them to exceed approved flat fees while patients were only reimbursed according to tariffs. The number of sector I practitioners[44]—those who kept abiding by approved fees—consequently declined rapidly, especially for specialists. This resulted in very significant increases of patient charges in ambulatory care. Sector II expansion was, however, subsequently stopped after 1990.

The detrimental effect to the poorest was all the more damaging in that it came on top of other converging reforms: increases in patient charges' for hospital and ambulatory care within sector I, and exclusion from reimbursement of a growing number of prescriptions. Thus, from 1975 to 1993, patients' direct contribution to costs climbed from 20 percent to 25 percent of overall costs (for ambulatory care), and has peaked at 30 percent since the 1993 reform.[45]

All this resulted in growing "individualization" and, while costs were shifted over to patients, expenditure was not significantly contained. However, because of *"mutuelles,"* costs were not "privatized" in a proper sense. Mutuelles are work-related, nonprofit health insurance organizations ("friendly societies") that employees join on a voluntary basis. As most French employees are members, costs were shifted to mutuelles, which were increasingly functioning as supplementary insurance funds (see table 3.8), thus sustaining the level of "socialized" spending. But because lower income groups join mutuelles less frequently,[46] this process of individualization and privatization significantly increased inequality.

Table 3.8[47]
Financing Healthcare and Prescriptions

Total Health-care Funding	1975	1980	1985	1990	1993	1996	1997	1990 nb[48]	1995 nb	1998 nb
Social Security	73.2	76.5	75.5	74.0	73.9			76.0	75.5	75.5
State	4.1	2.9	2.3	1.1	0.9			1.1	1.0	1.1
Total Public	**77.3**	**79.4**	**77.8**	**75.1**	**74.8**	**74.4**	**73.9**	**77.1**	**76.5**	**76.6**
"Mutuelles"	4.8	5.0	5.1	6.1	6.3			6.1	6.8	7.1
"Socialized" Spending	**82.1**	**84.4**	**82.9**	**81.2**	**81.1**			**83.2**	**83.3**	**83.7**
Private Insurance		1.5		3.1	3.6			2.6	3.1	3.0
Households share		14.1		15.7	15.3			14.2	13.6	13.3

Sources: Lancry, 1995; Rochaix, 1995; Rupprecht, 1999; Geffroy and Lenseigne, 1999.

As table 3.1 showed earlier, retrenchment strategies (either incentives for patients to "self-adjust" or hospital budgets' annual capping) failed to really stabilize expenditure (from 9.1 percent of GDP in 1983, it grew to 9.6 and 10 percent during the 1992-93 recession). For reasons of both inefficiency and inequity,[48] the individualization trend had to be reversed after 1993. Current reform orientations combine supply management for ambulatory care, a return to healthcare planning and an extension of universalism under increased state control. Paradoxically, these reforms have tended to limit traditional liberal practice. The 1995 Juppé Plan (see box 3.1) systematized these new orientations.

This wide-ranging project drawing on previous piecemeal reform[49] renewed the impetus for change in a systemic way (Join-Lambert et al., 1997). Because of fierce opposition, some of its recommendations were cancelled and courts challenged some of its regulations, but fundamental elements have lasted.

Box 3.1

The "Juppé" Plan for Healthcare

- Parliament is constitutionally empowered to fix annual spending limits with the imposition of penalties on doctors who exceed these caps (maintained but not fully implemented so far). A 1996 constitutional amendment provides for an annual Parliament vote of a "Social Security Financing Bill" (LFSS). LFSS fixes national spending targets and a national objective for healthcare funds (ONDAM) (the first such objective was passed in 1997).
- Healthcare funds managing boards are restructured. Against the *paritariste* tradition, the government nominates fund executives and qualified experts are introduced (maintained).
- A universal health-insurance regime is created, encompassing all nineteen existing regimes. The work (or work-related) conditions for benefit entitlement are substituted by residence requirements (adapted through CMU, see further).
- Funding principles are altered. State contribution is increased through CSG. Health social contributions are extended to taxable pensioners and the unemployed whose benefits exceed the minimum wage. Additional taxes are imposed on the pharmaceutical industry and use of "generic" drugs' is encouraged (implemented). Family benefits become taxable (not implemented).
- Healthcare cost management procedures are introduced (maintained). An individual healthcare file is created to restrict patients' "nomadism" and access to specialist practitioners (not implemented).
- Regional administration agencies are created to administer hospitals; evaluation procedures are extended as well as coordination between public and private sectors (maintained).

This is especially the case for the steps taken to unify the different healthcare *régimes,* which led to the introduction of a *couverture médicale universelle* (CMU-universal medical coverage), later passed by Parliament in July 1999. This is also true of the accounting and cost controlling content of the plan, in spite of pending technicalities.

The Juppé Plan clearly demonstrated that structural opposition by practitioners could not be easily put aside. Because of the medical associations' opposition, and because legal technicalities are still pending, an adequate mix of practitioners' accountability and overall spending limits has not yet been (fully) achieved. However, new cost control mechanisms are currently being devised to try and settle the internal conflict existing between liberal medicine and "socialized" expenditure. Specific compulsory medical norms and good practice references (*maîtrise médicalisée des dépenses*) are gradually being implemented.[50]

The 1995 Juppé Plan and subsequent 1996 Parliament acts have also introduced important changes in hospital care. Wielding general competence in matters of planning and financing for all hospitals, Regional Agencies (ARH) allocate regional resources according to LFSS standards and therefore are able to reduce previously entrenched imbalances and adjust resources to needs. In the long term, hospitals will have to comply with quality-care standards.

Finally implemented in 1999, *couverture médicale universelle* (CMU) is supposed to address the system's previous failings in terms of social exclusion and inequality of access to care. First it entails the creation of a universal additional subsidiary régime, for all those previously not eligible for fund membership (150,000 persons did not enjoy personal insurance rights nor took up free medical assistance). Second, CMU provides a complementary insurance scheme for an estimated six million low-income individuals excluded from mutuelles' membership. Entitlement to this insurance is income-tested (presently at a monthly 3500 FF[51]). Resources stem from a special tax on mutuelles and private health insurance, linked with incentives for these institutions to participate in the scheme.

CMU thus eventually emerges as consistent with the Bismarckian tradition. Despite being termed "universal," it strengthens the fragmentation of the system by adding a new "régime." Because this regime is subsidiary, healthcare's work-related base remains unchallenged. Indeed, the Bismarckian tradition remains firm because of the pivotal CNAM role and mutuelles' participation. Universalism is thus achieved through the creation of new schemes in the context of underemployment, while traditional links between "professional" solidarity and national solidarity are strengthened, and solidaristic assistance is integrated into social insurance.

*   *   *

All in all, developments in the French healthcare system for the last twenty years certainly could not be characterized as following privatization or individualization trends. Figures show long-term stability within the particular French welfare mix, which has always let individual choice and practice play an important role. At the same time, healthcare expenditure has remained high since 1993. Neoliberal influences that developed in the 1980s have been countered since. Reforms since 1995 also paradoxically give a new impetus to *paritarisme* (Catrice-Lorey, 1997; Hassenteufel, 1997). Far from only illustrating reinforced statism, they should also be considered as the tentative outcome of a new coalition being formed between social partners.[52] Current reforms have also stressed the crucial role ascribed to contracting mechanisms (between government and social security, between regional agencies and hospitals, etc.). CMU's creation demonstrates that the FSSP, at least in the healthcare area, has been able to draw a new balance from its hybrid Bismarckian/Beveridgean tradition.

Pensions: Resistance of the Pay-As-You-Go System or Development of Pension Funds?

The French pension system is almost entirely social insurance based and compulsory; it is based on a pay-as-you-go principle and very fragmented.[53] Three main groups of schemes account for nearly 90 percent of total pensions in 1997 (DREES, 1998: 41):

- The *régime général* (administered by CNAV) provides basic pensions to all private sector employees including executives and managers (cadres) (i.e., one-third of the total pension bill, for 8.5 million beneficiaries, amounting to 70 percent of the over 60 population). Government control is at its highest here.
- The *complementary régimes* (AGIRC and ARRCO) provide additional pensions to *régime général* beneficiaries, amounting to one-fifth of total pensions.[54] Social partners manage these schemes and government intervention is limited.[55]
- The *special régimes* for public employees amount to one-quarter of all contributive pensions. The government here acts as employer and negotiates with public sector trade unions on a neo-corporatist basis.

Pensions have been the main item in social spending since 1975: their current 43 percent share of total social expenditure was first reached in the early 1970s. The quasi-linear growth of pensions over the three periods under review, however, points to diverging causes. Until the early 1980s, pensions' value improved, while the number of pensioners grew slowly. Then pensions' value decreased while the number of pensioners grew very quickly. The pensions' ratio to GDP per capita consequently appears almost stable (Concialdi,

2000). Whereas pension policy remained generous until the early 1980s (retirement age was last reduced from 65 to 60 in 1982), it turned more restrictive from then on. The gap between GDP and pensions' growth rates has thus gradually been closing.[56]

As in other developed countries, the political debate about pensions, under the pressure of state élites and employers' associations, has mainly stressed the following economic arguments: (1) Long-term demographic trends threaten the financial sustainability of pensions; (2) Income distribution has developed in favor of pensioners, whose mean income now equals or exceeds the active population's mean income;[57] and (3) Low growth and massive unemployment as well as low employment rates jeopardize the financial prerequisites for pay-as-you-go schemes.[58]

As structural reform is particularly difficult to implement in this area because of fierce opposition by vested interests, retrenchment measures were limited to piecemeal action until 1993.[59] In 1993, structural reform began under Balladur's prime ministership. *Régime général* pensions saw their contribution period increase from 37.5 to 40 years for basic and complementary pensions (in the private sector). At the same time, an increase in the calculation period from 10 to 25 years was introduced and reference wages were indexed on prices instead of wages. In response to the reform, a third of employees postponed retirement for two and a half years while seeing their pensions reduced by 5.9 percent (Ralle, 1998).

Structural change also extended to *complementary régimes*. In these, additional pensions are calculated according to the number of *"points"* accumulated and not according to the number of contributing years. The complementary pension is thus akin to a defined contribution scheme as opposed to a defined benefit scheme. From 1983 to 1997, taxable pensioners have lost 10.4 percent for ARRCO and 14.4 percent for AGIRC vis-à-vis the net wages (Dupont and Sterdyniak, 2000). This relative loss of value may be considered a "soft" adjustment of these pensions to demographic and socioeconomic pressures. But changes negotiated from 1993 to 1996, led to important modifications of the compromises between social actors (ApRoberts and Reynaud, 1998).

Social partners agreed on a substantial increase in contributions (and reduced pensions) in 1993-94, despite difficulties raised by conflicting interests between small employers and big corporations, while banking institutions were keen on paving the way for future pension funds. Meanwhile, division was also encountered among trade unions. New contracts were signed in 1996, aimed at balancing the régimes' accounts for the next ten years. Although in line with the existing tendency towards reducing pensions, these agreements did not increase contributions. This break from previous practice probably indicates that employers' associations and some trade unions at the time implicitly agreed to accept the creation of pension funds. Indeed, the government passed the Thomas Act a few months later. This Act allowed for private sector employees to join pension funds, offering generous tax incentives for employees' and employers' contributions. However, the Thomas Act was never implemented in the wake of December 1995 social movement and Juppé's failure. The entire trade union movement including the managers' and executives' union (CGC) strongly opposed the law, mainly on the ground that exemption of taxation on employers' contributions jeopardized existing compulsory complementary schemes. The new scheme being more substitutive than additional, left-wing parties promised to scrap it when elected.

So far structural reform has only spared the "special regimes" for public firms' employees (Juppé Plan measures that applied to them were cancelled). There is little doubt that along with the SNCF's reform, the proposal to raise the number of years of contribution on a par with private sector pensions caused Juppé's electoral debacle. Special *régimes'* participants enjoy favorable conditions in terms of replacement rates, calculation periods, pension indexation on wages[60] and even retirement age (55 or even 50 years for some categories of workers).[61] This comparison is all the more important in that since 1997 the new socialist government has embarked on a policy to equalize pension conditions in the public and private sectors.

In 1999, while commissioning expert reports, the Jospin government created a new reserve fund for the *régime général*. In March 2000, it issued clear signals as to the choice to abide by traditional pay-as-you-go principles. Pension funds were thus again put aside. The first of these reports published was the *Charpin Report*, which recommended a general extension of the contribution period from 40 to 42.5 years. This recommendation was met by fierce trade union opposition. Nevertheless, current government reform projects envisage extending the 40-year period already effective for private sector pensions to the public sector (notwithstanding special conditions for special regimes). Interestingly enough, the reform project stresses the importance of negotiating with social partners, while the financial aspects are downplayed. A new Pension Council (*Conseil d'orientation des retraites*) was put in charge of monitoring the negotiation process and proposing measures to guarantee the systems' coherence.

But on the whole, decisions have not yet been made, and the government is likely to postpone them until after the election (2002). Essential questions remain to be addressed. Will the 1999 reserve fund's role be temporary or structural? Will most trade unions (except CFDT) stick to their opposition to the 40-year contribution period? What is clear, however, is that contrary to the healthcare sector, parties disagree on what is to be decided. Resistance also remains strong against the introduction of pension funds within the French framework, in spite of strong pressure from international organizations (OECD, the European Commission) and the employers' associations [now under the influence of the insurance companies professional association (FFSA)].

The issue is currently being vigorously debated. Media insistence on a so-called "demographic time bomb" and relatively widespread support for the creation of private, voluntary pension funds have been unable to put an end to this debate. Issues at stake are the sort on which politicians must tread softly. Moreover, economic and demographic arguments are controversial and they remain a matter of political debate.

As time passes and decisions are delayed, the financial requirements appear second to political and social justice stakes. Thus, the financing problem is not of the same nature as in healthcare. There is no significant supply-side efficiency problem, despite the current debate on comparative rates of return of pay-as-you-go schemes and pension funds. Two fundamental questions remain presently open-ended: (1) What share of national income is French society prepared to allocate pensioners and what would a fair ratio be for the purchasing power of pensions against wages? (2) Do political and/or economic reasons exist that would necessitate private financial capital entering the pension sector, with the risks of financial instability and inequality? Whereas the answer to the first question is still a matter of debate, the answer to the second has clearly been negative thus far. It seems therefore unlikely that private funding schemes will develop on a large scale in France, at least for as long as present compulsory mainstream and complementary regimes keep providing reasonable pensions on an "interprofessional" solidarity basis. It has been argued that reforms will sufficiently reduce pension levels, as to create conditions for a future substitution of complementary schemes by pension funds (Palier and Bonoli, 2000). On the other hand "path dependency" supporters have argued that for mature systems such as the French, transition to funding schemes entails unbearable transition costs (Myles and Pierson, 2000). Our position is somewhere in the middle. The French system's hybrid nature is open to several long-term paths of evolution. Because of political obstacles, the neoliberal project of replacing pay-as-you-go schemes by pension funds administered by private insurance corporations is unlikely to succeed. However, capitalization principles are not totally alien to the French context as several instances demonstrate (existing, albeit marginal, public employees' funds but also large-scale life-insurance saving funds already act as individual and voluntary complements to pension schemes). Future political compromises between French parties will determine the eventual structure of the pension mix, under pressure from business and financial élites, international organizations and civil society. They probably will allow for a limited development of funding schemes, possibly as a new tier of schemes within coordinated policies at the European level.

A French Model of Activation: A Solidaristic Citizenship Perspective

Relationships between the labor market and social protection in France for the last twenty years have created a more complex pattern than before. In a period of mass unemployment and of scarce job creation, unemployment insurance proved inadequate. Innovations were necessary because an increasing proportion of the potential active population was underemployed and "exclusion" increased dramatically. *Revenu minimum d'insertion* (RMI), the main 1988 innovation, eventually emerged as a substitution benefit for unemployment insurance and as the main minimum income. Concurrently, employment policies and insertion programs expanded throughout the 1984 to 1993 period. Entirely new developments have emerged during the period from 1994 on: wide ranging social contributions breaks were implemented in order to foster job creation (for the low skilled and lower wages), part-time work was subsidized, the first steps were taken toward working time reduction, while extensive temporary employment schemes in the public and non-profit sectors were maintained. These features may be regarded as constituting a French approach to activation that, in a way, is more similar to the Nordic countries' model than to "Anglo-Saxon" workfare/welfare-to-work policies. This French model demonstrates its own way of implementing the traditional obligation of "actively seeking a job" for assistance claimants deemed to be "employable." This will be examined before analyzing both the innovations implemented in the French system of social protection, namely RMI with its associated "insertion" programs and the new contribution made by employment policies at the end of our second period (1983-1993) over to the current one. Developments in this section should be viewed in the context of the poor job creation performance in France for the last twenty years, a performance that has only been reversed since 1997. This is why we argue that one of the challenges for the French contemporary system of social protection involves implementing "work-to-welfare" strategies more than "welfare-to-work" ones.

Actively Seeking a Job in the French Context

Unemployment benefits through the insurance system (whether the standard entitlement or ASS) are available provided traditional eligibility conditions are met (availability, seeking work and being out of work).[62] To receive benefits,[63] the registered unemployed are required to participate in the various employment and training programs offered by the Employment Service. This applies for insurance and assistance recipients with sufficient employment background and contributions. On top of this, unemployment insurance benefit recipients may keep part of their benefit *temporarily* when they find a job with a wage differential.

As for other benefits, claimants do not particularly "need" activation procedures, because the major portion of the so-called "employable" among them is already active. In the mainstream assistance system (*aide sociale*, whether *aide sociale à l'enfance, aide sociale aux personnes handicapées*, or *minimum vieillesse*), the absence of a link between active job search and entitlements is obvious, notably because of the recipients' age or health conditions (Barbier and Théret, 2000).

Minima sociaux claimants (apart from ASS claimants) are neither compelled to seek work nor register with the Employment Service as unemployed. *Allocation de parent isolé* (API) serves single parents, who are under no obligation to seek work. Introduced in 1976 as part of family policy, this benefit was considered from the start as providing for transitory situations: single parents are entitled to API until their last-born child reaches the age of three. Indeed, beneficiaries—an overwhelming majority of women—actually work. While they take jobs, the wages they earn are deducted from the API benefit. Single parents present rates of activity are high and this is consistent with the fact that the French female participation in the labor market has been one of high activity and mostly full-time[64] for a long time.

Disabled persons eligible for AAH[65] (*allocation d'adulte handicapé*) are not likely candidates for "welfare-to-work" either. A significant proportion of them not only work in special institutions but also take standard jobs thanks to subsidization. Integration into jobs is regarded as a citizen's right for the disabled. Because disabled people experience disadvantages, employers are legally obliged to hire a quota[66] of them for solidarity's sake.

The RMI has had a dual nature from the start. A "social assistance" program, it is also the only one where special public-funded activities (*insertion* activities) are systematically implemented to help beneficiaries take jobs or enter training programs. All these activities are *voluntary* and access to *insertion* is legally entrenched as part of the basic citizenship rights. Employment schemes are dominantly wage-based (instead of assistance-based) although most participants work part time and are among the very low-wage group (the working poor). However, wage-based schemes imply that participants have access to standard social insurance rights.

RMI, "Insertion," and "Social Exclusion"

RMI[67] has quickly emerged as an important component of the FSSP, embodying Beveridgean tendencies towards universalistic assistance. Because it is disconnected from employment and the traditional Bismarckian features of the system, it has changed the philosophy of solidarity (Barbier and Théret, 2000). Moreover, it gave birth to a new type of *insertion* policy, and it is decisively linked to the emergence of "social exclusion" (whether exclusion from social participation, citizenship, the labor market).

RMI's main innovation, a *contrat d'insertion* is attached to the benefit. This contract is signed both by the administrative body (*commission locale d'insertion*) and the claimant, supposedly within a three-month period after claiming benefits. It describes a *projet d'insertion* upon which both agree, that is, a description of the type and scheduling of actions the recipient is supposed to undertake with social services' support. While the benefit is state funded, local authorities (*départements*) are legally obliged to fund *insertion* activities for at least 20 percent of the benefits paid in their jurisdiction. These activities encompass actions and schemes in the domains of health, housing, various forms of counselling and *insertion professionnelle* (employment and training activities). There is no "punitive" approach in the French context in contrast to the U.S. case (Morel, 2000; Barbier, 1998). Society's obligations include providing individuals with the necessary means to become (and remain) "integrated" within society without compelling them to be either "available" or to "actively seek work."

This explains why a strict translation of the term *"insertion"* into English is impossible. The use of the term in French social policy dates back to the late 1970s, but it took its present meaning from the late 1980s. The diverse meanings of the term certainly reveal present contradictions within the FSSP. *Insertion* is a social work objective targeted at the "socially excluded." Integrated social services that build on cooperation of various social institutions include efforts that support claimants to gain access to their full social rights, support their socializing through health and housing, but also involve counselling—not only training and employment schemes. Only part of *insertion* is employment-oriented (*insertion professionnelle*). *Insertion*, inasmuch as it also refers to the mainstream social process eventually leading all citizens to social integration, points to a universal citizenship right, as is explicitly stated in the 1988 RMI Act.[68] However, actual RMI program implementation has shortcomings that often limit the effectiveness of the universal citizenship element.

RMI and *insertion* provide a good example of the limits attached to applying a universalistic perspective to welfare reform (Giddens, 2000). Just when the RMI bill was passed in 1988, a controversy arose about whether the new benefit would be subject to any *"counterpart"* from claimants. Belorgey (1996) justly argues that RMI was eventually instituted as an explicit right, *universal rather than local, differential and unconditional.* However, he is right to point out the existing "ambiguous situation," where, in practice, the benefit is somehow in between a wholly unconditional benefit and a benefit dependent on the beneficiary's compliance with participation in *insertion* activities. Notwithstanding ambiguity, since 1988, roughly 50 percent of beneficiaries have not signed any *contrat d'insertion* and only a very small proportion (5 to 6 percent) have been sanctioned explicitly for not complying. Moreover, only a minority of *contrats d'insertion* so far have had an *insertion professionnelle* content.

RMI's developments point to the blurring of frontiers between traditional social policies and employment policies in France. Whereas the main social problem in the 1970s was to apply specific techniques to limited marginal groups and help integrate them, the current problem has involved tackling underemployment across a wide scope of people in the population. To date, institutions addressing this task, such as the public Employment Service, have proved somewhat inadequate (Barbier, 1995). In the present recovery period, RMI beneficiaries' and the number of long-term unemployed have not declined as quickly as the rest of the unemployed.

Through *insertion policies* (and despite a growing awareness of the gradual extension of a "working poor" component of the labor market) social policy has retained specific features in the "welfare-to-work" debate up to the present. Policy has kept encouraging "wage-based" schemes where standard employee entitlements (including unemployment insurance) are provided, rather than "second class" assistance status. The increase of "working poor" situations thus has not been linked to lower wages or diminishing social rights but to the shorter hours of contracts for *insertion* or employment schemes. Public employment schemes paradoxically have supported more flexibility at their participants' expense (Barbier and Nadel, 2000). Participation in these programs has nevertheless always remained voluntary whether in *insertion* programs or in the mainstream labor market programs. Despite a relatively high turnover of beneficiaries,[69] a significant proportion of the potentially active population fail to access or return to standard market jobs or regular state employment and remain "stuck" on a "second labor market." This population is difficult to estimate and cannot easily be distinguished from the standard labor market program participants of the last ten years.

The Emergence and Consolidation of a New Sector of Social Policy: Public Employment Policies (PEPs)

France has developed a broad array of specific labor market programs during the last twenty years (Barbier and Gautié, 1998). "Employment policies"[70] have gradually served for an increasing proportion of the active population to around 9 percent (roughly 2 millions),[71] which amounted to an expenditure of more than 300 billion francs in 1998 (compared to 10 billion in 1973) (DARES, 1996). The corresponding GDP proportion increased from 0.9 percent to 4 percent during the same period.

These programs mainly targeted the unemployed.[72] Among them are the long-term unemployed (30 to 40 percent of the unemployed, i.e., roughly 0.8 million at the end of 2000) and other disadvantaged groups (the young with low qualifications and the disabled). The least "employable" priority target groups have remained rather stable for the last ten years or so, notwithstanding a high turnover of schemes.

During the period from 1975 to 1983, schemes were mainly supposed to cater to the victims of retrenchments in restructuring industrial sectors, the young experiencing increased difficulties during their transition from school to work, and the long-term unemployed. Early retirement programs, training schemes, retraining programs, job subsidization, and temporary public employment (with an affirmative action focus) were launched on an extensive scale. Thus, a new employment policy has been constructed on the fringes of the traditional FSSP, which has resulted in a considerable transformation of the nature of public employment intervention, in a period of growing orthodox fiscal and monetary policies. On the whole, labor market schemes implemented have mainly consisted of five types as identified in box 3.2.

Box 3.2

Public Employment Programs

1. Temporary public-funded jobs (in public administrations and voluntary organizations);
2. Training for the unemployed and the low-skilled young;
3. Targeted subsidized jobs (affirmative action) in the private sector;
4. Specific *"insertion"* activities; and
5. Early retirement and other schemes that allow aged unemployed not to seek work when remaining entitled to ASS benefits.

The main scheme in the first category, the *contrat emploi solidarité*—CES (inspired from earlier Swedish programs) has been typical of the new French PEPs in the last fifteen years (first created as a training scheme in 1984, it was transformed into a wage-based contract in 1990). Its counterpart in the private sector, the CIE—*contrat d'initiative emploi*—has also been typical of these affirmative action programs targeting the long-term unemployed (first created as CRE—*contrat de retour à l'emploi*, in 1989).

At the same time, social policies have undergone other transformations. Tentative *"politiques transversales"* and *"politiques territoriales"* have been launched, consisting of integrated local actions combining employment and other social intervention, with a particular insistence upon partnerships. These policies (for instance, *plans locaux d'insertion économique*) may have a thematic basis (*politique de la ville*, urban development) and give birth to local organizational and political coordination while also using standard central government schemes. The Employment Service has also been involved in specific targeted campaigns of action.

This policy has often been dismissed by its French critics as *"traitement social"* (social treatment) and contrasted with an alternative *"traitement économique"* (economic treatment), using taxes and incentives. However, research has demonstrated the significant contribution it made to containing unemployment levels and recycling a significant number of participants into regular jobs (DARES, 1996).

This evolution has resulted in the construction of what amounts to a new "risk" area in French social policy despite the fact that it is not generally seen as directly pertaining to social protection. While "activation" was sought for with *insertion*, temporary jobs and training programs were supposed to compensate for the limited labor market performance in terms of job creation. Both Beveridgean and Bismarckian features have been at work here. Devising new intermediary statuses on the fringes of the labor market (temporary employment, training measures and subsidized private sector jobs, and also crucial early retirement schemes) amounted to creating new categories of clients in the French traditional Bismarckian logic. But at the same time, RMI and *insertion* have introduced universalistic solidaristic tendencies. Also typical of the hybrid nature of the FSSP has been the fact that a new social policy sector (namely the PEPs) has been created and administered mainly without union intervention and *paritarisme*, but also until very recently at odds with the education and initial training system.

While undergoing this evolution, the FSSP has retained some of its initial central statist characteristics, and its "employer of the last resort" orientation that distinguish it from many other European Union member states–as reflected in two PEP programs: the "Nouveaux services emplois jeunes" (five years temporary public employment for the young)[73] and working time reduction to a statutory week of 35 hours.

Thus, "social treatment" critics have not triumphed altogether, despite the fact that from 1986 onwards "economic treatment" has gradually held sway. An increasing amount of the budget has been devoted to reducing labor costs. This reduction has been implemented through diverse measures, be it social contribution reductions for part-time contracts (which resulted in a dramatic rise in part-time employment from around 10 percent in 1990 to 17 percent presently) or subsidies for hiring low-skilled people and the unemployed. Significantly enough, since 1998 working time reduction has been associated with labor costs reduction and increased flexibility. Employers who have to comply with the 35-hour regulation at the same time become eligible for additional subsidies and social contribution breaks for wages under 1,8 SMIC (the minimum wage), a very significant subsidy indeed. Although this policy is not targeted at individual contracts for assistance recipients, it has undoubtedly influenced the general functioning of the labor market. The degree to which job creation has consequently been eased for those excluded from the labor market is a matter of debate among experts (DARES, 1996) because of important deadweight effects. Such a policy must, of course, be interpreted within the national context of institutions we previously referred to, and especially the interrelation with social protection funding principles (insurance contributions). Within the French system, no general mechanism of tax credits, like the U.S. EITC program or the present tax credits in Britain, would be easily accommodated. One was nevertheless introduced for low-wage employees in mid-2000 (*Prime pour l'émploi*).

* * *

Thus emerges a rather specific and to a certain extent contradictory French model of activation. It combines elements consistent with an "employer of the last resort" orientation with indirect intervention to enhance job flexibility and reduce the influence of traditional Bismarckian elements—retrenchment of social insurance principles for unemployment benefits, solidaristic assistance developments through RMI, which tentatively attempt to enhance universal citizenship rights.

A New French Welfare Mix

In comparative welfare research, France has traditionally been grouped with Germany as an "industrial achievement performance" cluster (Titmuss, 1974). More recently it has been categorized as a "conservative" (or "corporatist-statist") welfare regime (Esping-Andersen, 1990), that is, as a "continental" model of social protection (Flora, 1986). We contend that these classifications are methodologically and empirically flawed in the case of France. Using clusters inevitably implies listing "hybrid" countries under one of the ideal-types. Important features of the hybrid cases are thus underestimated or even ignored, however determining they might be. Rather than strictly matching one of the three ideal-types (i.e., Germany, Sweden, and the United States), "hybrid welfare states" combine characteristics of them (Théret, 1996, 1997), and static clustering methodologies tend to be inadequate when change is considered. Dynamic trajectories indeed involve new combinations of these characteristics (Martin, 1998).

Until the late 1990s, international comparisons used to exclude France and empirical evidence was lacking. But recent research[74] has been available to compare the FSSP with other regimes. These studies point to some important features, notably its family policies, which contrast it with the German type and make it rather similar to the "Nordic," social-democratic Beveridgean regime (Bradshaw et al., 1994; Théret, 1996; Merrien, 1997; Martin, 1998). Indeed, it has adequately been described as a *Bismarckian system* with *Beveridgean objectives* (Palier, 1998, 1999). Such a qualification is consistent with the interpretation by Pierre Laroque—one of its founding fathers—of a compromise between both conceptions of social protection.

The FSSP exhibits four Bismarckian features: (1) It is extensively based *on social insurance principles* and funded through employers' and employees' social contributions; earnings related benefits are not focused at alleviating poverty for the non-working population; (2) It used to be functional to the *male-breadwinner family*, where coverage extends to the employee's wife and children; (3) It is *fragmented*, i.e., made up of a multiplicity of *"régimes;"*[75] and (4) It is relatively independent from the state and jointly administered by social partners (trade unions and employers' associations) under the *paritarisme*[76] model. However, the Bismarckian orientation has been tailored to achieve the three so-called Beveridgean "U objectives"—universality, unity, and uniformity (Kerschen, 1995). These have underpinned the historical development of the system since its foundation was set in 1945.

Rather than applying one single scheme to the entire population, universality has been pursued through the continuous creation of new schemes and benefits to gradually cover uninsured risks (such as the unemployment insurance in 1958), or to cover new categories of the population. Through this process, a wage-earner status gradually emerged as a pivotal reference.[77]

As for unity, it has been achieved under the symbolic *"Sécurité sociale"* flag instead of a centralized single-state bureaucracy. The multiple schemes (*régimes*) were made financially coherent (via *"compensation démographique"* mechanisms among them) into an overall system under central government's supervision (*tutelle*). They adopted an "isomorphic" administration pattern (*paritarisme*) as well. On top of this, all particular *régimes* have kept participating in national solidarity (Barbier and Théret, 2000).

Finally, contrary to Beveridgean flat-rate contributions and benefits, uniformity was nevertheless present in the French system via the existence of "ceilings" applied for calculating contributions.[78]

This hybrid development between Bismarckian and Beveridgean rationales has emerged as a key factor of the changing FSSP over the last twenty years. This process is consistent with the possibility of multiple paths of historical dependence. Whereas Bismarckian features (namely, social insurance, "weak-stateness," fragmentation) constantly prevailed throughout the system's building stages, Beveridgean features were also at work. Testimony of this is found in the gradually universalized access to healthcare and family benefits on the basis of residency. As internal and external challenges emerged, these Beveridgean features somehow acted as resources allowing for new potential compromises.

Analyzing the French system's coherence and its embeddedness in French society supports the assumption that the "dominated" Beveridgean features might provide internal resources for transformation. However, the French system's coherence should not be overestimated. Particularly when compared with the German ideal-type, the French welfare state appears very discordant, because many other French institutions are at odds with the Bismarckian model. *Paritarisme* is deprived of a functional equivalent for the German industrial relations system. French trade unions are divided and very weak; contrary to their German counterparts, they have no substantial say in company decisions (except for consultation procedures). French labor law, as part of a "social public order," is rooted in universal political rights rather than in a wage earner status, as in the German model (Mückenberger and Supiot, 1999). Social rights thus appear more to compensate for a deficit than to complement labor's economic and political rights. Because of the division within the trade union movement and the powers of state social bureaucracy, *paritarisme* between business and labor has often been more symbolic than substantial (Catrice-Lorey, 1997).[79]

Secondly, the French educational system (seldom considered part of the social protection system) is built on "liberal republican" principles—akin to Beveridgean, solidaristic and/or egalitarian principles (Renard, 1995; Kott, 1996; Bec, 1999). Its limited vocational training capacity is in stark contrast with the German system (Maurice et al., 1982; Verdier, 2000).

Consequently, the increasing influence of Beveridgean principles within the dominantly Bismarckian FSSP has resulted in growing internal tension. This is particularly clear for family policies. Historically, family allowances were administered directly by employers, which explains their subsequent inclusion within social insurance funds. However, as has already been said, the French state was for a long time involved in natalistic family policies. Hence, from the first stages of the FSSP, Bismarckian principles for financing family benefits have been used in a natalistic and universalistic perspective. Eventually, the transformation of family patterns eroded the legitimacy of social insurance principles to finance flat-rate universal allowances.

In the postwar context, Bismarckian forms of organization were supported by reformist trade unions and employers' associations whereas the "three Us" objectives, more in line with French republican tradition, were supported by political parties (Bonoli and Palier, 1995). Because full employment allowed for the overall extension of the wage-earner reference, compromises were possible. These proved both economically functional and socially efficient: social insurance and assistance principles were complementarily embedded into the basic scheme (*régime général*) (Renard, 1995; Bec, 1999).

However, the system subsequently became less efficient. It was first confronted with internal challenges (structural unemployment and "social exclusion"; the male breadwinner family's crisis; aging and inadequate containment of health costs). It also faced external challenges (globalization). Compromises between actors within the hybrid Beveridgean/Bismarckian mold have thus been destabilized and new compromises are presently needed. Nevertheless, the French welfare state's hybrid structure might well constitute a comparative advantage in confronting the new challenges. Using its internal resources for innovation, the FSSP could then eschew the polar choice between conservation (continuity) and revolution (radical change).

Indeed, the French system of social protection has undergone numerous innovative transformations since the eighties and the nineties. The very long list of acronyms according to which new schemes, instruments, institutions, financial mechanisms, etc., are named is instructive by itself. These new "institutional forms" all pertain to adaptations either to financial pressure or to labor market and demographic challenges. Since the end of the Fordist era, they have resulted from a process of trial and error, and the slow development of new conceptions of welfare. New forms emerged in the early 1990s after two periods during which expansionist social policies were pursued from 1975 to 1983 and financial retrenchment from 1984 to 1993. Structural reform in almost every policy area has been on the agenda during the current period, which started in 1993-94.

It is obviously too early to assess what the eventual outcome of current reforms will be, given that in many areas, crucial decisions or compromises are still pending. The general trend nevertheless seems clear. Rather than a radical shift in the traditional French Bismarckian model, what seems to emerge is a new Bismarckian/Beveridgean *welfare mix*. This particular mix appears as a logical extension of a pattern present from the early stages of the system in 1945. Change is path-dependent, but that path dependency does not prevent innovation in the French hybrid system. Although Beveridgean principles have influenced these developments crucially, the outcome in terms of institutions and rules is certainly not uniformly Beveridgean. A tentative new alliance is building up between the traditional *paritariste* spirit and state-dominated national solidarity.

If Beveridgean objectives were pursued with Bismarckian means during the early stages of French social security, Beveridgean instruments seem to be used presently for Bismarckian objectives. CSG, CMU, RMI, and the new employment policies undoubtedly all participate in the system's evolution towards universalistic social protection. But at the same time, these elements remain subsidiary within an overall Bismarckian architecture. Healthcare and pension reforms demonstrate its resilience. Significant adjustments in family and housing benefits and in poverty and employment programs result from adaptations to labor market developments, but, so far, do not dispense altogether with the traditional wage/benefit relationship.

External influences have been important, but probably not decisive. However, in the context of an increasing impact of European Union institutional building, national social policies will certainly become less independent (Maurice, 1999). What remains to be seen is whether the present structural welfare mix will be able to resist pressures from globalization, which clearly favor social protection liberal minimalist standards. All continental systems face this question that concerns the future of welfare provision quality and values (Barbier, 2000). Clearly, democratic and transnational mobilization of social actors will be needed to allow ambitious collective social investment strategies.

Notes

1. "Social expenditure" encompasses the entire social protection system (Barbier and Théret, 2000). When "social security" is used in the text, it refers to Sécurité sociale in the French sense, which is different from the U.S. and UK meaning, and closer to the German. Labor market programs expenditure is usually not considered part of the "social protection" budget. As will be seen later, it has nevertheless become an important element of social policy in France for the last twenty years.
2. When including public transfers of goods and services, such as education and culture, a "socialization ratio" of households' income amounts to about 45 percent.
3. The CCSS "Commission des comptes de la Sécurité sociale" (a supervisory body) was created in 1979. Cost containment thus entered the political agenda. Subsequently reformed, the Commission only embarked on an effective role from 1987. RMI was created in 1988 and CSG in 1991.
4. Including sickness and income compensation, disability and industrial accident benefits.
5. Part of one business cycle for the third period.
6. "Désinflation compétitive" refers to economic policies implemented in the period, mixing restrictive fiscal policies, trade liberalization, strict monetary policy and the disindexation of wages.
7. According to the Employment rates report, France appears as one of the intermediate member states. When adjusted, France's 60.8 percent employment rate in 1998 is 57.4 percent in full-time equivalents (EU Commission, 1998, 1999).
8. Perhaps because the proportion of poor children is comparatively low in France (7.3 percent as opposed to 20.5 percent in UK, 19.5 percent in Italy, and 18.8 percent in Portugal) (Chambaz, 1997).
9. Nevertheless, this is the lowest rate in Europe after Denmark (Lagarenne and Legendre, 2000).
10. Eleven percent if poverty is defined as under half the median disposable income by unit of consumption (Chambaz, 1997).
11. Low income is here defined as less than 60 percent of the median national income.
12. Excluding overseas territories.
13. Majnoni d'Intignano (1999) notes that only 17 percent of 14.4 million economically active households are couples with inactive women.
14. 1.7 million families in 1999 compared to 1.4 in 1990.
15. Notwithstanding, some cases were, especially in the second period under review, women's inactivity was obliquely encouraged, for instance through "allocation parentale d'éducation."
16. Life expectancy in France also remains very dependent on social status and occupation. For instance, life expectancy at 35 is 44.5 years for managers compared to 37 years for unskilled workers (Données sociales, 1999).
17. The Charpin report is one of a series of reports supposed to prepare government decisions.
18. As well as with 1988 OECD estimates for an anticipated tripling of health and pension expenditures, especially in Japan (Esping-Andersen, 1997).
19. Because accounting conventions changed for national accounts, rates are not strictly comparable.
20. Special taxes (on alcohol and tobacco, on insurance and pharmaceutical companies, etc.) were also transferred.
21. In the text, professional refers (along with "interprofessional") to a solidarity organized on the basis of a work-related insurance system, in various régimes, but also across all industries, trades, and professions.

22. Incidentally, this deficit is "in-built." As total expenditure is only known of after annual accounts are established, corresponding resources cannot be fixed ex-ante, which results in a permanent imbalance, either positive or negative. To balance actual expenditure, social contributions' rates for the different funds and régimes, as well as state subsidies have to be adjusted every year; hence a recurring dispute between state administration and social partners on the basis of these accounts.

23. A régime (a particular sector/scheme within the overall insurance system with specific eligibility rules and benefits) covers employees in a particular trade or industry (for example, railway employees) or a category of employees (for example, managers, etc.).

24. Structures of contributors and recipients vary considerably across the "régimes": "*Compensation démographique*" mainly refers to the special transfer mechanisms between régimes. These special transfers thus play a key role in the global coherence of the overall system.

25. Finally, although not part of the Family Benefits system, a new assistance benefit (*prestation spécifique dépendance*) has been added to cater to people over 60 in need of permanent care when they lose physical and/or mental autonomy. This benefit, which took over a previous one, has been means-tested from its inception in 1997. Contrary to the German example, loss of autonomy for old people was not established in France as a new fully fledged social insurance risk. It was instead included within the conditional differential assistance benefits administered by départements. However, in 2001 a new universal scheme was introduced, APA (*allocation personalisée d'autonomie*), which greatly extended central state funding.

26. Before 1975, only two minimum incomes existed: *minimum vieillesse* (a minimum for the old-aged) and minimum invalidité (a minimum for the disabled) were introduced in their present form in 1956 (Barbier and Théret, 2000).

27. Taxable income is divided according to the number of units in the family, so as to result in tax reduction for households with children. The reduction has been gradually capped since the late 1980s.

28. The limit was eventually never raised to 22.

29. It was somehow piquant to observe that the UK system retained a universalistic principle whereas the French government (temporarily) abandoned it.

30. Traditionally, only families of two or more children have been eligible for Child Benefit on a universal basis. But poorer families with one child have been entitled to it for the last twenty years.

31. Quantitatively, family benefits explicitly linked to labor market status have remained of limited importance.

32. When minima sociaux and housing benefits are excluded, the proportion of income-tested strict family benefits has remained stable at only 25 percent from 1973 to 1995.

33. Economic estimates show that no significant measurable impact has existed on fertility patterns for the last twenty-five years (Join-Lambert et al., 1997).

34. The maximum amount in June 2000 was FF 2500, i.e., a little under half the full-time minimum wage, SMIC (FF 5440 after contributions). The unemployed over 55 with 20 years of contributions or when they reach 57.5 and 10 years' contributions are entitled to a supplement. When over 55, recipients may be exempted from the actively seeking clause.

35. Whereas nearly 214,000 claimed it in 1984, less than 15,000 do it now.

36. The French unemployment insurance system was established only recently (1958).

37. At the time of this writing, new regulations are being devised that will eventually cancel the gradual reduction principle from 2001 onward (winter 2000).
38. *Paritarisme* here stands for an equal representation (parity) of employers' associations and labor unions on the Funds' boards (caisses). This principle has undergone many reforms since it was introduced in 1945.
39. As calculated by Daniel and Tuchszirer (1999) the rate includes all the registered unemployed, including those looking for a part-time or fixed-term contract. Using such standards (different from the ILO definition), 1.8 million unemployed are ineligible for unemployment benefits, strictly speaking. Many of them (the number is not known) are RMI beneficiaries either as main beneficiaries or as someone from their household.
40. With the current booming labor market, this number has again started to decrease in mid-2000.
41. *"Régime general,"* the mainstream and biggest caters for private sector employees (CNAM), accounts for 80 percent of total health spending. *"Régimes spéciaux"* are for civil servants and public enterprises' employees. There are also funds for farmers (MSA) and the self-employed (CANAM).
42. The level of patient reimbursement on ambulatory care and medicines was reduced.
43. In 1997, the number of beds in the public sector accounted for nearly 65 percent of the total and private services within public hospitals for 10 percent. Private beds accounted for one-quarter of the total (Deville and Lesdos-Cahaupé, 1999).
44. In 1980, 82 percent of all practitioners were in sector 1, and 68 percent in 1990 (respectively 70 percent and 51 percent of specialists).
45. Corresponding figures vary from 35 percent to 100 percent for prescriptions and 20 percent for hospital care.
46. Only 85 percent of the population join a supplementary insurance. Membership strongly varies with income levels and social groups (Rupprecht, 1999). In 1999, according to Volovitch (1999), 9.5 million people had no *mutuelle*, and only 2.5 million of them were 100 percent covered by social assistance for their healthcare.
47. New 1995 basis of social protection accounts.
48. Increasing inequality of access to care was experienced (despite targeted measures for the very poor—for instance RMI claimants in 1989). According to a 1995 survey, although nearly all interviewees had health insurance, 24 percent declared they had to give up certain cares, because of the inadequacy of the insurance coverage. Restrictions concerned dental care (12 percent), glasses (8 percent), and other medical cares (6 percent). Another study states that "the rate of renunciation to cares is more than 25 percent for households whose income is less than FF 6500 monthly, while it is half (12.5 percent) for those earning in between FF 20,000-30,000. Moreover, the rate of renunciation was higher than the mean rate for people belonging to groups with the highest degrees of morbidity" (Schneider-Bunner, 1995: 17).
49. In previous years there had been "a long genesis of a rushed reform" (Damamme and Jobert, 2000). In 1991, U.S.-inspired "diagnosis related groups" were adopted. Medically adapted spending control procedures were first implemented in 1992-93.
50. Various contemplated instruments are still to be finalized: compulsory standards for given pathologies (références médicales obligatoires, RMO), overall computerization of the system, experimentation of care networks, extension of generic drug use according to Drug Agency norms. Norms have been gradually and increasingly implemented since 1994. Their effectiveness is, however, dependent on further computerization of the healthcare system. Presently, only roughly one-third of general practitioners are connected by computers.

51. AAH beneficiaries (the disabled) and some minimum income beneficiaries are not eligible (2 million people) because their benefits are higher.
52. CFDT has replaced CGT-FO as MEDEF—the main employers' association's partner (accordingly in the unemployment insurance sector). The internal balance of interests within MEDEF has also been altered at the pharmaceutical industry's expense and the mutuelles sector has been able to assert itself within the coalition, while a new medical association, MG-France, emerged as a supporter of supply-side reforms (Damamme and Jobert, 2000).
53. A sum of 538 pension regimes cater to employees, the self-employed, professionals, farmers, managers and executives, each being organized according to different rules and delivering benefits of varying levels. Among them, one hundred *régimes spéciaux* cover 4.5 million public sector employees (20 percent of all employees). A very small proportion of these régimes are voluntary (the farmers', some large corporations schemes for executives, a few schemes for the self employed). It should nevertheless be stressed that life-insurance schemes, because of their very attractive taxing conditions have collected a significant part of savings.
54. Social partners (in 1947 and 1961) decided to complement the CNAV basic pension (which amounts to a 50 percent replacement of gross wages under a ceiling—a monthly FF 14,470 in 1999). As these complementary regimes have become compulsory for all employees, AGIRC, ARRCO, and CNAV form a quasi-integrated system. AGIRC caters to managers and executives.
55. For private sector employees, the system is two tiered (excluding a social assistance minimum pension). Non-civil servants in the public sector have their own complementary scheme, IRCANTEC (delivering an annual 5 billion francs pension bill altogether whereas AGIRC and ARRCO pensions amount to F. 180 billion (Ralle, 1998).
56. Since the 1980s growth deficit has accounted for the growth of the GDP pensions' ratio.
57. Given that current pensioners have benefited from inflation in the 1960s and 1970s, and from deflation and high interests rates on their savings in the 1980s, wealth distribution is even more distorted than income distribution according to age.
58. Not to mention a very generous use of early retirement schemes.
59. Taxable pensions for instance have been submitted to health contributions from 1983 on and to CSG since 1991. Pensions were subsequently re-evaluated according to inflation instead of wages and lost purchasing power (a drop of 15.4 percent or 11.2 percent to the net wage—Dupont and Sterdyniak, 2000).
60. Paradoxically, this latter disposition has proved less advantageous as public wages have lost purchasing power in the 1980s and 1990s: between 1987 and 1997, the mean loss was 0.4 percent a year (Dupont and Sterdyniak, 2000).
61. Nevertheless, these special regimes conditions are not so privileged because reference wages on which pension calculation is made exclude pay supplements (*primes*). They also are exclusive from complementary ones. These factors led to the creation of public employees' mutual funding schemes (PREFON and CREF) which constitute the only instance so far of French pension funds for employees enjoying tax deductions. They cover 400,000 contributors out of 5 million potential participants (Dupont and Sterdyniak, 2000).
62. Conditions are lifted for beneficiaries aged 55 or 57 who may not seek work; the condition of being out of work is lifted in certain cases when beneficiaries are employed for short spans of time (*"activités réduites"*).
63. When compared with the very strict benefit regime in the UK for instance, the French is much less strict. There are no targets in that domain; most leavers of the

unemployment count do it from their own choice. The monthly average of leavers for unknown reasons is much higher than the number of claimants sanctioned.

64. Notwithstanding the fact that part-time jobs have been increasing steeply as a proportion of all jobs during the 1990s. The current proportion is 17 percent of the active population (but more than 30 percent for women).

65. All AAH beneficiaries are presently about 800,000 (eligible from 20 to 65). This is comparable to the number of WAO recipients in the Netherlands, for a French active population of roughly 25 million. Six hundred thousand AAH beneficiaries are of working age. The activity rate of persons that declare being disabled is 54 percent (Brygoo et al., 2000).

66. Six percent for firms with a staff of over twenty.

67. RMI is a means-tested, differential, state-funded (paid by Family funds) benefit. At the beginning of 2000, a little more than 1 million claimed it. The maximum benefit ranges from FF 2552 for a single person with no child to FF 6636 for a couple with three children. The average monthly income of a RMI recipient was FF 4200 in 1995, RMI accounting for 46 percent of the total and housing benefits for 18 percent. The number of beneficiaries has grown dramatically since 1989 when it was only 407,000.

68. Article 2 of the law reads as follows: "Every person residing in France whose income...does not reach the amount of the minimum income...and who is at least 25 or is in charge of one or several child (ren)...and who accepts participation in the activities, determined with him/her, that are necessary for his/her social or professional insertion, is entitled to the RMI" (1988, 1992 revised Act).

69. For instance, a study of 1995 RMI recipients showed that if 70 percent of them had been claimants for one year, one-third of the 1995 claimants had left the rolls by the end of the year (CREDOC, 1996).

70. From a universalistic comparative point of view such policies would rank among "active labor market policy."

71. Including participants in the insertion *professionnelle* activities.

72. The rate of unemployment exceeded 10 percent of the active population for most of the last ten years, 12 percent in 1998, but 9.5 percent at the end of 2000. See figure 2.

73. From December 1997, the government started this new program aimed at creating 350,000 five-year public jobs for the young under 25 years; a small proportion of these was reserved for non-skilled youngsters and the ones "excluded" from the labor market.

74. Thanks to Palier, 1999, and MIRE (ministère des affaires sociales).

75. See previous note.

76. See previous note.

77. This interpretation of universality presumes a full employment society where wage earners enjoy citizenship and a status based on permanent/stable job tenure with social rights attached.

78. From the eighties on, for financial reasons, ceilings for contributions have gradually disappeared (except in limited areas, for instance for pensions—régimes complémentaires).

79. An exception is the complementary pension schemes for managers and executives (*cadres*) (Reynaud, 1996). Another one may be found within the public firms (Duclos and Mériaux, 1997) where it constitutes a sort of French neo-corporatism.

References

Abramovici, G., and Mathieu, R. (1999). Les comptes de la protection sociale 1995-1998. *Dossiers solidarité-Santé,* n° 4, oct.-dec. Paris, DREES, Ministère de l'emploi et de la solidarité.

ApRoberts, L., Daniel, C., Rehfeldt, U., Reynaud, E., and Vincent, C. (1997). "Formes et dynamiques de la régulation paritaire." *La Revue de l'IRES,* n° 24, numéro spécial, *Le Paritarisme. Institutions et acteurs,* pp. 19-42.

ApRoberts, L., and Reynaud, E. (1998). *Un panorama de la protection sociale complémentaire.* Paris, IRES, Rapport pour la MIRE, février, ronéo.

Barbier, J.-C. (1990). Comparing Family Policies in Europe: Methodological Problems. *International social security review,* n°3, pp. 326-341.

Barbier, J.-C. (1995). Politiques publiques de l'emploi: de la production des services à leur evaluation. In "Les politiques publiques d'emploi et leurs acteurs," *Cahiers du Centre d'Etudes de l'emploi,* n° 34, octobre, PUF, Paris, pp. 79-102.

Barbier, J.-C. (1998). La logica del workfare in Europa e negli stati uniti: i limiti delle analisi globali. *L'Assistenza sociale,* n°1, gennaio-marzo 1998, pp. 15-40.

Barbier, J.-C. (2000). "Juger l' 'Europe sociale' en termes d'efficacité et d'équité?" communication aux 20è journées de l'AES, Toulouse, septembre, 14p.

Barbier, J.-C., and Gautié, J. (eds.). (1998). *Les politiques de l'emploi en Europe et aux Etats Unis.* PUF, Paris.

Barbier, J.-C., and Nadel, H. (2000). *La flexibilité du travail et de l'emploi.* Domino, Flammarion, Paris.

Barbier, J.-C., and Théret, B. (2000). Welfare-to-work or Work-to-welfare? The French Case. In Neil Gilbert (ed.), *Welfare-to Work Policies in Social Assistance: A Comparative Study.* New Brunswick, NJ: Transaction Publishers.

Beaumel C., Kerjosse R., Tamby I. (1999). Démographie des pays industrialisés: la position de la France. *Données sociales,* Insee, Paris.

Bec, C. (1999). Assistance et égalité dans le système français de protection sociale. In MIRE, *Comparer les systèmes de protection sociale en Europe.* Vol. 4: Rencontres de Copenhague, Paris: DREES-MIRE—Imprimerie Nationale, tome I, pp. 135-147.

Belorgey, J.-M. (1996). "Pour renouer avec l'esprit initial du RMI," in "Vers un revenu minimum inconditionnel," *Revue du MAUSS semestrielle,* n°7, premier semestre, La Découverte, Paris, pp. 297-299.

Bonoli, G., and Palier, B. (1995). Entre Bismark et Beveridge. "Crises" de la sécurité sociale et politique(s). *Revue française de science politique,* Vol. 45, n° 4, pp. 668-698.

Boyer, R. (1999). *Le gouvernement économique de l'Europe,* Documentation Française, Paris.

Bradshaw, J., Ditch, J., Holmes H., Whiteford P., and Ray, J.-C. (1994). Une comparaison internationale des aides à la famille. *Recherches et Prévisions,* septembre (37), pp. 11-26.

Brygoo, A., Destéfanis, M., Fouquet, A. (2000). "Politiques actives et insertion dans le marché du travail des personnes handicapées: estimation du bénéfice net," Document de travail CEE 00/05, Noisy le Grand, 56p.

Catrice-Lorey, A. (1997). La Sécurité sociale en France, institution anti-paritaire? Un regard historique de long terme. *La Revue de l'IRES,* n° 24, numéro spécial, "Le Paritarisme. Institutions et acteurs," pp. 81-106.

CERC. (1999). Immigration, emploi et chômage, un état des lieux empirique et théorique. *Les dossiers de CERC-Association,* n°3, Paris.

Chambaz, C. (1997). La pauvreté en Fance et en Europe. *INSEE Premiére*, n° 533, juillet.

Chauvel, L. (2000). Entre les riches et les pauvres, les classes moyennes. In *Mesurer les inégalités*, DREES-Mire, Ministère de l'emploi et de la solidarité, Paris, pp. 53-63.

Concialdi, P. (1999a). Réformer la protection sociale? Le débat sur les retraites. *Cahiers français*, Emploi et protection sociale, pp. 107-116.

Concialdi, P. (2000). Débats et enjeux autour des retraites: un état des lieux. *L'Année de la régulation*, Vol. 4, pp. 78-208.

CREDOC (Isa Aldeghi). (1996). Les nouveaux arrivants au revenu minimum d'insertion, profils, parcours antérieurs, rapports à l'emploi et à la famille. Rapport n° 173, novembre, Paris.

Damamme, D., and Jobert, B. (2000). Coalitions sociales et innovations institutionnelles: le cas du Plan Juppé. *Innovations institutionnelles et territoires*, in Tallard Michèle, Théret Bruno, and Uri Didier (eds.), Paris, L'Harmattan, pp. 185-203.

Daniel, C., and Le Clainche, C. (coord.). (2000). *Mesurer les inégalités*, DREES-Mire, Ministère de l'emploi et de la solidarité, Paris.

Daniel, C., and Tuchszirer, C. (1999). *L'État face aux chômeurs, l'indemnisation du chômage de 1884 à nos jours.* Flammarion, Paris.

DARES. (1996). *40 ans de politique de l'emploi.* La documentation française, Paris.

DARES. (1997). *Premières synthèses,* n° 97.07, 27-1, "La politique de l'emploi en 1996."

Dehove, M., and Théret, B. (1996). La parole de l'Etat. A propos de la crise sociale qui a paralysé la France en novembre-décembre 1995. *Politique et Sociétés*, 15(30), special issue "Vers un nouvel Etat-providence?" pp. 53-90.

Deville, A., and Lesdos-Cauhapé, C. (1999). Les Comptes de la santé en 1998. *Etudes et Résultats*, DREES, n° 24, juillet.

Données sociales, INSEE, 1999, Paris.

DREES. (1998). *Les comptes de la protection sociale 1990-1997*, Paris, La Documentation française.

DREES. (1999). Les comptes de la protection sociale en 1998. *Etudes et Résultats*, n° 36.

Duclos, L., and Mériaux, O. (1997). Pour une économie du paritarisme. *La Revue de l'IRES*, n° 24, numéro spécial Le Paritarisme. Institutions et acteurs, pp. 61-80.

Dupont, G., and Sterdyniak, H. (2000). *Quel avenir pour nos retraites ?* Paris, La Découverte, collection Repères.

Esping-Andersen, G. (1990). *The Three Worlds of Welfare Capitalism*, Princeton, NJ, Princeton University Press.

Esping-Andersen, G. (1997). L'Etat protecteur à la fin du siècle, les conséquences de l'évolution du marché du travail, de la famille et de la démographie. In *Famille, marché et collectivité, équité et efficience de la politique sociale*, OCDE, Paris, pp. 65-83.

EU Commission. (1998). *Employment rates report*, Brussels, mimeo, 21p. + tables.

EU Commission. (1999). Employment report, mimeo, internet version.

Eurostat. (1999). Les transferts sociaux et leurs effets redistributifs dans l'UE. *Statistiques en bref,*, n°13, thème 3 (Population et conditions de vie).

Flora, P. (1986). Introduction. In P. Flora (ed.), *Growth to Limits. The Western European Welfare States Since World War II.* Berlin/New York: de Gruyter, pp. XII-XXXVI.

Geffroy, Y., and Lenseigne, F. (1999). Les Comptes de la santé en 1998. *Etudes et Résultats*, DREES, n° 33, septembre.

Giddens, A. (2000). *The Third Way and Its Critics.* Polity Press, Cambridge.

Hassenteufel, P. (1997). Le plan Juppé: Fin ou renouveau d'une régulation paritaire de l'assurance-maladie. *La Revue de l'IRES*, n° 24, numéro spécial Le Paritarisme. Institutions et acteurs, pp. 175-190.

Jobert, B., and Théret, B. (1994). La consécration républicaine du néolibéralisme. In *Le tournant néolibéral en Europe*, B. Jobert ed., Paris, L'Harmattan.

Join-Lambert, M.-T., Bolot-Gittler, A., Daniel, C., Lenoir, D., and Méda, D. (1997). *Politiques sociales*. Paris, Presses de Sciences Po et Dalloz, 2 ème édition.

Kerschen, N. (1995). L'influence du Rapport Beveridge sur le plan français de sécurité sociale de 1945. *Revue française de science politique*, Vol. 45, n° 4, pp. 570-595.

Kott, S. (1996). Communauté ou solidarité. Des modèles divergents pour les politiques sociales française et allemande à la fin du XIX ème siècle? In MIRE, *Comparer les systèmes de protection sociale en Europe*. Vol. 2: Rencontres de Berlin, Paris: MIRE—Imprimerie Nationale, pp. 41-60.

Lagarenne, C., and Legendre, N. (2000). Les travailleurs pauvres en France: facteurs individuels et familiaux. *Economie et Statistique*, n° 335, pp. 3-25.

Lancry, P.-J. (1995). Le financement de la santé en France. *Revue d'économie financière*, n° 34, pp. 167-181.

Lévy, M. L. (2000). "La population de la France au seuil des années 2000," *Population et Sociétés*, n° 355, mars.

Lollivier, S. (2000). Inégalités de revenus et de patrimoine en France: quels indicateurs? quels constats?" In *Mesurer les inégalités*, DREES-Mire, Ministère de l'emploi et de la solidarité, Paris, pp 21-30.

Majnoni d'Intignano, B. (1999). *Égalité entre femmes et hommes: aspects économiques*, rapport du Conseil d'analyse économique. Paris, La documentation française.

Martin, C. (1998). Le domestique dans les modèles d'Etat-providence. In J. Commaille and B. Jobert (eds.), *Les métamorphoses de la régulation politique*. Paris, LGDJ, pp. 361-380.

Maurice, M., Sellier, F., and Sylvestre, J.-J. (1982). *Politique d'éducation et organisation industrielle en France et en Allemagne*. PUF, Paris.

Maurice, J. (ed.). (1999). *Europe sociale*, Rapport au Premier Ministre, Commissariat Génral du Plan. Paris, La documentation française.

Merrien, F.-X. (1997). *L'État-Providence*, Collection Que sais-je? PUF, Paris.

Morel, S. (2000). *Les logiques de la réciprocité, les transformations de la relation d'assistance aux Etats Unis et en France*. PUF, Paris.

Mückenberger, U., and Supiot, A. (1999). Ordre public social et communauté. Deux cultures du droit du travail. In B. Zimmermann, C. Didry, and P. Wagner (eds.), *Le travail et la nation*. Paris, Éditions de la MSH, pp. 81-105.

Myles, J., and Pierson P. (2000). The Comparative Political Economy of Pensions Reform. In P. Pierson (ed.), *The New Politics of the Welfare State*. Oxford, Oxford University Press.

Palier, B. (1998). The French Social Protection System. In J.-C. Portonnier (ed.), *1997, Glossaire bilingue de la protection sociale. Social Protection: a bilingual glossary*, Vol. 1, Les termes français, Paris, MIRE, pp. 23-34.

Palier, B. (1999). *Réformer la Sécurité sociale. Les interventions gouvernementales en matière de protection sociale depuis 1945, la France en perspective comparative*. Thèse de doctorat, Institut d'Études politiques de Paris, ronéo.

Palier, B., and Bonoli, G. (2000). La montée en puissance des fonds de pension: une lecture comparative des réformes des systèmes de retraite, entre modèle global et cheminements nationaux. *L'Année de la régulation*, Vol. 4.

Paugam, S. (1999). Pauvreté, chômage et liens sociaux en Europe. In *La société française*, INSEE, Paris, pp. 472-479.

Quermonne, J.-L. (ed.). (1999). *Vers des institutions européennes légitimes et efficaces*. Rapport au Premier Ministre, Commissariat Général du Plan, Paris, Documentation française.

Ralle, P. (1998). Évolutions démographiques et retraites: éléments sur la réforme de 1993." In Conseil d'analyse économique, *Retraites et épargne*. Paris, La Documentation française, pp. 175-186.

Renard, D. (1995). Les rapports entre assistance et assurance dans la constitution du système de protection sociale français. In MIRE, *Comparer les systèmes de protection sociale en Europe*. Vol. 1: Rencontres d'Oxford, Paris: Imprimerie Nationale, pp. 105-125.

Reynaud, E. (1994). "Les différentes logiques de financement des retraites en repartition. *La Revue de l'IRES*, n° 15, numéro spécial Les retraites complémentaires, pp. 125-140.

Rochaix, L. (1995). Le financement par les particuliers: la boite de Pandore. *Revue d'économie financière*, n° 34, pp. 197-227.

Rupprecht, F. (1999). Evaluation de l'efficience du système de soins français. In Conseil d'Analyse Economique, *Régulation du système de santé*, Paris, La Documentation française, pp. 151-164.

Schneider-Bunner C. (1995). La justice sociale dans les systèmes de santé européens. *Futuribles*, septembre.

Théret, B. (1991). Néo-libéralisme, inégalités sociales et politiques fiscales de droite et de gauche dans la France des années 1980: Identités et différences, pratiques et doctrines. *Revue Française de Sciences Politiques*, vol. 41, n° 3, pp. 342-381.

Théret, B. (1996). De la comparabilité des systèmes nationaux de protection sociale dans les sociétés salariales: essai d'analyse structurale. In MIRE, *Comparer les systèmes de protection sociale en Europe*. Vol. 2: Rencontres de Berlin, Paris: MIRE—Imprimerie Nationale, pp. 439-503.

Théret, B. (1997). Méthodologie des comparaisons internationales, approches de l'effet sociétal et de la régulation: fondements pour une lecture structuraliste des systèmes de protection sociale. *L'année de la régulation*, Vol. 1, pp. 163-228.

Théret, B. (2000). Theoretical Problems in International Comparisons: Toward a Reciprocal Improvement of Societal Approach and "Régulation" Theory by Methodic Structuralism. In M. Maurice and A. Sorge (eds.), *Embedding Organizations. Societal Analysis of Actors, Organizations and Socio-economic Context*. Amsterdam–Philadelphia: John Benjamins, pp. 101-115.

Titmuss, R. (1974). *Social Policy*. London, Allen and Unwin.

Verdier, E. (2000). Analyse sociétale et changement institutionnel: le cas de l'éducation et de la formation professionnelle initiale. In M. Tallard, B. Théret, and D. Uri (eds.), *Innovations institutionnelles et territoires*, Paris, L'Harmattan, pp. 101-128.

Volovitch, P. (1999). L'accès aux soins pour tous. *Alternatives Economiques*, n°169, avril, pp. 44-47.

4

New Directions for the British Welfare State

Linda Bauld, Ken Judge, and Iain Paterson

Introduction

Between 1979 and 1997 there was a persistent perception that the British welfare state was under threat. Under a Conservative administration, the country experienced widening income inequality, the growth of private markets and limits on welfare spending. However, since May 1997, which marked the election of New Labour, there have been dramatic changes of emphasis in social policy, including a new commitment to reducing social exclusion. During its first 1,000 days in office an avalanche of policy initiatives emerged, many of which might be expected to have profound welfare consequences in future years. But despite the very real change of direction in social policy in recent years the impact of changes in government should not be exaggerated. There are also many long-term and often global influences that impact upon modern welfare states. The aim of this chapter is to evaluate some of the most significant trends in recent decades in Britain, and to reflect on what these imply for the future direction of the welfare state.

The first section traces some of the main economic and social trends in Britain that shaped and modified social policy between 1980 and the beginning of the new century.

Economic Trends, 1980–1998

The main economic and fiscal trends that influenced the changing shape of the welfare state are separated into three sections: changes in the economy, state spending and its constituent parts; trends in the availability and value of tax reliefs and allowances related to social policy; and significant patterns in the financing of the welfare state.

Public expenditure. In a famous statement, soon after she became prime minister in 1979, Margaret Thatcher declared that high levels of public spending lay at the root of Britain's economic difficulties. For the best part of two decades this belief and the values that underpinned it dominated domestic public policy. As a result public expenditure as a share of national income shrank from almost 53 percent in 1980 to 48.6 percent in 1990 and to 44.4 percent in 1998. But this pattern may be about to change. After three years of endeavor to establish its economic and fiscal credibility in financial markets the Blair government has announced a major expansion of investment in essential public services for the first quinquennium of the new century.

Table 4.1 shows the main trends in public expenditure between 1980 and 1998 (at constant 1995 prices). During this period net national income increased in real terms by 62 percent whereas public expenditure grew by only a fraction less than 36 percent. In contrast, spending on social welfare programs grew at almost the same rate as the economy as a whole and increased

Table 4.1
Trends in Public Expenditure 1980-98 (1995 Prices)

	1980	1990	1998	% change 98/80
Social protection	55914.29	89292.16	121922.1	118.0518
Education	28048.35	30869.36	34945.92	24.59171
Health	25567.03	33307.6	42502.29	66.23865
Housing	18569.23	9545.131	5148.488	-72.27409
Social Welfare	1280898.9	163014.3	204518.8	59.65694
Other programs	101109.9	114361	107173.2	5.996788
TOTAL PUBLIC EXPENDITURE	229208.8	277375.3	311692	35.98607
NET NATIONAL INCOME	433624.2	571292.2	702741.5	62.06235
Social Welfare as % public expenditure	55.88743	58.77028	65.61566	
Public Expenditure as % national income	52.88743	48.55227	44.35372	
Social Welfare as % national income	29.54146	28.53431	29.10299	

Source: ONS *United Kingdom National Accounts* 2000 Edition. London: The Stationary Office.

their share of total public expenditure from 56 percent to 66 percent. However, there were marked differences in the experiences of different social welfare programs during this period. Social protection expenditure was the fastest growing area, which more than doubled after 1980 (118 percent), and accounted for almost 60 percent of social welfare spending by 1998. In contrast, health spending rose by approximately two-thirds (66.2 percent) and education by almost one-quarter (24.6 percent). The main casualty was public spending on social housing, which declined by almost three-quarters (-72.3 percent). The main reason for this change is that the number of households renting from a local authority declined substantially after the introduction of "right to buy" legislation that resulted in the transfer of many properties from public to private ownership.

Tables 4.2 and 4.3 provide more detail about spending on social protection, the largest and fastest growing area of social welfare between 1980 and 1998. The data are taken from an official review of social security spending (DSS, 2000) and are not directly comparable with those shown in table 4.1. For example, they provide information about most of the significant social security benefits, but the coverage of social protection is not quite as comprehensive as that shown in table 4.1. However, the broad trends are consistent.

Table 4.2 compares spending over time on the main social security benefits. Total spending on the benefits listed increased by 87 percent between

Table 4.2
Expenditure by Benefit, 1978/79 to 1998/99 (£ Million, 1998/99 Prices)

	1987/79	1988/89	1998/99	% change 98/78
Retirement pensions	24258	28427	35574	46.65
Unemployment benefits	2030	1635	3557	75.22
Sickness benefits	2236	1611	26	-98.84
Invalidity/Incapacity benefits	2698	4963	7241	168.38
Maternity benefits	388	409	571	47.16
Disability allowances	926	3204	9812	959.61
Income support	5014	11192	11787	135.08
Child benefit	5705	6670	7295	27.87
Housing-related benefit	3556	7604	13601	282.48
SUB TOTAL	46811	65715	89464	91.12
Other	4175	4216	6117	46.51
TOTAL	50986	69931	95581	87.47

Source: Table B2, *The Changing Welfare State: Social Security Spending 1998/99*, Department of Social Security paper.

1978/79 and 1998/99. However, the most expensive benefit—retirement pensions—that accounted for 37 percent of total spending in 1998/99, experienced substantially below average levels of spending increase (47 percent). In contrast, the most rapidly expanding sub-programs were those related to disability and incapacity, housing and to a lesser extent income support, the main social assistance benefit. This picture is confirmed by an analysis of benefit expenditure by main client group shown in table 4.3. Total spending on elderly people increased by only 58 percent between 1978 and 1998 whereas expenditure on families and on people with long-term illnesses and/ or disabilities grew by well over 300 percent. Other significant trends highlighted in table 4.2 include the effective abolition of public spending on sickness benefits and the relatively modest rate of increase in spending on child benefit.

Tax expenditures. There is a very important area of public provision of social welfare benefits that is not shown in statistics of public expenditure. In the 1950s Richard Titmuss coined the term *fiscal welfare* to describe benefits provided to citizens through the provision of tax allowances and reliefs for a wide variety of purposes. More recently the term *tax expenditure* has been most commonly used in the international literature to describe this phenomenon. In the UK, Sinfield (1998) has suggested that "the terms tax benefit and tax welfare are probably the most appropriate to use to describe the advantages which result from tax spending, whether officially recognised or not" (p. 62). Whatever term is employed it is critical to consider the role of tax

Table 4.3
Social Security Expenditure by Client Group, 1978/79 to 1998/99
(£ Million, 1998/99 Prices)

	1978/79	1988/89	1998/99	% change 98/78
Elderly people	28113	34944	44507	58.31
People with long-term illness/disability	5687	10790	23848	319.34
Families	2428	5528	10139	317.59
Unemployed people	4458	7982	5367	20.39
Children	5782	6937	7297	26.20
SUB TOTAL	46468	66181	91158	96.17
Other	4518	3750	4423	-2.10
TOTAL	50986	69931	95581	87.47

Source: Table B4, *The Changing Welfare State: Social Security Spending 1998/99*, Department of Social Security paper.

allowances and reliefs when considering the role of the modern state in providing social welfare services. Sinfield (1998) argues, as shown in box 4.1, that there are four main reasons why this should be so.

Box 4.1

The Importance of Tax Expenditures

First, the costs of tax benefits affect the balancing of the budget just as much as public expenditure benefit or service. Second, tax benefits generally widen inequalities. The more limited the public provision, the more important and valuable tax benefits become for protecting some at the expense of others. They promote the social inclusion and privilege of some while limiting the resources available for meeting the needs of others. Third, high levels of unemployment and labour market insecurity increase the size of the groups, which are unable to benefit from the distribution of tax benefits through secure and regular income. Pressures on government revenues from growing needs increase the problems for public spending on social benefits and services. Those who have the economic resources take advantage of what tax benefits there are to subsidize their private provision. Recent governments have deliberately set out to stimulate private alternatives, using tax reliefs and other incentives, with little benefit to the poor and marginal groups who are most vulnerable to the cuts in public spending. This has reinforced the processes excluding the poor. Fourth, they weaken the legitimacy of collective, state provision. People are helped by concealed public subsidies to provide for themselves privately and to opt out of collective measures which pool risks and promote solidarity and integration.

Source: Sinfield, 1998.

Table 4.4 is a modified version of one presented to the House of Commons Social Security Committee in 1998 by Adrian Sinfield. It shows the main changes in the most significant tax allowances and reliefs during the past twenty years that are related to social policy within the limitations of the data that are available. During the 1980s there was a massive expansion (a three-fold real increase) of tax expenditures. This trend was associated with the Thatcher government's promotion of owner occupation as a cornerstone of its housing policy, and the even stronger emphasis on encouraging people to invest in occupational and personal pensions rather than rely on state retirement pensions, which were significantly reduced in real terms by the policy of linking changes in benefit levels to retail prices rather than average earnings. These trends did much to exacerbate the rising inequality in the distribution of income that was such a marked feature of British experience in the 1980s.

Table 4.4
Major Tax Allowances and Reliefs Relating to Social Policy,
UK 1980 to 1999 (£ Millions, 1995 Prices)

	1980/81	1990/91	1999/2000	% change 99/80
ALLOWANCES				
• Married couple's allowance	N/a	5700.71	1833.18	N/a
• Age-related allowances	183.19	688.84	1145.74	40.89479
• Additional allowances for one-parent families	186.81	332.54	137.49	-26.40319
RELIEFS				
• Pension schemes	2065.93	9976.25	11824.01	472.3326
• Life assurance premiums	1186.81	403.80	100.82	-91.50457
• Mortgage interest	4307.69	9144.89	1466.54	-65.95522
EXEMPTIONS				
• Child benefit and one-parent benefit	N/a	N/a	779.10	N/a
• Long-term disability benefits	340.66	760.10	1035.75	204.0419
• First £30,000 paid on termination of employment	N/a	N/a	1008.25	N/a
• Working families tax credit	N/a	N/a	1191.57	N/a
TOTAL: social policy related tax benefits	8901.099	27007.13	20522.46	130.5609

Source: Board of Inland Revenue *Inland Revenue statistics*. London: HMSO/The Stationery Office. www.inlandrevenue.gov.uk/stats/.

The pattern of investment in tax expenditures during the 1990s was a more complicated one. On the one hand, tax revenues were foregone because of the policy of subsidizing private pension provision continued to grow, albeit at a slower rate than in the 1980s. There were also a number of very significant new tax expenditures with rather different consequences for the distribution of income. The substantial subsidy associated with the termination of employment contracts tended to favor more affluent people. On the other hand, the introduction of the Working Families Tax Credit is very much part of New Labour's policy of encouraging low-paid workers back into the labor market, which should help to redistribute income to one of the poorest and most socially excluded sections of the community. However, the most striking feature of the 1990s has been the gradual phasing out of the tax reliefs associated with marriage and owner-occupied housing. These policies will help to redress some of the most striking inegalitarian tendencies of the 1980s.

Financing. At the time when Margaret Thatcher first became prime minister in 1979 academic and political debate was obsessed with discussions about the fiscal crisis of the state and the excessive burden of debt associated with the financing of state expenditures. These debates quickly became overlaid with ideological concerns about limiting the size and role of the state and the need to free citizens from excessive taxation to promote liberty and to stimulate the economy. One of the key features of the last quarter of the twentieth century in Britain was the extent to which the majority of politicians of almost all parties have been constrained by the perception that they needed to reduce headlines rates of direct taxation in order to win electoral credibility. Despite these efforts the structure of the income tax system has meant that revenues from this source have continued to grow as a result of fiscal drag. However, there has also been a gradual increase in the relative importance of expenditure rather than income taxes that has had a regressive impact on income inequality. At the same time, successive governments have continued to keep a tight rein on public expenditures. Somewhat surprisingly, the New Labour government elected in 1997 and headed by Tony Blair maintained firm restrictions on state spending during its first three years in office as it sought to establish economic credibility with the electorate and financial markets. One consequence of the sustained fiscal policies that have been put in place, combined with steady economic growth in the second half of the 1990s, is that by the spring of 2000 the Blair government found itself able to contemplate very substantial increases in public expenditure. An indication of how this largesse will be used is outlined in the final section of this chapter. The aim here is to summarize some of the main trends in terms of financing public expenditure in Britain during the last two decades of the twentieth century.

Table 4.5 shows that total government revenues increased in real terms between 1980 and 1998 by almost 44 percent. This is substantially below the 62 percent increase in national income recorded during the same period but comfortably in excess of the 36 percent increase in public spending (see table 4.1). These patterns help to explain the improved fiscal position of the government bequeathed to the Blair government as compared to the one that Mrs. Thatcher inherited in 1979.

Changes in the structure, level, and impact of taxation during the past twenty years have been numerous and complex. Table 4.5 simply highlights some of the main trends that are most clearly related to social policy objectives. Despite the emphasis on reducing headline rates of direct taxation the yield from this source has been slightly above the overall rate of increase in government revenues. However, the rate of increase has been much greater for both social security contributions (62 percent) and taxes on expenditure (79 percent). The rapid rise in expenditure taxes such as Value Added Tax (VAT), where the yield has more than doubled over the period, is a matter of concern

Table 4.5
Trends in Financing Public Spending 1980 to 1998
(£ Million, 1998/99 Prices)

	1980	1990	1998	% change 98/80
Income Tax	53430.77	65286.22	79272.23	48.36
Taxes on expenditure	62006.59	88668.65	111139.3	79.24
• Value added tax	26147.25	40197.15	52306.14	100.04
• Fuel taxes	7312.088	11086.7	19027.5	160.22
• Alcohol & tobacco	11597.8	12277.91	12461.04	7.44
Social security contributions	30635.16	40922.8	49626.03	61.99
TOTAL REVENUES	201578	241770.8	289500.5	43.62

Source: ONS *United Kingdom National Accounts* 2000 Edition. London: The Stationery Office.

in terms of trends in income inequality because these sources of revenue (see table 4.8) are much more regressive than income taxes. Somewhat surprisingly though there are some marked differences in the trends for different expenditure taxes. The income from duties on alcohol and tobacco, for example, has risen very slowly (7 percent) whereas the revenues from fuel taxes–driven in part by environmental concerns–have risen very sharply (160 percent).

Social Trends

In addition to the economic developments that have taken place in the period since 1980, British society has also undergone important changes. It is possible to identify a range of social trends, from demographic change, shifts in household and family structure, changes in the labor market and developments in relation to immigration and asylum seekers. Some of these changes have been more dramatic than others, but each has had an impact on debate and decisions surrounding social protection and public expenditure in the UK.

Table 4.6 illustrates a range of social trends since 1981. The size, age and gender profile of Britain's population has changed over this period. The population of the UK increased by almost three million between 1981 and 1998 to an estimated 59.2 million. In common with all Western countries, Britain has an aging population. There has been a steady rise in the proportion of the population who are over the age of 65, accompanied by a drop in the proportion of those under the age of 15. In 1981, 14 percent of the population was aged 65 and above, rising to 16 percent by 1998. This rise is due to the increase in the proportion of people aged 75 and over, which rose from 4 percent in 1981 to 7 percent in 1998. Conversely, the proportion of children under the age of 15 dropped from 24 percent in 1981 to 22 percent in 1998. These gradual demographic shifts differ slightly between males and females in the UK, as table 4.6 illustrates. Due to the longer life expectancy of women, they make up a significantly higher proportion of those aged 75 and over— 8 percent of females in 1998, compared with 5 percent of males.

The diversity of Britain's population has grown since the early 1980s. Table 4.6 illustrates the proportion of the population belonging to broad categories of ethnicity, as reported in the General Household Survey (a cross-sectional, annual survey based on a sample of approximately 25,000 people). The proportion of the population who describe themselves as "White" dropped from 95 percent in 1981 to 93 percent in 1998. There was an accompanying rise in the proportion of people who identified themselves as members of other ethnic groups, most markedly those from the Pakistani and Bangladeshi communities (from 1 to 2 percent) and those from a range of other groups not specifically identified in the GHS (from 1 to 3 percent). Although these changes are very small when presented as proportional shifts, they do represent a consistent growth—from 2 percent in 1971 to 4 percent in 1981 and 7 percent in 1998—in the number of people identifying themselves as members of ethnic minority communities in the UK.

What table 4.6 does not illustrate is the age profile of Britain's ethnic minority communities, as well as the concentration of these communities in certain parts of the UK. In contrast to the population overall, ethnic minority populations have a younger age profile. Whereas in 1998 21 percent of Britain's white population was under the age of 15, 36 percent of the ethnic minority population fell into this age bracket, with the Pakistani/Bangladeshi community containing the highest proportion of children (41 percent). In contrast, while 16 percent of the white population was over the age of 65 in 1998, just 4 percent of the ethnic minority community fell into this age bracket. These significant differences in age profile are due to a range of factors, but the most significant are the high influx of relatively young immigrants from the 1950s onwards and higher fertility rates among most ethnic minority groups. This has resulted in larger households—the mean household size among the white population is 2.4 people, compared with 3.1 people among ethnic groups overall—and will contribute significantly to the growing diversity of the UK's population in the future.

It is worth noting, however, that figures from 1998 do highlight significant divergence in the regional distribution of the ethnic minority population. Almost half—43 percent—of Britain's ethnic minority population live in London. Just 1 percent live in Wales and 1 percent in the North East of England, with 2 percent living in Scotland.

Table 4.6
Social Trends in Britain, 1981-1998

	1981	1991	1998
POPULATION			
Males			
0-15	25	23	24
16-44	41	41	38
45-64	22	22	24
65-74	8	8	9
75+	4	5	5
Females			
0-15	22	21	21
16-44	39	39	38
45-64	22	22	24
65-74	10	10	9
75+	7	7	8
ETHNIC GROUP			
White	95	94	93
Indian	2	1	2
Pakistani/Bangladeshi	1	1	2
Black Caribbean	1	1	1
Remaining Groups	1	2	3
HOUSEHOLD TYPE			
1 adult aged 16-59	7	10	13
2 adults aged 16-59	13	16	16
Youngest person aged 0-15	35	30	29
3 or more adults	13	12	9
2 adults, 1 or both aged 60+	17	16	17
1 adult aged 60 or older	15	16	16
FAMILY TYPE*			
Married/cohabiting couple	87	81	75
Lone mother	11	18	22
Lone father	2	1	2
SOCIOECONOMIC GROUP BY GENDER****			
Males			
Non-manual	38	44	51
Manual	62	56	49
Females			

Table 4.6 (cont.)

	1981	1991	1998
Non-manual	42	49	53
Manual	58	51	48
IMMIGRATION			
Acceptances for Settlement (thousands)	59	54	70
Asylum Seekers (thousands)***	4	45	46

Sources: ONS *General Household Survey* 1984. London: HMSO. ONS *Living in Britain: Results from the 1998 General Household Survey*. London: The Stationery Office. ONS *Social Trends* 2000 Edition. London: The Stationery Office.

* Family Type relates to families with dependent children

**1981 figures relate to 1979

*** No figures for asylum seekers were available prior to 1986. Thus, 1981 figures relate to 1986.

Growing diversity is also evident in relation to family structure in the UK. Table 4.6 provides two examples of evidence from the General Household Survey that suggests that shifts away from traditional family structures continued in the period from 1981. The first example in the table illustrates changes in household type. There has been a growth in the proportion of adults living alone and a drop in the proportion of households with children. In 1981, 7 percent of households were made up of a single adult of working age. This rose to 10 percent in 1991 and 13 percent in 1998. The proportion of single pensioner households also rose slightly over this period. In contrast, households with one or more child(ren) dropped from 35 percent of the total to 29 percent in 1998. Households with three or more adults (i.e., parents living with an older child, or elderly people living with younger relatives) have also become less prevalent since 1981, dropping from 13 percent to 9 percent of households.

The second example of changing family structure illustrated in Table 4.6 relates to family type. Three types of households are presented: those containing a married or cohabiting couple with children, and households containing either a single mother or single father with children. Since 1981, children in the UK are less likely to live with both parents. Families containing a married or cohabiting couple dropped from 87 percent in 1981 to 75 percent of households with children in 1998. In contrast, the proportion of families containing a single mother doubled—from 11 percent to 22 percent of the total. Other evidence from the GHS not shown in table 4.6 suggests that the largest proportion of these single mothers in 1998 were never married mothers, rather than widows or mothers who were divorced or separated from their partners. This is in contrast to 1981, when divorce was the most common cause of single parenthood. The dramatic rise in the proportion of families headed by a single mother has implications for social security and employment policies, a point we return to later in this chapter.

Since the early 1980s, there have been a number of significant shifts in the labor market in the UK. Fluctuations between periods of recession and relative economic prosperity have combined with changes in the structure and nature of employment to result in fluctuating rates of economic activity and unemployment. These changes have had important implications for family and individual incomes and thus for demands on social protection. As we show in the "Employment and Wefare-to-Work" section, for most of the period since 1980 Britain has struggled with historically high levels of worklessness associated with structural unemployment and rising rates of economic inactivity among men aged 50 and above, in particular. In the second half of the 1990s and especially since 1997, however, a combination of economic growth and active labor market policies has begun to address many long-standing employment issues. We discuss below the extent to which the New Labor government can take credit for these changes.

In addition to changes in economic activity and unemployment, the continuing shift away from traditional industries that Britain has experienced since the 1970s has combined with wider access to higher education to result in a significant change in socioeconomic groupings across the country. This shift is depicted in a very general way in table 4.6, which differentiates between non-manual and manual occupations for men and women from 1981 to 1998. For both men and women, the proportion of people of working age who described their occupation as manual (consisting of skilled manual, semi-skilled manual and unskilled manual jobs) has dropped. In 1979, 62 percent of working men and 58 percent of working women were in manual occupations. By 1998, this proportion had dropped to 49 percent for men and 48 percent for women. In contrast, the proportion of men and women in non-manual occupations, including professional, managerial and junior non-manual jobs, has risen significantly.

One final social trend that has been increasingly evident in Britain since the 1980s relates to immigration, particularly changes in the number of applicants for asylum in the UK. In common with other countries in Western Europe, the UK had witnessed a significant rise in the number of asylum seekers. This trend is illustrated at the bottom of table 4.6, along with general immigration statistics for the period. As the table shows, the number of immigrants accepted for settlement in the UK has fluctuated since 1981. In that year, 59,000 individuals were accepted for settlement in the UK. This represented a slight drop since 1976, when 80,700 were accepted. In the 1980s the decline continued, reaching a low of 47,800 in 1986. By the early 1990s numbers accepted for settlement had begun to rise again. This steady rise has continued, reaching 70,000 in 1998. Much of the rise since 1991 is due to asylum seekers. As table 4.6 shows, the number of individuals applying for asylum in the UK has risen dramatically from 4,000 in 1986 to 45,000 in 1991 and 46,000 in 1998. This rise can be attributed to a number of factors, including economic change and easier access to travel. However, there is little doubt that the single most significant reason for the rise has been conflict in Africa, the Middle East and most recently in Europe. Between 1991 and 1998 the number of asylum seekers from Europe rose from 3,700 to 17,700, with the greatest number of applicants in 1998 coming from the Federal Republic of Yugoslavia.

Income Inequality and Social Exclusion

Probably the most dramatic and significant of all of the economic and social trends in the UK since 1980 has been the growing concern about social exclusion that is closely associated with the substantial rise in income inequality and poverty. Social exclusion is a tricky concept despite the fact that ambitious attempts have been made to develop empirical measures of the phenomenon and to use them to map patterns in Britain in the 1990s (Burchardt et al., 1999). Nevertheless, in common usage the term certainly embraces those groups who are unable to fully participate in social and economic life because of long-term illness or disability, marital or relationship breakdown, inadequate social security benefits, fear and isolation in crime-ridden neighborhoods, and a lack of appropriate skills to be able to take advantage of opportunities in the labor market. Furthermore, what many of these groups have in common is sustained experience of low incomes and poverty. Indeed, it is the growth of poverty and income inequality in Britain since the early 1980s that is most closely associated with increases in social exclusion.

Table 4.7 shows the astonishing increase in income inequality that took place during the 1980s. During that decade the share of total equivalized disposable income going to the most affluent fifth of the population increased by more than 16 percent at the expense of the poorest 60 percent of the income distribution. The poorest fifth suffered the most losing 22 percent of its meager share between 1980 and 1990. A number of general indicators of the overall distribution of income that are shown in table 4.7 testify to the scale of the redistribution that took place. The Gini coefficient, probably the most widely used indicator of income inequality, increased by nearly 29 percent during the 1980s, and the P90/P10 ratio rose by 40 percent.

The causes of increases in income inequality are many. They include the macroeconomic influences of globalization that have seen the collapse of traditional industries and the dramatic decline in demand for unskilled male

Table 4.7
Trends in Income Inequality 1980 to 1998/99

	1980	1990	1998/99	% +/- 98/80
% shares of equivalized disposable income by quintile group				
Bottom	9	7	7	-22.2
Second	13	11	12	-7.7
Third	18	16	16	-11.1
Fourth	23	23	23	0.0
Top	37	43	42	13.5
Indicators of overall distribution of equivalized disposable income				
Gini coefficients[1]	28	36	35	25.0
P90/P1O Ratio[2]	3.5	4.9	4.5	28.6
P75/25 Ratio	2	2.5	2.3	15.0

Source: Tables 1-3, Appendix 2, ONS *Economic Trends* No. 558, May 2000. London: The Stationery Office.

manual labor in particular. At the same time discretionary changes in fiscal policy have unarguably exacerbated the external influences. During the 1980s in particular, the Thatcher governments abolished or reduced social security benefits, slashed the highest rates of direct taxation, and set in train significant shifts towards a greater reliance on expenditure taxes. All of these policies had a regressive effect; they benefited the rich and further impoverished the poor. Nowhere is this more apparent than in the dramatic and unprecedented rise in child poverty. Piachaud and Sutherland (2000) have shown that:

> Over the period since 1979 for which consistent data are available, the number of children in poverty has tripled...the latest figures for 1997/8 show that...one-quarter of the population...were living below half the mean income level...one in three children were living in poverty. (p. 5)

More generally, it is important to acknowledge that since 1990 the statistics about income inequality have remained remarkably constant. There has been a very slight reduction in the degree of inequality but the revolutionary shift in the nature and extent of inequality that transformed British society in the 1980s has remained largely in place. It represents one of the biggest and most challenging issues to confront British social policy at the beginning of the twenty-first century.

As a result of the growing interest in and concern about social exclusion and the persistence of very high levels of poverty and income inequality, the

Joseph Rowntree Foundation has funded the collection and analysis of data to monitor the extent to which future government policies are able to address these issues. Fifty indicators of poverty and social exclusion have been identified and the second of what is intended to be a regular annual series of updates has been published, which summarizes emerging trends over both the medium term and the last year (Howarth et al., 1999). As yet, there is no clear evidence that the election of a Labour government has resulted in a radical change in the general direction of the indicators, although these are early days.

Allocation Principles: Targeting

Despite the growth in income inequality, it is worth asking to what extent are benefits in cash and in-kind targeted on the more disadvantaged groups in British society and how does this contribute to greater equality overall?

This question will be addressed by a summary glance at patterns of the overall distribution of benefits, followed by an analysis of the impact of cash benefits, benefits in-kind (the social wage) and finally the presentation of one detailed example relating to the targeting of social care resources for the elderly.

Overall Patterns

Targeting can be achieved in a variety of ways. These include the direct provision of services, the financing of flat rate benefits from taxes or contributions, means-testing, tax allowances, and the allocation of resources to local governments or agencies based on needs-assessment. Table 4.8 illustrates the overall distribution of taxes, benefits and incomes in 1998-99 for different households, based on their disposable income.

- The table does illustrate an overall pattern or redistribution towards those with lower incomes. The final column illustrates that the amount of income available to those in the 9th decile compared with the 1st. Benefits and taxes reduced the D90/D10 ratio from 17.43 for original income to 3.28 for final income.
- The table also shows that direct taxes and social security contributions are more progressive than indirect taxes, and that cash benefits are targeted to a greater extent than benefits in-kind.
- It is important to note that the overall redistribution towards those with lower incomes is not related entirely to income. The principle reason for this is that the demographic and economic characteristics of households vary between deciles in the income distribution (thus there are more retired people in the 2nd, 3rd, and 4th deciles, while there are more children in the lowest decile than others).

Table 4.8
Distribution of Taxes, Benefits, and Incomes: 1998-99: Decile Groups of Households Ranked by Equivalized Disposable Income

Income, Benefits And Taxes	Percentage of mean value attributed to specified decile groups										Mean Value	D90/ D10 Ratio
	1	2	3	4	5	6	7	8	9	10		
(1)	(2)	(3)	(4)	(5)	(6)	(7)	(8)	(9)	(10)	(11)	(12)	(13)
Original income	0.10	0.18	0.25	0.45	0.69	0.90	1.13	1.42	1.76	3.13	20936	17.43
Cash benefits	1.29	1.61	1.68	1.45	1.18	0.90	0.76	0.47	0.38	0.30	3314	0.29
Direct taxes	0.16	0.20	0.25	0.43	0.63	0.83	1.08	1.37	1.75	3.30	5020	10.91
Indirect taxes	0.56	0.54	0.60	0.74	0.90	1.02	1.16	1.28	1.39	1.80	3969	2.47
In-kind benefits	1.47	1.20	1.12	1.05	1.10	1.03	0.89	0.79	0.70	0.64	3130	0.48
Final income	0.43	0.53	0.58	0.67	0.81	0.91	1.03	1.19	1.42	2.44	18391	3.28
Final as % of original	274.94	158.35	105.10	32.09	4.12	-10.88	-19.98	-26.60	-29.36	-31.62	-12.16	

Source: Derived from ONS *Economic Trends* No. 558, May 2000. London: The Stationery Office.

Cash Benefits

Just under 30 percent of total UK government expenditure is allocated to cash benefits, which include retirement pensions, income support, child benefit and housing benefit. Each of these is targeted in quite different ways.

Evidence suggests that income support and housing benefit in particular are more clearly targeted on those with the lowest incomes, whereas the relative value of benefits from retirement pensions and child benefit reflects the demographic profile of groups.

That said, the targeting of cash benefits has clearly taken place in the UK since 1980 and has contributed to the reduction in inequality between income groups. In relation to income inequality, original incomes between 1987 and 1998 were more unequally distributed than post-tax incomes. The availability of cash benefits made the largest contribution to achieving greater equality and direct taxes were more fairly distributed than indirect ones, with the redistribution benefiting retired households in particular.

In-Kind Benefits

The targeting of specific services has also grown since 1980. Welfare services overall constitute one-third of government spending and include the

National Health Service, education, the personal social services and subsidized social housing. The combined receipt of these services can be thought of as an income in-kind and is often referred to as the "social wage."

Analysis of the distribution of the social wage since 1979 (Sefton, 1997) indicates that it has been "pro-poor," or distributed in favor of those with lower incomes, although the extent to which this is the case varies between services and is affected by demographic change.

Table 4.9 illustrates the distribution of the social wage in 1993 among income groups. The value of benefits in-kind received by the poorest fifth of the population was about 70 percent greater than for the richest fifth. As the table shows, this varies between services, however:

- Housing and the personal social services were strongly "pro-poor,"
- Schools and health care were moderately "pro-poor,"
- Higher education was strongly "pro-rich."

The distribution of the social wage, like cash benefits, also varies with demographic factors. These factors are, however, often a good indicator of the need for particular services—such as healthcare and personal social services among older people. If differences in service use related to age and gender are controlled for, the "pro-poor" bias in the overall distribution of benefits in-kind is considerably reduced, although there is still an underlying pro-poor bias.

When changes in the social wage between 1979 and 1993 are analyzed, it is evident that expenditure on services increased, and thus the overall value of the social wage increased by about 30 percent in real terms, which benefited all income groups. Table 4.10 illustrates changes in the distribution of the social wage for this period.

Table 4.9
The Distribution of the Social Wage, 1993

| Service | Ratio of spending per person on the bottom quintile group to that of the top quintile group | |
	Actual	Demographically adjusted
NHS	1.3	1.1
Schools and further education	2.2	1.1
Higher education	0.5	0.7
Subsidized social housing	9.9	6.2
Personal Social Services	7.9	1.1
Total	1.7	1.2

Source: Derived from Sefton (1997), Table 8.1.

Table 4.10
Changes in the Distribution of the Social Wage, 1979-93

Year	Percentage Share of the Social Wage received by the poorest 50% of the population	
	Actual	Demographically adjusted
1979	56.0	52.9
1993	60.1	53.7
% Change	7.3	1.5

Source: Derived from Sefton (1997), Table 8.3.

As table 4.10 shows, the proportion of the social wage received by the poorest half of the population increased by 4 percent between 1979 and 1993. However, most of this increase was due to demographic factors rather than government policy.

More in-depth analysis does suggest, however, that changes in the social wage have helped offset the increased inequality in cash incomes over the period. Using the Gini coefficient as the indicator of income distribution, the increase in inequality since 1979 is smaller by around one-fifth, after the effect of the social wage is taken into account.

Social Care for Older People

One area of welfare provision in which clear targeting effects can be seen is social care for older people. The budgets of local authorities, which are responsible for financing home care services for older people and younger disabled people, have been increasingly restricted since the late 1980s and particularly since the passage of the 1990 NHS and Community Care Act. The 1990 act transferred to local authorities lead responsibility for coordinating all community care services, including institutional care. Some transfer of resources from the NHS to local authorities following the closure of long-stay hospital beds did take place, but authorities have consistently found it difficult to finance both institutional and domiciliary provision in the 1990s, both of which are provided largely free of charge to users who satisfy a means-test. The result has been a reduction in the amount of funding available to pay for home care, both through the local authority's own service and that provided by private care agencies but paid for by public funds. Budgetary restrictions have been exacerbated by demographic factors and the implementation of social policy designed to maintain people in their own homes that have increased the demand for domiciliary services.

Local authorities have responded to these pressures in two main ways. Firstly, they have placed budget caps on social care packages that have limited the amount and frequency of service available to maintain people in their own homes. Secondly, they have introduced eligibility criteria designed to limit the number of people who receive domiciliary care. These criteria effectively screen out potential users who may require only a limited service in favor of those in "genuine need," in other words, those who may be at risk of admission to institutional care or whose care needs may be placing their informal caregivers under significant strain. The result of these policies has been a pattern of increased targeting of home care services on fewer users since the early 1990s, while offering a more intensive level of provision to those who qualify for service receipt (Bauld et al., 2000; Davies and Fernandez, 2000).

Table 4.11 illustrates this targeting of services on those with more complex needs. Among households receiving home care, the number of contact hours has increased since 1992. When both local authority and independent sector services are considered, it is evident that there has been a significant increase in the number of home care hours received per 10,000 households, from 899 hours in 1992 to 1,405 hours in 1997. Much of this increase in service intensity has been borne by private and voluntary sector providers, as table 4.11 illustrates. This is consistent with government policy designed to encourage a mixed economy of care, which we discuss in the next section.

Table 4.12 shows changes in the number of households receiving home care between 1992 and 1997. In contrast to the evidence relating to service intensity, table 4.12 shows that the number of households receiving services per 10,000 has dropped, from 282 to 255 for all sectors. This reduction is due to a significant drop in the number of households receiving local authority home care, whereas there has been a slight increase in the number of people receiving services from private and independent sector providers. More recent data from 1999 suggest that this trend has continued since 1997 (Department of Health, 1999). Thus, in relation to publicly provided services, tables 4.11 and 4.12 illustrate clearly a pattern of targeting higher levels of home

Table 4.11
Contact Hours of Home Help and Home Care per
10,000 Households by Sector in England

Year	Local Authority	Independent	All Sectors
1992	878	21	899
1993	903	47	949
1994	952	228	1180
1995	900	377	1277
1996	924	527	1451
1997	803	603	1405

Source: Department of Health *Community Care Statistics, England*, 1994 and 1997.

Table 4. 12
Households Receiving Home Help and Home Care per 10,000
Households, by Sector in England

Year	Local Authority	Independent	All Sectors
1992	276	6	282
1993	264	10	274
1994	255	32	287
1995	224	50	274
1996	216	70	287
1997	179	77	255

Source: Department of Health *Community Care Statistics, England*, 1994 and 1997.

care on a limited number of households—those containing users with more complex needs—in order to avoid the higher costs associated with admission to residential or nursing home care which could result if adequate domiciliary provision is not available.

Shifting Axis of Benefit Delivery: Welfare Mix

The British welfare state has always included some forms of private sector involvement, both in the finance and provision of services. In 1980, just under half (48 percent) of all welfare spending was on services with some private sector involvement.

The election of a Conservative administration in 1979 marked the beginning of a period in British social policy in which the growth of private welfare was actively encouraged in a variety of ways. The Labour government elected in 1997 is continuing to support this involvement, although the mechanisms to maintain or control it are currently the focus of reform.

It is worth examining the balance between public and private finance and delivery of services in three ways. Firstly, overall changes in the boundaries between public and private between 1980 and 1996 will be summarized. Secondly, the mechanisms used by previous administrations to encourage the growth or private welfare will be examined, particularly focusing on the concepts of quasi-markets in health. Finally, the example of independent sector provision in long-term care is presented as one area in which there has been significant change in the public/private mix of services.

Overall Shifts in Public and Private Welfare

The relationship between the public and private sector in welfare has several dimensions. In order to capture this, Burchadt and colleagues at the LSE devised a typology that distinguishes between the type of provider of the service, the finance used to purchase the service, and the type of "decision" governing purchase of the service. The locus of decision concerns who chooses the service; for example, a service is privately decided if it is chosen directly by the consumer from a range of similar alternatives. When this breakdown is applied to the range of welfare services, eight possible combinations of relationships arise. Table 4.13 illustrates these by welfare sector.

Table 4.13 illustrates that, despite significant policy developments, the overall shift in the welfare mix has been relatively minor. If the final column in the table is considered, the overall change has been away from "pure public" (publicly provided, financed and decided) and towards "pure private" welfare. Whereas in 1980 the pure public sector (publicly provided and financed) accounted for 54 percent of total welfare spending, this proportion had fallen to 49 percent by 1996. In contrast, the privately financed and provided sector rose from 25 percent in 1980 to 30 percent 1996.

These aggregate shifts however do disguise important changes within sectors, as table 4.13 also shows. This is particularly the case for the housing and personal social services sectors. In housing, the overall shift has been from pure public to pure private welfare, with privately provided, financed and decided services accounting for 9 percent of the total in 1980, but rising to 15 percent by 1996. This reflects the sale of council houses and growth in the private rented sector in the 1980s and early 1990s. As a consequence of these policies, rents to local authorities declined significantly, which accounts for the drop in the public provision, private finance and public decision category from 9.1 percent to 3.7 percent. In the personal social services, the overall shift away from pure public provision has been significant, a reduction of almost 30 percent between 1980 and 1996. While pure private services grew, a significant change is also evident in the private provision, public finance and decision category, which rose from 11 percent to 34 percent over the period. This category captures the huge rise in private residential and nursing home provision for older people whose care was financed by the state following means-testing.

In education, health and social security the broad shifts all involve pure public and pure private welfare. Changes in social security have been characterized, as we have already discussed, by a significant growth in public benefits, particularly in relation to income support. This is evident in the growth from 57 percent to 66 percent in the pure public sector. Conversely, the shifts in education and health have been in the other direction, towards privately provided, financed and decided services. This change arose as a result of Conservative social policy from the mid-1980s to early 1990s, when the concept of quasi-markets was introduced in order to stimulate a mixed economy of care, through contracting out, the separation of purchasing and providing functions within public services and the replacement of some previously public forms of provision with private services.

Table 4.13
Changes in the Boundaries between Public and Private Welfare, 1979/80-1995/96, by Sector

Welfare mix	Education		Health		Housing		Soc. Security		PSS		All Sectors	
	1979/80	1995/96	1979/80	1995/96	1979/80	1995/96	1979/80	1995/96	1979/80	1995/96	1979/80	1995/96
Public provision, finance & decision	65.5	52.4	70.5	62.9	18	10.4	57.2	66.1	70.2	41.1	53.6	48.7
Public provision & finance, private decision	0	0	0	0	0	0	9.7	3.5	0	0	4.7	1.4
Public provision, private finance, public decision	0	0	0.8	0.5	9.1	3.7	0	0	9.9	3.9	2.4	1.2
Public provision, private finance, private decision	0	0	0.4	0.5	0	0	0	0	0	0	0.1	0.1
Private provision. Public finance & decision	23.4	25.1	18.3	18.9	0.9	2.3	0	0	11	34.2	4	8.7
Private provision. Public finance, private decision	2.9	4.9	0	0.5	13	13.4	13.7	15.3	0	0	9.9	9.8
Private provision and finance, public decision	0	0	1.3	1.7	0.9	1.5	0	0	0.5	5.1	0.4	0.9
Private provision, finance & decision	8.2	17.7	8.8	15	58.1	68.6	19.4	16	8.3	15.6	24.9	29.2

Source: Burchart, T., Hills, J., and Propper, C. (1997).

Quasi-Markets in Health

The introduction of quasi-markets represented a major offensive by the Thatcher government against what was perceived as the bureaucratic structures of state welfare provision. Quasi-markets were so called because the policy changes involved the replacement of monopolistic state providers with competitive independent ones. They were "quasi" however because they differed from conventional markets in one or more of the following ways:

- Nonprofit organizations competed for public contracts, sometimes in competition with for-profit organizations.
- Consumer purchasing power was either centralized in a single purchasing agency or allocated to users in the form of vouchers rather than cash.
- In some cases, consumers were represented in the market by agents (such as care managers) instead of operating for themselves.

Quasi-markets operated by retaining the state finance of the service concerned but changed priorities by decentralizing decision-making and introducing competition. This was achieved by the state becoming primarily a purchaser of services with state provision replaced by a system of independent providers. The idea was that providers would compete with each other in internal markets.

The introduction of quasi-markets began with a set of reforms to primary and secondary school education introduced as part of the Education Reform Act in 1988. In health, quasi-market mechanisms were proposed in the 1989 White Paper, "Working for Patients." and later implemented following the 1990 NHS and Community Care Act. Three main structural changes were involved. The first gave GPs the option of becoming "fund-holders," responsible for their own practice budget which could be used to purchase services from a variety of providers, including private hospitals. The second structural change involved the creation of self-governing Trusts, hospitals whose management arrangements were separate from the Health Authority and who acted as "providers" of services to both GPs and health authorities. Finally, the creation of Trusts involved the separation of the purchasing and providing functions of Health Authorities. This split was implemented in most parts of the UK by 1992, by which point 160 NHS Trusts had also been established and 600 GP Fundholding practices had been formed. Figure 4.1 illustrates the relationship between the different components of the NHS internal market.

The opportunities and problems associated with the introduction of quasi-markets are too numerous to examine here, but it is evident from the overall welfare expenditure figures presented above that their introduction, along with other policy changes in the health service, was instrumental in shifting provision away from the public sector towards a greater range of providers.

Figure 4.1
The NHS Internal Market

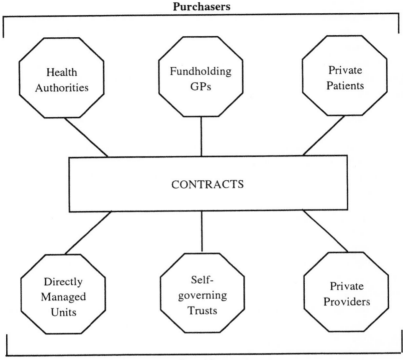

Since 1997, a number of features of quasi-markets in health have been dismantled by the Labour government, including the abolition of GP fundholding. Other aspects of the internal market, including the separation of purchasing and providing functions, however, have been retained, and it remains to be seen to what extent changes introduced in the 1980s affect the structure of the NHS in the longer term (Ham, 1999). One area in which there is more consistent evidence of a significant shift towards a mixed economy is long-term care, to which we turn in the next example.

Residential and Nursing Home Care

Responsibility for long-term care for older people in the UK has traditionally been divided between local authorities, which provided residential care, and the NHS, which provided long-stay hospital beds and to some extent the voluntary sector. Private provision was relatively marginal until the 1980s.

Indeed, the profit motive perceived as inherent in private sector provision was seen as incompatible with the provision of services for older people and other vulnerable groups.

Since the 1980s, however, private sector institutional care in Britain has expanded at a rapid rate. Private and voluntary agencies are now the dominant providers of nursing and residential care for older people. As Hardy and Wistow (2000) recently observed:

> so established is private sector provision in these sectors that its dominance is virtually unchallenged and apparently irreversible. (p. 46)

Table 4.14 illustrates the reduction in publicly provided (local authority) residential care places and the increase in private and voluntary residential and nursing home places in the UK between 1980 and 1998.

As table 4.14 shows, the number of private sector places in residential care homes rose from 37,400 in 1980 to 180,100 in 1998, a rise of almost 500 percent. In contrast, the number of residential care places provided by the public sector (local authority) fell from 134,500 to 64,100 in the same period. The result of these changes is that the private sector's share of the residential care market rose from 17 percent in 1980 to 48 percent in 1990 and to 61 percent in 1998 (Hardy and Wistow, 2000). The growth of voluntary sector residential homes has been more modest. The number of places has risen by 25 percent since 1980, partly reflecting the overall expansion of a mixed economy in residential care, but at the same time the voluntary sector's share of the residential care market has fallen slightly.

Table 4.14 also illustrates the rapid expansion in voluntary and private sector nursing home places since 1980, although figures for each sector were not separately available until 1987. The number of voluntary and private nursing home places rose from 26,900 in 1980 to 123,000 in 1990 and to 224,200 in 1998. The expansion was most marked from the mid-1980s on-

Table 4.14
Residential and Nursing Home Places for Elderly, Chronically Ill, and Physically Disabled People, U.K, 1980-1998 (000s)

	Residential Care Places				Nursing Home Places		
	LA	Private	Vol	Total	Private	Vol	Total
1980	134.5	37.4	42.6	214.1	*	*	26.9
1985	137.1	85.3	45.1	267.5	*	*	38.0
1990	125.6	155.6	40.0	321.2	112.6	10.5	123.1
1995	80.0	169.3	56.7	306.0	193.4	17.9	211.3
1998	64.1	180.1	53.2	297.4	205.6	18.4	224.2

no breakdown of figures by sector available. Source: Laing and Buisson (1998).

wards, with growth in the private sector alone amounting to a rise of 295 percent between 1987 and 1998 (Hardy and Wistow, 2000).

The reasons for the growth in private and voluntary provision of institutional care are complex. Demographic change and the resulting rising demand for long-term care have played a role. What is most clear, however, is that the changes are not primarily associated with a reduction in public sector expenditure. Instead, the nature of public funding has changed. The state has withdrawn from funding long-term care for older and disabled people through the National Health Service. This withdrawal began with the closure of long-stay hospitals in the 1960s and 1970s but accelerated in the 1980s and early 1990s. Between 1970 and 1993, the number of long-stay hospital beds fell by 18 percent. Between 1993 and 1998, the number reduced by an additional 36 percent. This reduction in long-term NHS care has combined with fiscal pressures and other changes in the health service to result in substantially shorter lengths of stay and early discharge for older and disabled people admitted to hospital. This "vicious circle" of emergency admissions, shorter lengths of stay, early discharge and an absence of rehabilitation and chronic care beds has left a significant void in the continuum of care for older and disabled people—a void that was at least partially filled from the 1980s onwards by an expansion in private and voluntary sector institutional care (Audit Commission, 1997).

An additional reason for the growth of the "mixed economy" in institutional care is the growth in public funding of the independent sector. Early growth in the number of private and voluntary residential and nursing home beds was fuelled by the availability of public finance. From the early 1980s, changed perceptions of the availability of social security funding from central government (through Supplementary Benefit and later Income Support) helped anyone with less than £3,000 capital and who qualified on income grounds to apply for benefit to pay for their care in a residential or nursing home of their choice. No assessment of need was required. In effect, the central government had set up a voucher system for the public funding of private and voluntary care homes. The result was that public expenditure on independent sector institutional care through income support payments rose from £18 million to more than £2 billion in 1992 (Laing, 1993). This fanned political and professional concern about the perverse incentive to encourage institutional care. The consequence was that the growth in private sector homes and public financing of this growth was restricted from 1993 onwards, when the full implementation of the NHS and Community Care Act had taken place and entry to institutional care became more limited on the basis of both needs assessment and more stringent means-testing. However, the dramatic change in the balance of provision has not been reversed. State funding of private sector care remains important, with 46 percent of independent sector residential and nursing home residents publicly funded in 1998. Private and voluntary sector homes remain the dominant form of institutional care for older people in the UK, representing one policy area in which there has been a significant shift from public to private welfare.

Direction of Future Policy

It is apparent from the evidence presented above that, with the exception of several policy areas in which the growth of private welfare has been substantial, overall shifts in the welfare mix have been slow to take place. Despite over two decades of government policy aimed at "rolling back the frontiers"of the welfare state, the bulk of welfare services in the UK are either financed or provided by the public sector. It is still unclear how policies introduced by the new Labour government will affect the balance of provision. The government's "third way" includes a commitment to a strong welfare state, but where exactly the boundary between public and private provision will lie is yet to be determined.

Employment and Welfare-to-Work

Background

Although Britain experienced several years of sustained economic growth during the mid- to late1990s, it continues to face a number of serious employment problems, some of a deep and long-standing nature. First, the second half of the twentieth century has witnessed a marked gender difference in employment trends. Whereas female participation in the labor market has steadily increased there has been a marked reduction in employment levels among men. Secondly, there remains a hard core of long-term unemployment especially among young people and members of many ethnic minority groups. Unemployment rates often exceed 20 percent among these groups and they can easily reach 50 percent and more in the most disadvantaged parts of the country. Thirdly, there has been a dramatic increase in the numbers of people entirely dependent on state benefits and who have lost all contact with the labor market. For example, one million single parents, nearly all of which are women, are not in work. Similarly, approaching 2 million people, mainly men, are dependent on long-term sickness or incapacity benefits. The size of both of these groups has doubled since the late 1980s.

Table 4.15 provides some historical background to patterns of economic activity and unemployment since 1984 when the series of *Labour Force Survey* statistics began to be published. In terms of recent trends in unemployment there are some marked discontinuities over time and between gender groups. As far as male unemployment is concerned the rates display a clear cyclical pattern between 1984 and 1997. In 1984 unemployment rates were recovering to some extent after the recession of the early 1980s, before increasing rapidly after the boom of the late 1980s fizzled out. As the economy improved between 1992 and 1997 so the rates fell for all groups. What is perhaps most striking, apart from the very high levels of youth unemployment throughout the period, is the marked decline in unemployment rates after the election of the Blair government in 1997. We discuss below the extent to which new investments in active employment policies are responsible for this change.

Table 4.15
Trends in Economic Activity Rates by Age and Gender,
Spring 1984 to Spring 2000

	Spring 1984	Spring 1993	Spring 1997	Spring 2000
MALE				
Unemployment rate				
16-24	20.54	28.67	22.9	13.96
25-49	9.43	14.81	10.4	4.69
50-64	9.42	14.83	9.35	5.1
65+	7.87	11.79	7.8	n/a
Inactivity rate				
16-24	17.57	21.95	23.36	23.86
25-49	3.94	5.53	7.1	6.94
50-64	22.55	26.51	27.13	27.55
65+	91.46	92.03	92.19	92.0
FEMALE				
Unemployment rate				
16-24	18.1	13.13	10.97	11.39
25-49	10.25	6.71	5.05	4.6
50-59	7.04	5.76	4.34	3.0
60+	7.23	3.79	2.07	1.82
Inactivity rate				
16-24	30.08	33.15	33.57	31.73
25-49	32.77	25.29	24.38	23.25
50-59	41.03	37.23	36.3	34.11
60+	92.03	91.79	91.67	91.64

Source: ONS *Labour Force Survey Historical Supplement* 1997. London: HMSO. ONS *Labour Force Survey Quarterly Supplement* 10, August 2000: London: The Stationery Office

Female unemployment rates differ from those for men in that they have shown a steady improvement throughout the whole period since 1984 for all age groups, with just a small upward blip in the rates for very young women between 1997 and 2000. Among both young men and women the period has seen a steady increase in rates of economic inactivity as more young people have been encouraged to take advantage of new opportunities to participate in further and higher education. However, among older adults there are clear gender differences over time in trends in economic inactivity rates. For women between the ages of 25 and 60 these rates have fallen quite substantially, whereas for men of similar ages the rates have risen steadily especially for men over the age of 50.

Welfare-to-Work

In response to these and related problems there has been a growing interest in the UK in what are generally described as welfare to work or active employment policies. There is nothing particularly new about the adoption of such policies to address the economic and social costs of long-term unemployment. Prior to 1997, the Thatcher and Major governments invested considerable amounts of political capital in promoting welfare-to-work policies. But there has been a dramatic change in the ordering of political priorities since Labour's election in 1997. Welfare reform in general and welfare to work in particular are at the very center of New Labour's domestic policy agenda.

Alan Deacon (1997) suggests that welfare-to-work strategies have three main goals. First, to increase job opportunities for those reliant on social security benefits by providing employment subsidies, creating new jobs or offering training and work experience schemes. Secondly, to change the characteristics and motivation of long-term welfare recipients through the provision of a range of advice and counselling services and training and development opportunities. Finally, to reform the structure of the tax and benefit system so that welfare claimants have clearer incentives to take advantage of work opportunities. To varying extents all three of these distinct aspects of a welfare-to-work strategy can be found among changes implemented or planned by the Blair government since 1997.

In March 1998 the Blair government published a consultative paper on welfare reform (Cm 3805, 1998) that set out a number of key principles that ought to guide the future development and adaptation of the British welfare state. The first of these principles emphasized the central importance of work. "The new welfare state should help and encourage people of working age to work where they are capable of doing so" (Cm 3805, 1998: 2). Starting from this principle the government set itself the task of rebuilding the welfare state around work. It aims to do this in five main ways (Cm 3805, 1998: 23):

- Helping people move from welfare to work through the New Deals and Employment Zones;
- Developing flexible personalized services to help people into work;
- Lowering the barriers to work for those who can and want to work;
- Making work pay, by reforming the tax and benefit system, including a Working Families Tax Credit, reforming National Insurance and income tax, and introducing the national minimum wage; and
- Ensuring that responsibilities and rights are fairly matched.

The Blair government has embarked on a very ambitious agenda of social reform and many of its new policy initiatives are expected to have beneficial consequences in terms of increasing employment opportunities. However, two strands of policy development are probably the most significant. The first is a series of "New Deals" for particular groups where long-term unemployment is regarded as especially serious. The second element reflects a more general commitment to "making work pay."

The biggest single investment of public expenditure and political capital made by the Blair government during its first phase in office has been made in a large-scale welfare-to-work program focused on five main groups:

- Young unemployed people;
- Long-term unemployed people;
- Single parents;
- People with a disability or long-term illness; and
- Partners of the unemployed.

To date, most of the investment and attention has been concentrated on the first two of these so-called New Deals, although employment programs for the other groups are now in place.

The means by which the government intends to "make work pay" include: The introduction of a national minimum wage; reducing the starting rate of income tax and the threshold for national insurance contributions; and the replacement of Family Credit by Working Families' Tax Credit (WFTC) in October 1999.

Evaluation

It is too early to offer a comprehensive review of welfare-to-work policies as some new initiatives such as the New Deal have been in place for less than two years. The government itself claims that they are working (HM Government, 2000):

The New Deal has already helped over 210,000 young people to find work and long-term youth unemployment has more than halved across the UK. We have extended the New Deal to lone parents, disabled people and older people. So far over 850,000 people have joined the New Deal and 300,000 have gone on to find work.... The supportive economic climate has encouraged firms to set up or expand with confidence. This, together with welfare reforms to reduce poverty and make work pay, means that, compared to May 1997, over 970,000 more people are in work.

However, the latest research suggests that out of 146,000 people on the New Deal who found work lasting more than three months, 106,000 would have found work anyway, as the direct result of strong economic growth (*The Guardian*, 14/7/00). Furthermore, a report by the House of Commons Education and Employment Committee found that 25 percent of those who obtained jobs through the New Deal found themselves in "false start" jobs and out of work within thirteen weeks (*The Guardian*, 11/7/00).

More generally, we can point to two independent pieces of evidence available with which to make a tentative assessment of the impact of welfare-to-work policies. The first, produced by the authoritative Institute of Fiscal Studies, is a simulation exercise that attempts to evaluate government claims that the Working Families' Tax Credit would improve work incentives and encourage people to move into employment. The second is a summary of the most recent independent assessment of the New Deal.

Working single parents are most likely to benefit from the WFTC reform. Nearly 80 percent of single parents in part-time paid employment (between 20 and 30 hours) will benefit from the new tax credit. For women in couples where the male partner is in work, the WFTC will be most generous to households in which the women are not in paid employment; around one-third of this group will benefit, while this figure falls to 5 percent for women in part-time work. As table 4.16 suggests, the participation rate for single mothers will increase by 2.2 percent, corresponding to 34,000 individuals. The participation rate for married women with employed partners will decrease by 0.57 percent, corresponding to around 20,000 individuals. In all, the combined behavioral effects of the WFTC imply a small increase in overall participation by just under 30,000.

The second piece of evidence comes from the Joseph Rowntree Foundation's assessment of the effectiveness of New Deal, published in July 2000. Box 4.2 describes the various forms of New Deal and the level of participation in each.

The New Deal for Young People is targeted to those aged 18 to 24 and unemployed for at least six months. It is compulsory and includes a "gateway" period of advice and support followed by one of four options (subsidized employment, full-time education and training, voluntary work, and environmental work). As box 4.2 shows, less than half (45 percent) of the total young people who had joined the scheme by February 2000 had found jobs, and around half of those who did would have found work anyway. The New Deal for Unemployed People (for those 25 plus and unemployed for at least

Table 4.16
WFTC Participation Rates by Household Type (percent)

Household type	Non-work to work	Work to non-work	Part-time to full time	Full-time to part-time	Changes in participation
Single mothers	2.2	0.0	0.5	0.2	(+2.2)
Women in couples, partner working	0.2	0.7	0.0	0.1	(-0.57)
Women in couples, partner not working	1.3	0.0	0.4	0.1	(+1.32)
Men in couples, partner working	0.0	-0.3			(-0.3)
Men in couples, partner not working	0.4	0.0			(+0.37)

Source: Blundell et al., (2000).

12 months) received 238,000 people over the same period but only 16 percent (38,000) had found jobs. The voluntary New Deal for Single Parents recorded a more successful rate of employment at 39 percent. Key barriers for finding work varied between groups; for the young they included lack of skills and work experience. For the long-term unemployed, the barriers were a mismatch of skills and what was required, or outdated skills. In both of these compulsory programs, the study found that the requirements to move into options was sometimes experienced as too rigid, and the gap between the individualized assessment and the fixed option that followed was felt to be too large. The fact that every participant is assigned a personal adviser, rather than dealing with a range of staff, has been found to be extremely important, both in the client's perception and induction into the initiative, and in the employers' demands for suitable staff. The JRF report suggests that the New Deal will have to work harder in order to support and inform those with multiple disadvantage and special needs. It concludes that, in two years it is still too early to fully assess the impact of the New Deal.

Box 4.2

The New Deals: The Experience So Far

- **The New Deal for Young People (NDYP).** Just under 440,000 young people had been through NDYP by February 2000 and in total about 200,000 had found jobs. Of these, about 146,000 lasted 13 weeks or more (34 percent of all participants). It is estimated that the first year saw youth unemployment go down by about 30,000. About half of those who found work would probably have done so anyway. It is projected that about 250,000 young people will find work over the four years planned for the program.
- **The New Deal for Long-Term Unemployed (NDLTU).** Around 238,000 people had been through the NDLTU by February 2000 and in total about 38,000 people found jobs. About 32,000 of these jobs lasted 13 weeks or more (around 13 percent of all participants). Over half of those who leave the program return to Job Seekers' Allowance/Income Support.
- **The New Deal for Lone Parents (NDLP).** About 133,000 lone parents had attended an initial NDLP interview by February 2000. Just over half (54 percent) came from the target group and 37 percent came forward before being invited to interview. Of those who have left the NDLP, 39 percent have gone into employment and 43 percent are again claiming IS. Almost half of those in employment are continuing to receive personal adviser support. The number of those who would not have found work without the program was estimated at 20 percent for the prototype program.
- **The New Deal for Partners of Unemployed People (NDPU) & The New Deal for Disabled People (NDDP).** The numbers going through the NDDP and NDPU are relatively small. Over the first three months of the NDPU about 1,400 people were interviewed, 6 percent of whom found jobs. Over about 15 months of the NDDP pilots and innovative programs, just over 10,000 people had initial personal adviser interviews and almost 6,600 had drawn up personal action plans. About 3,000 had been accepted onto innovative programs and just over 2,000 had found jobs.

For young people, the key barriers to work were lack of skills and work experience, ineffective job-seeking, low pay, and access to and costs of transport. For the long-term unemployed, the key barriers were a mismatch between their skills and what was required, outdated skills and lack of transport. For disabled people, the barriers were special needs and employer attitudes, while for lone parents childcare and money issues were paramount. For partners, it was also childcare and a concern about role reversal.

The most important thing in the way people perceived the programs was the personal adviser. Their role is pivotal and both groups would like them to do even more. Employers want advisers to prepare more people and be more selective on their behalf. Clients want practical help with their specific needs. These demands may potentially conflict. The New Deal process is dynamic and the routes people take through the process have to be flexible in order to meet

continued on next page

continued from previous page

> people's needs. The New Deal programs will have to work harder in order to reach those with multiple disadvantages and special needs.
>
> New Deal is having an impact for a range of different groups. It suggests that the personal adviser approach has had an impact on both participants and providers. However, these evaluations have mainly been in relation to the prototypes and the initial stages of national implementation. The next stage of research will be able to show more about whether and how this picture holds when the national programs for all these groups are fully up and running.

Source: Millar, 2000.

Implications: Shifting Boundaries

The electoral success of the Labour party in May 1997 following eighteen years of Conservative government may mark the beginning of a significant shift in the direction of British social policy. While it is too early to begin to fully assess the implications of reforms currently being introduced by the new administration, it is possible to reflect on early evidence regarding the changing balance of priorities that New Labour represents, and to consider how this contrasts with the approach to social welfare adopted by previous governments since 1980. Current changes appear to be shifting the boundaries of relationships within the welfare state between:

- Left and right ideologies (the third way)
- The "haves" and the "have-nots" in British society (social exclusion)
- Organizations and agencies within the welfare state (news forms of partnership)
- National and subnational levels of government (devolution)

The Third Way

Britain's New Labour government is particularly eager to distinguish and distance itself from what it describes as the weaknesses of traditional political values and approaches from both the left and the right. Statements coming from the new government argue that the series of reforms to social policy currently being introduced represent a new approach, one that has learned from past failures on both sides of the political spectrum and thus represents a "third way" in welfare. Anthony Giddens (1998), a British sociologist closely associated with the development of the approach and its application within government, is honest about the somewhat varied history of the concept:

> ...the term "third way" is of no particular significance in and of itself. It has been used many times before in the past history of social democracy, and also by writers and

politicians of quite different political persuasions...The phrase seems to have originated as early as the turn of the century, and was popular among right-wing groups in the 1920s. Mostly, however, it has been used by social democrats and socialists. (p. vii)

The third way as interpreted by New Labour is a broad ideology that aims to occupy a middle ground between the free market liberalism of recent Conservative governments and the traditional left, state-centered policies that characterized old Labour. At its heart, the third way is an attempt *to reconcile the promotion of growth in the market system with social democratic goals* (Taylor-Gooby, 2000). A 1998 pamphlet by Tony Blair (1998) outlines four essential values within the approach:

- Equal worth
- Equality of opportunity rather than equality of outcome
- Rights and responsibilities
- Community

Traditional concepts of equality are expanded within third way discourse in two important ways. Firstly, equality between individuals is based around the concept of worth. This means that social justice is founded on the equal worth of each individual, whatever their background or ability. By implication, the government therefore has an important role to play in tackling prejudice and discrimination. Secondly, equality of opportunity is promoted as another essential third way value. Thus, "enabling" individuals, families, and communities to exploit opportunities becomes an important objective, in contrast to the more traditional leftist concept of the importance of equality of outcome for all.

The concept of rights, be they political or social, is linked in discussions of the third way with responsibilities. As Blair (1998) describes: "for too long the demand for rights from the state was separated from the duties of citizenship...The rights we enjoy reflect the duties we owe" (p. 4). This "redefinition" of rights and obligations implies a new form of relationship between the individual and the state. Blair has claimed that "old-style" democracy treated rights as unconditional aims, but in a more modern context this needs to be matched with a recognition of individual obligations. This stress on responsibility is apparent across a range of policies introduced by the Labour government, particularly in relation to welfare-to-work and the New Deal.

Finally, third way values promote the primacy of the concept of "community" and the importance of protecting, promoting and involving communities and their members. As Driver and Martell (2000) note:

In a decent society, individuals should not simply claim rights from the state but should also accept their individual responsibilities and duties as citizens, parents and members of communities. A third way should promote the value of "community" by supporting the structures and institutions of civil society—such as the family and voluntary organisations—which promote individual opportunity and which ground "responsibility" in meaningful social relationships. (p. 151)

Local solutions to local problems are to be sought, implying a "bottom-up" approach rather than one that relies on central control. This is closely related to the concept of subsidiarity, and involves re-examining and re-structuring a series of relationships within the welfare state, including between levels of government as witnessed by the process of devolution.

Social Exclusion

A key issue for the Blair government is to tackle social exclusion and to promote social justice. Many of the government's social policy initiatives introduced in the past two years have addressed these issues. Key policy developments have included welfare-to-work schemes, broadly based regeneration investments in blighted urban areas, a drive to improve educational standards in disadvantaged areas, and a renewed emphasis on tackling health inequalities.

Some illustrations of the approach being adopted by the Blair government are set out below. The first describes the rationale for and the remit of a Social Exclusion Unit that has been established at the center of government. The second describes some aspects of the government's response to the growing problem of child poverty. Finally, in this section, we review the extent to which New Labour has made or is likely to make any progress in reducing income inequality and poverty as a result of new policy initiatives during its first three years in office.

The Social Exclusion Unit

The creation of a Social Exclusion Unit in the Cabinet Office was one of the first acts of the Blair government after its election in May 1997. It defines social exclusion as:

...a shorthand label for what can happen when individuals or areas suffer from a combination of linked problems such as unemployment, poor skills, low incomes, poor housing, high crime environments, bad health and family breakdown. The Government has policies that are targeted at reducing all of these individually, but Government programs have been less good at tackling the interaction between these problems or preventing them arising in the first place.

The purpose of the Social Exclusion Unit is to help break this vicious circle and coordinate and improve government action by:

- improving understanding of the key characteristics of social exclusion, and the impact on it of government policies; and
- promoting solutions by encouraging cooperation, disseminating best practice, and where necessary, making recommendations for changes in policies, machinery or delivery mechanisms.

One of the clearest examples of where the Social Exclusion Unit (2000) has started to make an impact on government policy is the work that it has completed in developing a *National Strategy for Neighbourhood Renewal.* A consultative document published in the spring of 2000 set out a long-term vision as well as detailed plans for the revitalization of the most disadvantaged neighborhoods in the UK. As we show in the conclusion to this chapter many of the policy proposals have been incorporated in the government's radical new public expenditure plans for the next three years.

Child Poverty and Educational Opportunity

The government believes that the rapid rise in the numbers of children growing up in poverty and a lack of educational opportunity are inextricably linked. Both need to be tackled in unison. As a result the government has implemented substantial increases in child benefit, committed itself to subsidizing child-care costs for the poorest families and introduced a number of educational initiatives targeted in various ways at the poorest children living in the most disadvantaged areas. These projects include: Sure Start for families with children under the age of four; educational maintenance allowances for 16-19 year olds; and the establishment of educational action zones.

1. Sure Start
Sure Start aims to "join-up" provision for families with children under four. Working with parents, Sure Start aims to promote the physical, intellectual, social and emotional development of children to make sure that they are ready to thrive when they go to school. In Sure Start areas, which are located in some of the most disadvantaged parts of the country, all local providers of services—voluntary, statutory and private—will combine with the local community to improve opportunities for families in ways that cut across old professional and agency boundaries and focus more on community needs. Sure Start local programs will form a universal and open access "gateway" to core services for all young children and their families in the area, covering childcare, early education and play, health services and family support.

2. Educational Maintenance Allowances
Partly to help teenagers for whom early prevention measures are already too late, the government is piloting Educational Maintenance Allowances (EMAs)

for 16 to 19-year-olds. The highest rates of EMA will be concentrated on the poorest families, where the scope for increasing participation, retention and achievement in post-compulsory education is greatest. If successful, EMAs will replace Child Benefit for this age group.

3. *Education Action Zones* (EAZs)

EAZs will use innovation and radical solutions to raise pupil attainments and tackle disadvantage, beginning with the basics of literacy and numeracy. Each Zone covers the three-four secondary and special schools together with their feeder primaries. Partners include businesses, parents, voluntary and community groups as well as schools and local education authorities. Twenty-five EAZs are already operational. And a second round of bidding for further zones started in January 1999. EAZs will provide tailored support for families and pupils, for example, by changing the school day or school year to estab-lish before and after school clubs, weekend and holiday classes, reading clubs and nursery facilities. They will work better with other local services to tackle social exclusion, for example, by linking with health or employment zones, and by providing access to health or social services for children within a school. Business and other organizations will offer new management and leadership expertise as well as opportunities for work-related learning. New incentives for teachers and additional non-teaching staff will also play a part in transforming the skills and lifetime employment opportunities of pupils in our most disadvantaged areas.

It is too early in the life of these initiatives to evaluate the extent to which they will make a substantial contribution to tackling social exclusion. How-ever, it is relatively easier to assess the impact of tax and benefit changes on income inequality and poverty, which we turn to next.

Tackling Poverty and Social Exclusion

There can be no reasonable grounds for doubting that New Labour is committed to trying to reduce poverty and social exclusion. However, many commentators have expressed concern that its approach is too cautious. Cer-tainly the evidence to date is indicative of only relatively modest progress.

Box 4.3 presents data compiled by the Institute for Fiscal Studies, which evaluates the redistributive impact of tax and benefit changes introduced by New Labour since it was elected in 1997. It shows that the poorest sections of the community and families with children have been the main beneficiaries of policies to date, but the overall impact has been quite small when com-pared to the massive increases in poverty and inequality that occurred in the 1980s and that have remained at historically high levels ever since.

In a separate analysis, Piachaud and Sutherland (2000) have carried out a macrosimulation study to analyze the impact on child poverty of New Labour's policies. They conclude that changes in tax and benefits and a new approach to active labor market policies, that were announced but not necessarily fully implemented between May 1997 and January 2000, might reduce the number of children living in poor households by about 1 million or one-third of the current level by 2002. The challenge for the Blair government is to develop sustainable policies that have a realistic chance of eliminating or at least substantially reducing poverty among the remaining two million children. Piachaud and Sutherland (2000) conclude that a reasonable start has been made towards reducing child poverty but they caution against complacency:

> ...it is important to stress that, while child poverty will be substantially reduced, the extent of child poverty that will remain in 2002 is extremely high by post-war Britain standards and by European standards. Child poverty will still be over twice as high as when a Labour Government was last in office. If the Prime Minister's declared aim of abolishing child poverty in a generation is to be achieved then it will not be enough to roll forward the policy initiatives taken so far, it will be necessary to maintain, even accelerate, the momentum of policy change and achieve further transfers of resources to families with children. (p. 32)

Box 4.3

Fiscal Reforms since May 1997

Since the May 1997 general election, the Labour Government has announced numerous reforms to the structure of the tax and benefit system in the UK. Using well-established simulation models the Institute for Fiscal Studies (IFS) is able to assess the distributional impact of the reforms, which can be directly assigned to individual households.

The IFS tax and benefit model, TAXBEN, is based on information from the Family Expenditure Survey. This is a representative sample of around 7,000 UK households. For the information on incomes and expenditures, TAXBEN can calculate the effect of tax and benefit reforms on each household in the survey. These can then be aggregated to analyze the effect of reforms on incomes of particular types of households and to examine aggregate distributional effects. The results presented here compare two fiscal systems. The April 1997 system is used as a benchmark. This is compared to a new system which includes all the budgetary measures that directly affect household income announced since May 1997, whether they have already taken effect or not. The two systems are indexed to 1999 prices.

Results show the effect of the changes on post tax income of households that are grouped into deciles, which are constructed by dividing UK households into ten equal sized groups, ranked by income adjusted for family size. So the first decile contains the poorest 10 percent of the population, while the tenth decile contains the richest 10 percent. The decile effects represent the average impact on households in each group. Results are presented for changes in direct taxes (both income tax and National Insurance), indirect taxes and for spending changes.

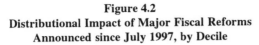

Figure 4.2
Distributional Impact of Major Fiscal Reforms
Announced since July 1997, by Decile

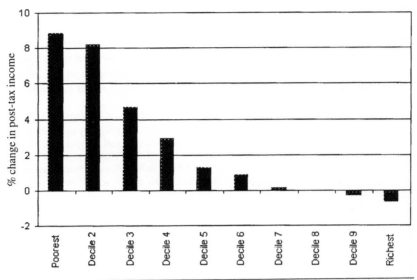

Source: IFS (http://www.ifs.org.uk/budgets)

The total distributional effect of the modelled reform package is shown in figure 4.2. On average, the package benefits households in most deciles. The results reflect the government's commitment to raising living standards of the lowest income households. The post-tax income of an average household in the bottom decile of income distribution is 8.8 percent higher if all measures announced since May 1997 are taken into account. Further deciles gain proportionately less on average and the richest 30 percent of households experience a fall in post-tax income once all of the reforms are considered.

The gains going to the poorest households are mainly due to benefit increases for those out of work, and to the introduction of the Working Families Tax Credit for those in work. The loss of income by households in the top decile is associated with increased National Insurance and the abolition of both mortgage tax relief and the married couple's allowance.

Figure 4.3 shows the results by family type. All types of families with children gain on average from the reforms. This largely reflects the impact of the introduction of the Working Families Tax Credit, the Children's Tax Credit and increases in child benefit and income support child allowances. Two-earner couples with children gain less than other types of families with children as they are least likely to benefit from the WFTC and income support allowances, and most likely to see the CTC withdrawn. No-earner couples

Figure 4.3
Distributional Impact of Major Fiscal Reforms since
July 1997, by Household Type

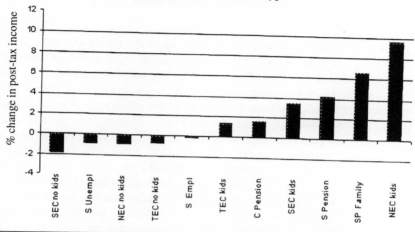

Source: IFS (http://www.ifs.org.uk/budgets)

with children gain most both relative to their total post-tax income as well as in absolute terms—an average gain of this type of family is £18.70 per week.

Both single and married pensioners are, on average, also net gainers. This is driven mainly by the policies aimed specifically at pensioner households (increased age-related income tax personal allowance, increased income-support premia, winter allowance, and retention of the married couples allowance for those born before April 1935). On average, a single pensioner household has gained £6.10 per week, while a pensioner couple £4.20 per week.

All non-pensioner households without children turn out to lose from the reforms. Withdrawal of the married couple's allowance and changes in excise duties are the largest element driving these effects, and reforms to National Insurance and direct tax rates, which benefit most earners, are insufficient to outweigh the negative effects.

New Forms of Partnership

In his first public speech after becoming prime minister, Tony Blair emphasized that a key element of the assumptive world of his government would be the recognition "that government has to learn to work more coherently."

In every poor housing estate you can encounter literally dozens of public agencies—schools, police, probation, youth service, social services, the courts, the Employment Service and Benefits Agency, TECs, health authorities and GPs, local authorities, careers services—all often doing good work, but all often working at cross-purposes or without adequate communication. This matters because it leads to poor policy and wasted resources—like schools excluding pupils who then become a huge burden for the police. Our challenge must be to overcome these barriers, liberating funds from their departmental silos so that they can be used to deliver the best results.

There is now substantial evidence pointing to the failure of public agencies to work together in coordinated ways to tackle social problems. Some of the early work of the Social Exclusion Unit has addressed this theme in its "national strategy for neighborhood renewal," pointing to the fact that poorly designed public policies have failed to meet the challenges of poverty and inequality. There are many causes for this failure. They include: the absences of effective national policies to deal with the structural causes of decline; a tendency to parachute solutions in from outside, rather than engaging local communities; and too much emphasis on physical renewal instead of better opportunities for local people. Above all, a joined-up problem has never been addressed in a joined-up way. Problems have fallen through the cracks between central government departments in Whitehall, or between central and local government. And at the neighborhood level, there has been no one in charge of pulling together all the things that need to go right at the same time.

Given this analysis, the Blair government is now committed to *making Whitehall work better* and to *joining it up locally.*

The need for this emphasis is highlighted, for example, by evidence that shows many of the problems that have bedevilled policy on poor neighborhoods in the past are deeply ingrained in the way Whitehall works. A number of steps are being taken to improve the quality of decision-making and the coherence of policy delivery. The Cabinet Office Performance and Innovation Unit has undertaken a major review of the links between central government and the regions, cities and towns, with a view to improving coherence and effectiveness of government policy. We summarize some of the key recommendations of this review below. In parallel, an external study is being conducted on streamlining the many different funding streams for areas, and on options for encouraging flexibility where this can deliver better results. Underpinning all this work is the principle that where Whitehall's rules and traditions obstruct solutions, these need to be looked at critically and not regarded as set in stone.

But more needs to be done to develop better awareness within Whitehall of how policy impacts at ground level and affects those in poverty. Furthermore, the general problem of the lack of coordination is endemic. For example, many thousands of people up and down the country are engaged in regeneration activity in poor neighborhoods. But there is no central source of training or advice on good practice, except in relation to specific regeneration programs. This means the wheel is being reinvented all the time, known mistakes are being repeated, and promising approaches are slow to be replicated. There is an urgent need for better ways of spreading knowledge and understanding. The January 2000 report of the Performance and Innovation Unit within the Cabinet Office has put forward a number of recommendations for all government departments that, if implemented, may begin to address these issues. The recommendations include (PIU, 2000):

- Emphasizing the importance of strong leadership from ministers and senior civil servants to create a culture in which cross-departmental policies and objectives are valued as highly as purely departmental ones.
- Improving the process of cross-departmental policymaking by involving outside experts and practitioners more fully at an earlier stage, and focusing on what users of public services actually need, not what it is convenient to provide.
- Equipping civil servants with the skills and capacity to handle the more complex relationships involved in partnership working.
- Making greater use of budgetary flexibilities, with development of cross-departmental budgets and pooling of funds where appropriate.
- Appreciating the role of audit in encouraging the greater risk-taking inevitable in cross-departmental work.
- Creating a strategic framework in which cross-departmental working can thrive.

Problems of coordination are just as serious at local level as in Whitehall. The recent White Paper *Modern Local Government* made clear the Government's commitment to build a more mature and cooperative relationship with local government. Councils have a vital role to play and should be at the center of local public service and local action to tackle social exclusion.

Some local authorities have already developed promising strategies to combat social exclusion at local level. The Local Government Association's New Commitment To Regeneration offers the prospect of developing systematic cross-agency strategies and encouraging better cooperation between national and local agencies. Local government reforms, including Best Value and the duty on local authorities to promote social and economic well being, will also foster this. Work currently underway on linking the various "Zones" (such as Health Action Zones and Employment Zones) should help, as should the priority given to local partnership working as a means of combating ill health. But all these different initiatives should be dovetailed so as to make local planning to tackle social exclusion the norm.

Devolution

In the period since 1980, there has been a growth in both regionalism and nationalism throughout Europe. These movements have put pressure on central governments to devolve power to subnational levels, and in some cases have led to considerable fragmentation of existing national institutions and boundaries.

The United Kingdom has not escaped this shift towards greater regional autonomy. Reforms have been implemented that have created separate assemblies in Northern Ireland and in Wales, and a separate parliament for Scotland. While political parties advocating outright independence from the UK exist in each of these regions, the push for devolution has been spearheaded by the New Labour government. Labour's commitment to devolution has complex origins. There is a historical link with home rule movements and trade unionism, which traditionally supported regional autonomy in Scotland and Wales. The last Labour government from 1974 to 1979 held referendums in both regions on the issue of devolution, although neither vote resulted in an endorsement of reform. The Labour party also has a record of electoral success in Scotland and Wales, and thus has prioritized issues relevant to both areas in order to retain this support. One outcome of Labour's strength in the regions has been the influence of both Scottish and Welsh MPs who were extremely effective in sustaining the party's basic commitment to some form of constitutional change through the years of Conservative government. These years were characterized by a centralizing rather than decentralizing approach to local government which was particularly unpopular in Scotland and Wales and thus contributed to current support for Labour's devolution agenda.

Subsidiarity

The transfer of authority and finance to the regions that devolution will involve is entirely consistent with the third way philosophy espoused by New Labour. Third way ideals support the concept of subsidiarity, which has been a dominant theme in European Union social policy since the early 1990s. In order to build cohesive communities, messages emerging from New Labour argue that power needs to be decentralized in key areas from central government to local organizations and structures. Community-level bodies are regarded as the new means for achieving desired goals. Subsidiarity is embraced in the belief that communities are better able to identify their own needs and implement appropriate strategies to address them, rather than relying on policy imposed from national government.

Implementing this principle of subsidiarity by the process of devolution is also intended by New Labour to offer communities more accountable and responsive government that is more open and inclusive. Thus, the new Parliament in Scotland and the Assemblies in Wales and Northern Ireland have been promoted in policy documents as institutions that will adopt "modern ways of working." They are to use new technology and new forms of communication in order to improve public access to information (one of the first responsibilities of the Scottish parliament was to formulate a new Freedom of Information Act) and encourage greater participation in decision-making by organizations and individuals. This emphasis on accessibility and account-ability also reflects the link Labour makes between subsidiarity and democ-racy, with the assumption that the parliament and assemblies will provide the people of Scotland, Wales and Northern Ireland with more opportunities to affect and influence policy decisions relevant to them. Devolved govern-ment as more democratic government is also reflected in the new voting systems with which the parliament and assemblies have elected their repre-sentatives—the UK's first experiment with a form of proportional representa-tion—the additional member system.

Devolution and Its Implications for Social Policy

How will the new assemblies and parliament affect social welfare? Powers to formulate and finance policy will differ significantly between the three new bodies. The main source of this difference lies in the fact that the Scottish Parliament has the power to make primary legislation, whereas the power of the assemblies is limited to the passage of secondary legislation in areas where executive functions have been transferred to them. The Scottish Parlia-ment also has tax-varying powers, which have the potential to provide an additional source of revenue that could be directed towards the expansion or reform of services, or indeed towards targeting or supplementing existing benefits for particular groups.

Despite the greater range of powers devolved to the Scottish Parliament in contrast to Northern Ireland and Wales, its ability to make any substantial changes to social protection will be limited. This is due to the fact that Westminster retains a range of powers that will limit the Parliament's ability to make any independent contribution towards addressing issues such as social exclusion or child poverty. Aside from the ability to vary the basic rate of income tax, the Parliament has no other powers in terms of taxation, so any large-scale redistribution of resources will not be possible. In addition, social security remains a Westminster responsibility, so no divergence will be pos-sible in terms of benefits or pensions. However, there are some areas of social policy in which the Scottish Parliament could potentially take a different path from the rest of the United Kingdom governments in years to come. Lindsay Paterson (2000) explains:

> The parliament...has extensive powers in relation to what economists call the supply side. It can do virtually what it wants in education...it can also do a lot in training; for example through its legislative responsibility for most of training policy, it could shape the New Deal in Scotland even though employment legislation is reserved to Westminster. It could promote health policies that would mitigate social and other inequalities.... The parliament is likely to want, and to be able, to promote social

cohesion. The explicit intentions of the reformers who have established the parliament are that it should renew Scottish pluralism. The high proportion (37 percent) of women among the 129 members is one signal of that. (p. 77)

Evidence to date of "distinctive" social policy in the devolved assemblies and parliament is limited. These new bodies have only been in place since the spring of 1999 and have spent much of their first year discussing and developing the processes of governance. In Northern Ireland, the political situation has meant that the Assembly has met for limited periods of time, and as yet has had little opportunity to make any impact. In Scotland however, there is to date at least a single clear example of the forging of a new direction in one area. In its first session, the Parliament reviewed the findings of an independent commission that examined the issue of funding in higher education. Following an earlier electoral promise, the Parliament chose to implement some of the findings of the commission and has now abolished tuition fees (which still exist in the rest of the UK) and restructured the maintenance grant system for all students studying in Scotland and for Scottish domiciled students studying elsewhere in Britain. It remains to be seen how this policy decision will be implemented in practice, and to what extent other such examples will arise.

Conclusion

Between 1979 and 1997 under successive Conservative administrations headed by Margaret Thatcher and John Major, the British welfare state and society experienced considerable change. As we have tried to show these changes included:

- Restrictions on the growth of the state;
- The growth of inequality and social exclusion;
- Experiments with quasi-markets, a new emphasis on the mixed economy of welfare and various attempts to target resources in more focused ways; and
- The development of a growing reliance on active labor market policies to deal with long-term unemployment.

For many years it looked as though the welfare state—if not actually in terminal decline—was in a state of siege. But all may be about to change. Indeed, a marked change of direction is arguably already underway.

Since May 1997 New Labour has hardly let a day pass without one or more policy initiatives being launched. Virtually every public agency in the land and many of the most disadvantaged communities have been subjected to more change and turbulence—or at the very least remonstration—than any of them have ever previously experienced. Inevitably of course there has been more evidence of rhetoric and promise than action and achievement. As one astute commentator has observed, Tony Blair's ministers are beginning to learn some hard lessons and

> ...a new caution and circumspection born of three years discovering how very hard it is to steer a rowing boat from Whitehall, let alone the ship of state.... It is not disillusion or loss of faith. It is certainly not cynicism. It is simply the weary discovery that...things are very much harder to implement than to devise. Out there the real world is messy, slow, obdurate, unyielding. (Toynbee, *The Guardian*, 12/7/00. http://guardian.chadwyck.co.uk)

And yet radical hopes may triumph over vested interests despite the difficulty of promoting social change in a complex and pluralistic world. Three years after it was elected the Blair government has announced a huge injection of public spending to reinforce its commitment to what is seen in third way parlance as the social investment welfare state.

In July 2000 the Chancellor of the Exchequer, Gordon Brown, published the results of the government's comprehensive spending review for 2001–4, which unveiled massive increases in spending especially on health, education and urban renewal. The government also pledged investment to provide universal employment opportunity and to take forward its long-term ambition to halve child poverty by 2010 and eradicate it in twenty years (HM Treasury, 2000).

It remains to be seen how many of these aspirations come to pass. What is clear is that the British welfare state is at least pointing in a new direction. Whether or not social policy is being transformed is open to genuine debate but it has an energy and a purpose not seen for many decades.

Notes

1. It takes a maximum value of one in a situation of complete inequality where all income is held by a single citizen, and it takes a minimum value of zero if income is equally distributed across the population with all citizens receiving the same share of income.

2. It measures the ratio of the income of the 90th percentile of the total distribution to that of the 10th percentile.

References

Audit Commission. (1997). *The Coming of Age: Improving Core Services for Older People*. London: Audit Commission.

Bauld, L., Chesterman, J., Davies, B., Judge, K., and Mangalore, R. (2000). *Caring for Older People: An Assessment of Community Care in the 1990s*. Aldeshot: Ashgate.

Blair, T. (1998). *The Third Way*. Fabian Pamphlet 588. London: Fabian Society.

Blundell, R., Duncan, A., McCrae J., and Meghir C. (2000). The Labour Market Impact of the Working Families' Tax Credit. *Fiscal Studies*, Vol. 21, No.1, 75-104.

Board of Inland Revenue. *Inland Revenue Statistics*. London: HMSO/The Stationery Office. www.inlandrevenue.gov.uk/stats/.

Burchardt, T., Le Grand, J., and Piachaud, D. (1999). Social Exclusion in Britain 1991-1995. *Social Policy and Administration*, Vol. 33, issue 3.

Burchardt, T. (1997). *Boundaries between Public and Private Welfare: A Typology of Maps and Services*. Paper for the ESRC Research Centre for Analysis of Social Exclusion.

Burchardt T., Hills J., and Propper, C. (1997). *Private Welfare and Public Policy*. York: Joseph Rowntree Foundation.

Cm 3805. (1998). *The Welfare Reform Green Paper*. London: The Stationery Office.

Davies, B., and Fernandez, J. (2000). *Equity and Efficiency Policy in Community Care*. Aldershot: Ashgate.

Deacon, A. (1997). "Welfare to Work": Options and Issues. *Social Policy Review, 9*, London: Social Policy Association, pp. 34-49.

Department of Health. (1995). *Community Care Statistics 1994: Day and Domiciliary Personal Social Services for Adults*. England.

Department of Health. (1998). *Community Care Statistics 1997: Day and Domiciliary Personal Social Services for Adults*. England.

Department of Health. (1999). *Community Care Statistics 1998: Day and Domiciliary Personal Social Services for Adults*. England.

Department of Social Security. (2000). *The Changing Welfare State: Social Security Spending 1998/99*.

Driver S., and Martell, L. (2000). Left, Right and the Third Way. *Policy and Politics*, 28(2), 147-161.

Giddens, A. (1998). *The Third Way: The Renewal of Social Democracy*. Cambridge: Policy Press.

Gregg, P., Jonson, P., and Reed, H. (1999). *Entering Work and the British Tax and Benefit System*. London: Institute of Fiscal Studies.

Ham, C. (1999). *Health Policy in Britain: The Politics and Organisation of the National Health Service*. 4th ed. London: Macmillan.

Hardy B., and Wistow, G. (2000). Changes in the Private Sector. In B. Hudson (ed.), *The Changing Role of Social Care*. London: Jessica Kingsley Publishers.

HM Government. (2000). The Government's Annual Report 1999/2000. *London: The Stationary Office*.

HM Treasury (2000). *Prudent for a Purpose; Building Opportunity and Security for All-2000* Spending Review: New Public Spending Plans 2001-2004. Cm 4807.

Howarth, C., Kenway, P., Palmer, G., and Miorelli, C. (1999). *Monitoring Poverty and Social Inclusion*. York: Joseph Rowntree Foundation.

Kvist, J., and Sinfield, A. (1996). *Comparing Tax Routes in Denmark and the United Kingdom*. Copenhagen: The Danish National Institute of Social Research.

Laing, W. (1993). *Financing Long Term Care: The Crucial Debate*. London: Age Concern.

Laing, W., and Buisson. (1998). *Care of Elderly People: Market Survey 1998*. Suffolk: Laing.

Millar, J. (2000). *Keeping Track of Welfare Reforms: The New Deal Programmes*. York: Joseph Rowntree Foundation.

Office for National Statistics. (2000). *Economic Trends No. 558*. May. London: The Stationery Office.

Office for National Statistics. (1984). *General Household Survey 1984*. London: HMSO.

Office for National Statistics. (2000). *Labour Force Survey Quarterly Supplement 10*, August 2000. London: The Stationery Office.

Office for National Statistics. (1997). *Labour Force Survey Historical Supplement 1997*. London: HMSO.

Office for National Statistics. (1998). *Living in Britain: The Results from the General Household Survey 1998*. London: The Stationery Office.
Office for National Statistics. (2000). *Social Trends* 2000 Edition. London: The Stationery Office.
Paterson L. (2000). Social Inclusion and the Scottish Parliament. *Scottish Affairs, 30*, 68-77.
Piachaud, D., and Sutherland, H. (2000). *How Effective is the British Government's Attempt to Reduce Child Poverty?* Case Paper 38. Centre for Analysis of Social Exclusion, London School of Economics.
Performance and Innovation Unit. (2000). *Wiring It Up, Whitehall's Management of Cross-Cutting Policies and Services*. London: Cabinet Office.
Sinfield, A. (1998). *Social Security through Tax Benefits: How Some Are Helped to Become Securer Than Others*. Evidence presented by Adrian Sinfield to the Commons Social Security Committee, 21 January 1998.
Sefton, T. (1997). *The Changing Distribution of the Social Wage*. STICERD Occasional Paper 21.
Social Exclusion Unit. (2000). *National Strategy for Neighbourhood Renewal 2000*.
Taylor-Gooby, P. (2000). *Risk, Contingency and the Third Way: Evidence from BHPS and Qualitative Studies*. Paper presented at the Social Policy Association Conference, Roehampton, London, 18-20 July 2000.

5

Social Welfare under Advanced Capitalism: The U.S. Response

Rebecca A. Van Voorhis

Development of the U.S. Welfare State

Since the mid-1980s, arrangements for social provision in the United States have undergone a radical restructuring due to philosophical, market-related, and demographic pressures, which are affecting the nature of social protection in many modern welfare states. An emphasis on personal responsibility has come to overshadow the standard of entitlement; privatization of social protection is increasing; the robust economy and low unemployment rate encourage the view from the right and left that individuals should be self-sufficient; and immense fiscal pressures posed by projected demographic change necessitate re-examination of the structure of social security. These patterns mark a significant break from the welfare state of the past sixty years.

The early history of public aid in the United States perpetuated rigid classifications established by the English Poor Laws, with limited relief available to the needy and no formal arrangements for social insurance. National government was not a source of social protection. Although assistance was available through local and state agencies, there was a high degree of regional variation in levels of support (Schneider, 1980). Without uniform national criteria to determine which groups comprised the most vulnerable members of society and the level of benefits to be dispensed, the early decentralized arrangements for support were functional only as long as limited demands were placed upon the institutions assisting the poor.

A public system of social insurance emerged when the system of social protection (which had relied upon family, church and local community) was unable to meet the manifest needs of contemporary industrial life. The U. S.

welfare state emerged amidst the high unemployment and economic instability of the Great Depression, which began with the stock market crash in 1929. This economic collapse stimulated the passage of public legislation, the objectives of which were "relief, recovery, and reform" (Leuchtenberg, 1963). This legislation was the concrete expression of President Roosevelt's " New Deal," which marked the beginning of significant federal support for social welfare in the United States—the birth of the American welfare state.

From 1933 to 1938 a set of reforms and policies were enacted, which established a wide spectrum of New Deal benefits and programs funded by the federal government. In time, the panoply of federally supported benefits came to include cash assistance to dependent children (Aid to Dependent Children), the elderly (Aid to the Elderly) and the blind (Aid to the Blind); unemployment compensation, employment services, child welfare, public housing, urban renewal, vocational education and rehabilitation, and grants for state and local public health work. Absent from this package were provisions for national healthcare or health insurance, lacuna only partly sealed by the establishment of Medicare and Medicaid in 1965.

The most enduring legacy of the Roosevelt era is the Social Security Act of 1935, the cornerstone of the New Deal social welfare legislation. The act established universal social insurance, Old Age Survivors and Disability Insurance (OASDI), and means-tested categorical direct-cash assistance programs for the aged, blind, disabled and poor families with dependent children. While the legislation was amended and reformed, for example, aid to the aged, blind and disabled was collapsed into Supplemental Security Income (SSI) in 1972, the beneficiaries of federal aid and their social rights remained virtually unchanged until 1996.

While some charge that the Social Security Act's provisions were relatively modest considering the demands that many groups had been making, the reforms initiated during the Depression signaled a change from a residual welfare state model to an institutionalized one, a shift with both philosophical and fiscal implications. International comparisons often present the American welfare system as predominantly residual in nature. Wilensky (1975), for example, refers to the United States as a "welfare laggard." This reputation is well-deserved in many respects. At a time when European countries had implemented public support systems for the poor with enumerated benefits, American relief was provided on an informal basis through familial networks, charities and churches. However, with the introduction of New Deal, and subsequent legislative developments, the American social insurance package supplies a broad range of aid including disability, medical, unemployment and other benefits which comprise a social support network similar to welfare systems implemented by "social democratic" or "corporate" countries, if somewhat modest in comparison (Esping-Andersen, 1990).

Social Expenditure: A Comprehensive Ledger of Public and Private Contributions

Prior to the New Deal, direct government expenditure for social welfare programs was largely nonexistent, less than 4 percent of the GNP in 1929. With the introduction of the New Deal, federal spending increased to 9.2 percent by 1940, and remained fairly constant throughout the postwar era during which time state and local contribution exceeded federal payments (Social Security Bulletin, 1979). Government spending for social programs rose dramatically with the introduction of the Great Society programs in the mid-1960s. Expenditure data from the annual report of the Social Security Administration (SSA) presented in table 5.1, reveal that the total direct government disbursements (from federal, state, and local sources) for social welfare programs surged from 11 percent of the GDP in 1965 to 18.2 percent in 1975 (hitting a then all-time high of 19.5 percent by 1976) as additional benefits were created through an array of new social legislation (Gilbert, 1995). Motivated by concern for the rapidly expanding federal obligation, Congress enacted ceilings on federal welfare programs in 1974 in an attempt to curb spending (Derthick, 1975).

From the mid-1970s through the mid-1990s, public social welfare expenditures remained fairly constant—18.2 percent of GDP in 1975 to 20.9 percent GDP in 1995. In comparison to the sharp rise in social spending from 1965 to 1975, the leveling off in spending from 1975 to 1995 was experienced very much as a "steady state." Most of the change in social expenditure from 1975 to 1995 is accounted for by the increasing cost of social insurance (which reflected an increase in the elderly population from 10 percent in 1975 to 12 percent in 1995) and to a lesser extent social assistance costs. At the same time, there was a proportional decrease in veterans' programs.

In regard to the expenditures on social assistance there have been two periods of AFDC caseload expansion since 1968—the initial increase began in the late 1960s through the early 1970s when the economy was strong and the general poverty rate was shrinking, with a second increase between 1989 and 1993 that is attributable to the growth of female-headed-households, and to a lesser extent, the weak economy (Peskin, et al., 1993). Besharov (1996) is more specific, linking the growth in out-of-wedlock births and the breakdown of traditional family structures to inflated welfare rolls, citing census survey research that indicates 70 percent of the new caseload between 1989 and 1991 were never-married mothers (Gabe, 1992).

Over the last decade it has become widely recognized that direct public expenditure is not the only method of government support for social welfare objectives. Tax expenditures constitute a large and growing share of public social welfare expenditures that are not counted in the official SSA or OECD social expenditure calculations. According to Christopher Howard's (1997)

Table 5.1
Social Welfare Expenditures under Public Programs

Item	1965	1970	1975	1980	1985	1990	1992	1993	1994	1995
Amount ($ millions)										
Gross domestic product	$701,000	$1,023,100	$1,590,800	$2,718,900	$4,108,000	$5,682,900	$6,149,300	$6,476,600	$6,837,100	$7,186,900
Total social welfare expenditures[1]	77,084	145,979	288,967	492,213	731,840	1,048,951	1,266,504	1,366,743	1,435,714	1,505,136
Social insurance	28,123	54,691	123,013	229,754	369,595	513,822	618,938	659,210	683,779	705,483
Public aid	6,283	16,488	41,447	72,703	98,362	146,811	207,953	221,000	238,025	253,530
Health and medical programs	6,155	10,030	16,535	26,762	38,643	61,684	70,143	74,706	80,130	85,507
Veterans' programs	6,031	9,078	17,019	21,466	27,042	30,916	35,642	36,378	37,895	39,072
Education	28,108	50,846	80,834	121,050	172,048	258,332	292,145	331,997	344,091	365,625
Housing	318	701	3,172	6,879	12,598	19,468	20,151	20,782	27,032	29,361
Other social welfare	2,066	4,145	6,947	13,599	13,552	17,918	21,532	22,670	24,762	26,558
All health and medical care[2]	9,302	24,801	51,022	99,145	170,665	274,472	353,174	381,710	408,780	435,075
As percent of gross domestic product										
Gross domestic product	100.0%	100.0%	100.0%	100.0%	100.0%	100.0%	100.0%	100.0%	100.0%	100.0%
Total social welfare expenditures	11.0	14.3	18.2	18.1	17.8	18.5	20.6	21.1	21.0	20.9
Social insurance	4.0	5.3	7.7	8.5	9.0	9.0	10.1	10.2	10.0	9.8
Public aid	.9	1.6	2.6	2.7	2.4	2.6	3.4	3.4	3.5	3.5
Health and medical programs	.9	1.0	1.0	1.0	.9	1.1	1.1	1.2	1.2	1.2
Veterans' programs	.9	.9	1.1	.8	.7	.5	.6	.6	.6	.5
Education	4.0	5.0	5.1	4.5	4.2	4.5	4.8	5.1	5.0	5.1
Housing	(3)	.1	.2	.3	.3	.3	.3	.3	.4	.4
Other social welfare	.3	.4	.4	.5	.3	.3	.4	.4	.4	.4
All health and medical care	1.3	2.4	3.2	3.6	4.2	4.8	5.7	5.9	6.0	6.1

Notes: Through 1976, fiscal year ended June 30 for federal government, most states, and some localities. Beginning in 1977, federal fiscal year ended Sept. 30. 1. Represents program and administrative expenditures from federal, state, and local public revenues and trust funds under public law. Includes workers' compensation and temporary disability insurance payments made through private carriers and self-insurers. Includes capital outlay and some expenditures abroad. 2. Combines "health and medical programs" with medical services provided in connection with social insurance, public aid, veterans', and "other social welfare" categories. 3. Less than 0.05 percent.

Source: Social Security Administration. Web: www.ssa.gov/statistics/Supplement/1999/tables/index.html.

estimate, in 1995 tax expenditures (on health, housing, social services, education, and income security) amounted to $400 billion. His figures show that between 1967and 1975 tax expenditures grew (5.9 percent) at a little less than 50 percent of the rate of direct social expenditures (11.4 percent). In contrast, between 1975 and 1995 tax expenditures grew (4.3 percent) at almost 130 percent the rate of direct expenditures (3.2 percent) (see table 5.2).

In addition to direct and indirect public expenditures, a comprehensive understanding of social welfare expenditures must take into account the increasing role of the private sector. The private sector voluntarily contributes to the provision of social welfare benefits through employment-related pensions, health insurance, disability insurance, paid sick leave, and social services.[1] Private spending for social welfare in the U.S. climbed from 9.3 percent of the GDP in 1980 to 13.5 percent of the GDP in 1994—a 45 percent increase in its share of the GDP over fourteen years. The definition of public and private social welfare expenditures gets fuzzy around the edges. In some cases contributions from the private sector are not voluntary, but mandated by public authority. And sometimes private spending is partially subsidized through tax deductions.

As noted earlier, the U.S. welfare state has been typically considered a laggard relative to other advanced industrial nations, based largely on comparisons of levels of direct public social welfare expenditures as a proportion of the GDP. Taking a broader more comprehensive view of social welfare expenditures, however, Adema's (1999) findings suggest that social spending among the advanced industrial welfare states is much closer than that based on comparisons limited to direct public expenditures. For comparative purposes, a comprehensive assessment of social welfare expenditures requires an enumeration of not only direct and indirect public spending and voluntary and mandated private spending, but also taking into account the extent to which social welfare benefits are subject to direct and indirect taxation. In many cases governments recapture a portion of direct social welfare expenditures by clawing back public benefits through direct and indirect taxes. As shown in table 5.2, when only counting direct public social expenditures the United States is by far the lowest spending welfare state and Denmark is the highest.[2] However, with a comprehensive and more exacting measure that factors in all of the considerations noted above, the range of social expenditures narrows considerably and the United States appears close to the middle, above Denmark.

The Broader Socioeconomic Context: Implications for the Nature of Social Protection

Since the mid-1980s powerful global economic and social forces have created new pressures on the welfare state and the nature of social protection

Table 5.2
Comparison of Social Expenditures 1995

Country	Gross Public Social Expenditure (% GDP)	Net Total Social Expenditure (% GDP)
United States	17.1	24.5
Denmark	37.6	24.4
Sweden	36.4	27.0
Netherlands	30.1	25.0
United Kingdom	25.9	26.0
Italy	26.5	22.3
Germany	30.4	27.7
Ireland	21.8	18.7
Finland	35.7	25.7
Canada	20.8	21.2

Source: Willem Adema, *Net Social Expenditures: Labour Market and Social Polic— Occasional Papers No. 39* (Paris: OECD, 1999), Table 7.

in most OECD nations. Where earlier changes in the dimensions of the welfare state grew out of increased expenditure and expanded eligibility, since the mid-1980s the "steady state" experienced changes driven by socioeconomic pressures and a philosophical debate concerning central government's role in the provision of welfare. These forces collectively represent the unfolding of a new era—here referred to as "advanced capitalism"—that has altered the contours of the welfare state in the United States, resulting in change as profound and far-reaching as that experienced during the Industrial Revolution. As illustrated in table 5.3, there are six areas in which there have been dramatic breaks since 1985, which impact the demands and adaptations for social protection in the U.S. welfare state. Ideological concerns focus on market and quasi-market alternatives to public provision; globalization of the economy has replaced the emphasis on industrialization; migration patterns have been elevated to an international scale; and changing demographics and labor force participation require a reconsideration of spending priorities.

In the United States adaptation of social welfare policies to the socioeconomic developments under advanced capitalism is exemplified by three policy trends: (1) an increased emphasis on targeting; (2) movement toward the privatization and decentralization of service delivery; and (3) implementation of contractual obligations between the state and beneficiaries (e.g., workfare). These movements are observable across social insurance and social assistance programs alike, and together demonstrate a significant break from the welfare state of the 1980s and before.

Table 5.3
Transitions from the Industrial Age to the Era of Advanced Capitalism Which Generate New Social Welfare Demands and Adaptations

	Industrial Era (1940- 1985)	Advanced Capitalism (late 1980s to present)
Ideology	Social Provision by Government	Social provision through market and quasi-market (Privatization)
	Welfare	Workfare
	Entitlement	Emphasis on rights and responsibilities
	More expansive categorical assistance	Targeting
Economy	Domestic Autonomous	Globalized economy Interconnectedness
	Competition between command and market ideology	Dominance of Market economy
Migration	Rural to urban	International
	Unskilled migration	Immigration of skilled labor
Labor	Male dominated work force	Increased female participation Part-time work
Demographic Adjustment	Expanding population	Decreasing birth rate Increasing life expectancy
Family Structure	Stable nuclear	Divorce and serial monogamy Single parent families

Targeting: Towards More Restrictive Criteria

A prominent feature of the U.S. welfare state in the era of advanced capitalism is the trend towards more restrictive eligibility criteria. This tendency is apparent in a number of policy changes affecting both social insurance and social assistance programs, which denotes a departure from the industrialized welfare state with its emphasis on expansion and inclusiveness. Measures that limit access to and consumption of social welfare benefits involve the stricter application of both economic and social criteria such as: means-tests, "claw-back" taxes, more limited definitions of disability and restrictive conditions for entitlement.

Old Age and Survivor's Insurance (OASI)

The increased use of targeting is highly evident in several significant legislated changes to the eligibility parameters for OASI. When the Social

Security Act was passed, creating universal Old Age Insurance (OAI) in 1935, the retirement age was set at 65 years of age (a provision for Survivors was added in 1939). At the inception of OAI, few elderly benefited from the newly enacted Old Age Insurance program. In fact, between 1935 and 1950, Old Age Assistance (OAA), a program based on need rather than contribution, paid higher benefits and supported far more people than did Old Age Insurance (Achenbaum, 1986). Consequently, OAI continued to struggle to prove its political relevancy—with Congress refusing to implement scheduled payroll tax and taxable wage base increases throughout the 1940s (Derthick, 1979). Old Age Insurance did not exceed OAA in total amount of payments and total number of recipients until 1951. This progression was interpreted as evidence of the OAI program's viability, which increased its political support. The heightened political support for Old Age and Survivors Insurance paved the way for the expansion of the Social Security Act with the introduction of Disability Insurance (DI) in 1956.

From this uncertain beginning, OASDI has emerged as the largest single category of public social expenditure, with a total of 44.2 million recipients in 1998, and benefit payments totaling $375 billion. With total life expectancy as well as the total number of persons surviving to age 65 expected to rise well into the next century for both men and women and a decreasing support ratio, significant questions loom concerning the solvency of this pay-as-you-go program.

While the incentive to move older workers out of the labor force made sense at one time, this practice is problematic in light of the current demographic realities. Not only are people retiring earlier, they are living longer (and collecting more) than previous generations of retirees.

One immediate response to the problems confronting the Old Age pension system has been to raise the access threshold by lifting the normal age of retirement (NRA). Congress has legislated an increase in the NRA from 65 years of age to 67, with a gradual phase-in to be completed by year 2022 (recent proposals recommend raising it further to age 70). This change in the social definition of the "normal retirement age" of retirement targets benefits to an older cohort of recipients. Efforts to tighten access to social provision are also evident with respect to other social insurance programs such as Disability Insurance, where more stringent examinations and criteria are being employed to determine eligibility.

Another departure from the original policies which limits consumption of Old Age insurance concerns the tax status of Old Age pension benefits. Here an indirect method of targeting has been employed through ameliorative reforms that increase taxation on pension benefits for those in the upper income brackets. Although benefits were entirely exempt from taxation, amendments to the Social Security Act and tax laws in 1983 permitted including up to one-half of pension benefits in the taxable income of certain high-income households (Steuerle and Bakija, 1994). The proportion of benefits subject to income taxation was increased to up to 85 percent in 1993, dependent upon the beneficiaries total income from all sources (*Social Security Bulletin*, 2001). In this way what the government allocates with one hand it "claws" back through taxes with the other, targeting not at the point of allocation but the point of consumption.

Social Assistance

The United States has long relied upon direct targeting in the determination of eligibility for provision of aid to the needy—the Social Security Act of 1935 established three categorical assistance programs; Aid to the Blind (AB), and Old Age Assistance (OAA), as well as Aid to Dependent Children (ADC). Later, a provision for Aid to the Permanently and Totally Disabled (APTD) was added. In 1962, the ADC program was renamed Aid to Families with Dependent Children (AFDC), which reflected a change in policy intended to protect the family unit. (Prior to this time, children were ineligible for aid if an unemployed yet able-bodied parent/father was living in the home. The policy effectively established desertion as a condition for AFDC eligibility—the possibility that this might reward desertion inspired lawmakers to establish AFDC-UP (AFDC-Unemployed Parent), which allowed benefits to be given to two-parent families.

Through the early 1970s, Medicaid and the four categorical assistance programs, along with food stamps, formed the general core of public assistance in the United States (Gilbert, Specht, and Terrell, 1993). States were granted significant latitude in determining the size of the grants, though federal monies received were a function of states' wealth. This resulted in significant variations in eligibility and levels of assistance. However, the structure of categorical assistance was significantly revised by an amendment to the Social Security Act in 1972. This amendment consolidated Old Age Assistance (OAA), Aid to the Blind (AB), and Aid to the Permanently and Totally Disabled (APTD) into a single program called Supplemental Security Income (SSI). Implemented in 1974, SSI removed state administrative authority, including eligibility requirements and grant size, resulting in a uniform cash grant to all recipients. While states were permitted to supplement federal grants with state-funded payments, SSI was fully under federal jurisdiction. AFDC remained under state administration, and was jointly financed through federal and state matching funding. While AFDC was often maligned, little was done to change the availability of benefits or alter the nature of delivery.

After the sharp increase in federal spending in the 1960s—a result of programs initiated during the War on Poverty—efforts to hold spending constant dominated welfare policy through the 1980s. The implementation of the Family Support Act (FSA) in the late 1980s signaled the beginning of efforts to tighten eligibility in AFDC. While the FSA stressed individual responsibility and focused on welfare-to-work approaches that introduced an element of participant involvement into the welfare equation, the Act is also noteworthy as it marks one of the first movements aimed towards limiting the number of recipients (Gueron, 1996).

Since the passage of the Social Security Act of 1935, categorical means-tested programs grew along several lines as benefits became more generous and the categories of those who might qualify for benefits expanded, resulting in a general increase in caseload. However, all this has come to a screeching halt under the brake of recent policy initiatives. The passage of the Personal Responsibility and Work Opportunity Act in 1996 (PRWO) dramatically altered categorical assistance programs. The PRWO was the culmination of several decades of welfare policy adaptation and retrenchment. This act targets public assistance-related benefits delivered through four different federal programs—Supplemental Security Income (SSI, means-tested public assistance for blind, aged, and disabled people), Food Stamps, Medicaid (means-tested health insurance), and AFDC—resulting in the most comprehensive welfare reform movement of the twentieth century. Two types of restrictive strategies are employed—the first aims to reduce the number of public assistance beneficiaries by tightening access through stringent eligibility criteria; the second aims to reduce the length of time beneficiaries remain on welfare rolls through the introduction of term limits for benefits.

Some see the sharp distinction between the "deserving" and "undeserving" poor under the English Poor laws being revived in the recent reforms of American welfare policy. The PRWO Act targets most intensely those people whom the public view as the "undeserving poor": able-bodied recipients of food stamps; unemployed adults with children; and recent immigrants. The implicit characterization of some as "undeserving" allows for a decrease in the welfare effort without repudiating obligations incurred under prior social legislation, and can be viewed as an attempt to target the neediest of the poor.

Under the Personal Responsibility and Work Opportunity Act of 1996 eligibility requirements for food stamps and Supplemental Security Income (SSI) were changed. Legal immigrants, for example, were denied access to SSI and food stamps. (These measures were modified to grandfather in those already on the rolls.)[3] Moving in the same direction, the Contract with America Advancement Act of 1996 severely restricted eligibility or eliminated it entirely for several categories of incapacity—for example, alcohol and drug addiction for adults and learning disorders and attention deficit disorder in children—previously covered by the Aid to the Disabled program (Berrick, 2001). The most significant impact of the Personal Responsibility and Work Opportunity Act of 1996 was to dismantle a cornerstone of federal protection for the poor, with the elimination of AFDC—the 61-year-old federal guarantee of cash assistance for the nations' poorest families. The withdrawal of AFDC, an open-ended federal entitlement, is a radical reform, reflecting an attenuation in tolerance for and social rights of the able-bodied poor. In place of the AFDC program, the PRWO Act created the Temporary Assistance for Needy Families (TANF) program, which provides time-limited cash assistance delivered by states and funded through federal block grants. TANF imposes a five-year limit on public assistance to any family during their lifetime, and requires most adults to work within two years of receiving aid. However, states can both set stricter limits and exempt up to 20 percent of families from the time limit for reasons of hardship. Food stamps to able-bodied poor without dependents are also reduced and term-limited (APWA, 1996).

In addition to the time limits, many of the TANF-initiated reforms have created a more restrictive definition of eligibility, predicted on recipients' behavior and participatory efforts. States have created a whole new range of requirements, incentives and sanctions that focus on parental behaviors—having children immunized, insuring that children attend school, reporting the father's name to welfare authorities; self-improvement such as requiring clients to enroll in high school degree programs and denying benefits for additional children born while on welfare (child exclusion laws); encouraging marriage by allowing benefits to continue even if the recipient marries (as long as it is not to the natural father of her child).[4] These examples illustrate the fact that in the United States mechanisms of targeting have moved beyond the simple determination of need to embrace a moral dimension of social behavior.

Rights Versus Responsibilities: Activation and Workfare

One of the most significant ideological changes experienced by modern welfare states in the era of advanced capitalism involves the recalibration of rights and responsibility. The early history of the welfare state, grounded in the tradition of social rights, has veered dramatically in the past two decades to a system under which individuals are expected to take significant responsibility for their own welfare and well being. Variously described as a shift from entitlement to obligation, a movement from the Keynesian Welfare State to a Schumpeterian Workfare State (Torfing, 1997), a change from a passive to active society (OECD, 1989), or from a welfare state to an Enabling State (Gilbert, 2002)—all of these descriptors allude to the broad range of policy changes affecting the nature of social protection. The implementation of policy promoting activation and workfare is evident throughout the major social insurance and social assistance based programs, although the strictest application has been reserved for means-tested programs.

Social Insurance

The OASDI system is built upon mandatory payroll taxes jointly paid by the employer and employee. Both taxes are set at the same rate, measured as a percent of the employees' earned income. A maximum taxable ceiling was also implemented under the original Social Security Act. In 1937 through 1939, the contribution of both employers and employees was 1 percent of payable wages, with a $3,000 ceiling. By comparison, in 1999 the tax rate is 6.2 percent for OASDI (5.35 and .85 for OASI and DI, respectively, with an additional 1.45 for HI) with an income ceiling of $72,600 (Social Security Administration, 2001). While tax rates have changed dramatically since the 1930s, the system continues to be guided by principles of equal employer-employee contributions, and a maximum taxable income.

In recent years, the contractual nature of the relationship between generations inherent in the OASDI pay-as-you-go finance system has fallen prey to the issue of intergenerational equity. The first generation of beneficiaries received far more in benefits than they "earned" through contributions— since a worker retiring in 1940 paid little into the new national system, recouping whatever was paid in payroll taxes plus accrued interest in about six months (Morris, 1996).[5] The steady increase in payroll taxes from 1950 to 1990 perpetuated the trend that retirees received more from the system than they paid in contribution tax. For example, according to figures from the SSA, a beneficiary who turned 65 in 1996 contributed $21,518 in 1996 dollars (employee's share only), but can be expected to receive over $73,703 in benefits, which amounts to a monthly benefit of approximately $890. (Most agree that the true measure of contribution is both the employer and the employee share since employers tend to factor the contribution tax into the employee salary [Hurd, 1997; Steuerle and Bakija, 1994]).

Using OASDI Board of Trustee data, Steuerle and Bakija (1994) show that all low, average and high-income earners retiring prior to 1995 receive a large positive net-transfer—that is, the total benefit they receive from the Social Security system exceeds their contribution. However, the largest positive transfers have been granted to those who retired prior to 1995. Beginning with the cohort born in 1930 (who retired in 1995) some members will have contributed more to Social Security than they can expect in benefits, and the number of beneficiaries for whom Social Security becomes a negative investment is expected to rise (although many future retirees will continue to receive significant, if more modest, transfers). Similar conclusions are reached by Chen and Goss (1997) who found that individuals retiring from 1960 to 1968 receive a 12.5 percent real rate of return on their tax contribution, whereas workers retiring between 1982 and 1987 receive a much lower 5.9 percent return, with future retirees experiencing an even lower real rate of return. These figures vividly demonstrate the disproportional benefit received by the current generation of retirees compared to their contribution, contrasted with the expected situation of future retirees. The disparity between cohorts predicted by the SSA and others, has fueled the issue of intergenerational equity, and in the process has lent weight to an increasing emphasis on activation of the elderly.

The relationship between contribution and participation is important, and will become more relevant in the coming years as policy changes designed to activate—promote or prolong the working life of—the elderly gain momentum. As previously mentioned, the Normal Retirement Age (NRA) has already been increased to age 67—designed to encourage labor market participation among the elderly, or at least somewhat curtail the period of recipiency. Other examples of the heightened emphasis on individual responsibility are evident when examining OASDI replacement rates and the reform of the limit on earnings sometimes referred as the retirement test. The diminishing replacement rates provided by benefits have already begun to place new pressures on individuals to supplement retirement income, either by continuing to work or by making private arrangements to provide for one's own retirement. At the same time the elimination of the earnings test for workers who begin collecting social security benefits at the normal age of retirement allows them to continue working without having to pay any penalties (which involved loss of $1 in benefit for each $2 of earning above an annual exempt amount). And as an incentive to postpone collecting social security benefits at the normal retirement age, the monthly benefits are increased by 3 percent for each year an individual works past the normal retirement age without claiming benefits. All of these modifications are reforms that require individuals to play a more active role in providing for their own support in old age. Disability Insurance offers an additional example of the shift towards activation. In 1999, the regulatory threshold for the amount of earnings necessary for a disabled individual to be considered as engaged in Substantial Gainful Activity (SGA) increased from $500 per month to $700 per month. This modification was issued as part of a package of reforms designed to encourage people with disabilities to return to the workforce (Social Security Administration, 2001). The renewed emphasis on employment and activation has emerged during a period of relatively low levels of unemployment in the United States.

Social Assistance

The most dramatic shift from entitlement toward individual responsibility occurred in the context of means-tested programs. By the late 1980s, deliberations surrounding the nature of entitlement programs dominated the agenda of the U.S. welfare state. At issue was the appropriate balance between the social right to entitlement, and the social responsibility incurred upon receipt of benefits. This ideological discussion evolved into a practical debate as policy analysts and politicians entered the arena.

Introducing an element of participant involvement into the welfare equation, the Family Support Act of 1988 (FSA) was one of the first attempts in the era of advanced capitalism to promote individual responsibility, and welfare-to-work approaches (Gueron, 1996). As such, the FSA reflects policymakers' heightened efforts to connect welfare benefits and incentives to work (Gilbert, 1995). The act required mothers with children over the age of three to enroll in work-training or education programs, and seek employment when the programs were completed. The explicit message was that policymakers expected AFDC recipients to become self-sufficient, with the benefit of education or job-training, and thus no longer be a burden to the state. In order to assist in the transition from welfare recipient to employee, day care services, and a year-long continuation of Medicaid insurance were offered as incentives for successful entrants to the work world. While most attempts to cultivate personal responsibility focused on encouraging recipients of AFDC to work and move off of welfare rolls, other movements toward parental responsibility are noteworthy. A component of the FSA required that paternity be established upon birth of a child to an AFDC mother so that fathers could be held responsible for child-support payments, demonstrating renewed efforts on support collection (Garfinkle and McLanahan, 1990).

The centerpiece of the Act was the Job Opportunity and Basic Skills (JOBS) program, envisioned as the vehicle of deliverance from dependency to self-sufficiency for poor families. The JOBS program provided new federal matching funds for state welfare-to-work initiatives. Consistent with the trend toward decentralization, goals for targeting and participation were identified; however, program specification and other requirements were largely undefined (Gueron and Pauly, 1991). The relative freedom afforded states in program design is attributable to both delivery modifications in the 1980s, as well as an attempt to disassociate from prior attempts at workfare. This was not the first governmental attempt to encourage poor parents to leave welfare for work. In 1967, Congress created the Work Incentive program (WIN) to reorient parents from welfare toward work. However, the legacy of WIN was judged unsuccessful, more often resulting in registering recipients to work than actually involving them in program activities or employment (Gueron and Pauly, 1991). By contrast, the initial outcome of JOBS related programs was more encouraging; state projects demonstrated that employment-directed services and mandates for single mothers on AFDC could be implemented effectively and be somewhat successful in encouraging work and self-support (Gueron, 1996).

Since the mid-1980s, efforts have been made to define the parameters of both rights and responsibilities in relation to welfare benefits. While the contested boundaries are subject to political, social and fiscal influences, there appears to be no retreat from the initial movement toward balancing the equation. Rather, an ongoing attempt to formulate a normative consensus concerning rights and obligations dominates welfare-based discussions. Although the debate often tends to reflect conservative rhetoric, it is important to note bipartisan support exists for exacting obligations from public aid recipients. President Clinton's 1992 campaign promise, "end welfare, as we know it," focused on this balance (Ellwood, 1996). Attempts toward contraction of welfare obligations previously have been the jurisdiction of conservatives, never embraced by liberal philosophy. The defection from welfare advocacy by the Democratic Party in some ways signified a dramatic movement, which some suggest leaves the poor without a voice (Teles, 1996). The Clinton administration "ended welfare as we know it" with the passage of the Personal Responsibility and Work Opportunity Act of 1996 (PRWO), marking the culmination of several decades of adaptation and retrenchment. As already noted, AFDC was abolished and a new program, Temporary Assistance for Needy Families (TANF), was created which provides numerous incentives to work along with time-limited cash assistance delivered by states and funded by block grants. Welfare reform was accompanied by an unprecedented decline in the public assistance caseload, which fell by over 50 percent from 1994 to 2001. This remarkable development is attributed in part to opportunities provided by a strong economy in the 1990s, during which the unemployment rate fell to an historic low of 4.3 percent, and in part to the demands and constraints emanating from policy reforms (Besharov and Germanis, 2000).

The shift toward increased individual obligation reflects what many policymakers see as the need for a more balanced relationship between social rights and civic responsibilities. This view is emphasized by the communitarian movement, which asserts that a civil society demands both accountability and participation from its members. Contribution and active enrollment in the community are prerequisites to deservedness (Etzioni, 1993). The communitarian model challenges the assumption that citizenship alone confers social rights—a belief that shaped the contours of federal policy since the 1960s (Marshall, 1963).

The Changing Welfare Mix: Added Privatization

Under advanced capitalism, most modern welfare states are no longer increasing levels of public expenditure and are moving, at various speeds but in the same direction, towards increased private arrangements for the provision and allocation of social welfare.[6] Globalization and increased competition demand new levels of efficiency that put pressure on social expenditure. The dawn of the global market economy has converted the capitalist promise of increased economic prosperity for each successive generation popularized by the Industrial Revolution to a Darwinian struggle of competition between workers and nations during the era of advanced capitalism (Leonard, 1997). In this context social welfare policies in the United States are being designed with an increasing emphasis on personal responsibility, flexibility of labor, and privatization.

The shifting balance between public and private delivery of social welfare has been going on since the mid-1970s, spurred by purchase-of-service arrangements with public agencies for services such as child welfare, daycare, health, nursing care, homemaker aides, housing, and meals for the elderly. By 1980, for example, 58 percent of the financial support received by private *nonprofit* agencies came from federal agencies (Gilbert, 1995). However, more recently the expansion of privatization has moved from contracting with voluntary nonprofit agencies to contracting with *profit-making* agencies. Between 1982 and 1987 the number of paid employees in for-profit social service agencies (child welfare, daycare, homemakers, nursing homes, etc.) increased by 38 percent compared to a 19 percent increase of employees in voluntary social welfare agencies. In addition to enlarging the sphere of private social welfare through publicly financed purchase-of-service arrangements with voluntary and for-profit providers, direct private spending has also increased, climbing from 34 percent to 39 percent of the total proportion of the GDP allotted to social expenditures between 1980 and 1994 (Social Security Administration, 2001).

Proponents suggest privatization infuses the delivery of welfare services with a degree of competition found in the private market, which leads to increased efficiency (Gilbert, 1983). Those opposed to privatization argue that the element of market competition and the corresponding tendency to increase profit at all costs, is a dangerous combination for vulnerable populations who are less able to defend themselves against the inequalities that the free-market creates (Abramovitz, 1986). Although privatization may suit some social services better than others, the trend has enjoyed considerable popularity in many program areas, most notably daycare, nursing homes, child welfare and job training services. To date, the outcome of this trend is mixed, as illustrated by research on daycare and nursing home services. While proprietary programs have increased consumer choice and in some cases lowered costs, privatization of child-care has resulted in diminished standards of care, and a decline in quality of service (Kisker, et al., 1991; Kamerman and Kahn, 1987). In nursing homes, for example, Weisbrod and Schlesinger's (1986) findings show that for-profit providers tend to charge less than nonprofit homes, but that the ratio of staff to clients was higher under for-profit services as was the administration of sleeping medication to clients.

In the mid-1990s, with the advent of TANF, the movement toward privatization gained momentum as many states began to contract-out their job training efforts. In Texas, corporate giants such as Andersen Consulting and Lockhead Martin bid on a contract to manage the state's entire public welfare operation, budgeted at over half a billion dollars annually. The federal authorities disallowed this because of concerns that private agencies performing the function of eligibility determination might be tempted to deny eligibility to applicants and keep the "profits." However, private corporations can contract with the states for all other functions, such as case management, training, and payment, related to the TANF program. Arranging for the delivery of welfare benefits via a fixed-price contract with corporate sponsors offers an attractive option to states faced with decreasing budgets and financial penalties for failure to meet new employment requirements (Bernstein, 1996).

In addition, many states are exploring ways to develop "partnerships" with private employers as an alternative form of privatization. For example, some states are experimenting with use of employer wage subsidies and tax credits that may encourage businesses to hire recipients (Kilborn, 1996). The transactions appear to benefit all parties: the employer receives a financial incentive, the recipient a job and the opportunity to develop skills, and the state the possibility of decreasing welfare enrollment. However, there may be hidden costs to public subsidies of low-end wages. Subsidies may encourage employers to hire only TANF recipients, since the employers' expenses would decrease for every subsidized worker hired over an unsubsidized worker. In regard to subsidizing low-wage employment, it should be noted that tax transfers that benefit the working poor are currently offered in the United States through the Earned Income Tax Credit (EITC). Under this scheme, low-income earners are eligible for a maximum $3,756 refund from the government, even if they pay no income taxes. The value of EITC rises by 40 cents on every dollar earned up to $9,390; it levels off there and then begins to decline after earnings go above $12,250. In addition to the federal EITC, a number of states have initiated State EITCs for their residents.

Finally, under the Bush administration a concerted effort is being launched to partially privatize social security, with about 2 percent of the contributions being invested in individual accounts. A rigorous political debate is brewing in response to the work of the President's Commission to Strengthen Social Security, which was appointed by President Bush to prepare proposals for partial privatization.[7] As Robert Solow (2002) notes in his review of the discussion of "retirement security" in the 2002 *Economic Report of the President*: "Notice that the topic is not 'social security'; it is precisely the administration's goal to take as much of the 'social' out of 'social security' as it can" (p. 20). This observation offers a clear signal of where the U.S. welfare state is headed for the immediate future—toward market-oriented solutions that involve increasing commodification of labor; greater reliance on private initiative; greater demands on personal responsibility of social welfare recipients; and a decreasing consideration for social rights.

Notes

1. For a detailed discussion of the definitions of private social welfare expenditures in the United States, see Kerns and Glanz (1991).
2. It should be noted that the SSA data differ somewhat from the most recent OECD figures for social expenditure, mainly due to the inclusion of educational spending in the U.S. data.
3. One of the reasons for this push was the considerable increase in noncitizen uptake on SSI, particularly for the aged. For example, in 1982, noncitizens accounted for 5.9 percent of the recipients of the federal payments for SSI for the aged; this rate increased dramatically to 32 percent by 1995 (declining slightly to 27 percent by 1997). Many of these recipients were the elderly parents of young immigrants, who were brought to the U.S. by their children. In the category of SSI for the blind and disabled noncitizen recipients, increased from 1.6 percent in 1982 to 6.3 percent in 1995. One of the consequences of the citizenship requirements in the welfare reform legislation was to multiply the numbers of legal immigrants signing up to qualify for U.S. citizenship.
4. For an analysis of the various measures implemented among the states, see Rowe (2000).
5. The first person to receive a Social Security check was a retired legal secretary named Ida Fuller who paid in less than $100 in payroll taxes, before receiving her first benefits' check in 1940, and who collected more than $21,000 in Social Security cash benefits before her death in 1975 (Kingson and Schulz, 1997).
6. In the mid-1990s social expenditure as a percent of GDP began a slight decline in a number of the advanced welfare states. See OECD (2000). The drift toward the market is observable among a wide range of countries and across programs designated as both social insurance and social assistance. For example, Great Britain and Sweden have already privatized portions of their retirement programs, with similar plans under consideration in the United States. Currently, many OECD countries are routinely involving private enterprise in efforts to end welfare dependency by contracting out benefit delivery and workfare programs. (See, for example, Gilbert, 2002.)
7. For the flavor of this debate, see Aaron, Blinder, Munnell, and Orszag (2001).

References

Aaron, H., Blinder, A., Munnell, A., and Orszag, P. (2001). *Perspectives on the Draft Interim Report of the President's Commission to Strengthen Social Security*. Washington DC: Center on Budget and Policy Priorities and The Century Foundation.

Abramovitz, D. M. (1986). Privatization of the Welfare State: A Review. *Social Work* 31 (4) 257-264.

Achenbaum, W. A. (1986). *Social Security: Visions and Revisions*. New York: Cambridge University Press.

Adema, W. (1999). *Net Social Expenditures: Labour Market and Social Policy—Occasional Papers No. 39*. Paris: OECD.

American Public Welfare Association (APWA). (1996). *The Personal Responsibility and Work Opportunity Reconciliation Act of 1996, Summary*. Washington, DC.

Bernstein, N. (1996). Giant Companies Entering Race to Run State Welfare Programs. *New York Times*, 15 September, p. 1, col 1.

Berrick, J. D. (2001). Targeting Social Welfare in the United States: Personal Responsibility, Private Behavior and Public Benefits. In N. Gilbert (ed.), *Targeting Social Benefits: International Perspectives and Trends*. New Brunswick, NJ: Transaction Publishers.

Besharov, D. (1996). Poverty, Welfare Dependency and the Under Class: Trends and Explanations. In M. R. Darby (ed.), *Reducing Poverty in America*. Thousand Oaks, CA: Sage.

Besharov, D., and Germanis, P. (2000). Welfare Reform–Four Years Later. *The Public Interest, 140* (Summer): 17-35.

Chen, Y-P, and Goss, S. C. (1997). Are Returns on Payroll Taxes Fair? In E. R. Kingson and J. H. Schulz (eds.), *Social Security in the 21st century*. New York: Oxford University Press.

Derthick, M. (1975). *Uncontrollable Spending for Social Services Grants*. Washington, DC: Brookings Institute.

Derthick, M. (1979). *Policy Making for Social Security*. Washington, DC: Brookings Institution.

Ellwood, D. T. (1996). Welfare Reform as I knew It. *The American Prospect*, May/June.

Esping-Andersen, G. (1990). *The Three Worlds of Welfare Capitalism*. Princeton, NJ: Princeton University Press.

Etzioni, A. (1993). *The Spirit of the Community*. New York: Crown.

Gabe, T. (1992). *Demographic Trends Affecting Aid to Families with Dependent Children (AFDC) Caseload Growth* (CRS Report to Congress). Washington, DC: Library of Congress: Brookings Institute.

Garfinkle, I., and McLanahan, S. (1990). The Effects of the Child Support Provisions of the Family Support Act of 1988 on Child Well-Being. *Population Research and Policy Review, 9*, 205-234.

Gilbert, N. (1983). *Capitalism and the Welfare State*. New Haven, CT: Yale University Press.

Gilbert, N. (1995). *Welfare Justice: Restoring Social Equity*. New Haven, CT: Yale University Press.

Gilbert, N. (2002). *Transformation of the Welfare State: The Silent Surrender of Public Responsibility*. New York: Oxford University Press.

Gilbert, N., Specht, H., and Terrell, P. (1993). *Dimensions of Social Welfare Policy*. 3rd ed. Englewood Cliffs, NJ: Prentice Hall.

Gueron, J. M. (1996). Welfare and Poverty: Strategies to Increase Work. In M. R. Darby (ed.), *Reducing Poverty in America*. Thousand Oaks, CA: Sage Publications.

Gueron, J. M., and Pauly, E. (1991). *From Welfare to Work*. New York: Russell Sage Foundation.

Howard, C. (1997). *The Hidden Welfare State*. Princeton, NJ: Princeton University Press.

Hurd, M. D. (1997). Adequacy and Equity Issues: Another View. In E. R. Kingson and J. H. Schulz (eds.), *Social Security in the 21st century*. New York: Oxford University Press.

Kamerman, S. B. and Kahn, A. J. (1987). *Facing the Hard Choices*. Dover, MA: Auburn House.

Kerns, W., and Glanz, M. (1991). Private Social Welfare Expenditures, 1972-88. *Social Security Bulletin, 54*:2, 2-11.

Kilborn, P. T. (1996). Previously Reluctant States Moving on Welfare Changes. *New York Times*, 16 December, p. 1, col. 1.

Kingston, E. R., and Schulz, J. M. (eds.). (1997). *Social Security in the 21st Century.* New York: Oxford University Press.

Kisker, E. et al. (1991). *A Profile of Child Care Settings: Early Education and Care in 1990–Executive Summary.* Washington, DC: U.S. Dept. of Education.

Leonard, P. (1997). *Postmodern Welfare.* London: Sage.

Leuchtenberg, W. E. (1963). *Franklin D. Roosevelt and the New Deal.* New York: Harper and Row.

Marshall, T. H. (1963). *Sociology at the Crossroads and Other Essays.* London: Heinemann.

Morris, C.R. (1996). *The AARP.* New York: Times Books.

OECD. (1989). Editorial: The Path to Full Employment: Structural Adjustment for an Active Society. *Employment Outlook.* July.

OECD. (2000). *OECD Social Expenditure Database.* Paris: OECD.

Peskin, J., Tapogna, J., and Marcotte, D. (1993). *Forecasting AFDC Caseloads with an Emphasis on Economic Factors.* Washington, DC: Congressional Budget Office.

Rowe, G. (2000). *Welfare Rules Databook: State TANF Policies as of July 1999.* Washington, DC: Urban Institute.

Schneider, D. M. (1980). The Patchwork of Relief in Provincial New York, 1664-1775. In F. R. Bruel and S. J. Diner (eds.), *Compassion and Responsibility*, pp. 64-94.

Social Security Administration. (1979). *Annual Statistical Supplement, 1979-1979.* Washington DC: Government Printing Office.

Social Security Administration. (2001). *Social Security Bulletin: Annual Statistical Supplement 2001.* Washington, DC: Government Printing Office.

Solow, R. (2002). The Party Line. *New York Review of Books* (11 April), 19-22.

Steuerle, C. E., and Bakija, J. C. (1994). *Retooling Social Security for the 21st Century.* Washington, DC: Urban Institute Press.

Teles, S. M. (1996). *Whose Welfare?* Lawrence: University Press of Kansas.

Torfing, J. (1997). From the Keynesian Welfare State to a Schumpeterian Workfare Regime—The Offensive Neo-Statist Case of Denmark. Paper presented at the 9th International Conference on Socio-Economics, Montreal, Canada, 5-7 July.

Weisbrod, B., and Schlesinger, M. (1986). Nonprofit Ownership and the Response to Asymmetric Information: The Case of Nursing Homes. In S. Rose-Ackerman (ed.), *The Economics of Nonprofit Institutions.* New York: Oxford University Press.

Wilensky, H. L. (1975). *The Welfare State and Equality.* Berkeley: University of California Press.

6

Back on Track—To the Future?
The Making and Remaking of the Swedish
Welfare State in the 1990s[1]

Sven E. O. Hort

"The new economy has also jolted the famous
Swedish welfare state, fueling a national debate
over whether the economics reform introduced
over the past decade went too far or not far
enough. And it will cause the rest of the world
to pause and take positive notice of Sweden
once again."—*Newsweek*, 7 February 2000

Introduction: The 1990s—*Decennium Horribile*
of the Model Welfare State?

Among social science analysts of large-scale change, 1989 to 1991 marks
the end of history, or at least a great divide differentiating the twentieth
century from the next to come (Fukuyama, 1989, 1992; Hobsbawm, 1994).
The 1990s indicate the starting-point of a new era, a run-up to the future of the
new millennium. This scenario also applies to Sweden and its welfare state,
which had been seen as a model of social policy during most of the postwar
period. Until the fall of the Berlin wall, the trajectory of the Swedish welfare
state was often described as advancing from civil and political citizenship
rights to social rights. Over the last decade things have changed dramatically.
The possibility of a rupture or dismantling of the comprehensive welfare
state, came to be seen as a viable option by some foreign and local experts
(Castels, 1997; Lindbeck et al., 1994).

Entering the twenty-first century, the Swedish welfare state has in the most
recent decade gone through rough seas. The 1990s saw the worst economic

recession in Sweden since the Great Depression and, of course, it hit the national welfare state and many of its citizens as well. Although there had been some fairly severe economic ups and downs since the mid-1970s, 1991 may be looked upon as a watershed after several decades of almost unbroken—at the end rather flat—growth trends. In that year, most, if not all, macroeconomic indicators showed a decline and continued to be bleak for most of the decade. Growth had been rather sluggish for two decades, and in the early 1990s it became negative and remained so for three consecutive years. Unemployment tripled and, if including those "on a measure," reached double-digit figures, an unprecedented event during the Golden Age of full employment. Simultaneously, the state coffer began to drain as the number of taxpayers decreased and the majority of those who paid became poorer day by day. The slump went on for most of the decade although there was a sudden but brief economic upturn in 2000 (*Financial Times*, 11 May 2000).

For most of the 1990s there was also a dramatic drop in the level of consumption as many people received less money and started to conserve their resources for the hard times ahead. Declining income during the decade meant that large groups in Sweden faced financial difficulties. The problems in metropolitan regions were greater than elsewhere, as reflected in unemployment and social assistance statistics. Young households and single adults with children generally had greater difficulties than other groups, but financial vulnerability rose in every group except the very oldest (SOU, 2001: 79), and, of course, the tenth decile, that is, top end of the income and wealth distribution. Socioeconomic division within the greater metropolitan areas increased considerably throughout the decade and added to this was a distinct ethnic dimension.

In addition, conventional political stability gradually declined. The September 1991 election was labeled an "earthquake" election as the "national party" of Sweden, the Social Democrats, for the first time since the establishment of parliamentary democracy in the 1920s received less than 40 percent of the votes, and was unable to form a government (Rothstein, 1993). The break-up of the characteristic twentieth-century five-party pattern of politics that started in 1988 continued as two new right-wing parties entered Parliament in the first national election of the new decade. However, the ideological alternative to the government had been designed only by two parties—the Moderate-Conservatives and the Liberals. Their joint program, "New Start for Sweden," included some challenging features in regard to welfare policy. But the new government had to tackle a wide range of difficulties in 1991. There was no economic turnaround as the Social Democratic Minister of Finance had promised before election day, but rather a deepening of the recession. Nevertheless, for the first time since 1928 the leader of the once Conservative now neoliberal Moderate party became prime minister. "In his unsentimental way, Mr. Bildt is setting a new tone in Swedish politics," wrote the *Financial Times* (October 1991). "Gone is the familiar rhetoric about solidarity, equality and collectivism in what became known as the Social Democratic People's Home. Instead, here is a Swedish Prime Minister enthusing without guilt about the profit motive, private enterprise and competition."

The economic slump and the political upheaval were accompanied by another crack in the Swedish system: at the crossroads of economics and politics peaceful industrial relations had been a basic characteristic of the corporatist "Swedish model." During the 1980s, the breakdown in peak wage negotiations was one-sidedly engineered by the Employer's Confederation against the wish of the trade unions (Pontusson, 1994). This was pursued as a counterattack after the long battle by the labor unions to introduce wage-earners funds and economic democracy as a fourth stage on the road to democratic socialism. These funds were financed by profits and originally designed to produce far-reaching transformation in the ownership structure and control of enterprises. In a watered down version they were legislated in 1982 by the returning Social Democratic government. Nevertheless, they became the most hated symbol of red-hot domestic totalitarianism, not only to private capitalist employers and the representatives of big business but also to the non-socialist parties. Implementing one of their main election promises, in late 1991, the new government immediately started to dissolve these funds making research and technological development—R&D—the main beneficiaries of billions of Swedish kronors.

Thus, it was no coincidence that the once-famous Swedish welfare state— a prime example of the social democratic "policy regime," the middle way or the third road to welfare capitalism (cf. Esping-Andersen, 1990)—became a favorite target of proponents of the victorious ideology of the 1980s. The Swedish welfare state was ridiculed in mainstream media with observations that the "milestone had turned into a millstone." The international business press competed in similarly pungent headlines from *Business Week*'s (1992) "Sweden Fights to Come in from the Cold" to *Forbes'* (1993) "The Swedish Disease" and the *Economist*'s (1993) "Farewell, Welfare." Also in Sweden, right-wing think-tanks began to penetrate the rocky soil of welfare state capitalism. Their agenda included the dismantling of the comprehensive welfare state, along with the pursuit of egalitarian social policies—not only traditional redistributional policy but also policies aimed at gender and ethnic social inclusion and equal opportunity—in a capitalist market economy.

The Making of the Welfare State

The welfare state is a political artifact composed of social institutions as well as welfare programs, which are shaped by social forces that emerge from historical experience in a specific cultural context. As an unintended consequence of the growth of the welfare state new social forces emerge such as the organizations of pensioners and the trade unions of female public welfare employees. Yet, the making of the welfare state has been pointedly described by the Columbia-trained Swedish sociologist Hans L. Zetterberg (1967) in a somewhat critical perspective.

> The welfare state may be unlikely to flourish except in a civilization in which values of neighborly love and charity have been preached for generations; yet its establishment in Scandinavia is mostly the work of a generation of atheists and lukewarm believers. (p. 16)

The foundation of the Swedish welfare state goes back roughly a century to a time when the old form of social support—the municipal poor relief system—was gradually complemented and later overshadowed by the modern forms of welfare provisions. The modern welfare state took shape as active labor market measures, social insurance, social housing, and universal personal social and medical services were enacted by national legislation based on general agreement among the four main political parties of twentieth-century Sweden (cf. Olsson, 1986, and the references therein). Apart from popular mobilization in domestic civil society, Bismarckian social legislation gave the impetus to social reform in this "northern province" of the new but short-lived German empire. More important, having twice stayed out-of-war, Sweden went undamaged into the build-up of both prewar and in particular postwar Europe. Its export industry benefited tremendously from this state of affairs and became the economic foundation for social reform. Thus, while the system of social policy dates back to the early twentieth century, it was only in the postwar period, after the defeat of Nazi Germany and the increased influences from Beveridgean ideas, that the new mix of central state and local government provisions came to dominate Swedish state and society.

The new, enlarged and amalgamated municipalities became organizational cornerstones in the administration of social policy (Stenius, 1999; Ramel, 1998) along with some new central state agencies, in particular the crucial National Labour Market Board. At the national level local authorities formed powerful quasi-private lobby organizations such as the National Association of Local Authorities and the Federation of County Councils. The quasi-public organizations of social insurance have been less noticed, but are far from insignificant. These national lobby organizations include the Federation of Social Insurance Offices as well as the National Organization of Unemployment Benefit Societies, which is closely affiliated with the trade union movement.

Another important feature of the emerging welfare system was the increased degree of civil society involvement where the distinction between private and public often was blurred or deliberately obscured. In particular, trade unions and employer associations became very active in the setting up of labor market services and unemployment insurance (solely the business of unions through the above-mentioned benefit societies) while housing cooperatives and tenants association occupied a similar role in the strongly state-subsidized housing sector (Strömberg, 1992). Furthermore, without the active involvement of farmers' organization in the heavily state-regulated agricultural sector the "historical compromise" of the 1930s would probably not have survived the socio-political turbulence of the time (Odhner, 1992; cf. also Therborn, 1983-84).

In addition, during the first part of the twentieth century the Christian revivalist and the Sobriety movements were both crucial elements in obtaining social citizenship as an extension of universal civil and political rights, as well as a restrictive alcohol policy; the latter was for decades an essential element of Swedish welfare policy, but at the end of the 1990s it dissolved with the entrance of Sweden into the winelands of the European Union (Sutton, 1999). Thus, laymen as well as professionals were involved in the daily activities of the welfare state. The erosion of the traditional social popular mass movements and their backing of the welfare system, its social capital, is a significant feature of late twentieth-century Sweden with definite implications for the beginning of the new millennium (Rothstein, 2000).

As late as in the mid-1960s, Sweden was *not* on top of Harold Wilensky's (1975) welfare state league, that is, not the high tax haven/grinder/hell *(select one!)* later expressed in the vocabulary of Friedmannian monetarist economics. It was in the mid-1960s that the notion of a cradle-to-grave welfare state got off the ground. Prior to that time, the great pension battle of 1957-58 around the proposals to introduce a supplementary and earnings-related Superannuation pension system on top of the basic pension scheme (or Bismarck on top of Beveridge) had shaken up traditional consensus politics between left and right. The Social Democratic-Center party coalition government that had governed the country since 1951 dissolved in 1957. With the legislation of a supplementary pension added to the existing system of social protection, the basic framework of social security was in place (cf. Olofsson, 1994). What remained was a fine-tuning of a system that would "mature" (cf. Flora, 1986) in the 1970s and 1980s. The fine-tuning of important modifications such as an increased emphasis on gender-neutrality was seen, for instance, in the introduction of parental insurance in the mid-1970s.

The decisive general election in 1960 can be viewed as a turning point, since no serious political alternative came in sight for a full decade. Indeed, the Social Democrats remained in power for another sixteen years, altogether forty-four years without interruption (1932-1976, with the exception of the summer of 1936). At the same time as the pension battle, the government had successfully strengthened the financing of the welfare state by re-introducing a VAT (Value Added Tax) (in existence during World War II). It had tested the capacity of the active labor policy during the first postwar recession in the late 1950s, and the potential of its social housing program. These policy areas, together with the agricultural policy worked out during the 1950s in close cooperation with the Center party and the farmer's production cooperative movements, formed the basis of what would become the mature welfare state policy.

In addition, the Social Democrats instigated a major public sector program by enlarging and improving personal medical and social services: education, health, child day care, disability, and old age services. Through rather generous central state grants the institutions of local government—county councils and municipalities governed by elected politicians of different color—cooperated in a massive build-up of social services of the welfare state whereby women en masse came to enter the labor force (Acker et al., 1992; cf. also Liljeström and Dahlström, 1982). Often the system of social protection in the narrow sense—social insurance/security—came to be involved through various complementary cash benefits related to in-kind services and administered by the Social Insurance Offices. The subsequent growth of the welfare state thus included a great number of cash and in-kind social benefits as well as other kinds of welfare provisions organized by a variety of sub-units and populated by a diversity of more or less professional street-level bureaucrats (Ahrne, 1990; Johansson, 1992; Hort and McMurphy, 1997).

The Social Democrats pursued this program at the helm of central government, supported both at the national as well as the local levels by the middle-of-the road parties, the Liberal party and the Center party, and later on also by the Left Communist party which gradually came in from the cold in the 1960s. The Left Communist party became a junior partner of Social Democracy after the constitutional reform in 1970, as the parliamentary situation became more polarized. When the three non-social-democratic parties achieved a parliamentary majority in 1976 under leadership of the Center party, they still had not agreed upon alternatives in regard to welfare state policies. On the contrary, they hesitated to increase taxes when they faced a state budget deficit, and instead continued to pursue Keynesian macroeconomic policy at a time when academic economists declared Keynes dead and switched to Friedmann-inspired monetarist policy recommendations. These parties adhered to the basic principles of universal welfare policy throughout their period of government (1976-1982), fine-tuned various parts of it, and made a few small but extremely controversial cutbacks.

Furthermore, when the economy declined they even increased efforts to curb unemployment through active manpower policy measures—becoming even more social democratic than the Social Democrats—and nationalized basic industries that had gone out of business (Benner, 1997). However, such policies created great tension within this majority, and during this period four different coalitions were at the helm under either Center or Liberal party leadership. This pattern of government completely reversed power relations within the group of non-social-democratic parties as the Moderate (Conservative) party was moved from a marginal into a center-stage position later to challenge the party of government.

The Social Democrats restored their claim to be the natural party of government in Sweden—though in most cases as a minority cabinet—by scoring three successive election victories in the 1980s, and continued to encourage, initiate, and oversee a number of reforms of welfare state programs in the 1980s (Therborn, 1992a, b). The institutional structure of the Swedish welfare state had five pillars: (1) tax policy as the foundation of social expenditure, (2) labor market activity—full employment—as the foundation of fiscal efficiency, (3) in-cash social insurance/security benefits as adjacent to labor market participation, (4) in-kind personal social and medical services as a complement or replacement of for-profit market activities, and (5) finally, large-scale state subsidies to certain sectors of society, chiefly housing and agriculture, not always regarded as part and parcel of universal welfare policy. In all these areas more or less major reforms were proposed and/or implemented.

This broader context of social policy is necessary to bear in mind to understand the workings of the Swedish system of social protection in a narrow sense (social security). Sometimes this larger picture is viewed as a dual system of cash and in-kind benefits whereby the fundamentals of financing a social welfare system may get obscured. As an analytical divide, the five pillars of the welfare state are intended to transcend the dichotomy of the social insurance state versus the social service state (Anttonnen, 1990). In any case, this is the "big" welfare state that came under mounting criticisms in the 1990s in particular from the profession of academic economists but also from the business community.

Social Expenditure in the 1990s: The Financing of the Welfare State

Cost containment was already a dominant feature of Swedish social policy consideration in the 1980s. Measuring welfare state development by social expenditure and GDP data—the Wilensky approach—has long been considered a risky business and many attempts have been made to come to terms with the shortcomings of such an approach. Nevertheless, crude social expenditure data show that as a percentage of GDP there were only marginal annual changes in Sweden during the 1980s and 1990s. Roughly 33 percent of GDP was spent on social programs except education (NOSOSCO, 2001). Including spending on education the annual figure would increase to and fluctuate around almost 40 percent.

Thus, fiscal prudence was already characteristic of the 1980s. Within Social Democracy a growing section around the Minister of Finance became worried by slackening productivity and the lack of efficiency in the public sector. A minor civil war named the "War of Roses" occurred within the labor movement and focused, among other things, on the financing of the national as well as the local welfare state. Fiscal decentralization increased the responsibility of local government, which came under strong pressure to make delicate priorities. In some sectors such as healthcare and care of the elderly, cost containment was fairly successful. In others, such as sickness insurance and housing policy it was obviously less so. Thus, at the end of that decade, the national government ran into severe difficulties in the financing of the welfare state.

Sweden's macroeconomic performance in the early 1990s differed in a number of fundamental respects from its performance during most of the postwar period. Distinctive features of macroeconomic developments in the early 1990s included the deepest and longest economic recession since the 1930s; a rise in the overall unemployment rate to levels substantially above those previously experienced by the country; a ballooning in the public sector's overall budget deficit to an extent rarely encountered in member states of the Organization of Economic Cooperation and Development (OECD); and a decline in the value of the currency to levels below those reached immediately after Sweden's 1981-82 devaluation. As has increasingly been recognized in Sweden, these macroeconomic developments raise questions about the country's capacity to sustain the comprehensive welfare state that has evolved in the postwar period. (IMF, 1995:1)

In Sweden, fiscal crisis of the state was an almost unknown phenomenon until the 1990s, although the late 1970s saw a significant budget deficit and an increase in public debt. This is not to say that there were no flaws in the system during the postwar period. Already in 1981, the third non-social-democratic government in consensus with the Social Democratic opposition reached an agreement to lower marginal tax rates and make the taxation of real estate solely a central state obligation by abolishing municipal levies. While the reform was implemented it led to the breakdown of the governing coalition as the low-tax Moderate-Conservative party left. Thus, it was a (fourth) Center-Liberal minority cabinet, followed by the 1982 Social Democratic government that had to implement "the wonderful night" (as this reform came to be known).

This minor tax reform set the stage for extensive tax negotiations between the political parties that started at the end of the 1980s and resulted in what was labeled "the tax reform of the century." Compared to the introduction of income taxation in 1901 this was, of course, an exaggeration. However, like so many other countries at this time, Sweden embarked on a tax reform designed both to secure the strength of a welfare state saddled with heavy financial commitments and to improve the performance and efficiency of the Swedish economy. At the time, it was considered an international success. To avoid various forms of black and gray labor, and to make the country internationally competitive by stimulating work, business, and not the least, private savings, marginal tax rates were again lowered. Income taxation became solely a municipal prerogative as the progressive state income tax was abolished for most citizens. The scope of indirect value added taxes was widened, and capital taxation became more transparent.

The tax reform of 1990-91 was an example of the kind of broad-based compromise across party lines on pivotal national issues that have characterized so much of Swedish welfare policy, and it pointed to subsequent changes in areas such as pensions. On the tax issue, the Social Democrats allied themselves with the Liberals, who were immediately criticized by the Moderate-Conservatives for their stance. However, the 1991 government under Moderate-Conservative leadership accepted the deal already in the joint program "New Start for Sweden," and although both parties paid lip service to a decrease in general taxation, their joint government platform called for no major tax decrease. After the cabinet was formed some minor changes were introduced by the new government, which mainly benefited the owners of stocks and capital.

To summarize briefly, while the macroeconomic problem of the late 1980s was an overheated economy—unemployment below 2 percent and a labor shortage—by 1990 things changed, and the government had to face recessionary signs. After a rather dramatic regrouping within the Social Democratic leadership in January 1990—the Minister of Finance left the cabinet in an unprecedented manner—a new accord with the Liberal party was made which included cutbacks in sickness daily benefits, the first time ever a Swedish Social Democratic government decreased cash benefits. Housing subsidies were scrapped and, thus, a major part of traditional welfare state policies abandoned without further consideration. Later that year, in a last ditch effort by the Social Democrats to save the overvalued krona before the general election, the labor government announced that fighting inflation had become top priority of the government at the expense of the traditional full-employment target. In a similar vein, an application for membership in the European Union was submitted which would improve the possibility of carrying out coherent macroeconomic policy, thus financing the welfare state. Thus, EU-membership was suddenly a joint political elite project to promote simultaneously economic growth and protect costly social programs.

However, the new non-socialist government did not have the same legitimacy as guardian of the welfare state as the old one and ran into severe difficulties as the recession went deeper and deeper. For most of the postwar decades state revenues met public expenditures. Only at the end of the period, from the late 1970s, did the public debt increase considerably, and when the long recession started in the early 1990s the weakness of the tax reform became visible. The reform was quickly labeled under-financed. Nevertheless, the new government did not take any bold initiatives to raise public revenues, but relied on deficit spending as no major cutbacks in public expenditure occurred. However, due to the September 1992 accord between government and opposition during the currency crisis, social expenditure did not grow as cost control was achieved in the traditional budget item—actually the early 1990 changes in sickness insurance contributed to a surplus in this branch of social insurance and the minor item of workmen's compensation was more or less slashed—while the cost of unemployment became highly visible in the growth of unemployment insurance expenditures. Thus, the government increased public borrowing daily and accumulated a significant public debt. Interest payments on the public debt finally became a significant budget item.

Thus, in advance of the general election in 1994, and in sharp contrast to mainstream election competition—"rational choice"—theories, the Social Democrats advocated not only cutbacks in welfare benefits to come to terms with the ballooning budget deficit, but also tax hikes (Palme and Vennemo, 1998). These election promises were promptly delivered, although the Social Democrats initially had a hard time finding sustainable support in Parliament. After several months of wheeling and dealing with the Liberals to the right, the Greens in the middle, and the Left Party probably to the left, the Social Democrats were finally able to strike an accord with their traditional twentieth-century partner, the still agrarian but now tiny Center party. Even if this accord is currently forgotten by both sides, in retrospect, it will probably prove most decisive for the long-term development of the welfare state. Although the legitimacy of the welfare state was never in question among the great majority of the population (Svallfors, 1996), the fact that two main players at the top level took full responsibility in restoring a sound fiscal basis for its main social programs meant that the winds of the neoliberal critique faded. The growth of the public deficit, including the growth of unemployment costs, came under control.

The problems generated by the recession of the 1990s put many taxpayers out of work, which created tremendous pressures on the other pillars of the welfare state. Although many of them continued as tax-paying unemployment assistance recipients they paid less in tax and had less money to spend on the market. Those who became social assistance beneficiaries paid no taxes and in most cases had even less to make the consumption wheel go around. But well in advance of the 1998 election the growth of the budget deficit had come to a halt, as most social benefits had been reduced at the beginning of the election period but restored at the end, or benefit rules made stricter, while taxes increased. At the end of the decade there was even a rather substantial surplus in public revenues. The public debt still is considerable, and although within the limits of EMU membership (which in itself is postponed into a distant future) it would be potentially volatile in another recession. The possibility of another fiscal crisis of the Swedish welfare state remains, although the time is not yet ripe to frighten the populace with the ghost of state bankruptcy.

The Growth of Unemployment and the Shaky Return of Full Employment Policy

Earlier I reviewed the structure of the five pillars of the (Swedish) welfare state. Summarizing the mature welfare state, instead of the cradle-to-grave analogy, the Swedish welfare system can be described as a blend of the above-mentioned five elements or public policy mechanisms. Apart from tax policy, the most important element is the active labor market policy or the so-called Rehn-Meidner-model developed in the 1950s by two trade union economists and since that time administered by the powerful National Labour Market Board. This keeps unemployment at bay and promotes structural change by encouraging wage labor among both women and men which makes the great majority of the economically active population not only wage laborers but also taxpayers needed to sustain rather expensive, universal social programs.

The historical origin of the active labor market policy was the Lutheran work ethic coupled with its ungenerous poor relief system, which separated the deserving poor from the undeserving ones (Olsson Hort, 1992). This blend of public work ethic and extremely ungenerous poor relief brought the established state and state-church into conflict with the emerging social movements in civil society. The right to laziness of the early, spontaneous labor movement rapidly gave way to the demand for a decent job and a fair wage as the—institutionalized—movements approached state power. In the 1920s, when the long rule of Social Democracy slowly and gradually started in Sweden, the right to work and full—male—employment became a top priority of working class politics in municipalities as well as on the central state level. With the establishment in 1948 of the National Labour Market Board and its regional and local chapters, the labor movement was armed with an executive organ of considerable power (Rothstein, 1980). Throughout the postwar decades this agency enlarged its arsenal of active manpower measures, although these measures were not enough when Sweden was hit by the worst recession since the Great Depression.

In the 1990s the rate of employment fell from well above 80 percent of the population group aged 20 to 64 to less than 75 percent. Roughly half a million jobs disappeared, at first in the private sector but later also in the public. Unemployment, which during the postwar period never exceeded 4 percent of the labor force, suddenly reached double-digit figures. At the culmination of the crisis, open unemployment reached over 8 percent while another 6 percent were in active labor market measures (sheltered jobs). Elsewhere, I have outlined the civilized version of workfare in Sweden or the work-to-welfare practices based on the postwar active labor market policy, and the more recent attempts to combat labor market marginalization through various activation measures such as work rehabilitation and linking work requirement to welfare benefit recipiency. The changing role of unemployment insurance in response to active labor market policy measures was also scrutinized (Hort, 2001).

Suffice to say, the right to work inscribed in the 1974 Constitution of Sweden, was based on the previous experience of an active labor market and later full-employment policy. In the 1990s, active labor market policy was expanded—in connection with rising unemployment—as the number of persons engaged in individual measures rose sharply in the first half of the decade. But in relation to the number unemployed, the scale of labor market measures actually declined when unemployment was increasing most strongly, the reason being that the number of unemployed persons increased more rapidly than the individual measures. As municipal authorities became more responsible for the active labor market measures, the range of measures was broadened. In general, this resulted in an attenuation of the active measures in the sense that a growing proportion of participants were in programs that were comparatively inexpensive. At the end of the decade, however, this trend was broken as labor market authorities turned their attention towards skill development and education.

From 1990 to 1993, open unemployment shot up from under 2 percent to almost 9 percent as the number in employment fell by over a half million persons. The level of unemployment remained broadly unchanged from 1993 to 1997, but a marked reduction began in 1998. The overall effect of the recession was harshest in manufacturing and construction, while employment in private services actually rose in the course of the decade. In the second half of the 1990s, employment fell most in the public sector, in health and medical care and in social services. Unemployment increased most among youth and this trend was most marked in the first half of the decade; in 1994 one person in three, aged 16 to 23 years, was out of work at some time during the year. In the rest of the period, however, open unemployment fell in this group. The labor market difficulties for youth are also evident in the growing proportion who are not participating in the labor force. This upward trend lasted longer than the increase in youth unemployment. The number of persons aged 20-to-25 years who were outside the labor market virtually doubled from 1990 to 1997. No other age group was anywhere near this level. One explanation is that young people tend to remain in school when job opportunities are lacking. The proportion of students among 20-to-25-year-olds did, in fact, double in the 1990s, compared with the second half of the 1980s. Another notable feature is that in the oldest active age group (56-65 years), the proportion excluded from the labor market did not rise in the 1990s (cf. Olofsson and Pettersson, 1994). Besides youth, unemployment hit migrants in particular, though not uniformly. Compared with immigrants from other European countries, those born outside Europe experienced a sharper increase in unemployment. But even for these groups, unemployment stopped rising around the middle of the decade. Broken down by sex, unemployment rose more among men than women in the early 1990s, having been evenly spread at the end of the 1980s. The differences narrowed again from 1994 to 1996, but in the decade as a whole, unemployment hit men somewhat harder than women.

Measures to combat unemployment during the first half of the 1990s were not sufficient to result in any lasting achievements. The non-socialist government of this period had a hard time coping with the unemployment situation. Although the Social Democrats made fiscal stability their top priority when they returned to power in late 1994, the latter could easily refer to their overall postwar achievement in dealing with employment policy. However it was not until 1996 that the new Social Democratic government, together with its partner of the 1930s and 1950s the agrarian Center party, presented a joint plan to cut unemployment in half before the end of year 2000 (Swedish Government, 1996). To this author, the 1996-98 period represents a short but decisive phase in the development of welfare policy in Sweden in the 1990s as confidence and trust in public finance was restored and unemployment levelled off under the auspices of a highly legitimate, broad-based and less partisan political leadership. In sharp contrast to the shaky road of the early 1990s, the joint plan to reduce unemployment marks the birth of the resilient welfare state of the late 1990s whereby other alternatives were subordinated to the long-established path of the Swedish model. This plan was amended by the Social Democrats after the 1998 election when the still Social Democratic government declared that the employment level should be restored to 80 percent of the labor force at the end of year 2004. The second goal is for obvious reasons still too early to evaluate. But the first goal was roughly achieved due, above all, to a favorable world market, in particular in telecom and related technologies, as well as to increased efforts by the still strong National Labour Market administration in cooperation with other related state agencies such as the Social Insurance Offices. Finally, in the 1990s the monopoly of the labor market authorities in providing job seekers with job alternatives gave way to private employment agencies. Since then, so-called flexible employment has grown as an increasing number of employees have become employed in firms that dispatch casual workers to other firms.

Social Security—Towards Privatization?

A comprehensive social security network is another pillar of the model welfare state, sometimes regarded as the core of the welfare state. In Sweden, the five branches of social insurance—work injury insurance; sickness insurance; old age pensions; unemployment insurance and various family cash benefits such as parental insurance and general child allowances—are all closely related to active labor force participation or a "productivist social policy," which leads more to continuous recommodification of labor than to the well-known decommodification. Except for unemployment insurance, test programs are administered by regional social insurance funds, with the political backing of the National Federation of Social Insurance Offices, under the supervision of the National Social Insurance Board.

In an earlier analysis of targeting in universal welfare policies during the 1990s I provided an overview of the measures employed within the various branches of social insurance in Sweden, that is, reforms of occupational injury insurance, sickness, and parental insurance as well as the public pension system (Hort, 2000). I will not repeat the details of the analysis here. In general, however, during the 1990s governments of various colors introduced reforms that left their marks on social security; in these, changes to systems were greater than in earlier decades and generally restrictive in nature, that is, less generous provisions and decreased coverage. During the first half of the decade, there were also some expansionary changes, perhaps most notably regarding disability services promoted by the Liberal party in particular, but overall their number was consistently exceeded by the restrictive changes or retrenchment measures. The most important rule changes concerned replacement levels and eligibility criteria.

The changes in replacement levels involved a general pattern of decline in levels up to and beyond the middle of the decade and then some improvements in the final years of the twentieth century. In the pensions system, for example, economies were achieved by adjusting the indexing arrangement in 1993 and 1996, with a return to full indexing as of 1999. This meant that for most of the 1990s pensions were lower than would otherwise have been the case, for early retirement as well as old age pensions. The replacement levels for old age pensions were also lowered by decisions in 1995 and 1997, but this was accompanied by a supplement to the basic pension increment in order to protect persons with small or no national supplementary pension (ATP). Another field where numerous changes were made is sickness insurance, where replacement levels were lowered several times (1991, 1993, 1996), followed in 1998 by a return to the level in 1993 (80 percent of previous earnings). Moreover, the duration of sickness cash benefits was shortened by the introduction of one waiting day in 1993. Replacement levels in unemployment insurance were changed in the same way, together with the reintroduction of an initial no-benefit period of five days (back to pre-1987 rules).

The forms of support that are aimed more directly at families with children have also undergone many changes. In parental leave, for example, replacement levels were adjusted to much the same extent as and more or less concurrently with the changes in sickness insurance. The level of child allowances was raised a couple of times early in the decade; this was followed in 1996 by a nominal cut—a most symbolic event as it was the first time ever that such a cutback occurred in this subsystem of cash benefits—and the withdrawal of the supplement for more than two children. In 1998 child allowances were largely restored to the earlier level. Housing allowances were improved at the beginning of the 1990s but restrictions were introduced in the middle of the decade: people over 29 years of age without children ceased to be entitled and the system was tightened in general, along with lower allowances.

The eligibility criteria were more stable in general than the replacement levels. In some respects, however, the changes were important in principle. One instance is the early-retirement or disability pension: in 1995 specific labor-market and age-related criteria were abolished and the right to a pension formulated to rest on purely medical grounds. Another instance is the basic pension: in connection with Sweden's adherence to the European Economic Agreement (a brief predecessor to EU membership), the rules were tightened so that at least 40 years' residence in Sweden is now required for a full basic pension. Furthermore, a more restrictive definition of what constitutes work injury was followed by a dramatic fall in the number of work injury cases that qualify for compensation.

From a short-term perspective, the major change in the Swedish social insurance system during the last years of the twentieth century involved the sharp growth of long-term sickness insurance recipients. As the number of unemployment insurance recipients declined the number of recipients in the sickness insurance system rose. The small increase was already visible in 1997 and has grown tremendously since. The government was able to contain costs through downsizing other parts of the system—most important, of course, the cost of unemployment insurance—but more active measures will be required most likely in the years to come.

From a long-term perspective, it is probably the reform of the pension system in 1994 that will stand out as an exemplar of the resilient welfare state. Although the Social Democrats had to back down from generous earnings- and benefit-related supplementary pension schemes (ATP) and make an agreement with the four non-socialist parties ahead of the election of that year, the new system is still universal, but with stronger ties to previous labor market participation. The new system is also quasi-contributory-related. Its public nature is somewhat diminished as a minor part of contributions are set aside for investment in private funds and solely dependent on market returns. Thus, the new pension system has opened up an avenue for private financial investors such as banks and insurance companies to enter a previously public domain. There is, however, also a public fund for those who abstain from active choice and decline participation in the market. As this part of the system was introduced at the start of the most recent stock-market downturn, most investors have failed to reach break-even, while the public fund has managed to avoid major losses. So far, most active pension savers have become poorer while the overall distribution of income has become more even.

Finally, a few words about social assistance, which can be treated either as a functional supplement to social security—"the last resort"—or as an institutional part of the municipal welfare system. (Here it is being seen as a supplement to social security.) In the 1990s social assistance expenditures rose, the duration of assistance became longer and more people qualified (Salonen, 1994; Johansson, 2001). The changes were dramatic in many respects and unparalleled in modern times in Sweden. The upward trend was strongest up to the end of 1994, after which it slackened and then turned downwards in 1997. The increase was particularly marked for expenditure on social assistance; the figure of SEK 12.4 billion in 1997 was more than twice the level in 1990. In this period the proportion of recipients rose from 6 percent to 8.5 percent of the total population. It is noteworthy, however, that in 1998 the number of recipients decreased to such an extent that the proportion fell back to the level in 1993. This trend continued during 1999. The average duration of assistance lengthened from just over four months in 1990 to five months in 1999 and this was accompanied by an appreciable increase in the proportion of recipient households that can be classified, using various definitions, as being dependent on social assistance in the longer run. No reduction of the latter group occurred in the end of the decade.

The growth of social assistance in the 1990s was so extensive that an increase was noted in virtually every group. Two groups in particular stand out from the rest: youth and immigrant households. The proportion of 18 to 24-year-olds receiving social assistance almost doubled in the period studied here. However, there was a downward trend in 1998 and 1999, which was particularly clear among young people. In regard to immigrant households, the increase was mainly connected with the waves of immigrants in the first half of the decade. From 1990 to 1995, the number of nonresident households receiving social assistance rose from 25 percent to 30 percent of all recipient households and the share of expenditure from 47 percent to 52 percent. After that the relative importance of this group tended to fall. The risk of needing social assistance is crucially connected with sojourn in Sweden: the need is markedly elevated among persons who have been in Sweden for one or two years, whereas for those who have spent fifteen years or more in the country it is essentially the same as for people born in Sweden.

The expansion of social assistance in the 1990s was accompanied by changes in rules and municipal policy. Briefly, the trend can be said to involve a less generous approach and tougher eligibility criteria. As a result of judgments in the Supreme Administrative Court and the amended Social Services Act (from 1998), the standard for social assistance was eroded by degrees and made to include a growing element of detailed assessments. The amended act also restricted the individual's possibility to appeal social assistance decisions. At the same time, municipalities were given wider powers to require participation in their labor market programs of various kinds, particularly in the case of young people, and they tightened their interpretation of what it means to "be at the disposal of the labor market." On the whole, municipalities stepped up their undertakings in regard to active labor market programs and strengthened the explicit link between these programs and the efforts of the social services on behalf of social assistance recipients (Hort, 2000).

Public Sector Reform—Between Decentralization and Privatization

A large public service production sector—by and large universal but sometimes "targeted" at the point of access—in the spheres of health, personal social services, and education under the auspices of local governments (municipalities as well as county councils) was built up from the 1960s onwards. In the 1980s a trend towards decentralization began, succeeded by a trend towards privatization. During the 1990s, changes in the legislation in Sweden concerning the provision of welfare have increased the responsibilities of local and regional authorities. Since the non-socialist government came into power in 1991, in particular after it introduced block grants in 1993, which also opened the way more widely for nonpublic providers, local and regional authorities have been given greater freedom to choose how the money received from central government for welfare services can be allocated. National cleavages spread to and became more pronounced in particular at the level of greater metropolitan politics. The dialectics of decentralization and privatization are likely to continue as the Stockholm model has been put against the Swedish model half a year in advance of the 2002 national election by the local—Moderate-Conservative—government in the capital of Sweden (cf. Olsson Hort, 2001).

This system of social provisions comprises a broad set of child and youth as well as adult elderly personal social, educational, and medical services administered by local and regional authorities and governed by guidelines following national legislation. Below follows a summary of the development of the main part of such services organized or under the supervision of the municipalities and the county councils (in some cases transferred from one to the other). To give a broad picture of privatization potential within the Swedish welfare system, I think it is necessary to be fairly detailed regarding such different welfare systems as health and medical services, education, as well as personal social services for children and families, disabled and frailed elderly (cf. also Blomqvist and Rothstein, 2000). Furthermore, it should be emphasized that two administrative structures are on the same level of authority, that is, the county councils are not superior to the municipalities, and they have in recent time formed new quasi-public organizations for cooperation among themselves. At the national level, county councils have their own influential lobby organization in the National Association County Councils as have the municipalities in the National Association of Local Authorities (cf. Ramel, 1998). Since the 1994 general election, both organizations are headed by public sector delivery minded Social Democrats.

Since the 1960s medical services have been the sole prerogative of the county councils—public health—complemented with a rather small sector of private practitioners and a rather large sector of dental practitioners. However, sickness insurance is also involved as a partial financer of this system. During the 1990s, there were major changes in this area (Olsson Hort and Cohn, 1996). Many components of the care provided by county councils were transferred in a series of reforms to the municipalities; the most important was the so-called Ädel Reform in 1992, which included the transfer of nursing homes and long-term care. Control and ownership of medical care also changed considerably; a majority of county councils introduced purchaser/provider models with performance-related reimbursement, while private providers became more common, particularly in primary care (Gustavsson, 2000). In 1998, private practice accounted for almost one in five primary care consultations with a doctor (SOU, 2001: 3). Throughout the decade, in the greater metropolitan regions health policy and the privatization of health care has been a bone of contention between the political right and left. Although, where it is in power the left in general has accepted some private, sometimes only nonprofit, providers.

During the decade, total healthcare expenditure (including medicine and dental care) was comparatively constant. Thus, public cost containment was successful. Although the tendency was upwards, a growing share of expenditure was financed with user fees. From 1983 to 1999 patient contributions for medical and dental care and medicine rose 30 percent; most of the increase was a result of higher charges for dental care and medicine. The broadly unchanged level of total healthcare expenditure accommodated a very sharp increase in the bill for prescribed drugs; this doubled in current prices during the 1990s, from just over SEK 10 billion to rather more than SEK 20 billion. The increase was due mainly to the large-scale introduction of a number of new and comparatively expensive medical drugs such as Losec.

The trend in healthcare expenditure was accompanied by a declining number of hospital beds and an appreciable shortening of hospital stays, processes that also had to do with the above-mentioned Ädel Reform. But sizeable reductions were made even in activities that were not affected by that reform. The number of medical consultations was, however, relatively unchanged during the decade. Personnel cuts in the 1990s were comparatively large, even excluding staff transfers in connection with the Ädel Reform. A majority of the cuts affected groups with comparatively little training, such as assistant nurses and medical orderlies, and at the end of the decade there was considerable worry regarding the possibility of future recruitment to this work-heavy sector.

The legislation on care of the disabled was amended to a substantial extent in the early 1990s. The Liberal party actively pressed this issue. The Disability Reform in 1994 made a distinction between the Social Services Act (SoL) and a new act concerning Support and Service for Persons with Certain Functional Impairments (LSS), accompanied by a new act concerning Compensation for Assistance (LASS). Whereas SoL applies to anyone in "need" of help, LSS and LASS are restricted to individuals with certain degrees of specified types of functional disability. Moreover, support under LSS and LASS is free of charge as a rule, while user fees charged under SoL rose sharply in the 1990s.

Together with a reform of psychiatric care, the Disability Reform accentuated the trend towards decreased institutional care that had started in earlier decades. The psychiatric reform, introduced in 1995, extended the municipalities' responsibility for persons with mental disorders that constitute a functional impairment; municipalities are accountable, for example, for costs of patients for whom treatment is deemed complete after an uninterrupted period of three months in psychiatric care. Virtually all institutions for the mentally retarded were closed during the 1990s and more than 6,000 persons were transferred to group homes or dwellings of their own. Moreover, during the 1990s the number of psychiatric beds was reduced from over 14,000 to little more than 6,000 (SOU, 2001: 3). As an unintended consequence, homelessness increased.

Total public expenditure on support and services for persons with severe functional disorders is estimated to have risen by 40 percent from 1993 to 1997. The scale of municipal inputs under LSS and LASS was stepped up in the late 1990s, while expenditure under SoL has been declining ever since the 1980s. Even so, the number receiving LSS support is only half the predicted level; part of the discrepancy has been attributed to the LSS stipulation that support has to be applied for actively by the individual in question, which can be difficult for many of those with functional disorders, particularly the mentally disabled. Concerning other consequences of the Disability Reform, there are signs of an improved situation for persons whose functional impairments are very extensive, particularly those who have obtained personal assistants under LASS. But the strong focus on clearly defined categories does entail a risk that support is not provided for persons whose problems are less severe. The more restrictive approach in systems such as home-help services and transport services has probably also been a disadvantage for the latter.

Public care for the elderly changed appreciably in the 1990s (SOU, 2001: 52; cf. also Eliasson-Lappalianen and Szebehely, 1996; and Olsson Hort and Ahn, 1999). In connection with a reform in 1992, responsibility for nursing homes and for patients who still need care after their treatment has been completed was transferred from county councils to municipalities. Pressure on the care system also grew as a distinct increase in the number of elderly people coincided with a reduced supply of hospital beds. As the pressure grew, the municipalities generally tightened assessments of need and accorded priority to people with the most severe needs. A growing proportion of inputs were concentrated on the most needy groups, while groups of elderly persons who had previously been recipients of public care now turned, to a growing extent, to relatives for help or purchased private services. The coverage of services in the home was reduced in particular, accompanied by more hours of assistance for the remaining recipients. In the late 1990s, recipients of services in the home were considerably older and needed more care than before.

Moreover, the municipalities raised the fees paid by care recipients and there was a growing tendency to relate fees to income. One consequence of this is that for persons with a relatively large pension and a moderate need of help, it usually pays to buy help in the private market instead of obtaining municipal care for the elderly. At the same time, the level of fees causes as many as one pensioner in ten to refrain for applying for home-help services; this is particularly common among women with a small pension. Furthermore, retrospective assessments of the 1992 reform have found shortcomings in the various forms of municipal care as well as in the links between hospital care and care at home. Access to medical staff and resources in nursing homes had decreased even though the care requirement had grown. Elderly persons receiving care in various forms of specialized accommodation are in a worse state physically and mentally than was the case before the 1992 reform. Another shift in the 1990s was that private entrepreneurs provided a growing proportion of the publicly financed care (Sparks, 1995).

A landmark decision was made in 1989 by Parliament when the more-than-century-long joint central state-municipal administration of primary and secondary schooling (actually introduced already in 1842) was abolished and the municipalities became solely accountable for the organization and operation of the school system. As of 1993, moreover, the new form of accountability was accentuated and the municipalities were given the power to decide the allocation of resources for schools. This decentralization led to variations in the way in which municipalities and schools organize their activities, as well as in how much money they spend in this field. In general, expenditure decreased sharply in the early part of the 1990s, followed by a levelling off and, as of 1996, some increase. The fluctuations applied to compulsory education (9 years, starting at age 6 or 7) in particular, while expenditure on the comprehensive secondary education system (next 3 years) was more or less constant. The increase in the latter part of the period largely followed the rising number of pupils in compulsory schooling at that time. Calculated per pupil during the decade, total expenditure on schools declined by 9 percent. Expenditure was reduced mainly by cutting resources for teaching and after-school activities. In compulsory schooling, teaching expenditure in 1997 was little more than 80 percent of the level in 1991. One consequence of this was that teacher density per 100 pupils in compulsory schooling declined from 9.1 in 1991 to 7.5 in 1997 (SOU, 2001: 3). Expenditure on teaching materials and similar items fluctuated moderately earlier in the decade and then rose after 1996 as part of a new central grant and largely in connection with an information technology (IT) drive for schools. Excluding the IT expenditure, the trend on spending for teaching materials was, if anything, downward.

Schools run by nonpublic bodies—nonprofit as well as for-profit—were given access to municipal grants-in-aid in 1992 and this led to a rapid increase in the number of private—or as the terminology has become in Sweden—"free" schools. From 1992 to 1999 the number of such schools trebled. At the start of the new century, private schools have only around 4 percent of the total number of pupils in Sweden. Applications to establish independent schools are, however, still rising strongly. This was the case for schools with a sharp reduction of expenditure at the beginning of the period, followed by some levelling off and then an increase as of 1996; but total expenditure per pupil still decreased appreciably. Expenditure on child daycare was largely unchanged, but this was accompanied by a very marked increase in the enrollment of children, and a cut in expenditures per pupil occurred, mainly in the first half of the decade.

Thus, child daycare was another eventful sector in the 1990s. Responsibility for the activities was transferred from the social services to the school system and as of 1995 the municipalities were made legally accountable for providing places without delay for children of working or student parents. Most municipalities adapted to the new responsibility but many also introduced regulations that limited the child-care rights of the unemployed. The level of child-care expenditure hardly changed during the decade while, at the same time, the number of children in child-care facilities rose continuously, by over 30 percent. With such an increase and unchanged resources, funds per child were bound to dwindle. At constant prices, during the decade expenditure per child in pre-school care was cut by about 14 percent (SOU, 2001: 3). The number of children per group and per staff member rose markedly in pre-school care and even more so in leisure-time centers.

The municipal fees paid by parents for child daycare also climbed in the 1990s. The share of gross child-care expenditure that these fees covered rose in the period from 10 percent to 17 percent. The above-mentioned unchanged resources accordingly involved a decreased public commitment and an increased financial burden on parents with children. In addition, municipalities made considerable changes in the structure of fees, mainly by introducing various systems based on parental income and the duration of care. Fees have become directly related to the duration of care in nearly every municipality, but the level of fees varies greatly across municipalities. Child-care facilities run by the private sector also expanded in the 1990s. During the decade these facilities grew in relation to the total number of places in child daycare from 4 percent to 12 percent. The most common form of privately run child care is still the parental cooperative, but since the law was changed in 1992, so that child care organized as a for-profit company qualifies for government grants, the corporate form of child care has expanded and in the late 1990s made up approximately a quarter of the private side.

In Sweden, matters to do with vulnerable children and youth have been a traditional duty for local authorities and open to heated public debate. On a global level, the Swedish government has been actively involved in the 1989 declaration of the UN Convention on the Rights of the Child (Bartley, 1998). The establishment of a Children's Ombudsman in Sweden attracted increased attention to conditions for children (Olsson Hort, 1997). The amended Social Services Act meant that in the related social welfare activities for children and youth, greater consideration has to be paid to the child's situation. With the amended act (1998), the obligation of specified professionals to report children at risk to the social services was widened and time limits were set for child welfare investigations. Three years later, however, only a few municipalities had adopted new guidelines for work concerning children and youth; moreover, the child's perspective was missing in many investigations according to reports by the Ombudsman.

Another tendency in social welfare for children and youth in the 1990s is that both the number of reported child welfare cases and the number of investigations have risen. The reasons for this are uncertain. Certain but conceivable explanations are that problems have become more common, the propensity to report cases has grown, reports are registered to a greater extent than before, and school-related problems are now defined more often as child welfare problems. Clear-cut conclusions are, thus, difficult to draw from what is currently known in general about the extent of problems among children and youth. There are no reliable data on the situation for children at risk, and statistical deficiencies make it difficult to form a picture of the social welfare trend for children in terms of personnel or total resources. Still, the available data do indicate relatively clearly that cuts were not imposed on this field. Municipal expenditure on placements for children and youth rose during the 1990s. This was accompanied by some shift from care in families to more costly institutional care, as well as by an appreciable increase for care in private institutions (Hort, 1997).

While the central state left primary and secondary education in the early 1990s, all over the country it increased its presence and ambitions in tertiary education in the wake of the youth unemployment situation. The higher education system expanded strongly in the 1990s; new universities and university colleges were opened and old ones enlarged, and from 1990 to 1999, the total number of students at universities and university colleges rose by well over 50 percent. The increase was achieved by greatly enlarging the intake, but this was accompanied by such a strong growth of demand that it still became difficult to obtain a place at the end of the decade. The financing of tertiary education partly shifted from central state budget planning to exam results as a method of reimbursement to the universities. There are still no tuition fees but students have had to adapt to lower student loans (compared to benefit levels in the social insurance schemes).

Subsidies—The Dismantling of Housing Policy and the Short-lived Reform of Agricultural Policy

Significant public regulations and subsidies in such areas as agriculture and housing have contributed tremendously, as already emphasized, to the legitimacy of universal welfare policies. Throughout the twentieth century, farmers and agrarian organizations have consistently defended state intervention in competitive markets and supported nonmarket institutions in such sectors as health and education. Although in no sense "socialist" in orientation, these organizations have had an egalitarian and solidaristic stance that have distanced them from traditional market liberalism. In particular, agriculture—the production of such essentials as meat and dairies—has been regulated by price negotiations between the state and the collective organizations of farmers. Through their producer cooperatives, the farmers have had a major stake in the production of a great number of consumer products. Moreover, the main political representation of farmers, the Center party, has throughout most of the twentieth century had a much stronger position in local politics than at the national level, and as already emphasized, has been pivotal to the rebirth of the welfare state project in the mid-1990s.

In the early 1990s, government subsidy of major areas such as agriculture and housing came under scrutiny, subsidies then decreased somewhat in agriculture and substantially in housing. Both areas are extremely important to the functioning of the overall welfare system. The process of reforming and downsizing these areas was not entirely without conflict (cf. Wetterberg, 1988). Agriculture was made to be more dependent on the market and maybe also more consumer-oriented but not more environmentally minded. Although the initial objective of this reform was achieved in the time of Sweden's entry (in 1995) into the European Union, the latter has resulted in most subsidies being retained through the Common Agricultural Policy (CAP).

The near abolition of housing policy contributed to overall cost containment of welfare expenditure. At the same time, decreased subsidy of housing was a contributory factor in the stagnation of the domestic economy in the early 1990s (see, for instance, SOU, 1999: 148, and SOU, 1996: 156; cf. also Franzén and Sandstedt, 1993). At the end of the decade, the housing subsidies have only marginally been re-introduced. Instead of an overheated construction sector and an overall housing surplus, the situation changed dramatically as private housing production—single-family houses as well as multi-dwelling apartments—more or less disappeared in the first half of the 1990s. Only expensive private accommodations were constructed as state subsidized loans disappeared. In particular, in the greater metropolitan areas some new fancy buildings and apartment blocks have seen the light of day, while in the remote areas of Sweden, housing has been deconstructed or transformed to summer cottages as people have moved to the cities for jobs.

The sudden dismantling of housing policy can be, and has been, taken as an indicator of a paradigmatic shift in welfare policy (Carson, 2001). Still it remains to be seen if the re-introduction of such subsidies at the start of the new century—on a much smaller scale than during previous decades—is an example of the durable or resilient welfare state (Nordlund, 2002).

While housing policy disappeared from the political agenda at the start of the decade, housing segregation has been discussed most thoroughly at its end. Yet there is a general lack of systematic studies of segregation's roots and consequences. Analyses of developments in the 1990s show an increase in housing segregation along economic as well as ethnic lines. The pattern of economic segregation is particularly evident in the greater metropolitan regions, with a growing geographic concentration of low-income groups. This tendency, which was most pronounced in the first half of the decade, amounted to a growing proportion of persons with low incomes in the districts with the lowest average income level, and a diminishing proportion in districts with a high average income. This led to an increased geographical divide between individuals with high and low incomes, respectively. Ethnic segregation in housing grew in the three metropolitan regions in the first half of the 1990s. The geographic divide between people born in Sweden as opposed to abroad was more marked in Malmö and Göteborg than in Stockholm. In the metropolitan regions, ethnic segregation continued to grow during the second half of the decade. At the end of the decade, the government, with the support of all parties in Parliament in late 1998, initiated a "new" urban policy aimed at community renewal—in particular new jobs and better schooling—in the suburbs and inner city areas affected by socioeconomic and ethnic segregation in the greater metropolitan areas (Bunar, 2001; Andersson, 1999).

Welfare Developments in the 1990s

How can welfare trends in the 1990s be summarized? In February 1999, the government appointed a State Commission, headed by the son—himself a pension expert and welfare state scholar—of the brutally murdered Prime Minster Olof Palme and composed of a group of social science welfare researchers. In marked contrast to the situation in the early 1990s, no professional economist was involved in this endeavor. This commission presented its final report in October 2001. This section is entirely based on this investigation, reported in SOU 2001: 79 and its related documents. (Although this discussion may be too heavily dependent on these sources, no other major research is presently available, except for a few reports by advocacy groups such as Save the Children—cf. Åhnberg and Salonen, 2002). Overall, the trends in the first half of the 1990s clearly represented a more negative path for individual welfare and more far-reaching cuts in public welfare systems than was the case in the latter part of this period. But this general pattern contains many different details.

In general terms, unemployment followed a pattern that in many respects was typical for the period: a sharp increase in the first three years followed by a relatively stable phase and then a clear fall after 1997. The pattern for income was somewhat different, with a fall until 1995 and a recovery after that. The number of social assistance recipients rose rapidly in the first four years of the decade and then more moderately until 1997, followed by a very marked drop. But in all these developments there are deviant cases. Unemployment among single women with children went on rising when it fell for other groups, income inequality grew throughout the period and this tendency was accentuated when income levels recovered in general; the average duration of social assistance did not become shorter when the number of recipients fell.

The picture provided by the indicators of individual welfare is generally less uniform. Here, too, there are admittedly features that show a deterioration early in the decade, followed by stabilization or an improvement in the latter part. Examples are self-rated health, mental well being, and the incidence of working conditions involving mental strain. But in other respects the levels of welfare were broadly unchanged during the period studied. This applies to, for example, social ties and housing conditions such as overcrowding and forms of ownership. A consistently negative trend was found for the incidence of stressful jobs, particularly among women. Mortality, on the other hand, continued to fall in the 1990s at the same rate as in earlier decades.

Social security and family support were affected by so many different decisions that developments here cannot be described in simple, clear-cut terms. However, the dominant characteristic from a year or so into the decade up to the end of 1997, was decisions that lowered replacement levels and tightened the criteria for obtaining benefits. In 1998 and 1999 there were a number of decisions in the opposite direction with regard to levels, but as a rule, they did not fully restore the levels from the beginning of the decade. In some sectors, changes occurred in the distribution of resources across activities and categories of recipients. In care for the elderly, for instance, the coverage of home-help services was reduced and a growing proportion of the inputs was concentrated to those with the greatest needs; this was essentially a process that continued throughout the decade. In medical care, resources were redistributed in favor of medicines, accompanied by a shorter duration of care and staff cuts; this, too, was a comparatively continuous trend.

The changes in welfare services in the 1990s were characterized by decentralization, a growing element of private operations and a shift towards a market approach to the organization of work. That makes it all the more remarkable that so little is known about the consequences of these changes for the activities and the persons concerned. Besides dealing with the levels of welfare, the overall picture presented by the State Commission is very much concerned with distributional aspects. The most relevant question is perhaps whether some groups can be identified whose living conditions deteriorated more than those of others in the 1990s. The survey revealed a deterioration for three groups in particular: persons born abroad, single mothers, and youth. Levels of employment fell markedly for these groups and this is mirrored in their higher frequency of financial problems. Moreover, all three groups were hit harder than others with regard to other aspects of welfare. Mental well being, for instance, seems to have deteriorated among young people in particular. Persons born abroad were found to have particular disadvantages in terms of political resources and social ties. Single mothers were more likely than other groups to be exposed to violence and threats of violence. It should be added that the economic situation for the long-term unemployed became increasingly precarious during the decade.

Summarizing trends in the 1990s, it is fair to say that in many respects, the level of welfare today is lower than at the beginning of the decade, even though there are examples of the opposite. However, many developments at the end of the century point in a favorable direction and it is conceivable that in a number of years they may reach and even surpass the earlier levels. It is therefore relevant to ask whether the loss of welfare and the problems with resources Sweden has experienced are just a temporary deviation as opposed to the beginning of a more permanent change of course. In the coming decades, is it plausible to look forward to a continuation of the general improvement in welfare that has essentially characterized Sweden for half a century, or will economic and political conditions force social welfare policies down a different path?

The Commission concludes by stressing that it is reasonable to suppose that people's welfare will continue to depend on many circumstances that are not included in traditional welfare policy. But experience from the 1990s provides no grounds for supposing that welfare policy in Sweden will not remain highly important for the level of welfare and perhaps above all for its distribution. The picture reveals a number of shortcomings and trends that are not just a consequence of the economic crisis but also have to do with welfare policy's construction. It will therefore probably be necessary to formulate some positions in principle about the construction of policy and its direction.

While the supply of resources will no doubt be important in this context, so will the uses to which the available resources are put. In this sense, at the beginning of the twenty-first century, welfare is at a crossroads.

Expert Opinion, Public Support and Attitudes to the Welfare State

Although the legitimacy of the universal welfare state never was in question among the great majority of the population, attitudes changed among the elite at the beginning of the decade. In particular, the profession of academic economists mounted severe criticisms against the "big" welfare state from the start of the 1980s, and in the early 1990s managed to get a reform mandate by the incoming non-socialist government. The Bank of Sweden was given a stronger position to combat inflation at arms length from the Ministry of Finance. Further independence of the central bank was seen as a measure to strengthen the role of economic expertise of the democratically elected and thus mass dependent populist politicians. The so-called Lindbeck commission, headed by Assar Lindbeck, chairman of the Bank of Sweden prize committee in memory of Alfred Nobel, presented in 1993 a full-scale plan for a major overhaul of the welfare system (1994 and 1997). However, most of its proposal came to nothing. It is too early to tell if the measurements of the next generation of welfare state expertise—the above-mentioned State Commission headed by Joakim Palme—will have more of an impact.

In contrast to a swing among the elite, attitudinal research has shown consistent popular support for most welfare programs throughout the 1990s, and in particular for universal social programs in Sweden (Svallfors, 2001, 1996). In contrast, means-tested benefits lacked similar backing in public opinion and were subject to a considerable degree of suspicion of misuse by welfare scroungers. Furthermore, surveys concluded that there was majority support for increased or unaltered spending on all social programs. This majority also supported general taxes and social contributions from employers—payroll taxes—as the main source of financing various social services. Likewise, there was a majority in favor of the state or local authorities as the main provider of healthcare and care of the elderly while the delivery of child daycare services was the exception from this public pattern. In toto, there was no indication in attitudinal research that adherents of leftist parties endorsed a new trajectory for the Swedish welfare state while sympathizers of non-socialist parties displayed a stronger tendency not to support the welfare state to the same degree as left-wingers. However, social groups that tended to show weak support constituted only a limited fraction of the public (Nordblom, 2002).

However, the traditional backers of welfare programs were not unaffected by the wave of economic criticisms. The main opponents to the idea of a dismantling of the welfare state were mobilized networks of feminist activists at least partly outside the confines of traditional party politics. Some of these networks threatened in the run-up to the 1994 election campaign to form a women's party to fight the dismantling of the public sector and its welfare services where most employees were females (Stark, 1997; cf. also Jensen and Mahon, 1993). Such a party was never formed but it can be argued that the threat of such a party had an impact on other forces in the public arena. To gain a wider audience the network of female activists distanced itself from parties sympathetic to its ideas and positioned itself outside traditional party politics; it thereby succeeded in influencing the platform of most political parties. In the mid-1990s, only one or two political parties defined themselves as feminist in orientation, while in the early twenty-first century almost all the major parties do so.

The Return of Civil/Welfare Society and the Politics of the Welfare State: Still Between Left and Right?

Throughout this chapter the role of social forces and movements as well as political actors in the making and remaking of the welfare state have been stressed. Apart from cost containment, taxation and the financing of active labor market measures, a solid social insurance system as well as personal social, educational and medical services, what was on the agenda among old and new actors and movements with a view on the workings of the welfare state? Were there any ideas or issues—such as the People's Home of the 1930s—which energized public opinion and created heated intellectual controversies? The road from the red-green decade of the 1930s to the colors of the *decennium horribile* has given a hint of the respective strength of red, blue, yellow, and green in contemporary Swedish welfare politics, policymaking and implementation.

In 1988, the earlier characteristic five-party system disappeared with the advent of a new political party in Parliament, the environmentalist Green Party, in an election in which welfare issues did not top the political agenda. During the first half of the 1980s, the Green Party had entered the town halls of well over 100 municipalities and considered itself outside the confines of the old right-left cleavage structure. Although it disappeared in the next national election (1991), it would remain in focus for the coming decade, returning to Parliament in 1994 to become a junior partner in the Social Democratic-led pro-welfare state coalition after the 1998 election. However, its stance on welfare issues was closer to the international movement for a citizen wage as a foundation for individual prosperity than to the priorities of the traditional working-class movement.

In the meantime, in the general election of 1991 two other more or less new parties managed to enter Parliament and in similar ways influenced welfare policy away from the neoliberal scenario. First, the right-wing populist party,

New Democracy had a forceful but nevertheless rather unarticulated or incoherent anti-bureaucratic, anti-immigration, anti-taxation and anti-welfare agenda. Typical for Swedish politics, and for populism in general, at the end of the party's brief life the anti-welfare agenda was actually turned around and became a pro-welfare agenda defending those who were hit by the cuts made by the non-socialist government. This government, which did not have a majority of its own, had to rely on conditional and unreliable support from the newly formed and hence extremely Parliamentary unexperienced New Democracy. Furthermore, this party would more or less completely disintegrate during the electoral period. Thus, it is no coincidence that throughout this chapter the imprint on the rest of the decade of the weakness of this government has been aptly demonstrated.

Second, a new, social conservative Christian Democratic party not only entered Parliament but also became part of the four-party non-social-democratic coalition cabinet that took over at the helm in 1991. As a newcomer in politics and within government, this party initially had a hard time adapting to its share in power, but over time, emerged as a defender of traditional family policy and came out as the opposite of the futuristic welfarism of the gender-neutral and anti-sexist Liberal party. Thus, this government managed to propose both an extra father's month of leave within parental insurance, and a special care allowance for those housewives who wanted to keep their kids out of institutional child daycare. This was rather characteristic for the kind of compromises that such a government had to achieve to remain in power, and subsequently the neoliberal strength dwindled as the Moderate-Conservative party had to work out the compromises between their junior partners. Nevertheless, the non-socialist government of 1991-1994 opened the way for market solutions, in particular, in the sphere of welfare provision and delivery. Government subsidies to local authorities were opened up for private contractors of welfare provision. For-profit welfare became part of the new package. In particular, female entrepreneurs were singled out as future role models.

Still, it was not domestic affairs but the international situation, in particular the dissolution of the Soviet empire, under which the prospect of a second or third round of the middle way withered away. In central and Eastern Europe, civil society had become the rallying cry of oppositional intellectuals (the once famous dissidents) against state and party dictatorship as no truly voluntary associations were allowed to exist by the rulers of the Evil empire. In the 1980s, the Tocquevillian idea of a civil society attracted many Western intellectuals on the left as well as the right. Outside the realm of academic economics, instead of the prospect of a for-profit welfare society, it was the prospect of a civil welfare society that inspired most non-socialist or former socialist intellectuals in the early 1990s. Profits and welfare were kept apart, and rational public planning was separated from voluntary associations and informal social networks in civil society. Actually, in the process of rethinking the past of the Swedish welfare state, rationality and social engineering was equated with racism and radical eugenics. In an attempt to purify the Arian Nordics, nurturing the strong and eradicating the weak part of the population, a fair number of Swedish women were subject to forced sterilization from the 1930s to the early 1970s. As with the case of the supposedly Swedish Children's Gulag in international media in the early 1980s (cf. Gould, 1989), the domestic debate about the sterilization issue attracted similar global media attention in the mid-1990s. These repressive policies—akin to Nazi Holocaust—constituted the hidden side of the emblematic welfare model according to anti-welfare state crusaders in Sweden as well as outside.

The vision that challenged traditional welfare state policies also opposed the hopes and dreams of the social engineers. Civil society became a vision espoused by Hans L Zetterberg, for a brief period in the early 1990s, as editor-in-chief of *Svenska Dagbladet*, the main Conservative daily in Stockholm. Together with his collaborators at the City University think-tank he produced more than a dozen volumes on social policy and welfare reform in the early and mid-1990s. Human dignity, not equality and redistributional social justice, should henceforth be the primary goal of a public welfare policy. Civil society was presented as the dignified successor to the overburdened welfare state (Zetterberg and Ljungberg, 1996). However, at the end of the day this project's impact on Swedish society was marginal as the Social Democrats had returned to power and the non-socialist parties became deeply divided between the traditional public road to welfare and the neoliberal for-profit road aggressively pursued by the Moderates in the greater metropolitan regions.

This is not to say that the politics of the welfare state has had an altogether distinct left-right mark. The non-socialist government of the early 1990s, already during the currency crisis of the autumn of 1992, had to strike an accord with the oppositional Social Democrat party (Olsson, 1993a), which limited its possibility to pursue a distinct neoliberal agenda. This government was also internally divided between neoliberal market enthusiasts and much more traditional social liberals and conservatives. The familiar rhetoric about solidarity, equality and collectivism that became known as the Social Democratic People's Home was far from gone, and although the Swedish prime minister enthused without guilt about the profit motive, private enterprise and competition he did not manage to set a new tone in Swedish politics. Instead, it was the vice premier and leader of the Liberal Party, Bengt Westerberg, who kept the old tunes alive singing the virtues of a solidaristic and universal social policy (Olsson Hort, 1994). As an unintended consequence, he prepared for the brief but important Social Democratic-Center agreement of 1996-98 when public finances were restored and a return to perceived normality was achieved.

Summary and Conclusions: The Return of Economic Growth and the Remaking of the Welfare State

The picture given in this chapter reveals a fairly successful approach to cost containment and austerity measures; a half-hearted but nevertheless partial return to full employment and in particular to the active manpower policy; a far from mature, rather premature, trend towards privatization of the main part of the social security system, the pension system; a fairly stable pattern of less generous income maintenance provisions; a more obvious struggle between decentralization and privatization in regard to the delivery of education, personal social and medical services; and finally an abolition of housing policy measures while agricultural subsidies were restored by EU membership. Moreover, the level of welfare decreased among the great majority of the population and inequalities widened, in particular at the start of the decade, while the support for the welfare state has been rather stable throughout the decade in attitudinal surveys.

The author's perspective on Swedish social policy has been consistently long-term and skeptical towards any premature death-sentence for the welfare state (cf. Olsson, 1990, 1993). This perspective is supported by the Rokkan-inspired idea of the maturation—or constant transformation—of the welfare state together with an emphasis on the role of lukewarm, atheist social forces advocating social justice, neighborly love and reciprocity. Based on its formative moment(s) the welfare state is in constant change, but the bigger and more all-encompassing it has grown, the more it runs into a state of maturity. Nevertheless, as a political structure the welfare state is always open to adaptations and adjustments to new social and economic conditions as well as to extended cultural horizons and new normative environments. Of course, there is also the possibility of a more or less full-scale dismantling, but then such a change must be—as in the opposite case of "maturation"— deliberately imposed by existing or newly shaped social forces rather than evolving out of sheer necessity.

Still, is the Swedish welfare state really "back on track"—on the road to the future toward which it was once intended? The brief but sharp economic upswing of the late 1990s and first year of the twenty-first century has fuelled a national debate over whether the economic reforms—deregulation of previously controlled activities such as telecom as well as cutbacks in welfare benefits—introduced over the past decade went too far or not far enough. And, as the international press immediately noted at the climax of the IT-revolution, it has caused the rest of the world to pause and take positive notice of the welfare state model once again. Economic growth— and the financing of the welfare state—has resumed its number one position on the political agenda; the productivist relationship between work and welfare has been re-addressed and restated (cf. J. Andersson, 2002).

Nevertheless, the causes behind the crisis of the Swedish welfare state have to be taken seriously. They can be analyzed in political, economic, as well as demographic terms. So far, economics and politics have dominated this analysis. In an attempt to excavate the future, I will end in the reverse order by deconstructing the demographic outlook. During the 1990s, changes in the composition of Sweden's population have had direct consequences for the system of state-supported welfare. The number of elderly pensioners rose sharply, a large number of refugees immigrated in the first half of the decade and births decreased markedly from the mid-1990s. The increase in the number of elderly pensioners in the 1990s was confined to the over-80s, for whom it amounted to 17 percent; the number of younger retired persons actually tended to fall. The increase continued a trend that had started some decades earlier (Cnaan et al., 1990). This age group uses a relatively large proportion of the available resources, particularly for public health and social care, and will do so for the foreseeable future.

Refugees arrived in Sweden in a series of waves in the 1990s in connection with various international conflicts and civil wars. By far the largest inflow occurred in the period 1992-94 as former Yugoslavia fell apart. Immigration in the rest of the decade was on much the same level as in the late 1980s, although an increase was visible at the turn to a new century. Of those who obtained residence permits in the 1990s, more than half came from former Yugoslavia. The arrival of the large groups of immigrants coincided with the most unfavorable phases of the Swedish economy and labor market. This meant that the newcomers had very limited possibilities of earning a living in the regular labor market; in the virtual absence of other safety-nets, this group was largely left to make do with social assistance and thus became a heavy burden on local government budgets. At the end of the decade, the government increased its efforts to activate and mobilize this labor reserve, in particular in the greater metropolitan regions where housing segregation was considered an obstacle to adult—in particular female—labor market participation as well as to overall integration in Swedish society especially for children and school leavers without sufficient knowledge of the Swedish language (Axelsson, 2002). The outcome of this mobilization of the ethnic working poor or underclass may turn out to be decisive for the future of the solidaristic welfare state.

Furthermore, fertility in Sweden has fluctuated widely in recent decades. At the beginning of the 1990s the total fertility rate was 2.1 children per woman, which by European standards was comparatively high. As of 1992, however, the rate began a very rapid decline and was, at the end of the century, 1.5 children per woman, an all-time low in Sweden's history. Births have fallen most markedly among young women and there has been a successive upward shift in the child-bearing age. Moreover, the birth rate is relatively low among women with low incomes and low education. All in all, there are many indications that in the 1990s, having children has been increasingly a question of material resources. A partial exception to this pattern is the fertility rate among newly arrived immigrants giving the demographic outlook an ethnic dimension. An important consequence of the marked decline in the number of births is that the annual cohorts now vary greatly in size: the largest cohorts at present are around the age of ten, while the cohorts of preschool children are considerably smaller. With the economic upswing at the start of the new millennium, birth rates have increased somewhat for three consecutive years.

The changing landscape of the Swedish welfare state is visible in recent research and analytical interpretations. Following Sunesson et al. (1998) and based on investigations of the most recent evolution of social assistance, Clapton and Pontusson (1998) have argued that a fundamental shift, a rupture or paradigm shift, has occurred as the universal policies of the postwar period have been recently overtaken or replaced by residualist practices. Also, perhaps, the most ardent defender of the universal model in Sweden has in recent time pointed in this direction and emphasized the necessity of concerted action and working-class mobilization (Korpi, 2000). In contrast, those focusing on policy implementation and patterns of institutional change have underlined inertia—"institutional sclerosis" according to others—and path dependency and, thus, been more reluctant to admit the possibility of a failure of the "irreversibility thesis." The idea of a durable or resilient welfare state points in that direction (cf. also Kuhnle, 2000: Stephens, 1996).

Following Titmuss's (1974) distinction, I have argued that targeting social benefits has different implications in the universal model compared to the residual, where social assistance—despite its recent growth—plays a marginal role in the general Swedish system of social protection. Although scrutiny of welfare beneficiaries in various branches of social insurance has become much more stringent and benefits less generous during the 1990s, the tendency towards increasing reliance on social assistance reflects the extreme circumstances of the mid-1990s and cannot be taken as a sign of "paradigmatic shift" (Hort, 2000). Focusing on work-to-welfare practices in Sweden, I would suggest that despite a certain downgrading due to streamlining along the European montarist policy path, the good of full employment has remained high on the political agenda (Hort, 2001). In particular the announcement in 1996 of a government target to cut unemployment in half by the year 2000 and the achievement of this goal along with a second government goal to increase the rate of employment to the pre-1990 level in year 2004 point in this direction. Growth and public sector efficiency has returned to the forefront of a "productivist" welfare policy at a time when economic growth has recovered from the sluggishness and deep recession of the early and mid-1990s. However, whether the end of the 1990s was more than an end to the *decennium horribile* remains to be seen.

All these aspects of the development of the Swedish welfare state must be taken into account to understand the present development of the system of social protection in a more narrow sense, that is, social insurance or security (sometimes also called income maintenance policy). In a similar vein, developments within other related policy areas have to be included in a reconsideration of welfare state development in the 1990s and beyond. Throughout this chapter, the dialectics of decentralization and privatization visible from the late 1970s have been stressed. So has the importance of continued public financing of welfare services including active labor market measures. However, if there is any sign of a new institutional pattern in the Swedish welfare system, to this author it is within the branches of social insurance, where the pension reform of the most recent decade, or at least parts of it, point in a direction not followed previously. Still, this is an institutional reform within the confines of a domestic policy process that may or may not be influenced by exogenous variables. Thus, this broader picture must be kept in mind to answer the questions: "Where is the welfare state of the twenty-first century headed?"

The end of history proposed by Francis Fukuyama slightly more than a decade ago never materialized. The end of the Swedish welfare state and more generally the welfare state model is in sight. Maybe this model is wounded, even severely wounded. However, it has survived the deadly threats of the 1990s and as the century turns the future of the durable or resilient welfare state has seen the light of day.

Note

1. This chapter was prepared as a paper for the Research Team "Continuities and Changes in the Welfare State," headed by Neil Gilbert, and the Conference "The Changing Landscape of the Welfare State: Implications for the Future of Social Protection," Villa Serbelloni, Rockefeller Foundation Study and Conference Center, Bellagio, Italy, 5-11 August 2000, co-sponsored by the International Social Security Association (ISSA) and the Center for Comparative Research on Family Welfare and Poverty, University of California at Berkeley. I would like to thank the participants at that meeting for comments and criticisms. The paper was revised February-March 2002.

References

Acker, J. et al. (1992). *Kvinnors och mäns liv och arbete*. Stockholm: SNS.

Åhnberg, A., and Salonen, T. (2002). Vart femte barn lever fattigt. Stockholm, *Dagens Nyheter* 18 March.

Ahrne, G. (1990). *Vid byråkratins gränser*. Stockholm: Rabén and Sjögren.

Andersson, J. (2002). *Mellan tillväxt och trygghet*. Uppsala: Ekonomisk-historiska institutionen (diss).

Andersson, R. (1999). Skapandet av svenskglesa bostadsområden. In L. Magnusson (ed.), *Den delade staden—segregation och etnicitet i stadsbygden*. Umeå: Borea.

Anttonen, A. (1990). From the Social Insurance to the Social Service State. In L. Simonen (ed.) *Finnish Debates on Women's Studies*. Tampere: University of Tampere.

Axelsson, C. (2002). *Arbetslinjen i storstadsarbrtet–Huddinge, Stockholm, Södertälje.* Huddinge: Södertörns högskola.

Bartley, K. (1998). Barnpolitik och barns rattigheter.Ph.D. diss., Department of Sociology, Goteborg.

Benner, M. (1997). The Politics of Growth—Economic Regulation in Sweden 1930-1994. Lund: Arkiv (diss.).

Blomqvist, P., and Rothstein, B. (2000). *Välfärdsstatens nya ansikte: demokrati och marknadsreformer inom den offentliga sektorn.* Stockholm: Agora.

Boje, T. P., and Olsson Hort, S. E. (eds.). (1993). *Scandinavia in a New Europe.* Oslo: Scandinavian University Press.

Bunar, N. (2001). Skolan mitt i förorten. Stehag: Symposion (diss).

Carson, M. (2001). *The Paradigmatic Shift: Swedish Welfare Policy in the 1990s.* Uppsala: Department of Sociology.

Castels, M. (1996). The Information Age: Economy, Politics and Culture. Volume II: The Power of Identity. Oxford: Blackwell.

Cnaan, R., Olsson Hort, S. E., and Wetle, T. (1990). Cross-National Comparions of Planning for the Needs of the Very Old: Israel, Sweden and the United States. *Journal of Aging and Social Policy,* Vol. 2, No. 1.

Clapton, R., and Pontusson, J. (1998). Welfare State Retrenchment Revisited. *World Politics* Vol. 51 (October): 67-98.

Eliasson-Lappalianen R., and Szebehely, M. (1996). Äldreomsorg, kvalitetssäkring och välfärdspolitik. In J. Palme and I. Vennemo (eds.), *Generell välfärdspolitik.* Stockholm: Välfärdsprojektet/Ministry of Health and Social Affairs.

Esping-Andersen, G. (1990). *The Three Worlds of Welfare Capitalism.* Cambridge: Polity Press.

Flora, P. (ed.). (1986). *Growth to Limits–The Development of the West European Welfare States Since World War II.* Berlin: Walther de Gruyter.

Franzén, M., and Sandstedt, E. (1993). *Välfärdsstat och byggande.* Lund: Arkiv.

Fukuyama. F. (1989). The End of History. *National Interest* (summer).

Fukuyama, F. (1992). *The End of History and the Last Man.* New York: Free Press.

Gilbert, N. (ed.). (2000). *Targeting Social Benefits.* New Brunswick, NJ: Transaction Publishers.

Gilbert, N. (ed.). (2001). *Activating the Unemployed: A Comparative Appraisal of Work-Oriented Policies.* New Brunswick, NJ: Transaction Publishers.

Gould, A. (1989). *Conflict and Control in Welfare Policy—The Swedish Experience.* London: Longman.

Gustavsson, R. (2000). *VälfärdsTjänstearbetet.* Göteborg: Daidalos.

Hobsbawm, E. (1994). *The Age of Extremes–A History of the World 1914-1991.* New York: Pantheon.

Hort, S. E. O. (2001). Sweden–Still a Civilized Version of Workfare? In N. Gilbert (ed.), *Activating the Unemployed: A Comparative Appraisal of Work-Oriented Policies.* New Brunswick, NJ: Transaction Publishers.

Hort, S. E. O. (2000). Sweden—from a Fenerous to a Stingy Welfare State? In N. Gilbert and R. Van Voorhis (eds.), *Targeting Social Benefits.* New Brunswick, NJ: Transaction Publishers.

Hort, S. E. O. (1997). Advancing for Children in the Advanced Welfare State: Current Problems and Prospects in Sweden. In G. A. Cornia and S. Danziger (eds.), *Child Poverty and Deprivation in the Industrialized Countries.* Oxford: Clarendon Press.

Hort, S .E. O., and McMurphy, S. C. (1997). Sweden. In N. Mayades, T. Watts, and D. Elliott (eds.), *International Handbook on Social Work Theory and Practice.* Westport, CT: Greenwood Press.

IMF. (1995). *Challenges to the Swedish Welfare State*. Washington, D.C.: International Monetary Fund.

Jensen, J., and Mahon, R. (1993). Representing Solidarity: Class, Gender and the Crisis in Social-Democratic Sweden. *New Left Review*, No. 201 (September/October): 76-100.

Johansson, H. (2001). Det sociala medborgarskapet. Lund: Arkiv (diss.).

Johansson, R. (1992). Vid byråkratins gränser. Lund: Arkiv (diss).

Korpi, W. (2000). Sveriges upplysta opinion halkar efter den internationella forskningsfronten. *Ekonomiska samfundets tidskrift*, Vol. 52, No. 1.

Kuhnle, S. (ed.). (2000). *The Survival of the Welfare State*. London: Routledge.

Liljeström, R., and Dahlström, E. (1982). *Arbetarkvinnor i hem-, arbets- och samhällsliv*. Stockholm: Tiden.

Lindbeck, A. (1997). *The Swedish Experiment*. Stockholm: SNS.

Lindbeck, A. et al. (1994). *Turning Sweden Around*. Cambridge, MA: MIT Press.

Misgeld, K., Molin K., and Åmark, K. (eds.). *Creating Social Democracy—A Century of the Social Democratic Party in Sweden*. University Park: Pennsylvania State University Press.

Nordlund, A. (2002). Resilient Welfare States. Umeå: Department of Sociology No 32 (diss.).

NOSOSCO. (2001). *Social Protection in the Nordic Countries 1999*. Copenhagen: Nordic Social Statistical Committee.

Odhner, C-E. (1992). Workers and Farmers Shape the Swedish Model: Social Democracy and Agricultural Policy. In K. Misgeld, K. Molin, and K. Åmark (eds.), *Creating Social Democracy—A Century of the Social Democratic Party in Sweden*. University Park: Pennsylvania State University Press.

Olofsson, G. (1994). Det svenska pensionssystemet 1913-1993: historia, struktur, konflikter. *Arkiv för studier i arbetarrörelsens historia*, No. 58-59.

Olofsson, G., and Pettersson, A. (1994). Sweden: Policy Dilemmas of the Changing Age Structure in a "Work Society." In F. Naschold and B. Van der Vroom (eds.), *Regulating Employment and Welfare: Company and National Policies at the End of Worklife in Industrial Countries*. New York: Walther de Gruyter.

Olsson, S. E. (1986). Sweden. In P. Flora (ed.), *Growth to Limits–The Development of the West European Welfare States Since World War II*. Berlin: Walther de Gruyter.

Olsson, S. E. (1990). *Social Policy and Welfare State in Sweden*. (1st ed. 1990; 2nd ed. 1993). Lund: Arkiv.

Olsson, Hort. (1992). *Segregation—ett svensk dilemma?* Stockholm: Finansdepartementet.

Olsson S. E. (1993a). Postscript: Crisis, Crisis, Crisis—1990-1992. In Olsson 1993.

Olsson Hort, S. E. (1993b). Freiwillige Arbeitslosenversicherung und umfassende soziale Sicherheit—der Widerspruch der schwedischen Vollbeschäftungspolitik. In Lottes G. (ed.), *Soziale Sicherheit in Europa*. Heidelberg: Physica Verlag.

Olsson Hort S. E. (1994). Adolf Hedin och den nyliberala början på den socialliberala välfärdspolitiken. *Arkiv för studier i arbetarrörelsens historia*, No. 58-59.

Olsson Hort, S.E. (2001). La société civile, l'État e la sécurité sociale en Suède: centralisation et décentralisation dans le modèle social scandinave. In *Un siècle de protection sociale en Europe*. Paris: Association de l'étude de l'histoire de la Securitté sociale.

Olsson Hort, S.E., and Cohn, D. (1996). Sweden. In N. Johnson (ed.), *Private Markets in Health and Welfare*. Oxford: Berg.

Olsson Hort, S.E., and Ahn, S. H. (1999). The politics of old age in Sweden. In A. Walker and G. Naegele (eds.), *The Politics of Old Age in Europe*. Buckingham: Open University Press.

Palme, J. (1994). Recent Developments in Income Transfer Systems in Sweden. In N. Plough and and J. Kvist (eds.), *Recent Trends in Cash Benefits in Europe*. Copenhagen: Danish National Institute of Social Research.

Palme, J., and Vennemo, I. (1998). *Swedish Social Security in the 1990s*. Stockholm: Ministry of Health and Social Affairs.

Pontusson, J. (1994). Sweden—After the Golden Age. In P. Anderson and P. Camiller (eds.), *The West European Left*. London: Verso.

Ramel, C. (1998): The National Association of Local Authorities. Stockholm: Department of Sociology (mimeo).

Rokkan, S. (1999). *State Formation, Nation-Building and Mass Politics in Europe*. Edited by Peter Flora with Stein Kuhnle and Derek Unwin). Oxford: Clarendon Press.

Rothstein, B. (2000). *Det sociala kapitalet i den socialdemokratiska staten*. Arkiv for studier i arbetarrörelsens historia no. 79.

Rothstein, B. (1996). *The Social Democratic State—the Swedish Model and the Bureaucratic Problem of Social Reform*. Pittsburgh: Pittsburgh University Press.

Rothstein, B. (1993). The Crisis of the Swedish Model and the Future of the Universal Welfare State. *Governance*, Vol 6.

Rothstein, B. (1980). AMS som socialdemokratisk reformbyråkrati. *Arkiv för arbetarrörelsens historia*, No. 18.

Salonen, T. (1994). Margins of Welfare—A Study of Modern Functions of Social Assistance. Lund: Hällestad Press (diss.).

Sjöberg, O. (2001). Välfärdsstatens finansiering under 1990-talet. In SOU 2001:51. Stockholm: Ministry of Health and Social Affairs.

Sparks, S. (1995). *Privatisation of Social Services*. Stockholm: International Graduate School.

Stark, A. (1997). Swedish Women. In J. Mitchell and A. Oakley (eds.), *Women and Social Policy*. London: Routledge.

Stenius, K. (1999). Privat och offentligt i svensk alkoholistvård-arbetsfördelning, samverkan och styrning under 1900-talet. Lund: Arkiv (diss.).

Stephens, J. (1996). The Scandinavian Welfare States: Achievements, Crisis and Prospects. In G. Esping-Andersen (ed.), *Welfare States in Transition*. London: Sage.

Strömberg, T. (1992). The Politicisation of the Housing Market: The Social Democrats and the Housing Question. In K. Misgeld, K. Molin, and K. Åmark (eds.), *Creating Social Democracy–A Century of the Social Democratic Party in Sweden*. University Park: Pennsylvania State University Press.

Sunesson, S., Blomberg, S. Edebalk, P-G., Harrysson, L., Magnusson, J., Meeuwisse, A., Petersson, J., and Salonen, T. (1998). The Flight from Universalism. *European Journal of Social Work*, Vol. 1, No. 1, 19-29.

Sutton, C. (1998). Swedish Alcohol Discourse: Constructions of a Social Problem. Ph.D. diss., Department of Sociology, Uppsala.

Svallfors, S. (2001). Kan man lita på välfärdsstaten? Risk, tilltro och betalningsvilja i den svenska välfärdsopinionen 1997-2000. In SOU 2001:57. Stockholm: Ministry of Health and Social Affairs.

Svallfors, S. (1996). *Välfärdsstatens moraliska ekonomi*. Umeå: Borea.

Szebehely, M. (1997). Tjenestene og utviklingen i sammenheng. In S.O. Daatland, *De siste årene*. Oslo: Norsk institutt for oppvekst, velferd og aldring.

Szebehely, M. (1996). Vardagens organisering. Lund: Arkiv (diss).

Therborn, G. (1992a). A Unique Chapter in the History of Democracy: The Social Democrats in Sweden. In K. Misgeld, K. Molin, and K. Åmark (eds.), *Creating Social Democracy—A Century of the Social Democratic Party in Sweden*. University Park: Pennsylvania State University Press.

Therborn, G. (1992b). Swedish Social Democracy and the Transition from Industrial to Postindustrial Politics. In F. Fox Piven (ed.), *Labour Parties in Post-Industrial Societies*. Oxford: Oxford University Press.

Therborn, G. (1983-84). The Coming of Swedish Social Democracy. In Annali Giangiacomo Feltrinelli 1983-84. Milan: Feltrinelli (translated to Swedish in *Arkiv för studier i arbetarrörelsens historia*, No.41-42).

Titmuss, R. (1974). *Social Policy*. London: Unwin.

Wetterberg, G. (1988). *Alternativ i jordbrukspolitiken*. Stockholm: ESO.

Wilensky, H. (1975). *The Welfare State and Equality*. Berkeley: University of California Press.

Zetterberg, H. (1967). Sweden–A Land of Tomorrow? In I. Wizelius (ed.), *Sweden in the Sixties*. Stockholm: Almqvist and Wiksell.

Zetterberg, H., and Ljungberg, C-J. (1996). *Vårt land: den svenska socialstaten*. Stockholm: City University Press.

Official Documents

SOU 2001: 79. Välfärdsbokslut för 1990-talet. Stockholm: Ministry of Health and Social Affairs.

SOU 2001: 57. Välfärdens finansiering och fördelning. Stockholm: Ministry of Health and Social Affairs.

SOU 2001: 56. Funktionshinder och välfärd. Stockholm: Ministry of Health and Social Affairs.

SOU 2001: 55. Ofärd i välfärden. Stockholm: Ministry of Health and Social Affairs.

SOU 2001: 54. Barns och ungdomars välfärd. Stockholm: Ministry of Health and Social Affairs.

SOU 2001: 52. Välfärdstjänster i omvandling. Stockholm: Ministry of Health and Social Affairs.

SOU 2000: 83. Two of a Kind? Economic Crisis, Policy Responses and Well-Being during the 1990s in Sweden and Finland. Stockholm: Ministry of Health and Social Affairs.

SOU 2000: 41. Välfärd, ofärd och ojämlikhet. Stockholm: Ministry of Health and Social Affairs.

SOU 2000: 40. Välfärd och försörjning. Stockholm: Ministry of Health and Social Affairs.

SOU 2000: 39. Välfärd och skola. Stockholm: Ministry of Health and Social Affairs.

SOU 2000: 38. Välfärd, vård och omsorg. Stockholm: Ministry of Health and Social Affairs.

SOU 2000: 37. Välfärdens förutsättningar. Arbetsmarknad, demografi och segregation. Stockholm: Ministry of Health and Social Affairs.

SOU 2000: 3. Välfärd vid vägskäl. Stockholm: Ministry of Health and Social Affairs.

SOU 1999: 148. På de boendes villkor. Stockholm: Ministry of Finance.

SOU 1996: 156. Bostadspolitik 2000–från produktions-till boendepolitik. Expertrapporter. Stockholm: Ministry of Interior.

Swedish Government. (1996). *A Programme for Halving Open Unemployment by 2000*. Stockholm: Prime Minister's Office.

Newspaper Articles

Business Week, 1992.
Economist, 1993.
Financial Times, September 1991 and later.
Forbes, 1993.
Newsweek, February 2000.

7

Social Security and Welfare in the Netherlands Before and After the Year 2000

Piet Keizer

Context and Adjustment Problems

Introduction

After World War II most European economies recovered quickly. The Great Depression in the thirties and the war experiences in the forties convinced many people of the necessity of having strong government intervention with respect to the economy. In the first place, a system of collective bargaining had to guarantee a wage level that could meet conditions of economic efficiency as well as social fairness. In the second place, a commitment by the government was considered necessary to maintaining full employment, especially via the implementation of Keynesian macro-policies. In the third place, a system of social welfare had to be constructed, in order to protect people from having an insufficient amount of resources. From 1953 on, a long-term spell of full employment and a constantly increasing level of wealth allowed the government the opportunity to build a generous system of social welfare. In about twenty years, Dutch society constructed a social safety net for all citizens.

However, during the same period, global developments corroded the dominant position of the United States, most strikingly demonstrated by the un-linking of the dollar from gold. When the OPEC countries decided to quadruple the oil price in 1973, it was the beginning of a worldwide economic depression. Many economists consider 1973 a turning point, where a long term of growth turned into a long-term decline. Most EU economies went into a depression; the Dutch economy showed increasing unemployment from 1979 on. During the seventies Dutch economists disagreed about the character of the depression. Some interpreted it as post-Wicksellian, while others interpreted it as post-Keynesian (Kuipers and Wilpstra, 1983). In the period 1974-1982 Dutch politicians implemented a set of inconsistent measures, making the economic situation worse. In 1982, the situation had aggravated to such a degree that it was clear to everybody, including the trade unions, that strong cuts in government expenditures were necessary for the Dutch economy to recover. Employers' organizations and unions agreed to accept cuts in social expenditures, a moderate wage development and co-responsibility of the employers' organizations for the employment level of the economy as a whole [this agreement has become famous under the name "Wassenaar Akkoord"].

When looking at the results of the policy package the general opinion among economists and politicians is positive. There is agreement about the positive effects on economic growth and employment without having fundamentally dismantled the system of social welfare. But for the future, Dutch society has to face the existence of a number of persistent problems. In the first place, the number of inactive people who are entitled to receiving a social benefit is still high when related to the volume of the working population. Especially the number of so-called disabled persons is very high when compared with the numbers in other European societies. In the second place, there are a number of long-term unemployed people. The duration is part of the reason why they are still unemployed. This means a vicious cycle for these people, making it necessary for the community to offer them ample opportunity to return to active participation in society.

Besides economic and social developments other factors play a role as well, such as demographic developments. While in many countries in Latin America, Africa and Asia the population grows fast, we can observe a completely different picture in the Western world. The average number of children has been declining for a long period, leading to an increase in the average age of the Western population. If this trend continues, the number of pensioned people relative to the working population will become a financial problem of the first order. Several EU countries are already taking measures to deal adequately with this problem in the future. One of the consequences of the uneven demographic development is a flow of immigrants coming to the EU to look for a job. On the one hand, these people can be considered a problem. They might benefit from the welfare system more than they financially contribute to it. But they can also be considered a solution to the problem, contributing significantly to the Dutch and EU production and income, making the welfare system more viable. Moreover, an increase in the number of foreigners might induce feelings of rivalry among the indigenous people. This would make it more difficult for the Dutch and EU society to maintain a system of social transfers to those people who need some support in their attempts to fully participate in our society.

The "South"-"West" migration is one of the consequences of the ongoing processes of globalization. This process makes it difficult for economies with a more extensive system of social protection to compete with those that economize on benefits and the maintenance of social cohesion. Small open economies like the Dutch have hardly any opportunity to deviate from the level in other societies. The integration of European economies might lead to a level of social protection that is morally acceptable and economically payable, notwithstanding tough competition from other areas in the world.

The sustainability of the Dutch system of social welfare depends highly on developments in other economies that belong to the European Union. But on the other hand, the Dutch economic and social performance, together with Scandinavian and Central European performances, can affect the political opinion and policymaking in Brussels.

This chapter deals with the problem of the sustainability of the Dutch system of social welfare in the following ways. First, a sketch is given of important trends in the Dutch economy that played a role in the development of the social welfare system. Then an explanation is given of the internal as well as external developments that played a role in the changing of this system. In the next sections we discuss the changes in the system of social welfare that were implemented during the period 1982-2000. The generosity of social benefits was reduced, the organization of the execution was made more efficient and the relation between social system and the labor market was improved. In the nineties, the Dutch economy profited from the global downturn recovery more than the average of other EU economies. We then give a sketch of the Dutch social and economic developments in the period 1982-2000. Although the performance looks quite good at first, there are a number of persistent and growing problems that will need to be treated in the near future. The next section addresses the sustainability of the idea of "a welfare state in the context of a global economy." Several forces affect the possibility of maintaining the idea or paradigm of the welfare state as we had in the fifties when it was built up. Lastly, we draw the conclusion that a small welfare state in an open global economy can only maintain a sober and efficiently organized welfare system. The Dutch must pay more attention to their control systems to be able to maintain a decent minimum for all in the near future.

The Dutch Economy

After the Second World War Dutch labor market institutions were reshaped along corporatist lines. Tripartite consultation with respect to all relevant social economic matters led to a consensus about the main policy goals. The Dutch government declared itself responsible for reaching and maintaining full employment. The trade unions and the employers' organizations declared themselves responsible for having a moderate wage development, to be realized via a system of collective bargaining. In 1953, full employment was reached while continuing economic growth made it possible to construct an encompassing system of social security and assistance. In 1949, a law to provide benefits for the unemployed was adopted and reformed in 1952. In 1957, a state pension system was introduced, guaranteeing every citizen 65 years and older a pension. In 1965, a safety net was constructed: every person who appears unable to earn a living and for whom there are no other sources of income, gets a social assistance benefit. And, in 1967, a system was introduced for those who have become disabled. In 1976, this service was extended to the self-employed, who came under the jurisdiction of the Disability Law as well. Other social services that had existed already for a very long time, such as children allowance and widow/widower/orphan benefits were adjusted to the standards of the time.

Because the rates of economic growth were relatively high, these services were not very costly in the beginning. In good times generous insurance systems are cheap because of minimal use. But when the global long-term economic growth turned into a long-term decline, an increasing appeal to social services created a huge financial problem. But before a majority of people came to see that the welfare system was meant to be a solution to economic problems, it became a bottleneck to economic recovery and eight years of bad policies had been passed. In table 7.1 we present a number of key economic figures.

Table 7.1
Economic Development Indicators: 1960-1981

Table 7.1a: Key Variables of Social and Economic Development: 1960-1973

Time	(1)	(2)	(3)	(4)	(5)	(6)	(7)	(8)	(9)
1960	3.1	1.5	2.5	3.2	-1.4	50.6	34.2	12.9	0.30
1961	3.1	1.1	2.4	1.6	-2.5	49.5	35.3	13.2	..
1962	4.0	1.0	2.6	1.1	-4.0	47.9	34.8	13.7	0.29
1963	3.6	1.0	3.8	0.8	-3.9	46.6	36.1	15.7	..
1964	8.3	0.9	6.8	-1.2	-5.4	42.2	37.4	15.7	0.65
1965	5.2	1.0	4.0	0.1	-5.1	40.7	38.6	16.9	..
1966	2.7	1.2	5.4	-1.1	-5.2	40.5	40.1	18.3	0.72
1967	5.3	2.4	3.0	-3.0	-5.2	41.0	40.9	19.2	..
1968	6.4	2.2	2.6	0.3	-5.1	40.0	42.7	19.7	0.78
1969	6.4	1.7	6.3	0.2	-4.5	32.5	42.1	19.6	..
1970	6.7	1.4	4.5	-1.7	-3.8	31.1	44.4	20.3	0.79
1971	4.3	1.7	8.1	-0.5	-3.8	29.7	46.3	21.9	0.80
1972	3.4	2.8	8.4	3.1	-2.0	26.9	47.4	23.0	0.84
1973	5.7	2.9	9.0	4.2	-1.5	22.7	48.6	23.5	0.85

Table 7.1b: Key Variables of Social and Economic Development: 1974-1981

Time	(1)	(2)	(3)	(4)	(5)	(6)	(7)	(8)	(9)
1974	3.5	2.8	10.1	3.4	-2.9	20.5	52.2	25.1	0.87
1975	-1.0	4.0	10.7	2.7	-5.3	22.1	55.4	28.3	0.90
1976	5.3	4.3	8.8	3.5	-5.1	23.1	55.4	28.5	0.93
1977	2.4	4.1	6.0	0.8	-4.0	24.3	56.6	29.4	0.92
1978	2.7	4.1	4.5	-0.9	-4.2	27.6	53.8	30.4	0.92
1979	1.8	4.1	4.5	-1.4	-5.3	31.2	55.8	31.5	0.91
1980	0.6	3.9	6.9	-1.6	-7.2	34.1	58.1	32.1	1.00
1981	-0.7	4.3	6.5	2.8	-8.3	38.9	59.3	33.4	1.05

(1) Economic growth (real GDP growth);

(2) Unemployment as a percentage of the labor force;

(3) Inflation (percentage);

(4) Balance of payments deficit as a percentage of NNP (+ is surplus and - is deficit);

(5) Governmental budgetary deficit as a percentage of NNP (+ is surplus and - is deficit);

(6) Governmental debt as a percentage of GDP;

(7) Taxes and social premiums as a percentage of NNP;

(8) Social expenditures as a percentage of GDP; and

(9) Inactivity ratio, that is the number of benefit recipients divided by the number of workers.

All the indicators illustrate the message of an increasing structural imbalance. Economic growth and unemployment figures show the turn towards recession. The tax burden shows a structural increase. Unemployed people do not contribute to production, but receive a social benefit instead. This implies an increase in the tax burden. When business is in trouble, leading to a higher tax burden, something must be done to break this vicious circle. In 1982, tripartite consultations led to the so-called Wassenaar Akkoord. The social partners agreed to a policy of limiting the system of social security and assistance, while the employers' organizations explicitly committed themselves to cooperate in a common employment policy. In the next section we discuss the reasons why a structural reform of the social welfare system was unavoidable.

The Welfare State in the Seventies and Its Flaws

The construction of a welfare system. As already noted, the experiences of the thirties and forties led many people in Europe to conclude that the government had to intervene in the economy to reach and maintain full employment. Moreover, a social policy had to be implemented to support those who appeared unable to earn a living themselves. Full participation of all citizens became a cornerstone of social economic policy in most West-European countries. Full employment policy was mainly interpreted as Keynesian monetary and budgetary policies. Social policy was mainly interpreted as the construction of a safety-net for everyone, so as to keep all people in financial trouble at the standard of living before their economic difficulties.

The most important measures taken by the Dutch government were:

1. A law on *illness*. Such a law was first implemented in 1930. But in 1953 the Law on the Organization of Social Security was passed to integrate a whole set of illness-related benefits already in place. The level of the benefit was 70 percent or 80 percent, depending on the group to which an employee belonged. Over time, in a number of industries, the negotiating partners in the collective bargaining system agreed to a benefit level of 100 percent of the wage rate. For instance, all civil servants were entitled to a 100 percent benefit in case of illness.
2. A law on *disability*. In 1967, a law was adopted that entitled people who were ill for a year to receive a disability benefit. These people were assumed to be unable to return to work, so society had the social obligation to entitle these disabled persons to a social benefit for the rest of their life until they reached the age of being pensioned. The level of the disability benefit was set at 80 percent of last earned income. In 1976, the law was structurally adjusted; not only employees but also the self-employed became entitled to receive a benefit in case of lifelong injury.
3. A law on *unemployment*. In 1949, a new unemployment law was adopted replacing legislation that was established in the beginning of the twentieth century. The level of the benefit was 60, 70 or 80 percent of last earned income, the specific percentage dependent on the level of the income of the recipient's spouse. The duration was set at 126 days. Only those who had worked for more than 78 days during the last year before their unemployment were entitled to a benefit. In 1965, the benefit rate was set at 80 percent for all workers, and the maximum duration was set at 156 days, which was reduced to 130 days in 1967.
4. A law on *state pensions*. In 1957, the government adopted legislation that guaranteed a benefit from the state to all people in the Netherlands who reached the age of 65. At the moment of implementation there were 750,000 beneficiaries, who received a fixed amount of money, the level of which was determined by what was considered a necessary minimum. Later the level was linked to that of the net average wage.
5. A law on *health cost* insurance. In 1964, a law was adopted arranging the obligation of employers to pay insurance premiums for all workers who earned a relatively low income. The law was accepted by Parliament under the condition that specific legislation would be developed to solve the problem of severe and costly health risks. In 1967, a special fund was erected to provide premium payments and benefit transfers to those in need of special medical treatment. In contrast to the regular service, which covered only employees, all citizens were covered by this special service.

6. A law on *family allowance*. For wage earners there was a law that gave them the right to an allowance since 1941. In the 1950s, the government began discussions about trying to supplement this arrangement by covering the self-employed. Finally, a new law was adopted in 1963, under which every citizen was entitled to receive an allowance, not only for a third or more than the third child, but also for the first and second child.

7. A law on *relatives*. In 1901, the government adopted a law that entitled widows and orphans a benefit. However, this law only covered employees, not the self-employed people. In 1948, the government started preparations to improve legislation in this respect. Finally, a new law was adopted covering all widows and orphans. Those widows, who can be expected to have a job and earn a living themselves, were excluded from the arrangement. The level of the benefit was linked with the average income level, so as to keep the incomes of these people in line with the incomes of the rest of the population.

8. A law on *social assistance*. In 1912, the so-called Poor Law was adopted. It functioned as a social safety-net. After the Second World War, however, an increasing number of people opted for a restructuring of the law, to adjust to modern ideas about the role of the government in social affairs. Over time a shift had taken place from "care of the poor" as a matter of charity, primarily executed by the church and other private institutions to "care of the poor" as a matter of solidarity, primarily executed by the government. In addition, a poor law is a service of last resort for those who are not supported by other social services, while unable to earn their own living. In 1963, a new law was adopted, entitling all citizens to receive social assistance in case other services are not sufficient for a decent living. The local government was the executor and kept its discretionary power to decide upon what level of benefit had to be considered as necessary and decent. In 1971, temporary legislation set a maximum on the level of the social assistance benefit. In 1974, one nationwide norm for the benefit level was set.

These arrangements are the important building blocks of the Dutch welfare regime as it was constructed after the Second World War. They show an evolution in political philosophy. Under the pressure of wars and depressions the government was increasingly considered to be the societal institution primarily responsible for the achievement and maintenance of fair and harmonious social relationships. The building of a generous welfare system is the material expression of the idea of solidarity. Until the sixties, the confessional parties were quite reluctant to accept the solidarity view. They stressed individual responsibility and the social duties of private persons to support the poor via charity. But during the sixties they changed their political and philosophical ideas, moving towards those of the Social Democrats.[1] In parliament they voted in favor of an important increase in coverage of the various social arrangements.

As long as the use of the social welfare system is limited, generosity is cheap. But when in the seventies an increasing number of people became inactive and entitled to receive a benefit, a high price had to be paid for the generosity of the politicians during the sixties.

The system of collective bargaining. During the first half of the twentieth century Dutch unions succeeded in their attempts to introduce a system of collective bargaining with respect to the determination of wages. In 1907, a law was adopted giving the right to unions to bargain on behalf of their members about their labor conditions. In 1927, a law was adopted extending the negotiation results of a majority of the employees in a firm to all workers of the firm. Finally, in 1937, a law was adopted extending or nullifying the negotiation results reached by a majority of the employers in a particular industry to all employers and employees of that particular industry. So a large majority of the Dutch work force was covered by the system of collective bargaining. After the Second World War, the government decided to unilaterally determine wages and salaries because of the extraordinary circumstances. In 1950, the government institutionalized regular tripartite consultations about wages and other important social issues. This made the employers' organizations and unions co-responsible for the social economic policies of the government. During the period 1950-1953 the wage rule that was set meant an increase in the nominal wage equal to the rate of inflation. The wage rule that determined macro-wage increases in the period 1953-1959 meant a real wage increase equal to the rise in the labor productivity of the private sector. In the period 1959-1963 tripartite consultation led to differentiation in the real wage increases, depending on the industrial productivity increase. The next period can best be described as a period of anarchy; employers' organizations as well as unions refused to accept government intervention in the process of wage determination.

While the government was expected to abstain from interference with respect to the content of the labor contracts, the social partners still expected the government to extend the validity of the contracts to nonmembers of the employers' organizations and unions. In 1970, a new Law on Wages was adopted that institutionalized more or less the conditions under which government interference in wage determination was socially acceptable. Political and social considerations of responsible politicians made it impossible to implement sound Keynesian policies and supplementary wage policies. Only because the global economy as a whole was in a long-term upswing, Dutch economic growth still continued. The solvency of the Dutch private sector, however, showed a structural decline, which appeared disastrous when there was a downturn in the global economy.

The difference between micro and macro insurance. When OPEC quadrupled the oil price in 1973 many Western countries had trouble. Most of them reacted in a Keynesian way: no expenditure cuts, while accepting an increase in a governmental budget deficit. International financial institutions considered themselves responsible for the organization of proper investment of all the additional oil dollars that went to the OPEC countries. But Keynesian policy can only be effective if price structures are reflecting supply and demand relations on free markets in equilibrium. For the Netherlands these conditions were not met. Labor had become too costly and structural increases of social expenditures were financed by temporary increases in gas revenues. Thus, after a number of years the Dutch economy was in serious trouble; it developed what came to be called the "Dutch disease."By the end of the seventies, the unemployment rate started to rise and, unavoidably linked to that, the number of social benefit recipients rose sharply. Other European countries showed, although less pronounced, more or less the same development. Now the generosity of the welfare system as it was constructed in the fifties, sixties and seventies meant a huge increase in social expenditures and premiums. This process aggravated the problem via ongoing increases in the costs of labor.

What would have happened if all Western governments had implemented proper Keynesian policies, that is, a consistent set of measures in the field of monetary, budgetary, and macro-wage policies? If we could have avoided a structural rise in unemployment, we would have avoided a massive use of social benefits. In that case the welfare state could have functioned in the way it was meant to. But proper policies were implemented and the massive use of the welfare system made clear that the system was not a robust one. If the micro foundations of the economy are unsound because of inappropriate macro-social and economic policies, then not only the welfare system, but also the economic system as a whole is in trouble.

A principal problem is the difference in character between micro and macro insurance. An example of a micro insurance is an insurance against the negative financial effects of a robbery. In most cases the macro crime rate is constant or it changes quite slowly over time. This means that the insurance-premium is a constant or changes quite slowly over time. But in case of *macro insurance* the situation is quite different. Here the use is close to zero over a particular period of time; at the time a sudden sharp increase in the use of the insurance takes place. The funds are not sufficient to pay the benefits and the premium rate must be adjusted significantly. If the organization of premium payers is able to evade (partly) the payment of the increase, the price of labor will increase, affecting employment negatively. This creates a situation in which a decreasing number of people are able to maintain their jobs, against a decreasing wage rate, while the system has to finance an increasing number of benefit recipients. To stop these processes investors must discover indications of improvement in the financial health of the private sector. Practically, such a system can only return to a healthy situation if there are positive external forces.

There is another characteristic problem with social insurance and that is its *solidarity*. The element of solidarity in the system implies that all workers are obliged to pay a premium level which is independent of their personal risk. If workers perceive a risk that is much lower than is reflected by the premium they have to pay, these individuals start thinking about strategies to avoid the payment of these high premiums.

A comparison between obligatory car insurance and obligatory social insurance may clarify the problem. The first insurance is of a micro character and the premium varies with the number of times the insurance is used by the premium payer. The obligatory character stems from the fact that nearly nobody is able to pay the costs in case of very serious damage. Moreover, every reasonable person admits that he bears the risk of causing serious damage. This makes obligatory car insurance with a "no claim discount" acceptable for a homo oeconomicus. The case of an obligatory social insurance with premium rates reflecting solidarity is a different affair. Here many premium payers, workers as well as employers, might make a strict economic calculation showing that the premiums are quite high given their individual risk pattern. This creates a strong incentive to search for strategies that are more beneficial.

An increasingly popular strategy appeared in the form of tax evasion. In general, there are several ways to avoid regular payment of social premiums.

1. Individual workers move (partly) to the *informal sector*; they spend their time as volunteers or are paid in-kind.
2. Individual workers move (partly) to the *black sector*; they or their employers do not pay taxes and social premiums over their income anymore.
3. Individual workers move (partly) to the *foreign sector*, which means that they go abroad.
4. Workers become members of a union and *demand higher gross wages* to be compensated for the income loss resulting from increases in the premium rate.

All these strategies generate a beggar-thy-neighbor policy. The more successful some workers, the heavier the tax burden for the other workers. Macroeconomically this is not a solution to the problem; it only aggravates it. Only sound macro policies can solve problems created by a macro insurance system with a significant solidarity element in it. The increasing recognition of the misinterpretations and inappropriate policy reactions functioned as a necessary positive external force breaking the vicious circle of increasing unemployment and tax rates. In the Netherlands such an external force was the political recognition that in the construction of the welfare system economic considerations were not taken very seriously. Social democratic considerations of fairness dominated the construction of welfare policies, ignoring questions about microeconomic reactions of persons who became entitled to receive a benefit. Another reason why the system crashed, namely the refusal of politicians to ask the population to pay the welfare bill, has never been recognized as a major factor explaining why the Dutch economy was infected by such a serious disease.

The Dutch government, unions and employers' organizations agreed to a social contract in which they developed a new and more consistent framework of responsibilities and strategies. This agreement has become known as the so-called Wassenaar Akkoord (1982).

Shifting Axis and Benefit Delivery

Economizing and Restructuring the System

Introduction. The main elements of the Wassenaar Akkoord were as follows:

1. The government agreed not to use its legal instruments to affect the wage rate directly. Only under very special circumstances would intervention be acceptable. A main indicator for these "very special circumstances" was the so-called inactivity ratio, that is, the number of inactive people entitled to receive a benefit divided by the number of active, that is, working people; this ratio had to be higher than 87 percent to justify intervention;
2. The social partners accepted a long-term policy of economizing the welfare system, which had to lead to a significant reduction in social expenditures;
3. The employers' organizations accepted co-responsibility for the macro employment level; active participation in labor market policies was promised, including measures such as early retirement and general labor time reduction; and
4. The unions accepted cooperation with a long-term policy of wage restraint.

In this section we first discuss the measures taken by the government to economize the welfare system. The attempts to re-organize the system are then discussed. Next, measures taken by the government to link social policy to labor market policy are examined. Finally, we show some figures that illustrate the changes in social and economic development over the period 1982-2000. Of course, the changes cannot be attributed to the effects of the Wassenaar Akkoord only. The recovery of the global economy, especially that of the Western economies, had a significant effect on Dutch performance. When we compare, however, the seventies, characterized as the "Dutch disease," with the performance at the end of the nineties, characterized as the "Dutch miracle," the difference definitely involves the Wassenaar Akkoord and the resulting social and economic policies.

Economizing the welfare system. Important changes in policymaking always take a long period of time. After years of preparation, especially by the Ministry of Social Affairs and Employment, the first pieces of new legislation were implemented in 1986. In the first place, benefit rates were cut to reduce expenditures per recipient and the number of recipients, by making it less attractive for the homo oeconomicus—benefit recipient to remain on the payroll of society. In the second place, the government tried to reduce the number of potential recipients by a more effective targeting policy. The conditions under which people have the right to receive a benefit were significantly narrowed. The following changes were among the most important ones.

1. *Illness.* With respect to the illness benefits:

   a. A decrease of the benefit rate from 80 percent to 70 percent of the earnings, in 1985;
   b. The implementation of the rule that in the first six weeks the employee only gets paid the official minimum wage, in 1987; and
   c. The rule that the employer (that is, the firm, not the industry anymore) has to pay the benefit during the first six weeks, in 1992.

Because many industrial unions were successful in their attempts to negotiate a supplement on top of the official sickness benefit, the effectiveness of official policy was significantly reduced. In reaction to this policy the government urged the social partners to get the illness rates down. A new Law on Illness (1996) placed complete responsibility for the financial position of ill workers on the individual employers.

2. *Disability.* With respect to the disability benefit:

   a. In 1987, benefit rates were decreased to 70 percent of last earned income, for a fully disabled worker;
   b. In 1993, a law was adopted aimed to reduce the appeal of disability by medically re-examining all the benefit recipients younger than 50 years; and
   c. In 1992, a law was adopted that introduced a so-called bonus-malus system; employers who would hire a disability benefit recipient would get a subsidy. Employers who would fire a person into a disability fund would pay a penalty.

The changes led to a benefit reduction for about 60 percent of the medically re-examined persons and 10 percent of the 60 percent were successful in finding a job.

3. *Unemployment.* With respect to the unemployment benefit:

   a. In 1985, the benefit rate was reduced to 70 percent of last earned income;
   b. In 1987, a new Law on Unemployment was adopted in which a relationship was created between the duration of employment and the duration of the benefit. In case of an employment contract of more than 60 months the right to a benefit was extended to 3 months. In case of employment longer than 480 months, the extension of the benefit duration was to 54 months; and
   c. In the same act rules were made creating a wider sphere of action for job searching; refusal to take a vacant position became more difficult than before.

4. *Relatives.* With respect to the widows and orphans benefits:

   The Law on Widows and Orphans, the entitlements formulated in the Law of 1959, appeared to be a costly affair; not so much because of economic developments, but more as a result of the high level of the benefit and the absence of any means-testing. So from 1990 to1996 small adjustments were made, especially in the level of the benefit. Then, in 1996, a new law was adopted, the so-called General Relatives Act. The goal was to limit eligibility. There are two structural barriers to entry: The first restriction limits the transfer to widows with children younger than 18 years, and the second restriction limits the transfer to widows who are disabled for more than 45 percent. For people older than 46 years a transitional rule was made, providing benefits until these people become pensioned. At the moment the standard benefit is linked to the net minimum wage.

5. *Social Assistance.* With respect to the social assistance benefits:

   In the beginning of the eighties the number of people on social assistance rose sharply. From 1985 the number shows a slight decrease, until 1994. Then there was a slight increase in the period 1994-1996. The law of 1965 established a benefit level of 70 percent of net minimum wage. The arrangement was means-tested, making it impossible for wealthy people without a job to make use of the system. The basic philosophy behind this law was to be a social service of last resort. The income offered had to be sufficient for a minimum living. The changes brought about in 1996 were induced by a different philosophy. Now the law interprets the service as a temporary income service for people who are on their way back to the labor market. So recipients are constantly put under pressure to search for a job. Only single parents with children younger than five years are entitled to a benefit without having the obligation to search for a job. The discretionary room for local government to have their own anti-poverty policies has been enlarged. Local municipalities are allowed to increase benefits to 20 percent of the national standard, on the basis of tailor-made arrangements for individual recipients.

Restructuring the organization of social security. To understand the organizational structure it is necessary to know which political groups put pressure on the government to intervene in the economy. In the first place, there are socialist-oriented unions and political parties. They aim for a revolutionary or evolutionary reform of the political and economic system. A centrally planned economy under the leadership of a socialist political party should be organized in such a way that social justice could be reached and maintained. Meanwhile, unions had to struggle for improvement of the situation of workers and their families: wages, social transfers, employment, labor time, working conditions, healthcare, and education.

In the second place, there are *confessional* unions and political parties. They aim for a re-organization of society in the direction of a corporatist structure. Corporatism is an organizational philosophy that is based on a functionalist view of society. This means that unions are considered the natural representatives of the workers, whether or not they are members of that particular union. The same holds for employers' organizations and the government, representing the employers and the citizens. The main problems of the economy must be discussed by unions and employers' organizations on the national level. The corporatist term for these two organizations perfectly expresses the supposed interrelationship—social partners. These social partners are supposed to finance the necessary social transfers for workers. The government then, is responsible for the material well-being of those who do not belong to the group of workers. As far as coordination is necessary bi- or tripartite consultations on the national level must create the necessary consensus about the strategy to be followed. The specification of this strategy then, is a task for the social partners.

In the third place, are *conservative* liberals, who were impressed by Bismarck's success in "buying" social stability by organizing a system of social transfers, which kept the social hierarchy within the working-class intact.

These political groups were able to compromise on a growing number of social issues, including the organization of the administration and execution of the social welfare system. Because the organizational compromise contained, and still contains socialist, conservative, and liberal ideas, it is difficult to construct a logically consistent and efficient system.

At the end of the Second World War, the Dutch government decided to take responsibility for the construction of a sophisticated system of social security. Many temporary measures were taken while preparing more lasting legislation. In 1952, a law was adopted arranging the organization of the system. The Ministry of Social Affairs delegated her responsibility to administer the system to a tripartite body, in which unions, employers' organizations, and government were represented (the so-called Social Security Council). This council exercised control over the typical employee insurance, executed by bipartite industry associations, as well as over the social insurance related to all citizens, executed by the Social Insurance Bank. So we can conclude that the social partners dominated the bipartite-organized execution of social security, while the tripartite-organized administration was highly influenced by them. In other words, the corporatist views of the confessionalists were decisive in the construction of the social welfare system.

If a system is organized along strict corporatist lines, it is assumed that the various corporatist associations are exchanging information on their highly interrelated tasks. In practice, communication is far from perfect. Especially relevant is the fact that policymakers and controllers are badly informed about the cost structures that would exist in the case of perfect efficiency. Economists call this phenomenon *"asymmetric information"* and analyze what happens if this asymmetry appears to be persistent. The result is that social services are delivered at monopolistic prices. The Dutch system operated more or less like such a monopolistic structure. All decisions to increase social premiums were easily accepted by the Ministry of Social Affairs. It simply did not dispose of relevant information on the basis of which it could have decided differently, and so with the Parliament.

During the eighties, discontent about execution and control of social services was growing. In reaction to that Parliament decided to organize a Parliamentary Interview, in which a parliamentary commission was entitled to interview important execution and administration officers under oath. The results were shocking. There was hardly any control over many important and costly decisions, especially physicians' decisions to determine the degree of a worker's disability, which were made quite autonomously. Because employers were interested in easy ways to fire "unproductive" people, and workers were more interested in disability benefits than in the lower unemployment benefits, physicians knew that their immediate bosses would not criticize a degree of generosity in their medical judgments.

The Buurmeijer Commission, which conducted the interviews, blamed the social partners in particular, for the unacceptable rise in the costs of the system. In its proposals to restructure the system, the role of the social partners was considerably diminished. In 1994, a new law on the organization of social security was adopted, which was implemented in 1995. The tripartite Social Security Council and the Social Security Bank were replaced by a completely independent organization, the Commission for Control over Social Security (CTSV), responsible for control of the administration and execution of all social insurance. In 1997, the law was reformed. The bipartite industry associations were replaced by an independent organization, the National Institute for Social Security (LISV). The Institute was allowed to outsource the executive tasks to private firms.

Although it is more logical to discuss the advantages and disadvantages of the different structures of organization first, the Dutch seem to like it the other way around. After the introduction of a number of re-organizations the discussion about the efficiency of different organizational structures started. The main issues in these debates concerned the relative efficiency of public versus private provision, of bipartite versus tripartite and of centralized versus decentralized structures. In general, we can say the following about these different forms.

1. *Privatization* is an efficient means if we can expect competition to play an important role and if the good or service to be delivered can be clearly described in terms of quantity and quality. A simple substitution of a public by a private monopoly makes the situation worse. And if quantity and quality of the product is difficult to specify, a market relation will not turn out to be efficient, because of the lack of monitoring devices. Only if the government is able to clearly formulate under which conditions a social insurance, administered by a private insurance company, must function, privatization might work. If the government is not able to guarantee some degree of solidarity, social security is transformed into a private insurance system; in other words, the system is not social anymore.

2. *Corporatist structures* will function efficiently if the three parties involved are democratically organized and are able to reach consensus (internally as well as externally) about the solution to the "solidarity versus individual choice" dilemma. Moreover, the monitoring of such a structure must take place by the "members" of the different corporatist associations. If these people are not committed to function according to the typical rules of a corporatist system, the administrative oligarchy has monopolistic power, which could make the system more expensive. A special problem in case of corporatist structures is the question whether a tripartite or a bipartite (no government!) structure should be preferred. In general, we can say that business internal affairs should be treated bipartitely, while business affairs with significant externalities must be treated tripartitely.

3. *Decentralization* is efficient if the execution of policies requires expertise with respect to problems that differ highly among industries or regions. In that case central administration and monitoring must be supplemented with responsibilities on a lower level of administration. Some discretionary room on lower levels means that the center must formulate rules and allocate budgets in such a way that industries or regions can select among different forms of services, dependent on the characteristics of the local situation.

The Dutch government is constantly making new plans! In November 1999, the Minister of Social Affairs and Employment announced important changes in the organizational design of social welfare. The core of the new proposals is a diminished role for the social partners and a dominant role for the government especially in the administration and delivery of services. The private market is introduced with respect to the re-integration of benefit recipients in the labor market. In the following subsection we will turn to this re-integration issue. In figure 7.1, two organizational structures are presented: one reflecting the current situation and the other presenting the structure according to the governments' latest plan.

The figure shows that the current structure is a mix of private, public and tripartite elements. The organization of social security is separated from the organization of labor market policies. In the latest plan of the cabinet, the role of the social partners is reduced to advising governmental agencies. The government takes full responsibility for the efficiency of social security and as we will also see in the next subsection, it holds itself fully responsible for an efficient coordination of social and labor market policies.

Social Activation and Work-Oriented Policies

New Active Labor Market Policies

To get a sober regime of social security and welfare it is not enough to lower benefits and to limit eligibility to those who really need the support from society. In many cases a return to the labor market must be considered. It is obvious that the distinction between those who can and those who cannot

Figure 7.1
Organizational Structure of Social Security

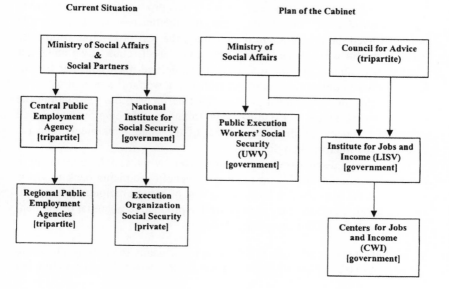

return is very difficult to make. In some cases it is clear that it is possible: ill people, short-term unemployed, some early retired, some people with a small handicap or lack of specific skills. In other cases it is clear that a return is impossible: people with a severe handicap, very old people. In many cases, however, it may be possible to get people back to work, but it takes a good deal of time and scarce resources to achieve this goal.

One of the dilemmas is the trade-off between reducing poverty among the unemployed on the one hand, and the necessary financial rewards of returning to work, on the other. Social considerations lead to the conclusion that the level of benefits must make it possible for recipients to participate fully in our society. Economic considerations, however, lead to the conclusion that all persons, including benefit recipients, are utility maximizers and will only accept a job if the (financial) rewards are significantly higher than unemployment benefits.[2]

Another problem that plays an important role is the behavior of the employers. Employers perceive their situation within the context of a competitive market. This implies that there is no financial room for paying attention to social considerations. If a firm has a vacancy, the most productive applicant must be hired. It is difficult to predict the productivity of an applicant, particularly if the applicant is unknown to the employer as well as to people in the labor market. This makes it difficult for an outsider to get a job, compared to insiders.

There is a third dilemma. Suppose there is an economic downswing. Firing less productive workers may be a solution to the financial problems of a particular firm, but only holds under the ceteris paribus clause. If all firms have the same considerations and are firing less productive people, then via the payment of social benefits and premiums, the business sector as a whole has not solved the problem. On the contrary, the less productive people receive a benefit in exchange for no productivity at all. Thus, if we make our cost/benefit calculations for society as a whole, we must consider the dilemma between micro and macro rationality in a welfare state context.

In conclusion, government policies must be focused on: (1) funding the optimal benefit levels, (2) finding ways to ensure that employers are well informed about the productive potential of the benefit recipients, and (3) resolving the micro-macro dilemma.

Now we will discuss several measures taken by the Dutch government in an attempt to get a significant number of benefit recipients back to work. Most measures are aimed at limiting the cost of benefit recipient-job searchers. Some other measures try to improve the productive potential of the benefit recipients as perceived by the employer.

1. In 1993, the cabinet made the decision to medically re-examine all recipients of disability benefits. The expected effect was a decrease in number

of disabled persons as well as a decrease in the degree of disability of the recipients. This unavoidably led to an increase of the number of recipients of unemployment and of social assistance benefits. To decrease these numbers, other measures were planned.

2. In 1993, a series of measures were implemented to create new job opportunities for low-skilled people. (At least one-third of benefit recipients do not have more than a basic school level education.) These measures included:

   - To stimulate employers to hire more low-skilled people, the government increased the *Special Reduction* in taxes for people who earn a wage that is lower than 115 percent of the minimum wage. For workers who are unemployed for longer than one year and are going to earn a wage that is lower than 130 percent of the minimum wage, there is a Supplementary Reduction. In total, the reduction is maximally f 8,160, which is about 23 percent of the wage.
   - To stimulate benefit recipients to accept a job, two laws were adopted, the Law on the Use of Job Seekers and the Law on the (Re)-integration of Handicapped People. These laws were meant to create jobs both in the private and in the public sector. Private employers are subsidized if they create *special* jobs that do not compete with regular jobs. Most special jobs are found in the public sector however. In 1994, the government asked the local municipalities to make employment plans for, in total, 40,000 jobs in the period 1994-1998. Later, social benefit budgets were re-allocated to the local governments for another 20,000 jobs. In 1998, the government decided to make another increase of 10,000 jobs in the level of created employment. Some of the jobs are so-called *work-experience* jobs. These are temporary, at least for the worker who fulfils the job. The employer receives a subsidy from the local government in these cases.
   - The Law on Social Employment Creation was renewed at the beginning of 1998. Until then "social employment" meant that people worked in special firms or agencies. The renewed law makes it possible to subsidize jobs that are adjusted to the possibilities of the handicapped worker anywhere (so-called *adjusted jobs*), for both physically and mentally handicapped people. Besides adjusted jobs, there is also the possibility of a *guided job*, especially for those who lack work experience.
   - Moreover, employers can get subsidies if they are willing to create jobs on an experimental basis (so-called *experimental jobs*). These jobs are provided to long-term unemployed social assistance benefit recipients for two years.

3. The organizational design of labor market policies was subject to heavy political debates over the last decade. In 1990, a new structure was intro-

duced on a tripartite basis. A central organization was responsible for administration and control. Active labor market policies were executed on the regional level. The connection between job search and the execution of the benefit transfers was a weak point in the structure. In 1997, new plans were recommended. Then in November 1999 the cabinet announced a totally new design, in which the role of the social partners was significantly reduced. In figure 7.2 the current situation is compared with the latest plan. A well-functioning coordination between social security, social assistance and job search support means that *every person between 15 and 65 years old who is willing to work will fall under the responsibility of a particular organization.* This responsibility involves an obligation to co-search for a job, while in the meantime delivering a benefit, if the person involved is entitled to it. So if a worker is taken ill, the employer is responsible for the payment of an illness benefit. If a worker becomes unemployed, an employer remains responsible for him for a particular period of time during which the employer must help in a job search and continue to pay wages (at the moment this is 13 weeks, but there are proposals to make it 26 weeks). Then a person becomes unemployed and falls under the responsibility of the organization that must pay him the benefit to which he is entitled. As long as the person is unemployed and entitled to the benefit, this organization is co-responsible for job-search activities. If these organizations do not have the expertise, then they must buy job-searching services on the market. This means that getting a benefit is, in most cases at least, considered a temporary affair. In this institutional design it is clear who is co-responsible for the job search at every stage in the process. The organizations in charge of particular activities must get budgets that are allocated in such a way that the budget system has a consistent set of incentives for the organizations to strive for the achievement of the official goals as efficiently as possible. To discover what constitutes efficient budgets, markets must be introduced in all cases where performance can easily be measured and the scale of production does not lead to a monopoly. As already noted, this law is in preparation, and subject to hot debates in periodicals, newspapers, and television programs.

At the moment the most important reason why it takes so much time to get new policies adopted and implemented is the political disagreement about the organization of the necessary coordination. The old contradiction between classical liberals and social democrats plays a role here. The Dutch cabinet is a coalition of a classical liberal party (VVD), a smaller continental liberal party (D66), and a social democratic party (PVDA).[3] The VVD has an ideological bias towards more privatization and market coordination. The PVDA has an ideological bias towards organizational cooperation. And D66 is too weak to create consensus or to formulate a consistent compromise.

Figure 7.2
Integration of Welfare and Job Search

Current Situation

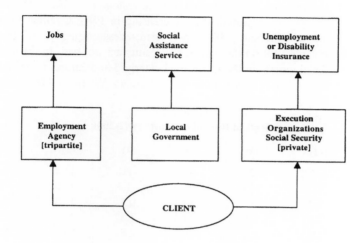

Latest Plan of the Government

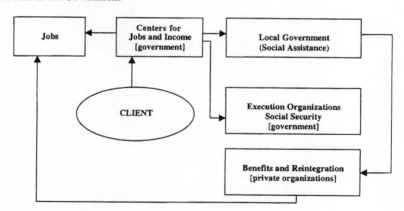

Emerging Borders of the Welfare State

Problems in the Near Future

Recovery in the period 1982-2000. Table 7.2 illustrates a number of variables that reflect Dutch economic and social performance from 1982 to 2000.

Two principal forces are responsible for developments over this period: On one hand, the recovery of the global economy in the nineties and, on the other, the significant policy changes with respect to government budget, labor market and the social security and welfare system. In the first column we see that Dutch economic growth starts increasing in 1984. Cyclical fluctuations show that in 1987 and 1993 a short-term recession pushed the growth figures downwards. But on the whole, the results are not bad. In the second column the development in the wage level clearly demonstrates the effect of the wage restraint policy of the three social partners. When we take columns

Table 7.2
Effects of the Policy Shift: 1982-2000

Time	(1)	(2)	(3)	(4)	(5)	(6)
1982	-1.2	-2.2	95.1	-2.1	11.4	46.7
1983	1.7	-3.6	92.9	-1.3	12.0	47.4
1984	3.3	-1.1	89.3	0.5	11.8	45.8
1985	3.0	1.5	88.4	1.3	10.6	45.6
1986	2.8	2.4	86.0	2.5	9.9	46.1
1987	1.4	1.5	86.7	1.6	9.6	48.5
1988	2.6	1.1	84.2	2.3	9.1	48.7
1989	4.7	2.1	81.0	1.8	8.3	45.6
1990	4.1	2.4	80.7	3.0	7.5	45.7
1991	2.3	0.2	82.4	2.6	7.0	47.5
1992	2.0	0.5	84.5	1.6	5.6	46.5
1993	0.8	0.6	86.5	0.7	6.2	46.8
1994	3.4	-0.5	84.0	-0.1	6.8	44.8
1995	2.3	-0.3	81.8	2.2	6.9	43.5
1996	3.0	0.8	82.8	2.4	6.3	40.5
1997*	3.8	0.7	81.5	2.8	5.2	41.5
1998*	3.7	0.9	81.0	2.5	4.0	41.0
1999	3.6	1.1	82.8	2.5	3.1	40.6
2000	4.0*	0.8*	82.8*	2.3*	2.3*	42.0*

(1)	GDP, in percentage change;
(2)	Real wages, in percentage change;
(3)	Labor share as a percentage of total income;
(4)	Employment in percentage change;
(5)	Unemployment rate, standardized; and
(6)	Taxes and social premium payments in percentage of GDP;
*	Estimate

Source: CTSV (1992), CEP (1996), CTSV (1996), MEV (1996), OECD (1996); SOZAWE (2000), CEP (2000).

one and two together the implication is a significant growth in the profitability of the business sector. The size of this growth depends on the growth in (labor) productivity. Column three shows the development in the labor share, which is equal to 100 percent, minus the capital income share. The fourth column shows a recovery in the employment level. From a yearly decrease at the end of the seventies and in the beginning of the eighties, the trend turns to positive figures during the eighties and nineties. Column five demonstrates that the problem of unemployment has become less severe. The last two columns show that the measures taken in the area of social security and welfare had significant effects on the level of social expenditures and premiums. The social welfare system has become much less costly now.

Important revisions took place in 1995, making these time series less fitted for detailed econometric research.

In the next series of subsections we will deal with a number of problems that must be faced by the Dutch. The developments in the demographic burden and the increased number of immigrants/asylum seekers, in particular, are important in this respect.

Demographic Developments. Like most Western countries the Dutch population is getting older on average. When we take the birth-rate and the death-rate together, it is quite easy to predict that the demographic burden is increasing. This burden is defined as the ratio reflecting the number of people of 14 years or younger plus the number of people 65 years or older, divided by the number of people between 14 and 65 years. In table 7.3 we have presented some figures, including two extrapolations.

Table 7.3
Demographic Burden

Year	1997	1998	1999	2000	2010
Burden	60.6	60.8	61.0	61.2	63.2

Source: CPB, 1999

Three factors have an important effect on the demographic development[4]. Firstly, the fertility rate affects the number of people of an age in the range 0-14. The share of this group in the population taken as a whole has structurally declined over the last century. In 1900, this share was 34.7 percent, while in 1991 it had declined to 18.2 percent. The period 1940-1960 appears to be an exception. Especially after World War II, there was a baby boom. This means that in 2010 the first baby-boomers become pensioners. Secondly, the *life expectancy rate* is an important factor. The longer people live, given a pension age, the larger the number of pensioners will grow. The share of people older than 65 was 6 percent in 1900. But in 1991, the share increased to 12.9 percent. In the third place, *immigration* might affect the demographic composition. In general, we can say that if the average demographic burden of the incoming people is lower than the average of the country, immigrants are not a problem, but a solution to this demographic problem. In the nineties the number of yearly immigrants increased. In 1999, the Dutch population grew by 6.4 percent, of which 2.7 percent can be attributed to immigration.

The conclusion is that a decreasing number of people (in terms of age at least) able to earn a living must feed an increasing number of people (in terms of age again) expected not to be able to earn a living.

When we focus on the number of pensioners, we see a rise indeed; a rise that will undoubtedly continue in the near future. Because the Dutch developed an early-retirement policy, which was meant to be an anti-unemployment policy, the rise in pensioners became even greater than could be expected on the basis of demographic considerations alone. In table 7.4 we present figures about the development of the number of pensioners of 65 and the number of early retired.

Table 7.4
Pensioners and Early Retired: 1990-2002

	1990	1995	1996	1997	1998	1999	2000	2001	2002
(1)	1956	2079	2104	2127	2150	2172	2194	2217	2240
(2)	39	51	51	52	53	53	53	53	53

(1) number of State Pensioners (x 1.000 expected in benefit years)
(2) number of Early Retired   (x 1.000 expected in benefit years)

Source: Ministry of Social Affairs and Employment, Sociale Nota 2000, The Hague, 1999.

Anticipating financial problems in the future, the government decided to create a state pension fund, to which the government would contribute each year. The savings in this fund would be used for the payment of state pensions when these expenditures increased significantly. The fund is subject to heavy political debates. It is difficult to establish a yearly sum of money that must be paid into the fund. The amount must set the public's mind at ease. Economically speaking, there is no need for such a fund. Lowering governmental debts, increasing profitable public investment or lowering the tax rate on private investments are possible measures to make it easier for the next generation to finance increasing pension expenditures. But after 2010, when the baby boomers cause pension expenditures to rise, it would be politically more acceptable to refer to the special state pension fund for payment. Increasing taxes because of the growing number of pensioners might create unnecessary resentments among younger people.

Immigration. With respect to immigration the Netherlands follows more or less the EU policy: immigration is not allowed, unless particular conditions are fulfilled. If a foreigner can prove that an employer wants to hire him and this employer can prove that he is unable to find that type of worker within the EU, the foreigner is allowed to immigrate to that particular EU country. Family reunification is another reason for officials to allow immigration. Once accepted, foreigners are entitled to use all public services in the same way as Dutch citizens. In table 7.5 we have presented figures on the number of non-national citizens who are in the Netherlands.

Table 7.5
Stocks of Non-National Citizens (*1000)

1986	1987	1988	1989	1990	1991	1992	1993	1994	1995
553	568	592	624	642	693	733	758	780	757

Source: Statistics in Focus: Population and Social Conditions: Migration Statistics, Ecostat, 1996.

When we talk about immigration we must include figures about the number of asylum seekers that get permission to stay and the number of illegal immigrants. The number of asylum seekers has increased significantly during the nineties. One of the reasons is the relative generosity of Dutch asylum policy. The annual number of asylum seekers entering the Netherlands multiplied from 5,000 in 1985 to almost 50,000 in 1998.

The number of illegal immigrants is, by nature, difficult to measure. Many indications suggest that the group of illegal people is large and growing.

Europeanization and globalization of the Dutch economy. The prior subsections explained the problems that affect Dutch social and economic performance significantly. These were:

1. The number of pensioners relative to the size of the working population will continue to grow. The postwar baby-boom will be pensioned from 2010 on; the peak will be reached at 2035.
2. Immigration flows will grow, if not legally, then illegally. Depending on the age structure and on the level of health and skills, this immigration flow is a problem or a solution to the problem as formulated under (1).
3. The level of the inactivity ratio of the Dutch economy remains high, notwithstanding the significant decline during the last decade (1990: 82.1; 2000: 66, CEP, 2000). Besides the already mentioned number of pensioners, the number of disability benefit recipients remains unacceptably high.

In tackling these problems it is important for the Dutch to recognize that their economy is increasingly dependent on developments in the EU area and in the world as a whole. The EU integration implies an increasing competition between the EU economies, which makes it more difficult for one country to deviate from other countries, also with respect to the size of the social welfare system. Moreover, the globalization of the economies makes it difficult for EU economies to deviate from other economies in the global economy.

In the following section we will deal with the question of the sustainability of the welfare state. Here we will formulate more precisely under which conditions the paradigm of the welfare state as it was developed in the 1950s can be maintained during the first decade of the twenty-first century.

Do We Need a Paradigm Shift?

Introduction. In earlier sections we saw that West European societies constructed their social welfare systems in a period that was characterized by long-term economic growth. Production, employment, and wages were constantly growing; and so was the level of tax and premium receipts. But the number of benefit recipients was not growing as fast. Hence, the future of the welfare state seemed bright. But in the seventies this long-term growth turned into a long-term economic downswing. The subsequent growth of the number of unemployed had a strong and positive effect on the level of social expenditures. Politicians were unable to stop this process without any structural reform of the social welfare system. In 1982, the three parties involved in the social economic policy process agreed upon the conditions under which structural reforms in the social system were acceptable. After two decades of policy reform and under the influence of a recovery of the global economy, Dutch performance significantly improved. However, given the problems mentioned in the previous section, we can ask ourselves whether the welfare state, as we knew in 2000, is sustainable. If not, then we have to think about ongoing structural reforms.

One important indicator of the price of a decent welfare state is the level of the collective burden. We must ask ourselves what the threats of a relatively high collective burden mean. As seen earlier, we can distinguish between several strategic options individuals and organizations have in this respect. In the first place, there is the possibility of substitution of *informal* for formal activities, as in barter exchange or volunteer activities. In the second place, there is the possibility of substitution of *black* sector activities for normal market activities. It goes without saying that it is illegal not to pay taxes and premiums in cases of particular productive activities. The same holds for receiving benefits while one is not eligible for them. In the third place, workers can substitute *leisure* for work. This kind of substitution takes place if the net wage is considered insufficient to compensate for the disutilities derived from the effort of working. In the fourth place, labor as well as capital services can be *exported*. If the collective burden is higher than in neighboring countries, labor emigration as well as border commuting might be profitable. In general, we can say that more informal activities and more leisure are not bad for society. The growth of a black sector, however, is definitely an unwelcome situation. Migration is intrinsically neutral; whether it turns out to be a problem or a solution to problems depends on the specific conditions of the flow of people. We deal with these two problems in more detail below.

The black sector. The size of the black sector and its elasticity with respect to social economic developments is a crucial restriction to further growth of the social welfare system. A welfare state necessarily implies a relatively large number of people who are "consuming, while not producing." Economic logic then, leads to the conclusion that there must be a group of people being prepared to "produce, while not consuming." If levying taxes and social premiums to pay this transfer leads to large-scale evasion, the solidarity transfer will not be realized. If many people are consuming without producing while not being eligible to receive a social transfer, the same process of undermining the welfare state takes place; the collective burden will reach prohibitive levels. Two possible policies are imaginable in this case. First, a more sober and efficient social welfare system would lead to a lower collective burden, making tax evasion less profitable. Secondly, more monitoring and penalizing misuse of the system would make illegal tax evasion less attractive. These options complement each other; it is not necessary to choose between the two.

With respect to size, Dutch empirical research leads to an estimation of the black sector activities being about 1 to 3 percent of GDP.[5] Research conducted by the EU Commission, however, leads to an estimation of a Dutch black sector of 5 to 14 percent, with an EU average of 7 to 19 percent of GDP. In terms of the number of persons involved in black sector activities, different research projects all indicate about one-third of the workers or social assistance benefit recipients who work are involved in fraud. Another remarkable finding is the fact that fraud is positively correlated with the level of skills and income! Thus, the black sector in the Netherlands is not an area where the poor try to improve their material well-being. It is an arena where the better-off fight their status battles.

While the Dutch have made their social welfare system more sober, it appears to be very difficult to improve monitoring and control. People are affected by a lack of discipline, as are the controllers who must be recruited from the same set of people! We will return to the issue of discipline in the last section.

Migration in a global economy. The Dutch economy becomes increasingly integrated with the EU economy at large. This means that a relatively high collective burden might lead to an average labor cost level that is not competitive with the levels in other EU economies. Firms might "migrate" to other areas in the EU. If national wage policies are not successful in moderating wage developments, then net wage levels might not be competitive anymore in the EU labor market. The talented and productive workers might search for jobs in other parts of the EU. A significant counter-force might be the value productive people attach to a progressive social climate that is created by maintaining a decent social system. If this counter-force is weak, it could be wise to accept larger differences in income. Productive people must be rewarded according to their productivity to keep them within Dutch borders. Europeanization and globalization makes egalitarian ideas more costly. Such recognition has the advantage that another ideal, namely the realization of a decent social minimum, could be maintained. Another threat in the case of a relatively extensive social welfare system is its attractiveness for people with lower productivity. If some immigrants appear to be productive but they are allowed to take their whole family with them, a number of low-productive people might come in, who are allowed to use the social system. Even if the foreigners have their family in their country of origin, some benefits, such as family allowance, can now be used.

Intra-EU differences are relatively small, compared with many economies outside the EU. There are several forces at work that result in intra-EU differences being relatively small. In the first place, national economies can be imagined as firms that compete with each other on free markets. The *economic force of competition* leads to higher prices and lower sales for those economies that have a relatively high tax burden. If a decline in sales leads to lower levels of production and employment, resulting in continuing increases in tax rates, these economies are in an ongoing process of decline. In the second place, national economies can be imagined as social groups who rival each other in the marketplace. According to basic sociology, intra-group relationships are characterized by solidarity. Inter-group relationships, however, are also characterized by rivalry. Imitation of one group by another group is a very common rivaling strategy. In our case, different national groups of workers imitate each other with respect to wages and social transfers. While price competition leads to a convergence of wage and social benefit levels in a downward direction, will *social processes of rivalry by imitation* lead to convergence in wage and social benefit levels in an upward direction? In the third place, national economies can be interpreted as prestigious goods or assets controlled by politicians. To improve their control they might coordinate their policies with those of other groups of "controllers," to make their environment more predictable. It is the task of politicians to stabilize developments that are the result of the economic and social processes just described.

When considering the problem of the competitiveness of the EU economy in relation to other areas in the world, the same mechanisms play a role.

Competition on goods and labor markets lead to a downward process of convergence of social welfare systems. Imitation leads to an upward process of convergence. The developments that are the result of these two forces will be stabilized by political coordination on a global level.

Some reflections. During the global economic downswing of the seventies and eighties, the generous and extensive welfare states came into trouble. The Dutch succeeded in creating consensus between unions, employers' organizations and government (1982). The government would not interfere with the process of wage formation. The employers would cooperate in a series of employment policy measures and the unions would accept a moderate wage development and structural reform of the social welfare system. In 2001, the economy was flourishing, while the essence of the welfare state was still intact. However, the *inactivity ratio* was still high. Moreover, the *black sector* appeared to be a profitable business, although it is impossible to get a reliable picture of the magnitude of this problem. Looking at the development in the *age structure* we can predict a significant increase in the number of pensioners in the future. A growing problem in the EU area, including the Netherlands, is the growth of *(illegal)* immigration. The relative attractiveness of the EU area in social and economic respects makes it profitable for people from the former colonies to look for a decent living in the country of their former colonizers. A last element that plays an important role is the *globalization* of the economy. This makes it increasingly urgent for the EU economies to keep an eye on their competitiveness. Competition on global goods and labor markets makes it impossible to deviate greatly in terms of social expenditures. To a certain extent, differences in social welfare systems might reflect cultural differences. But if productive individuals do not appreciate the social policy of their country and they emigrate, and if the relatively unproductive people appreciate the social policy in a particular EU country very much and immigrate into the EU area, these processes make a sophisticated EU welfare state impossible. Figure 7.3 illustrates a national labor market (which is called the working room) in the context of a welfare state as a small open system.

There are many positions possible, besides having a regular job in exchange for a (market-clearing) wage. Every policy measure has its effects on "prices" and "quantities" of the different services that are distinguished in the figure. The positions that are costly for the state as a whole are shaded. This makes it immediately clear that there are lines in terms of inactivity ratios we dare not cross.

The Dutch experience with several decades of tinkering leads us to the following conclusions. In the first place, the attempts to create a more sober and efficient social welfare system must go on. Social benefits of non-low income earners can only temporarily be higher than the social minimum. All benefits must return to the lowest level that is acceptable in our society. Of

Figure 7.3
The System of Employment and Welfare

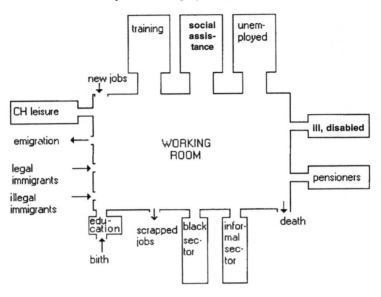

course every person is allowed to contract privately for supplementary insurance. These contracts, however, do not belong to the area of social security.

Secondly, the social minimum must be organized efficiently. Those who are physically and mentally able to work must be obliged to search for a job. If they refuse, penalties must be levied. If people are not able to work, they must be entitled to get a package of goods on the level of the social minimum. The social minimum must not only consist of monetary benefits, but society must offer a set of basic services to all citizens, for instance basic education, physical and mental healthcare and housing. Until now, Dutch society was quite egalitarian. But in a global economy a country does not have the instruments to achieve an egalitarian distribution. The highly talented and lucky people might have a strong inclination to move to the black sector or to other countries. To profit from the talented and lucky people we must be prepared to accept income inequality in the sense of having a small group of rich people, if necessary. The organization of a decent living is already very difficult, threatened as it is by the process of globalization of the labor market.

Third, perhaps the most important issue is that of the lack of discipline of people. Our prosperous and complex society can only function on such a high level if authorities set efficient and fair rules. Efficient control mechanisms are necessary to find out whether those in power are serving the interests of their "customers" as opposed to their own interests. In general, we can distinguish between three mechanisms of control. The first is the *political control* system. If people decide to adopt particular rules, the political control system has the task to guarantee the maintenance of the rules. Also, individual members of the group who were against the adopted policies have to obey the rules that are set. The second is the social control system. In all kinds of groupings some people are expected to fulfill the function of controller. Parents in the family, teachers at schools, reverends in churches, managers in firms all have the important function to guarantee the maintenance of rules. In the third place, we have an *individual control* mechanism. Each person has the task to control himself or herself. If a person sets rules for himself, he or she may experience internal turmoil or internal conflicts about these rules and develop forces that push the person to disobeying the rules set by the person himself/herself.

The three systems of control are highly interrelated. It means that lack of political control can affect the functioning of the social and individual control systems, and thus with the lack of social or individual control affecting the functioning of the other two systems. It appears that the Dutch (and EU?) mechanisms of control face a negative spiral of disobeyance.

*   *   *

The organization of a society must always offer an adequate answer to three primary and interrelated conditions or requirements, namely a minimum level of individual freedom, a minimum level of equality, and a minimum level of control. If not, it appears impossible to achieve a sufficient amount of individual prosperity, social peace and order. Figure 7.4 shows these three conditions in the form of corners of a triangle. As soon as a particular society moves to one specific extreme, the achievement of all three objectives will be threatened in the long term.

In modern societies, characterized by a process of individualization and secularization, there is strong emphasis on problems of individual freedom

Figure 7.4
Basic Characteristics of Society

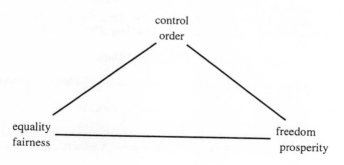

and social equality. This focus has affected mechanisms of control, making our society less effective in the achievement of its goals. Increasing attention should be paid to the consistent behavior of persons and groups. Politicians, bosses, and parents must evaluate their own commitments to see how they can function as the necessary "heroes" to be followed by others. Fraud and corruption at the top of organizations is worse than some theft at the bottom. In this respect we must develop a modern variant of a French saying: "Noblesse oblige."

Notes

1. For the results of empirical research with respect to this shift in ideology, see P .K. Keizer, Inflation as a Political-Economic Phenomenon, Stenfert Kroese, Leiden, 1982.
2. When anti-poverty policies reduce the gap between the financial benefits of unemployment and work, there is less incentive for the poorest to climb up the ladder. The habit of calling this increased difficulty a poverty trap is, however, quite misleading. The poorest are less poor because of the measures taken!
3. The distinction between classical liberal and continental liberal is from Hayek. See F. A. von Hayek, New Studies in Philosophy, Politics, Economics and the History of Ideas (London: Routledge and Kegan, 1978). Chapter 9 gives a detailed sketch of the historical development of liberalism as a political philosophy.
4. The demographic figures used in the text are found in a study by the Dutch scientific Council for Government Policy: WRR, Ouderen voor Ouderen, Demografische ontwikkelingen en beleid, The Hague, 1992.
5. A number of publications in this field (all in Dutch) are summarized and discussed in S. Boelhouwer, The Twilight Zone, A Theoretical and Empirical Approach to the Labour Market, Maastricht, Staatsdrukkerij, 1999.

References

Boelhouwer, S. (1999). *The Twilight Zone, A Theoretical and Empirical Approach to the Labour Market*. Maastricht: Universiteit Maastricht.

Ecostat. (1996). Statistics in Focus: Population and Social Conditions: Migration Statistics.

Hayek, F. A. Von. (1978). *New Studies in Philosophy, Politics, Economics and the History of Ideas*. London: Routledge and Kegan Paul.

Keizer, P. K. (1982). *Inflation as a Political Economic Phenomenon*. Leiden: Stenfert Kroese.

Kuipers, S., and Wilpstra, B. S. (1983). *Production, Growth and Distribution Theory*. Leiden: Stenfert Kroese.

Wetenschappelijke Raad voor het Regeringsbeleid, Ouderen voor Ouderen, Demografische ontwikkelingen en beleid, Den Haag, 1992.

Sources of Statistical Data

Centraal Planbureau (CPB), Central Economisch Plan (CEP). (2000), Staatsdrukkerij; The Hague, 2000.

MEV: MacroEconomische Verkenning, published by the CPB.

CTSV: Centraal Toezicht Sociale Verzekeringen.

OECD: Country Reports of the Organization for Economic Co-operation and Development.

SOZAWE: Ministry of Social Affairs and Employment; Annual Reports: Sociale Nota.

8

Half Way Through the Ford:
The Italian Welfare State at the Start
of the New Century

Valeria Fargion

Context and Adjustment Problems

Over the last two decades, the Italian welfare state went through two quite distinct—if not opposite—phases. Whereas the 1980s witnessed an apparent uncontrollable growth of social expenditure, during the 1990s Italy not only managed to achieve macroeconomic stabilization but also engaged for the first time over the postwar period in a comprehensive overhauling of its social protection system. Although the process is still largely under way and the end results are far from clear, the structural reforms passed from 1992 to 2001 represent a major breakthrough with respect to the institutional and policy legacy of the Italian social protection system. In order to place recent developments in perspective, I shall first provide some basic information on the social policies and politics of the eighties.

Ferrera (1997) suggests "the 1980s were a Janus-like and fairly tormented period for Italy's welfare state: a decade of both continued expansion and creeping (or better chaotic) retrenchment" (p. 236). Let's start by looking at the first side of the coin. Table 8.1 amply documents the steep rise in total public outlays, and particularly the role that income maintenance programs played in the overall growth of public expenditure. The relevant figures cover the period 1980 to 1992; notably, the latter year represents the turning point between the first Republic and the transition period inaugurated by the Amato Cabinet. As one can see, during the period under consideration total public expenditure went up from 42 percent to 55.9 percent of GNP. Total revenues—which were comparatively very low at the beginning of the eighties (32 percent of GNP)—also increased by 13 percent of GNP, bringing Italian fiscal pressure in line with EU averages. However, this was not enough to meet growing public expenditure. Within this context, deficit spending appeared as a palatable short-cut to solve the problem: *Pentapartito* governments did not hesitate in choosing this option, and in fact continued along this path, even when most other European countries moved to retrenchment policies. The effects for the Italian public finances were devastating: considering the budgetary deficit remained at around 10 percent of GDP throughout the decade, public debt skyrocketed from 57 percent to 108 percent of GDP between 1980 and 1992. Not surprisingly, debt service represented the fastest growing item of public expenditure.

Taking a closer look at the social policy component of public spending, one is immediately struck by the considerable rise in social insurance expenditure, which accounts for the largest proportion of the overall increase in social spending. Actually, when referring to income maintenance programs, in the Italian case, one is essentially talking about pensions. By 1980, the latter already represented as much as 80 percent of total social insurance spending, while family allowances, sickness and maternity benefits, work injuries, and unemployment compensation accounted for the remaining 20 percent (Ferrera, 1984). In detail, pension expenditure went up by over 3 percentage points of GDP as a result of both aging of the population and system maturation. The worsening ratio between active and retired workers is among the various factors underpinning this outcome. If we consider, for instance, the Private Employees Fund within INPS—the major Italian social insurance agency—the figures speak for themselves: whereas the number of workers paying into the system remained substantially the same between 1980 and 1990—going from 11.4 to 11.6 million—the number of pensions increased from 8,470,000 to 9,871,000. As a result, the fund, which until the early eighties managed to maintain a balanced budget, started to progressively accumulate deficits, which, in turn, required increasing state transfers. The financial situation was even worse in the case of pension schemes for the public sector. According to Artoni and Zanardi (1997), during the 1980s "...these pensions, in terms of GDP, rose by 84 percent, compared to 20 percent for the Private Employees Fund, and 33 percent for the entire social insurance system. The public sector, furthermore, accounted for the highest pensions: in 1993, 50 percent of the private employees pensions were less than 1,200 thousand lira a month, compared to 20 percent in the public sector" (p. 247). In short, spending increases were far from being evenly distributed across sectors, thereby confirming the inequities and distortions typical of the southern welfare model.

Turning to the other side of the coin, namely "chaotic retrenchment," health policy measures offer a good example. The National Health Service, originally established in 1978, became the object of a considerable amount of

Table 8.1

Public Expenditures and Social Protection, Italy 1980-1994

	1980	1981	1982	1983	1984	1985	1986	1987	1988	1989	1990	1991	1992
(As percentage of GNP)													
Total public expenditures	42,0	46,1	48,3	49,8	49,9	51,2	51,0	50,5	50,6	51,7	53,4	53,9	55,9
Expenditures for social protection	18,3	20,1	20,7	21,8	21,1	21,4	21,5	21,7	21,9	22,2	23,1	23,5	24,5
Social insurance	12,4	13,8	14,3	15,2	14,7	14,7	14,8	14,4	14,4	14,8	15,3	15,4	16,5
P₁blic assistance	1,1	1,3	1,2	1,3	1,4	1,5	1,7	1,7	1,7	1,7	1,7	1,6	1,7
Health	4,8	5,0	5,2	5,3	5,1	5,2	5,1	5,5	5,7	5,7	6,1	6,4	6,4
Budgetary deficit	-8,5	-11,4	-11,3	-10,6	-11,6	-12,6	-11,6	-11,0	10,7	-9,9	-10,9	-10,2	-9,5
Budgetary deficit net of social insurance deficit	-9,0	-10,3	-9,9	-8,6	-9,7	-10,5	-9,6	-9,3	-8,5	-7,6	-8,3	-7,7	-6,3
Ratio of social insurance deficit to current total public expenditures deficit	-9,7	16,8	19,4	30,3	26,9	30,1	30,5	26,7	36,4	42,0	42,7	41,5	43,3
(as percentage of total expenditures)													
Expenditures for social protection	43,5	43,5	42,8	43,7	42,3	41,9	42,2	42,9	43,3	42,9	43,2	43,6	43,9
Social insurance	29,6	30,0	29,6	30,4	29,4	28,8	29,0	28,6	28,7	28,5	28,6	28,6	29,5
Public assistance	2,5	2,7	2,5	2,7	2,7	2,9	3,4	3,4	3,3	3,3	3,2	3,0	3,0
Health	11,4	10,8	10,7	10,6	10,2	10,2	9,9	11,0	11,3	11,0	11,5	11,9	11,4
(as percentage of current expenditure net of debt service)													
Expenditure for social protection	56,4	57,1	57,4	58,4	57,2	57,6	57,6	57,8	58,2	58,4	59,6	60,0	61,2
Social insurance	38,3	39,3	39,7	40,7	39,7	39,6	39,5	38,5	38,6	38,9	39,4	39,4	41,1
Public assistance	3,3	3,6	3,3	3,6	3,7	4,0	4,6	4,5	4,4	4,5	4,4	4,2	4,2
Health	14,8	14,2	14,4	24,2	13,8	14,0	13,6	14,7	15,2	15,0	15,8	16,4	15,9

legislation aimed almost exclusively at cost-containment. The ruling coalition ignored the crucial problem, that is, the indequate functioning of the system that was reflected through opinion polls by the general discontent of the public. Instead of providing guidelines to reach adequate standards in the level of services, political attention focused on the introduction of patient co-payments for medicines, diagnostic tests, and specialist care. This opened the way to an intricate regulation of exemptions on the basis of age, income, and type of illness which was repeatedly changed—if not reversed—depending on the political pressures of the moment. In discussing the relevant measures, Cazzola (1994) reiterates Ferrera's (1984) view by commenting "...it was a chaotic legislation improvised and dictated by the necessity to remain within the national annual budget" (p. 145). Given that healthcare spending was, in fact, in line with other European countries, one can perhaps better appreciate the National government's emphasis on cost-containment measures by considering the power distribution between national and subnational levels of government in this particular area. As management responsibilities were primarily in the hands of regional governments and local health authorities, the passing of restrictive regulations by the National Parliament allowed them to shift the burden, and hopefully the blame, from the central to the local level.

Cost-containment measures were not confined to the health sector. Indeed, the neoliberal wind that was blowing in Thatcher's Britain started also in Italy, and certainly influenced the political debate. But what actually emerged was a particular version of neoliberalism, which soldered the necessity of rigor with Italian policymakers' traditional difficulty in using equitable criteria for the distribution of costs and benefits. We see a good example of this in family allowances, which were a traditional benefit widely distributed but of minimal value. Law no. 79 of 1983 established an increase in the benefit depending on the family's income and size. In following modifications thresholds were introduced, and a rather low-income ceiling was introduced. As a result, not only the middle classes but also the middle-lower class were excluded from the scheme: specifically between 1983 and 1987, the number of employees receiving family allowances dropped from 4,758,000 to 2,882,000. As resources were concentrated on the poorer and larger families, the share of benefits going to the southern part of the country increased from 39 percent to 50 percent of total expenditure. However, to get a complete picture we must also look at the financial implications. Due to the cutting of beneficiaries, which was by no means compensated by the improvement in benefit levels, expenditure rapidly decreased. But since no changes were introduced with respect to the social contributions financing the scheme, in-coming funds remained more or less the same. In 1987, the Istituto Nazionaledella Previdenza Sociale (INPS)—which was responsible for running the scheme—received 12,000 billion lire from earmarked contributions and only spent

4,000 billion lire for the relevant family benefits. The money saved was diverted to other programs, first of all, to cover the pension deficit. In short, the selection of beneficiaries aimed at containing expenditure went side by side with improper use of social insurance schemes and lack of transparency. Moreover, this certainly did not help solve the chronic problem of high labor costs.

Summarizing, in the Italian case the 1980s were characterized at best by a makeshift approach to welfare state restructuring. The basic features of the southern model appeared to be largely reinforced: not only did the Italian welfare state become even more of a "pension state" but emerging problems such as growing unemployment and changing family needs were hardly tackled at all. In the former case, the social protection system continued to respond primarily to the interests of the industrial labor force core sectors, while the vast majority of the unemployed remained unprotected. In the latter case, although fertility rates were progressively dropping to the bottom of European rankings, and families proved increasingly unable to meet the care needs especially of their frail elderly members, the National government essentially limited its action to restricting eligibility criteria for family allowances, and left the responsibility of meeting the new social care demands to local government.

The 1990s: Structural Reforms under Emergency Conditions

If distributive politics and easy spending dominated policymaking throughout the 1980s, the 1990s look quite the opposite with Italy's public finances turning at last from a vicious into a virtuous cycle. The turning point was represented by the dramatic fiscal and monetary crisis of the summer of 1992. Under the threat of state financial collapse, Prime Minister Amato pushed through a "blood and tears" budgetary law and was later forced to leave the Exchange Rate Mechanism substantially allowing for a devaluation of the lira. During the following years, the picture improved steadily: the budgetary gap between revenues and expenditure narrowed to the point that Italy managed to meet the Maastricht criteria for entering the European Monetary Union—which was largely unexpected a year earlier. In 1997, the country reached the required threshold of 3 percent deficit, and in the next two years consolidated the downward trend even further. Moreover, the "technical experts" cabinets of the early and mid-nineties succeeded in curbing inflation and substantially reducing debt service. To appreciate these impressive results as well as the passing of a number of social policy reforms, which had long been procrastinated, a few words are in order on what happened within— in the political system.

Exogenous variables played a crucial role in reshaping Italian political competition. Particularly, the fall of the Berlin Wall made it impossible for the Christian Democratic party to uphold the popular image of a bulwark against Communism, and brought to the fore its forty-year record of corrupt and inefficient state administration. The final blow came from the "Clean Hands" investigations massively launched by the judiciary in the early nineties. The *Tangentopoli* scandal and its follow-up definitely delegitimated the old leadership as a large proportion of parliamentary members from government parties were charged with corruption and fraudulent behavior. Under these circumstances, the core parties of the First Republic which made up the *Pentapartito* coalition, that is, Christian Democrats, Socialists, Social-Democrats, Republicans and Liberals, almost vanished after the 1994 election. While the old parties were crumbling, two new political actors emerged: the *Lega Nord* which campaigned vociferously against state centralization advocating a federal system, and *"Forza Italia,"* the conservative political movement led by the media tycoon Berlusconi, who won the elections in 1994.

Bull and Rhodes (1997) suggest "...the meltdown of the old configuration of parties was by comparative standards extraordinarily rapid, so rapid, in fact, that it created a vacuum" (p. 6). It is precisely this vacuum that offered the Amato Cabinet an unexpected opportunity for establishing the primacy of the executive in decisionmaking, and for setting policy formation on new grounds. In describing his personal experience as prime minister in the first "transition" government, Amato (1994) openly acknowledged this view:

> I was aware it was increasingly difficult to build consensus through party channels and for that matter even through Parliament itself; I resorted to the social partners as an alternative channel which, at that point in time, was more directly in touch with public opinion. In a number of cases this allowed me to follow a totally new procedure in pushing through my policy measures: I discussed them with the unions; on the basis of their total or only partial consent I drafted a text which I then presented to Parliament, and—building on the consensus I had reached out of Parliament--I asked for a vote of confidence. (pp. 366-67)

Prime Ministers Ciampi and Dini adopted a very similar strategy. In short, when attempting to pursue relevant policy objectives, all three prime ministers resorted to extensive negotiations with workers' trade unions and employers, a practice that a number of authors describe as the resurgence of neo-corporatist arrangements. The literature amply documents the significant contribution offered to balancing public accounts by the tripartite agreement reached in July 1992 and the subsequent 1993 Protocol. It is against this backdrop that we also need to consider the social policy reforms passed during the first part of the decade, particularly in the health and pension sectors. Actually, starting with the elections in 1996 the political scene started to change, and political parties progressively regained a pivotal role. However, the reform trend inaugurated under the technocratic rule of the 1992-95 period was not interrupted. In fact, it witnessed a further acceleration during the Center-left governments headed by Prodi, D'Alema, and Amato.

Given these premises, one is able to (better) understand why the incremental and particularistic approach, which was typical of Italian social legislation up until the end of the eighties, was largely abandoned in favor of middle-to-wide-range structural reforms. The need to balance public accounts was certainly a driving force of the entire reform process, not only during the very first phase but also as the deadline for meeting the Maastricht criteria approached. Indeed, while the measures which Amato passed in healthcare and the pension sector need to be contextualized with respect to the 1992 fiscal and monetary crisis, the pension reform of 1995 and the social policy provisions initiated by the Prodi government certainly reflected the increasing pressure stemming from the European integration process.

Expenditure trends confirm the crucial relevance of budgetary adjustment problems in Italian social policymaking during the early and mid-nineties. According to Eurostat data, in the period 1990-96 Italy only increased social spending (in real terms) by 1.5 percentage points of GDP compared to an average increase of 3.2 percent for the fifteen EU countries. In greater detail, compared to a EU average of 4.7 percent in the years 1990-93 the relevant figure for Italy was only 2.8 percent, which further dropped to 0.3 percent in 1993-96 with respect to a European average of 1.8 percent. As a result, in the mid-nineties Italian social expenditure (including tax expenditure) was well below the European average, accounting for less than 25 percent of GDP compared to a EU average of 28.5 percent.

Within this context, pension measures and especially the 1995 Dini reform provided a significant contribution to the recovery of public finance, particularly in a long-term perspective. Whereas the old system was projected to generate public pension spending over 23 percent of GDP by 2035, current projections estimate instead that spending will peak at just under 16 percent. Table 8.2 offers an overview of net social outlays (thus excluding tax expenditure) over the more recent years in absolute terms and as a percentage of GDP. On the one hand, the data clearly show the slowdown in Italian social expenditure growth compared to the previous decade. But, on the other hand, the information in table 8.2 points to the overwhelming role which pension outlays still play within total social spending, and the limited expansion of hitherto neglected social policy areas. The latter consideration sheds some light on the shortcomings of Italy's social reform process over the 1990s. However, it appears premature to address the issue at this point and I shall return to it in my concluding remarks. To provide a balanced view of the pros and cons of Italian social policy during the past decade, the next sections will first discuss changes in allocation principles, the welfare mix, and the approach to unemployment. But before I elaborate on these issues, a few words are in order with respect to how the Italian social protection system is financed.

Table 8.2
Italian Social Expenditure (in absolute values and as a percentage of GDP) 1996-2000 (figures in billion lira)

	1996		1997		1998		1999		2000	
	Absolute Value	% of GDP	Absolute Values	Percentage of GDP	Absolute Values	Percentage of GDP	Absolute Values	Percentage of GDP	Absolute Values	Percentage of GDP
Pharmaceuticals	10,588	0.56	11,650	0.59	12,833	0.62	14,274	0.67	15,678	0.71
Hospital care	52,751	2.77	57,701	2.91	58,754	2.84	59,926	2.82	62,543	2.83
Other	29,455	1.55	31,035	1.56	32,040	1.55	33,029	1.55	34,314	1.55
Health	**92,794**	**4.88**	**100,386**	**5.06**	**103,627**	**5.01**	**107,229**	**5.04**	**112,535**	**5.09**
Pensions	266,073	13.99	288,010	14.52	290,675	14.06	309,900	14.56	326,058	14.76
Severance Pay	8,792	0.46	8,795	0.44	12,333	0.60	10,108	0.47	10,589	0.48
Sickness, Occupational Injuries, Maternity	5,341	0.28	5,532	0.28	6,189	0.30	6,588	0.31	7,065	0.32
Unemployment benefits	8,262	0.43	8,365	0.42	8,501	0.41	8,901	0.42	9,125	0.41
Other	8,404	0.44	9,870	0.50	10,144	0.49	10,696	0.50	11,591	0.52
Social Insurance	**296,872**	**15.60**	**320,572**	**16.16**	**327,842**	**15.86**	**346,193**	**16.26**	**364,428**	**16.49**
Social Assistance	5,838	0.31	5,721	0.29	5,803	0.28	6,135	0.29	6,237	0.28
Non-contributory pensions	3,431	0.18	3,606	0.18	3,720	0.18	4,048	0.19	4,277	0.19
Disability Benefits	16,238	0.85	16,066	0.81	15,951	0.77	16,050	0.75	15,988	0.72
Veterans Benefits	2,839	0.15	2,625	0.13	2,447	0.12	2,169	0.10	1,983	0.09
Other Assistance	1,745	0.09	1,818	0.09	1,694	0.08	2,405	0.11	2,676	0.12
Public Assistance	**30,091**	**1.58**	**29,836**	**1.50**	**29,615**	**1.43**	**30,807**	**1.44**	**31,161**	**1.40**

Financing Issues

Notably, the Italian welfare state always depended heavily on payroll taxes as a funding mechanism. According to INPS data, in 1992—that is, at the beginning of the transition period—social contributions accounted for as much as 66.5 percent of total social spending, while general taxation covered 31.5 percent, and other sources the remaining 2 percent. Moreover, the distribution of social charges placed most of the burden on employers, as the latter covered 76 percent of total social contributions compared to 24 percent provided by workers. Not surprisingly, the Center-left governments that came into office after the 1996 elections, emphasized the need to recalibrate funding sources in favor of general taxation, in order to reduce progressively nonwage labor costs thereby enhancing Italian competitiveness on international markets.

Albeit to a limited extent, payroll taxes were effectively reduced, especially after the 1998 Social Pact envisaged the progressive elimination of earmarked social security contributions for family allowances and maternity benefits, and established that relevant funding should be provided through general taxation. It is precisely in this direction that a variety of innovative social policy measures envisaged general taxation as a funding source: for instance the special allowance for families with three or more children, the new maternity benefit, the experimentation of a minimum income program, and the establishment of the National Social Fund to bolster the newly defined system of social care services. Nevertheless, the most significant changes refer to the funding of healthcare.

In 1998, a new regional tax on all productive activities, Imposta regionale sulle attivita produttive (IRAP) replaced compulsory health contributions. The following year, Law no. 113 on "fiscal federalism" delegated the executive to redesign completely financing arrangements for the National Health Fund (NHS). Consequently, the relevant Legislative Decree that D'Alema's Cabinet issued in February 2000 outlined an entirely new funding system to be phased in gradually, starting in 2001. The decree abolished earmarked state transfers that complemented regional resources. In the coming years the regions will instead participate in revenue-sharing with respect to VAT (25.7 percent going to the relevant region) and will be granted an increase in their share of gasoline taxes and—although to a minimal extent— personal income taxes, which remain largely in the hands of the central government.

Within this context, incoming revenues will not be earmarked for healthcare. But for the first three years the regions are required to guarantee the same amount of resources previously allocated to them through the NHS. It appears quite difficult to forecast what the effective implications connected with increased regional fiscal autonomy will be—especially on healthcare standards across the country. A special inter-regional fund is supposed to redress the unbalances stemming from the different fiscal capacity of northern and southern regions. But the system is just starting to take off, and it is perhaps too early to appreciate whether the current devolution process will actually increase the North-South cleavage—as most indicators suggest—or whether the central level will be able to counterbalance this trend.

Allocation Principles

The previous section suggested that in the 1990s Italy experienced a reorientation of social policy goals and principles. Considered path-shifting, these measures substantially affect one or more of the following dimensions: eligibility criteria, the nature of the benefit, funding mechanisms, and management arrangements (Palier, 1999); one can begin to notice how Italy passed legislation meeting these criteria in most social policy fields. Table 8.3 highlights the specific pieces of legislation that can be considered path-shifting in seven major social policy domains.

When trying to elucidate the underlying logic of this widespread reform process, it appears most useful to distinguish two distinct phases: the first largely corresponds to the transition period and the beginning of the Prodi government, while the second covers the period 1998 to 2001. During the early and mid-nineties budgetary preoccupations appeared of paramount importance and always accompanied the attempt to eliminate previous privileges and inequities: this holds true in the case of pension as well healthcare provisions. Pension measures introduced a set of changes clearly aimed at putting pension expenditure under control; a similar logic can be traced in the health sector. In greater detail, the basic purpose of the 1992 and 1993 health reforms appears twofold—to introduce managerial criteria in the health sector, thus improving efficiency and effectiveness in care provision, and to alter the center-local balance of powers by increasing regional responsibilities, particularly on the revenue side.

During recent years, attention shifted to those areas traditionally marginal to the Italian welfare state but increasingly crucial in light of current social, economic, demographic, and family changes. Hence, new regulations were introduced with respect to parental leave, part-time jobs, social care services, job placement for the disabled, and child benefits; but also with respect to taxation for low-income groups, work injuries, irregular work, and employment services. Overall, the new provisions attempted to redress progressively the traditional unbalances and inequities of the Italian social protection system by resorting to a mix of benefits and tax measures.

Leaving aside for a moment other relevant aspects, the remainder of this section considers policy changes directly affecting entitlements and/or benefit structure. Given space limitations, I shall concentrate on pensions, family

Table 8.3
Path-Shifting Provisions in the Italian Welfare State

Pensions	legislative decree no. 503, 1992
	law no. 335, 1995
	law no. 449, 1997
Healthcare	legislative decree no. 502, 1992
	legislative decree no. 517, 1993
	legislative decree no. 229, 1999
	law no. 133, 1999
Unemployment	law no. 223, 1991
	law no. 196, 1997
	legislative decree no. 469, 1997
	law no. 144, 1999
Family Benefits	law no. 448, 1998 (art. 65 and 66)
	administrative decree no. 306, 1999
Social Care Services	law no. 285, 1997
	law no. 328, 2000
Means-tested benefits	legislative decree no. 109, 1998
	legislative decree no. 237, 1998
Equal Opportunities	*law no. 53/2000*

benefits, disability and means-tested benefits, which provide a good indication of where the Italian welfare state is heading.

Old Age Pensions

As noted above, the Italian pension system suffered from a major problem of financial viability, but also increasingly came under attack for being highly inequitable and for granting an intricate maze of privileges, primarily within the public sector—most blatantly the so-called "Baby Pensions." According to the public employees' pension scheme, irrespective of age, civil servants were entitled to "seniority" benefits with as little as 20 years contribution, which for some female employees could be further reduced to12 years. Over the previous two decades, Parliament was almost permanently engaged in debating pension reform bills aimed at overcoming existing disparities and inequities, but no structural reforms were passed until the 1990s. More precisely, the major changes were introduced by three distinct pieces of legislation that the Amato, the Dini and the Prodi governments, respectively, passed in 1992, 1995 and 1997.

The first of these measures, namely Law 421 of 1992, while maintaining a defined-benefit system, paved the way for the 1995 pension reform by introducing the following changes:

- Minimum contributory requirements were increased from 15 to 20 years
- Retirement age—among the lowest in Europe—was increased from 60 to 65 for men and from 55 to 60 for women (to be phased in by 2002—a deadline subsequently anticipated to 2000).
- Instead of considering the last five years, the pension benefit was to be calculated on the basis of average earnings from the last ten years of working life.

Building on these premises, three years later, Prime Minister Dini was able to pass a comprehensive reform of the pension system. The reform replaced defined-benefit with defined-contribution schemes. According to the new formula, all contributions made throughout the working life would be duly revalued depending on the country's economic growth and inflation rate; the calculation of the benefit would also be linked to life expectancy at retirement age. Quite clearly, the reform aimed at achieving greater inter- and intra-generation equity, by overcoming previous marked differences among occupational categories. The crucial innovations introduced by the Dini reform were:

- shift from the old earnings-related to a new contribution-defined formula, to be phased in by 2013;
- introduction of a flexible retirement age (57-65);
- introduction of an age threshold for seniority pensions (57 years), valid for all workers and to be phased in by 2008;
- standardization of rules for public and private employees;
- graduation of survivor benefits according to income; and
- stricter rules on the cumulative receipt of disability benefits and incomes from work, as well as tighter controls on beneficiaries.

Although the 1995 reform certainly represented a turning point with respect to the distributive approach typical of pension legislation in the 1970s and 1980s, it also displayed some relevant drawbacks: the new method fully applied only to new entrants into the labor market. Workers with a contributory record of more than 18 years were and still are exempted from the new rules, while workers falling below this threshold combined the earnings-related formula (which applies to their past working career) with the contribution-defined formula for the years to come. In sum, the law established an artificial barrier between younger and older workers openly siding with the latter.

The Prodi Cabinet added another piece to the puzzle, by accelerating the convergence between public and private pension schemes, especially for seniority benefits, and tightened eligibility criteria even further. The combined effect of the above-mentioned measures set Italian pension programs on a new track. At last, uniform allocation principles had been established, but the transition to the new system appears unduly long, inevitably affecting the level of pension expenditures: this is largely why pensions continue to be on the political agenda.

Family Benefits

According to many scholars—particularly the former president of the National Commission on Social Exclusion, Chiara Saraceno—in the case of Italy it is only over the last five years that one can detect an explicit family policy. Even if—Saraceno (2002) maintains—such a policy does not yet reflect a fully coherent strategy.

Between 1996 and 2000 the total amount of resources allocated for family policies increased from 13,700 to 23,500 billion lira. This considerable increase resulted from a mix of old and new measures reflecting a rather different logic. Let's start by considering insurance-based family benefits. Following the 1984 reform, the Italian child benefit scheme was in fact limited to low-income employees, hence leaving the vast majority of Italian families with practically no support to cover child-raising costs. Although Center-left governments did not extend the scheme's coverage to other categories, thus continuing to exclude the self-employed, between 1996 and 2000 expenditure for this program rose from 6,500 to 9,500 billion lira.

On the other hand, tax deductions for family charges were also substantially increased. Over the same period the total amount went up from 7,200 to 13,000 billion lira. Notwithstanding, the relevant data also included tax allowances for the spouse, the child component witnessed an unprecedented upgrading. Tax allowances for children were increased by almost three times in just three years: a considerable effort, although by the end of the Olive Tree experience (Center-left party that ruled from 1996 to 2001) the amount of the relevant tax benefit was still largely insufficient and the overall strategy did not reflect a coherent universalistic approach.

Clearly, neither child benefits nor tax expenditures were designed for large poor families, often with the head of household unemployed or having a seasonal job in the agricultural sector. Considering the horrific record on child poverty, especially in the southern part of the country, Center-left governments introduced a new measure specifically aimed at alleviating poverty among large families. The budgetary law for 1999 established a special allowance for families with three or more children, below a given income threshold. However, whereas the National Commission on Social Exclusion suggested 2,000 billion lira were needed to complement existing tax allowances with a negative income tax aimed at poor families with children, the new program was only allocated 600 billion lira.

Summarizing, in contrast to the past, the political agenda of the 1990s—especially by Center-left governments—included family needs, particularly financial support to cover child-raising costs. However, compared to expenditure trends in other areas, first of all pensions, resources funneled to family policy could hardly be considered adequate; moreover, legislation hovered between selective and universal principles.

Invalidity and Disability Benefits

Until recently, invalidity pensions represented the most visible anomaly in the Italian social protection system. From 1960 to 1972, these benefits skyrocketed from 1 to 4 million, outnumbering old age pensions. The upward trend continued along the decade, and reached in 1978 a peak level of 5,300,000 recipients compared to just over 4 million beneficiaries of old-age pensions. Legislation allowed one to claim an invalidity benefit with just a five-year contributory requirement, and gave local commissions considerable discretionary power in processing relevant applications. As a result, invalidity pensions became the object of clientelistic exchanges, which thrived especially in the agricultural sector and in the most impoverished southern areas. Apart from building on patronage ties especially rooted in southern civil society, this kind of outcome was also fuelled by the totally inadequate coverage offered by unemployment compensation. Indeed, many authors suggest considering invalidity pensions as a functional equivalent of unemployment benefits.

In 1983, stricter rules were introduced in order to effectively link benefits to medical assessment, but throughout the eighties the decline in the number of invalidity pensions was more than compensated for by the sharp increase in public assistance disability benefits. It was only during the 1990s that the downward trend was effectively consolidated for both invalidity and disability means-tested benefits. In just six years, from 1995 to 2001 invalidity pensions dropped from 3,800,000 to 2,800,000.

Starting in 1988, restrictive regulations were also introduced with respect to disability benefits. Legislation passed in the mid-nineties strongly reinforced this trend; particularly, Law 425 of 1996 required all current beneficiaries to submit to the Treasury an affidavit in which they stated their health conditions and their particular disability, lest they be disqualified from the benefit. The measure also launched a special monitoring plan according to which ad hoc medical commissions were to check randomly 150,000 beneficiaries over the following year. The budgetary law for 1998 extended the procedure to 100,000 more cases to be checked by the end of 1999. Apparently, this was still not considered enough, and the budgetary law for 1999 envisaged 40,000 extra controls for the same year and a further 70,000 for the year 2000.

While reflecting the climate of moral rigor typical of this period, the political will to stop the entrenched misuse of both invalidity and disability benefits actually led to some excess in the opposite direction: a case in point was the requirement only recently abolished that all beneficiaries—no one excluded—confirm their effective disability each year: certainly an unnecessary and humiliating provision for a person suffering, for instance, from Down's syndrome.

Means-Testing

In a comparative perspective, means-tested benefits continue to represent a small proportion of total social spending. According to the 1999 edition of Social Protection in Europe (European Commission, 2000), during 1990-96 in Italy means-tested benefits remained practically stable at around 7 percent of total social expenditure, as compared to just under 10 percent for Germany and France, not to mention the UK in which the level was notably much higher. To appreciate Italy's reluctance in pursuing targeting strategies, one needs to consider the size of Italian tax evasion which largely delegitimated income levels as a reference point for rationing benefits and services (Saraceno 1993). Taking into account the general suspicion about tax declarations (particularly by the self-employed), and the entrenched misuse of targeted benefits such as invalidity pensions, the Prodi Cabinet attempted a fresh start by fixing an entirely new procedure based on both income and asset criteria to be used as a yardstick for all means-tested benefits and services, especially by subnational levels of government. The latter specification can best be understood in the context of the wide disparities existing in the criteria which local governments used in granting access and establishing user charges for a variety of social care services ranging from childcare facilities to elderly care services.

Apart from setting these uniform guidelines—which, however, did not apply to categorical public assistance under the responsibility of the national government, including non-contributory old age pensions and disability benefits—the cabinets in office during the second part of the 1990s effectively increased the variety of means-tested programs. As mentioned earlier, a special means-tested allowance for large families was introduced in 1999. Along similar lines, a new maternity benefit was established for all women without social insurance coverage and falling below an income threshold. Both programs were financed through general taxation and jointly administered by municipalities and the Italian major social insurance fund INPS.

Further, a minimum income program was launched on an experimental basis. The Ministry of Social Affairs selected 39 municipalities that were responsible for carrying out the new program for a two-year period ending in December 2000. On the basis of the evaluation by a special experts' commission, the scheme was supposed to be extended to the whole country. However, primarily for financial reasons this did not occur. Parliament instead decided to continue the experimentation by also including the local authorities, which were involved in territorial social pacts; and this is where the situation stands right now.

The Welfare Mix

We now turn to analyze the extent to which the mix of public, private, for-profit, and voluntary involvement in the delivery of social welfare provisions has shifted along both the public-private and center-local axis. In the Italian case this essentially means concentrating on health and social care services. In other areas, such as pensions, given the considerable financial weight of public programs, private complementary schemes remain still largely marginal.

Health

Over the past decade, Italian governments introduced major changes in the health sector affecting the public-private mix as well as the Center-local dynamics of the National Health Service. As mentioned earlier, during the 1980s opinion polls showed Italians expressing increasing discontent with respect to NHS performance and lamenting the poor quality of services provided, along with the red tape which entangled the whole system—causing all sorts of inequities and inefficiencies. Local Management Committees (made up of political members appointed by municipal councils) came under the strongest criticism. However, responsibilities were so intermingled that, in fact, Management Committees had no discretionary power over a large share of the local budget. For instance, the National government set the wages for hospital doctors, and all NHS personnel; it signed the relevant agreements with general practitioners for primary care, and decided what medications were free of charge. On top of this, regional governments were responsible for deciding investment plans within their jurisdiction and for assigning personnel to the local units, by establishing well-defined ceilings for each category.

On the other hand, legislation endorsed a perverse public-private mix. Public hospital doctors were allowed to operate freely in both the public and the private sector, and since their paycheck was totally unrelated to performance and much lower than what they earned if they practiced privately, this arrangement provided a formidable indirect incentive for maintaining public inefficiency. Be it for diagnostic tests, specialist or hospital care, doctors could use their public position as a springboard to increase the stock of private clients. Keeping performance standards low in the public sphere would, in fact, divert increasing numbers of patients to private facilities that the doctors themselves often owned or where they might work on a part-time basis.

The financial crisis of September 1992 opened up the political opportunity for the Amato government to push through what is usually referred to in Italian debates as "the reform of the reform." The legislative decree passed in December 1992 was integrated the following year by an act initiated by Prime Minister Ciampi (see table 8.3). The original 659 Local Health Units were transformed into 199 Local Health Enterprises (ASL) with more operating autonomy, commercial accounting procedures, and performance auditing (Maino and Maioni, 1999). Moreover, the links between Local Health Enterprises and municipal councils were severed by replacing the old Management Committees with a General Manager appointed by the region on the basis of a five-year contract. Taking the British experience as a model but, in fact, attaining quite different outcomes, a number of elements typical of managed competition were also introduced into the system. Particularly, hospitals were allowed to set up independent bodies that could sell their services to the Local Health Enterprises on a tariff basis. However, it was left to the regions to decide how far they wanted to pursue the separation between purchasers (the ASL) and providers (the Hospital Enterprises). As a result, while Lombardy promoted formation of autonomous Hospital Enterprises, most of the other regions opted for an integrated model, which kept the majority of hospitals under the jurisdiction of Local Health Enterprises.

The latter comment sheds some light on the decentralizing goals, which represent the other crucial aspect embedded in the health reforms of the 1990s. Most clearly, by increasing regional responsibilities on the financing as well as the spending side, the provisions passed in 1992 and 1993 were aimed at overcoming the reciprocal accusations between the central government and the regions with respect to deficit spending in healthcare. According to the new rules, the regions were held responsible for covering expenditures exceeding healthcare standards set by the National Health Care Plan. However, only the policy measures passed in 1999-2001 effectively bolstered regional financial autonomy.

The changes introduced in 1992-93 were complemented by the third reform wave initiated by Health Minister Bindi, which culminated with legislative decree no. 229/1999. This piece of legislation for the first time addressed straightforwardly the perverse mix between doctors' private interests and public responsibilities. As mentioned above, doctors had no incentive to increase public sector efficiency: quite the contrary, they could take advantage of any inefficiency in the public sector to attract patients in the private sphere where they earned much more. The new rules attempted to reverse the situation, by combining public healthcare improvement with doctors' economic interests: medical personnel were required to work on a full-time basis for the NHS or to opt out of the public system. Doctors opting to work exclusively for the NHS were granted a very substantial salary increase and were allowed to practice privately within public premises, on top of their contractual working hours. Consequently, Local Health Enterprises were required to reorganize public hospitals in order to allow also for private practice by hospital doctors (so-called *intra-moenia* professional activity). According to the present regulations, doctors' private fees are agreed upon with Local Health Enterprises and the latter retain part of such fees to cover staffing and equipment costs. On the other hand, doctors opting to maintain—on top of their contractual obligations with the public sector—an independent activity outside the NHS (*extra-moenia*) can do so without been subject to any specific regulation by Local Health Authorities, but are penalized, both from an economic and career point of view. They are not granted the above-mentioned salary increase and they are also excluded from all top positions within public hospitals.[1]

This very controversial measure opened Pandora's box, if you will. As a result of the heated debate on the reform's implications, especially for the medical professions, once D'Alema resigned in April 2000, Prime Minister Amato did not confirm Rosy Bindi as health minister. He appointed instead the worldwide known oncologist Umberto Veronesi, in the clear attempt to reach mediation with the medical professions, without stepping back on the crucial points of the 1999 reform. But the story has not yet come to an end. The current health minister within the Berlusconi cabinet apparently intends to reappeal the above-mentioned provisions, once more allowing hospital doctors to freely combine public and private practice.

Social Care Services

In order to understand the current welfare mix in social care services one needs to recall what the policy legacy is in the field, and particularly the role that charitable institutions played in Italy. The power of the Church and the strong Catholic tradition of the country gave rise to a greater number of these institutions than normally exist in other European countries. During the twentieth century, charities and institutions linked to holy orders continued to maintain a primary role, despite the considerable expansion in the scope of state action. Social assistance functions were spread over an impressive number of public agencies, which promoted the labeling and categorizing of people, while offering an attractive opportunity for patronage. Within this framework, local government had a marginal role. As the relevant legislation constantly limited direct provision of social services by municipalities or provinces, local authorities' role was mainly confined to funding institutional care provided by the charities or private bodies.

The establishment of the regions in 1970 (more than twenty years late with respect to the relevant constitutional provision) represented a watershed in the development of this policy area. According to the Constitution, the regions were, in fact, entrusted with legislative power in the field. But for as long as thirty years the Italian Parliament never passed the required guidelines, letting regional governments differentiate their policies to a greater extent than institutionally envisaged. Particularly, while southern regions maintained an archaic system mainly providing poor relief and institutional care, northern and central regions stimulated the expansion of a wide range of community services: home help for the elderly, rehabilitation and training for the handicapped, daycare centers, home nursing for sick and disabled people, etc. (Fargion, 1997). It is true these regions were helped by their interaction with a strong system of local government, with municipalities already playing an active role in experimentation and innovation of social services. Quite the opposite holds true for southern regions, given the traditional weakness and inefficiency of local government in the South.

The institutional context of regional intervention changed considerably with the passing of legislative decree no. 616 of 1977, which entrusted municipalities with full responsibility for the management and coordination of all social services operating at the local level. The act also provided for the abolition of a wide range of public agencies granting benefits and services to specific categories of people. The functions of these organizations were transferred to local governments, as well as personnel, financial resources, and assets. As a result, local authorities were suddenly overloaded with new responsibilities. At the same time, municipalities were confronted with rising expectations by the people, particularly in more developed urban areas. The climate of widespread social mobilization, which characterized Italian political life during the 1970s, definitely helped to increase social pressure for an expansion in the local provision of public social services.

At the beginning of the 1980s, even the more active local governments were just starting to meet the new demands and requirements stemming from the above-mentioned reforms. It is at this very stage, when the consolidation of community services was far from being attained in any part of the country, that municipal action was hit by severe restrictive measures enacted by the central government. As noted earlier, during the eighties Italian governments addressed budget constraints in a rather inconsistent, if not openly contradictory manner: while allowing public expenditure to increase considerably at the central level, the Cabinets in office did not hesitate to cut state transfers—

which represented, until recently, almost the only funding source for municipal activities. Furthermore, the National government imposed a freeze on the hiring of municipal personnel, therefore blocking any further expansion in the direct provision of personal social services.

Under these circumstances, local authorities increasingly turned to nonstatutory suppliers. The latter allowed a policy response, albeit limited, while short-circuiting the freeze on hiring. Considering that traditional charities were ill-equipped to meet new social care demands, municipalities often stimulated the creation of new types of not-for-profit organizations, particularly cooperatives. Cooperatives could easily provide a wide range of services including home help, while also addressing the increasing problems of youth unemployment. Two other policy areas witnessed a mushrooming of nonprofit initiatives: work-insertion programs for the disabled and long-term rehabilitation for drug addicts. Whereas in the first case cooperatives were again in the forefront, in the latter case the total lack of therapeutic communities in the public sphere opened the way for church organizations to take over the task.

The outcome of these different factors was an intricate web of public-private arrangements also in leftist regions such as Tuscany and Emilia Romagna, which originally attempted to create an Italian version of the Scandinavian model of social care services (Fargion, 1996). In the 1980s, even Communist-led regions gradually endorsed a pluralist welfare model shifting from a publicly centered approach to the mixed economy of welfare. What are the features of the system that emerged out of this winding process? Ranci (1999) insightfully suggests using the term "mutual adjustment" rather than privatization, when referring to the relationship between local authorities and the third sector in the case of Italy. According to the author, local political élites largely tended to develop clientelistic ties and partisan links with the third sector, thus reinforcing sheltered markets rather than prompting open competition.

However, the 1990s also represented a turning point in this area. Whereas the National government almost completely ignored social care policies in the 1980s, starting in 1991, Parliament issued regulations on voluntary associations and cooperatives, and also legislated on the highly sensitive issue of tax concessions to not-for-profit organizations. But the most important step taken by Parliament was the passing of a Reform Law in November 2000, which for the first time provided a comprehensive framework for the management of social care services, and established clear guidelines for regional legislation. The new rules created a responsibility on the part of municipal governments for guaranteeing a well-defined set of social care services and benefits within their jurisdiction. The list included home help, sheltered housing, and professional counseling by social workers, which are still unknown in the vast majority of southern municipalities. Of particular interest here is the public-private mix that the reform law endorsed. Law no. 328/2000 placed the greatest emphasis on the voluntary sector, but at the same time clearly stated a public responsibility in the field, and urged local governments to achieve greater transparency in the relationship with private and third sector service providers by resorting to vouchers, performance contracts and public regulation of service standards. Although Southern Italy continues to lag behind, especially in the Center-north, many municipalities had already undertaken this process, which, however, is still largely under way. The issues currently at stake are manifold: service specifications setting out the quantity and quality of inputs and outcomes; staff skills; monitoring and performance requirements; tendering procedures; and more generally, the degree and openness of the competition among suppliers. Whatever the results of these challenges, the fact remains that up until recently the Italian third sector almost entirely relied on public funding by local authorities and one can expect the picture to remain largely the same in the near future.

Fighting Unemployment: EU Pressures and Internal Dilemmas

Unemployment policies represent another area that traditionally experienced considerable distortions in the allocation of resources. However, it should be noted that this policy area consistently played a marginal role within the Italian system of social protection. This continued during the 1980s when the unemployment rate started to soar to double-digit figures. Throughout the decade, expenditure for passive labor policies never exceeded 1 percent of GDP, constantly placing Italy at the bottom of European rankings. The Italian social protection system did not (and still does not) offer any public assistance program for those workers whose ordinary unemployment benefits expired or for those who do not qualify, including first-time job seekers. Indeed, the lack of any social protection coverage for a young unemployed in search of first employment is considered by Ferrera (1996) as an indicator of a distinct southern model of welfare.

In contrast, temporary unemployment attracted a good deal of attention. The major Italian social insurance fund—the INPS—was entrusted with the management of short-term compensation, and a specific fund therein was set up for this purpose. During the seventies and the eighties the profile of the fund increased to the point that, in the eyes of the public, the *Cassa Integrazione Guadagni* (Wage Compensation Fund) became almost synonymous with unemployment policies altogether.

Eligibility for short-term compensation was subject to negotiation between trade unions and employers, and up until 1988, the program was financed entirely by the state. Consequently, the program soon became palatable to both unions and employers because it allowed for a freezing of firings

while allowing firms to externalize the financial and the social costs of industrial restructuring. Highly unionized large firms were also in a better position
to take advantage of the discretionary procedures involved in its operation.
The result was such that this type of benefit lost its temporary nature entirely.
Irrespective of whether or not the restructuring process would eventually
create new working opportunities within the firm, coverage renewals, especially in large industrial plants, were granted for up to as many as ten years.
Early retirement measures further reinforced the distortions typical of Italian
shock absorbers. Along with France, Italy is the country that used this measure most extensively.

The main provisions adopted from 1991 onwards clearly set unemployment policies on a new track. Law no. 223 of that year represented a critical
break with previous developments in the field, in particular with the misuse
of short-term earnings compensation. The law introduced "mobility" rolls as
a standard procedure to deal with redundancies. Registration of dismissed
workers on mobility rolls—while definitely severing every link with previous employers—provided a very generous twelve-month allowance. On the
other hand, workers were formally required to attend training programs or to
engage in "socially useful jobs," lest they be disqualified from receiving the
benefit. From a broader perspective, this clearly sanctioned some form of
conditionality and obligation in return for the benefit, as highlighted by
workfare ideology in both the Anglo-Saxon and milder European versions.
However, the 1991 law was actually implemented with less vigor than initially expected, and the punitive rules and sanctions were increasingly put
aside as passive policies continued to protect only a small proportion of the
unemployed (Fargion, 2001a).

The second half of the decade witnessed an overall acceleration in the
reorganization of this policy area. The acceleration was most clearly connected to the Prodi government which came into power in June 1996, and
especially to the very active stance taken by the Labor and Social Security
Minister Tiziano Treu, a leading Italian scholar in labor law and industrial
relations. The strong commitment by the minister to rationalize and innovate
labor policies and to bring Italy in line with the rest of Europe was reflected in
what is usually labeled "the Treu package." This is a comprehensive law
(Law no. 196 of 1997), which set the relevant guidelines and empowered the
government to revise legislation on a wide range of issues pertaining to labor
market policies.

Following the Amsterdam Intergovernmental Conference and reinforced
by the take-off of the Luxembourg process, the European Employment Strategy gained considerable influence on Italian policymaking. In line with European Union suggestions, the National Action Plans for 1999 and 2000
placed the greatest emphasis on active measures. Actually, in 1999 the proportion of spending on active programs represented 53 percent of total ex-

penditure on labor market policies (i.e., 15,300 billion lira compared to 13,800 billion lira for passive measures). Incentives provided to employers to hire unemployed workers accounted for 61 percent of total spending on active labor policies. However, given there are over 90 measures providing different tax and social insurance deductions, the system remains very complicated with both gaps and overlaps. The executive was empowered by Parliament to provide a comprehensive reform of current benefits to employers along with administrative streamlining. But the executive has not yet issued the relevant provision.

Furthermore, there is still a long way to go before the country effectively raises the number of people benefiting from active measures to improve their employability. The precondition for fulfilling this commitment was the radical restructuring of public employment services, which traditionally operated according to strictly bureaucratic rules and procedures. Law no. 469 of 1997 started the decentralization process of public employment services, entrusting the regions with a pivotal role in regulating active labor policies and public job placement. However, the effective shift of resources, facilities and personnel from the National Labor Ministry to the regional governments—which were responsible for organizing within their jurisdiction the new public employment services—occurred only starting in November 1999 and was completed in 2000.

In setting up the new system, Center-left governments were especially concerned with the possibility of the North-South gap growing even further, and therefore attempted to counterbalance the devolution process by setting clear national standards. Particularly, the representatives of the central, the regional and the local levels of government signed an agreement in December 1999 on the basic functions that the new local employment services were to perform. Following this intergovernmental agreement, the executive updated the legal definition of unemployment to current international standards, and provided guidelines for the operation of local employment services.

According to the new rules—which, however, are far from being implemented in large parts of the country—in order to qualify for the unemployment status, the person must be available immediately to take up a job. Furthermore, the unemployed person is subject to sanctions in case he/she refuses to accept a job offer by the employment service, provided the job offer is suitable with respect to worker's professional qualifications and is within a certain distance from his/her home. One can fully appreciate the rationale underpinning the new regulation when considering that a large proportion of people registered with the old job placement offices (which totaled over 6 million people) was not actively seeking a job, either because they were already working—perhaps in the gray economy—or because they were not in the labor force and were exclusively interested in acquiring seniority on the unemployment register. As a result, the figures for registered unemployment were always unduly inflated, and a reversal of this trend represents a major challenge for local employment services, especially considering their prospective monitoring responsibilities and that the personnel coming from the state are only used to perform administrative functions.

In line with the current approach aimed primarily at preventing long-term unemployment, local employment services are required to interview young unemployed people within six months of registration, and to provide an individually tailored labor market re-insertion or training program to: (a) women re-entering the labor market; (b) long-term unemployed and first-job seekers; and (c) beneficiaries of social insurance unemployment compensation (short-term, mobility, and ordinary benefit). This appears as a very demanding requirement, which is supposed to be phased in by 2003, according to the latest NAP. But considering the recent shift from Center-left to Center-right government following the May 2001 elections, it is questionable whether the schedule and the priorities set by the previous majority will be confirmed. The new labor minister appears eager to dismantle the whole system of public employment services, or at least to confine its action to the least employable, particularly the disabled and long-term unemployed.

Whatever the political choices of the near future, the extent to which the new local employment services are actually starting to perform the envisaged guidance and counseling role and to tailor personal support to individual needs varies considerably from one region to another. The chances for unemployed people appear quite different depending on the profile of active labor policies autonomously enacted by regional governments prior to the decentralization process triggered by the 1997 national law. Whereas most regions in Central and Northern Italy started in the early or mid-nineties to set up local services for the promotion of employment opportunities, this was not the case in Southern Italy.

But what is blocking the whole reform process halfway through is the lack of a comprehensive restructuring of passive labor policies. So far, Italian governments, including the current Berlusconi Cabinet, repeatedly postponed the "reform of social shock absorbers" originally envisaged by the experts' committee (known as the *Onofri Commission* by the name of the chair) which Prodi established in 1997 to provide guidelines for the overall reform of the Italian social protection system. In 1999, Parliament formally delegated the executive to provide a new regulation of unemployment benefits according to the three-tier system suggested by the *Onofri Commission*. In detail, the system was to provide: (a) insurance-based short-term compensation extending coverage to previously excluded categories; (b) ordinary benefits considerably upgraded; and (c) a public assistance safety net, which was entirely missing.

Due to budget constraints, the executive was to provide a "zero cost" reform, which soon proved an impossible task, especially considering the extremely inadequate protection offered by Italian unemployment schemes. According to Eurostat data, in the late nineties Italy was still at the very bottom of European rankings, by covering only about 25 percent of the unemployed. The labor minister of the time, Cesare Salvi, openly acknowledged it was a matter of resources and—one might add—of the political impossibility to shift resources from the over-funded pension sector to any other sector. Precisely the same kind of political difficulty prevented the minimum income program from being extended to the whole country, once the two years of experimentation expired in December 2000. The reform of social shock absorbers appears crucial also to fully implement the monitoring and sanctioning system envisaged for the newly designed employment services.

Given the delay in the overall reform, the Amato Cabinet passed a measure (decree no. 346 of 24 November 2000) which raised the ordinary unemployment benefit from 30 to 40 percent of previous wages, and extended the duration from six to nine months for unemployed over 50. But it certainly was not enough to upgrade the country's ranking with respect to social protection against unemployment: Italy remains, in fact, one of the least generous countries in the European Union.

Concluding Remarks: Political Change in the Midst of Welfare State Reform

The previous sections of this chapter document how the social policy reforms of the 1990s distanced the Italian welfare state from a number of features typical of the southern model. Notably, in trying to identify some common traits of the welfare states of Italy, Spain, Portugal, and Greece, Maurizio Ferrera (1996) pointed among others to "the persistence of clientelism and the formation—in some cases—of fairly elaborated 'patronage machines' for the selective distribution of cash subsidies." More specifically, in referring to invalidity pensions, Ferrera recalled how "the vast scope and the specific modes of operation of this clientelistic welfare market have been highlighted and documented most systematically for the Italian case" (p. 25). If we contrast the policy developments discussed earlier against this backdrop, it certainly looks like Italy has come a long way in overcoming the clientilistic practices still predominant during the eighties. However, as I previously suggested, the recent tightening of rules and procedures with respect to both invalidity pensions and disability benefits has brought about some negative effects in the opposite direction. At present, there are signs of inadequate take-up, especially with respect to cash transfer programs for the disabled; and, in fact, the decisions currently taken by the commission of appeal are increasingly reversing rejections by first-level medical commissions.

But this is not an isolated example. The evidence presented in this chapter documents how the legislation of the 1990s addressed a number of the anomalies that made the Italian social protection system so different from other continental European welfare states. Let's consider, for instance, the so-called "Baby Pensions" which traditionally granted seniority benefits to public sector employees with incredibly low contributory requirements. This privilege no longer exists. After twenty years of useless parliamentary debate on the need to reform the pension system by introducing equitable and uniform criteria across occupational categories, this result was achieved at last by the 1995 Dini reform. The transitional period to a new defined contribution scheme appears unduly long and I also object to the artificial barrier that the reform creates between younger and older workers. Nevertheless, the pension measures of the 1990s mark a definite turning point with respect to the previous intricate maze of privileges and inequities and to uncontrolled cost expansion.

Furthermore, our discussion of the health reform wave initiated by Health Minister Rosy Bindi—which culminated with legislative decree 229 of 1999—provides clear evidence of the strategy pursued by Center-left governments in order to put an end to the "highly collusive mix between public and non-public actors and institutions" lamented by Ferrera—with particular reference to the health sector—as a further typical feature of the Mediterranean model. The above-mentioned measure represents a major break with respect to previous legislation regulating the public-private mix in healthcare. However, in this case it would be misleading to conclude that Italy is now firmly proceeding along a new path. The new provisions caused harsh conflict from the outset, especially among hospital doctors, to the point that Rosy Bindi was not confirmed in the Amato Cabinet in the clear hope that the medical profession would soften its positions. Moreover, the changes envisaged by legislative decree 229 were manifold, thus requiring a complex and rather lengthy implementation process. The shift from Center-left to Center-right occurred while this process was still largely under way. Considering, on the one hand, the close association between the health minister's positions and doctors' interests, and on the other hand, the current government's strategy in favor of private welfare arrangements, it is highly questionable whether the end results of the Bindi reform will remain as originally envisaged. Particularly, there is a possibility doctors will regain all the prerogatives they lost over the last two years, once more freely combining public and private practice to the detriment of the quantity and quality of the services provided within the public sphere.

The change of the political majority following the elections of May 2001 will most likely affect many other crucial aspects of the wide-ranging reform process inaugurated during the 1990s. Let's consider, for instance, the devolution policies pursued by Center-left governments. Especially during the second half of the 1990s, the Cabinets in office passed a variety of measures that altered the center-local balance of powers by increasing the role and responsibilities of sub-national levels of government. Particularly, regional governments were granted primary responsibilities in three crucial social policy areas: labor market policies, healthcare, and social care services. Given the North-South divide—which really makes of Italy two countries in one, in social, economic, political, and cultural terms—decentralization policies could easily be expected to widen the gap between the highly developed Center-northern regions and the underdeveloped areas of the South. Precisely to counterbalance this possible outcome, and especially to avoid southern Italy drifting even further away from the rest of Europe, Center-left governments opted for a devolutionary strategy somewhat similar to the "command and control" inclination highlighted by Blair's third way (Powell, 2001). In greater detail, in each of the three policy fields mentioned above, the Center-left governments emphasized national standards and monitoring, and in a number of cases also granted the central level of government substitutive powers with respect to "failing" local authorities.

The policy program and political priorities of the Center-right coalition currently in office do not reflect the same kind of preoccupation. Quite to the contrary, the action taken so far by the Berlusconi Cabinet moves in the opposite direction, underscoring the value of regional autonomy per se, especially when it comes to welfare state issues: in practical terms, this entails legitimating regional measures bolstering privatization not only in health and social care services but also in education; irrespective of the implications for the actual content of social rights in the different parts of the country. As a result, the initial attempts by Center-left governments to redress the territorial unbalances so deeply entrenched in the Italian welfare state might simply remain wishful thinking. And yet, one also needs to be cautious when assessing the overall achievements of Center-left rule. The electoral defeat of May 2001 abruptly interrupted the social policy reforms originally initiated by the governments of the Transition period and subsequently continued by Center-left Cabinets. But it was not just lack of time that hampered the Olive Tree coalition from completing the restructuring process and allowing the social protection system to adequately meet emerging social needs. Especially once the Prodi Cabinet managed to meet the Maastricht criteria and the external pressure stemming from the European integration process decreased, the executive increasingly found itself struggling with the veto powers of the workers' trade unions and of its own supporting majority. Notably, instead of providing adequate support to the executive, the Olive Tree coalition invested most of its energy in developing self-damaging internal conflicts. Under these circumstances, Center-left Cabinets proved far more effective in getting rid of old privileges and inequities than in designing new measures aimed at tackling traditionally neglected issues—such as poverty or unemployment—and new types of insecurity stemming from post-industrial working arrangements. Actually, a number of very innovative programs were introduced (for instance, parental leave, working insertion programs for the disabled, health and social services for immigrants), but the executive stopped short of solving two major problems of the Italian social protection system, which required a considerable financial commitment. In spite of the EU Recommendation on the subject, Italy is still without a public assistance safety-net and remains at the bottom of European rankings with respect to unemployment coverage. According to Eurostat data, in the case of Italy social transfers only manage to reduce the poor by 2 percent of the population compared to a drop of 20 percent in the case of Denmark. Notably, poverty is heavily concentrated in the southern part of the country and hits especially large families: as a result Italy shares with the UK the worse record on child poverty in the European Union. The cabinet in office at the end of the past legislature was painfully aware of these major shortcomings. As one can read in the economic and budgetary plan for 2001-2004, "a system which is unable to enhance social mobility and to provide sufficient protection against poverty can hardly be considered adequate." The fact remains that just as its predecessors, the Amato Cabinet was unable to build the consensus needed to provide the relevant allocation of resources.

Quite paradoxically, at least in one area, the current Center-right government might actually finish what the Center-left government left halfway, namely the reform of social shock absorbers. Berlusconi's decision to approach labor market issues by attacking—as a first move—article 18 of the Workers' Statute (which regulates unjustified dismissal) is apparently backfiring on him. The government's attempt to enhance greater labor market flexibility by simply canceling a protective rule which only covered a limited and decreasing share of the workforce, brought to the fore the lack of any kind of social protection for "atypical" workers. The latter are constantly increasing in numbers and by no means represent a marginal phenomenon. Indeed, following the legislation of the late 1990s, practically all new employment takes the form of highly flexible atypical work. To put it briefly, Berlusconi's confrontational style offered the workers' trade unions a formidable occasion to close ranks and raise the bidding by bringing millions of people into the streets of Rome and calling a general strike for the first time in twenty years. The unexpected outcome of this winding process will most probably be the funding of a comprehensive reform of passive labor market policies in next year's budgetary law.

The Italian case certainly supports the hypothesis that "politics matters": as major political change occurred in the midst of welfare state restructuring, it is hard to say where exactly the Italian social protection system will head in the near future: certainly, the reforms of the 1990s have moved the Italian welfare state from its original southern imprinting, but much remains to be done and the new governing majority hardly shares the goals and principles of the previous one: the approach to immigration is a case in point. As things stand now, Italy is half way through the ford in reforming its welfare state, and the future appears uncertain.

Note

1. Implementation difficulties stemming from the new regulation are manifold. Starting with Local Health Authorities (both Local Health Enterprises and Hospital Enterprises), the major problem is to guarantee doctors wanting to provide specialist or hospital care to private patients the facilities that are needed as well as the administrative and nursing personnel. In most cases, this means restructuring existing buildings—hence, substantial investments that cannot be carried out overnight. On these grounds, if the hospital was unable to provide the relevant facilities, hospital doctors choosing intra-moenia professional activity were temporarily allowed to treat private patients in their own studios or private clinics. In this case, they were granted a 10 percent deduction on taxable income to cover production costs. The whole arrangement caused much discontent on the part of medical personnel involved. The 10 percent deduction was considered far too low, but, first and foremost, hospital doctors resented that whereas every year doctors could switch from extra-moenia to intra-moenia, the contrary was not possible: according to legislative decree 229, opting for intra-moenia professional activity represents a lifetime choice. Medical associations have appealed the Constitutional Court on the issue, but for the moment, things stand as we have described.

References

Amato, G. (1994). Un governo nella transizione: la mia esperienza di Presidente del consiglio. *Quaderni Costituzionali*, 14 (3), 355-371.

Artoni, R., and Zanardi, A. (1997). *The Evolution of the Italian Pension System*. MIRE Comparing Social Welfare Systems in Southern Europe. Vol. 3, Paris.

Ascoli, U. (ed.). (1984). *Welfare State all'italiana*. Bari, Laterza.

Bull, M., and Rhodes, M. (1997). Between Crisis and Transition: Italian Politics in the 1990s. *West European Politics*, 20 (1), 1-13.

Cazzola, G. (1994). *Lo stato sociale tra crisi e riforme: il caso Italia*. Bologna: Il Mulino.

European Commission. (2000). *Social Protection in Europe 1999*. Luxembourg.

Fargion, V. (1996). Social Assistance and the North-South Cleavage in Italy. *South European Society and Politics*, 1 (3), 135-154.

Fargion, V. (1997). *Geografia della cittadinanza sociale in Italia*. Bologna: Il Mulino.

Fargion, V. (2001a). *Creeping Workfare Policies: The Case of Italy*. In N. Gilbert (ed.), *Activating the Unemployed: A Comparative Appraisal of Work-Oriented Policies*. New Brunswick, NJ: Transaction Publishers.

Fargion, V. (2001b). *Des Réformes negociées: le cas de l'Italie*. In C. Daniel and B. Palier (eds.), *La protection sociale en Europe. Le temps des réformes*. Paris: La Documentation Francaise.

Ferrera, M. (1984). *Il welfare state in Italia. Sviluppo e crisi in prospettiva comparata*. Bologna: Il Mulino.

Ferrera, M. (1997). The Uncertain Future of the Italian Welfare. *West European Politics* 20 (1), 231-248.

Ferrera, M. (1996). The "Southern Model" of Welfare in Social Europe. *Journal of European Social Policy*, 6 (1), 17-37.

Ferrera, M., and Gualmini, E. (1999). *Salvati dall'Europa? Welfare e lavoro in Italia.* Bologna: Il Mulino.

Gualmini, E. (1998). *La politica del lavoro.* Bologna: Il Mulino.

Levi, J. (1999). Vice into Virtue? Progressive Politics and Welfare Reform in Continental Europe. *Politics and Society*, 27 (2), 239-73.

Maino, F. (2001). *La politica sanitaria.* Bologna: Il Mulino.

Maioni, A., and Maino F. (1999). Fiscal Federalism and Health Care Reform in Canada and Italy. Conference Paper WS/93. European University Institute, Florence,

Palier, B. (1999). Beyond Retrenchment. Conference Paper WS/97. European University Institute, Florence.

Powell, M. (2001). *The Third Way in the UK: Concepts, Policies, Roots and Causes.* ECPR Joint Sessions, Grenoble.

Ranci, C. (1999). *Oltre il Welfare State. Terzo settore, nuove solidarietà e trasformazioni del welfare.* Bologna: Il Mulino.

Regini, M., and Regalia, I. (1997). Employers, Unions and the State: The Resurgence of Concertation in Italy? *West European Politics*, 20 (1), 210-230.

Rossi, N. (1997). *Meno ai padri, più ai figli.* Bologna: Il Mulino.

Saraceno, C. (1993). Alla ricerca di una difficile legittimazione: il welfare italiano nella prospettiva dell'Europa di Maastricht. *Stato e Mercato, 37,* 181-191.

Saraceno, C. (1998). *Mutamenti della famiglia e politiche sociali in Italia.* Bologna: Il Mulino.

Saraceno, C. (2002). Paradoxes and Biases in the Policy View of the Gendered Use of Time: The Italian Case. Presented at the Welfare, Work and Family: Southern Europe in Comparative Perspective conference, Florence, European University Institute, 7-8 June.

Trifiletti, R. (1999). Southern European Welfare Regimes and the Worsening Position of Women. *Journal of European Social Policy*, 9 (4), 63-78.

Vassallo, S. (2001). Le leggi del governo. Come gli esecutivi della transizione hanno superato i veti incrociati. In G. Capano and M. Giuliani (eds.), *Parlamento e processo legislativo in Italia.* Bologna: Il Mulino.

Visaggio, M., and Vitali, L. (1996). Il regime pensionistico a ripartizione in disavanzo: un contributo per il superamento dell'attvale sistema. In Padoa Schioppa Kostoris (ed.), *Pesioni e risanamento della finanza pubblica.* Bologna: Il Mulino.

Contributors

Jens Alber is professor of sociology at Free University of Berlin, and director of the Inequality and Social Integration research unit of the Social Science Research Center (WZB).

Jean-Claude Barbier is director of research (CNRS) (sociology) at the Centre d'études de l'emploi and associate professor at University Paris VII Denis Diderot.

Linda Bauld is lecturer in social policy in the Department of Social Policy and Social Work, University of Glasgow.

Valeria Fargion is associate professor in the Political Science and Sociology Department, University of Florence.

Neil Gilbert is Chernin Professor of Social Services and Social Welfare at the University of California, Berkeley, and director of the Center for Comparative Study of Family Welfare and Poverty.

Sven E. O. Hort is professor in sociology and vice president, Södertörn University College, Stockholm, Sweden.

Ken Judge is professor and director of the Health Promotion Policy Unit, Public Health and Health Policy Section, University of Glasgow.

Piet Keizer is associate professor of institutional economics at the Faculty of Economics and Business Administration, University of Maastricht.

Ross Mackay is principle advisor in the New Zealand Ministry of Social Development.

Iain Paterson is research associate in the Health Promotion Policy Unit, Public Health and Health Policy Section, University of Glasgow.

Bruno Théret is research director at the Centre National de la recherche Scientifique, France, and was director of the Institut de Recherche IRIS, Universite Paris Dauphine.

Rebecca A. Van Voorhis is assistant professor in the Department of Sociology and Social Work at California State University, Hayward.

Index